SATURDAY AM

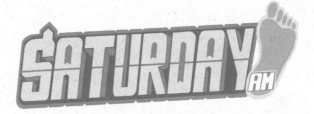

PRESENTS...

HENSHIN!

VOLUME 1: BLAZING PHOENIX

STORY AND ART BY **BON IDLE**

ROCKPORT

CONTENTS

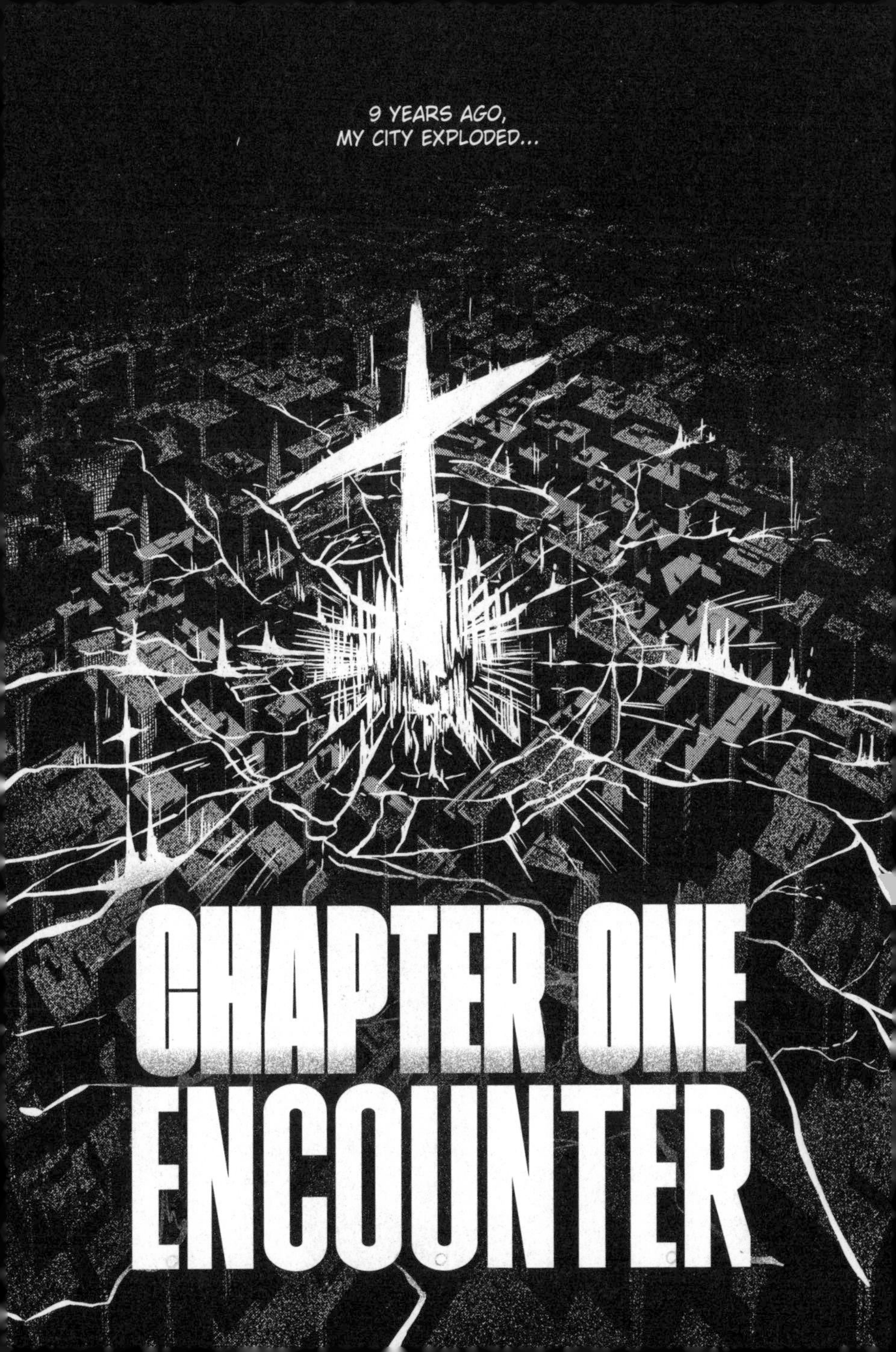
9 YEARS AGO,
MY CITY EXPLODED...
CHAPTER ONE
ENCOUNTER

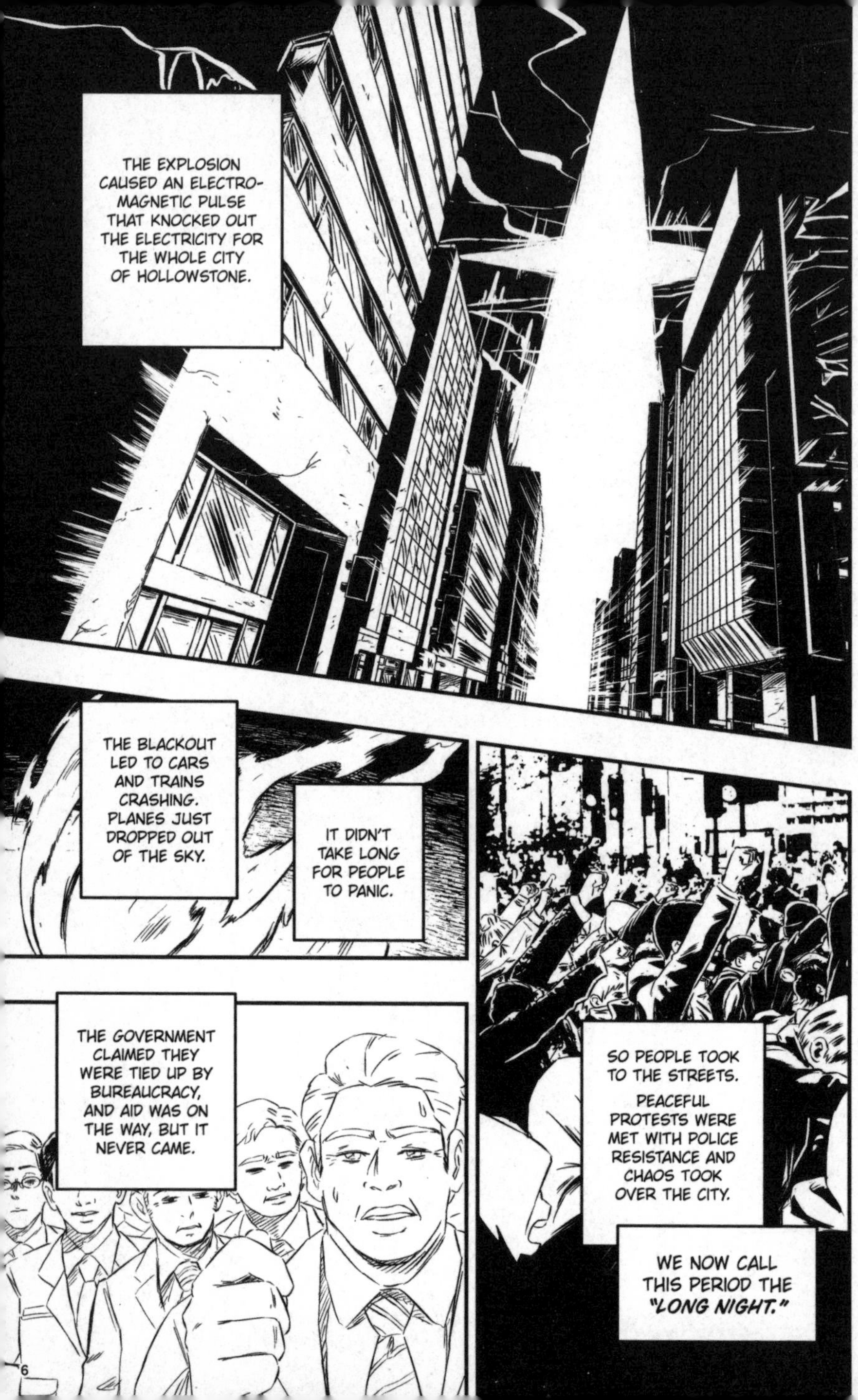
THE EXPLOSION CAUSED AN ELECTRO-MAGNETIC PULSE THAT KNOCKED OUT THE ELECTRICITY FOR THE WHOLE CITY OF HOLLOWSTONE.
THE BLACKOUT LED TO CARS AND TRAINS CRASHING. PLANES JUST DROPPED OUT OF THE SKY.
IT DIDN'T TAKE LONG FOR PEOPLE TO PANIC.
THE GOVERNMENT CLAIMED THEY WERE TIED UP BY BUREAUCRACY, AND AID WAS ON THE WAY, BUT IT NEVER CAME.
SO PEOPLE TOOK TO THE STREETS.
PEACEFUL PROTESTS WERE MET WITH POLICE RESISTANCE AND CHAOS TOOK OVER THE CITY.
WE NOW CALL THIS PERIOD THE *"LONG NIGHT."*

BUT THEN, OUT OF NOWHERE, OUR CITY'S SHINING KNIGHT, THE TECH BILLIONAIRE **ALTON GRIEVES**, ARRIVED.

HE WAS CHARISMATIC, ATTRACTIVE, AND IMPOSSIBLY WEALTHY. HE'D MADE A FORTUNE DEVELOPING A SOCIAL MEDIA PLATFORM CALLED G-PARTY.

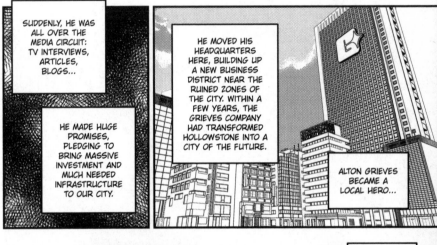

SUDDENLY, HE WAS ALL OVER THE MEDIA CIRCUIT: TV INTERVIEWS, ARTICLES, BLOGS...

HE MADE HUGE PROMISES, PLEDGING TO BRING MASSIVE INVESTMENT AND MUCH NEEDED INFRASTRUCTURE TO OUR CITY.

HE MOVED HIS HEADQUARTERS HERE, BUILDING UP A NEW BUSINESS DISTRICT NEAR THE RUINED ZONES OF THE CITY. WITHIN A FEW YEARS, THE GRIEVES COMPANY HAD TRANSFORMED HOLLOWSTONE INTO A CITY OF THE FUTURE.

ALTON GRIEVES BECAME A LOCAL HERO...

SO NOBODY BATTED AN EYE AS HE SLOWLY CREPT INTO EVERY ASPECT OF OUR LIVES.

PHONES, SOCIAL MEDIA, TV CHANNELS, ELECTRIC CARS...

...HELL, EVEN MEDICINE.

THERE IS NOTHING THAT GRIEVES DOESN'T HAVE A HAND IN...

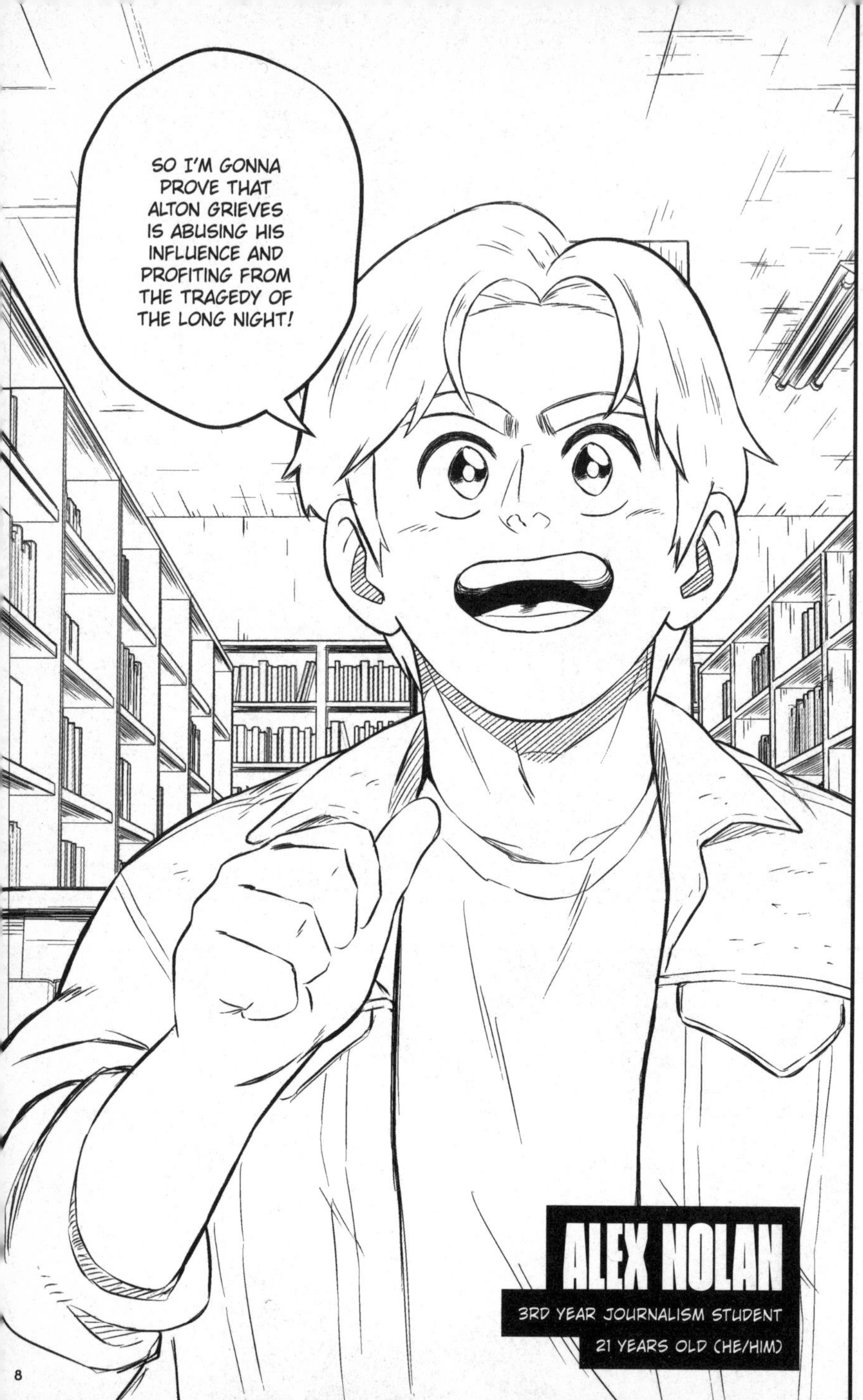
SO I'M GONNA PROVE THAT ALTON GRIEVES IS ABUSING HIS INFLUENCE AND PROFITING FROM THE TRAGEDY OF THE LONG NIGHT!
ALEX NOLAN
3RD YEAR JOURNALISM STUDENT
21 YEARS OLD (HE/HIM)

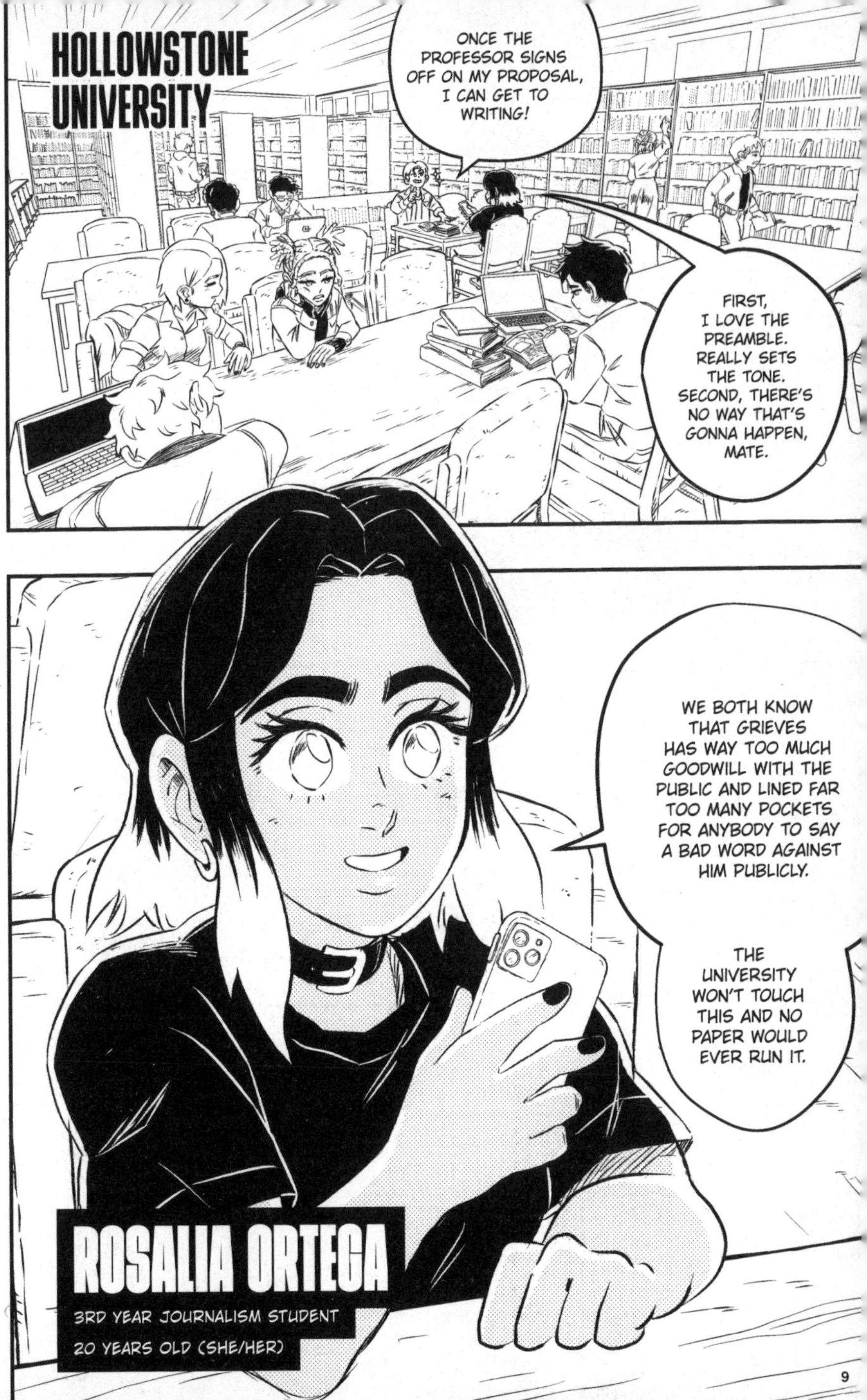
HOLLOWSTONE UNIVERSITY
ONCE THE PROFESSOR SIGNS OFF ON MY PROPOSAL, I CAN GET TO WRITING!
FIRST, I LOVE THE PREAMBLE. REALLY SETS THE TONE. SECOND, THERE'S NO WAY THAT'S GONNA HAPPEN, MATE.
WE BOTH KNOW THAT GRIEVES HAS WAY TOO MUCH GOODWILL WITH THE PUBLIC AND LINED FAR TOO MANY POCKETS FOR ANYBODY TO SAY A BAD WORD AGAINST HIM PUBLICLY.
THE UNIVERSITY WON'T TOUCH THIS AND NO PAPER WOULD EVER RUN IT.
ROSALIA ORTEGA
3RD YEAR JOURNALISM STUDENT
20 YEARS OLD (SHE/HER)

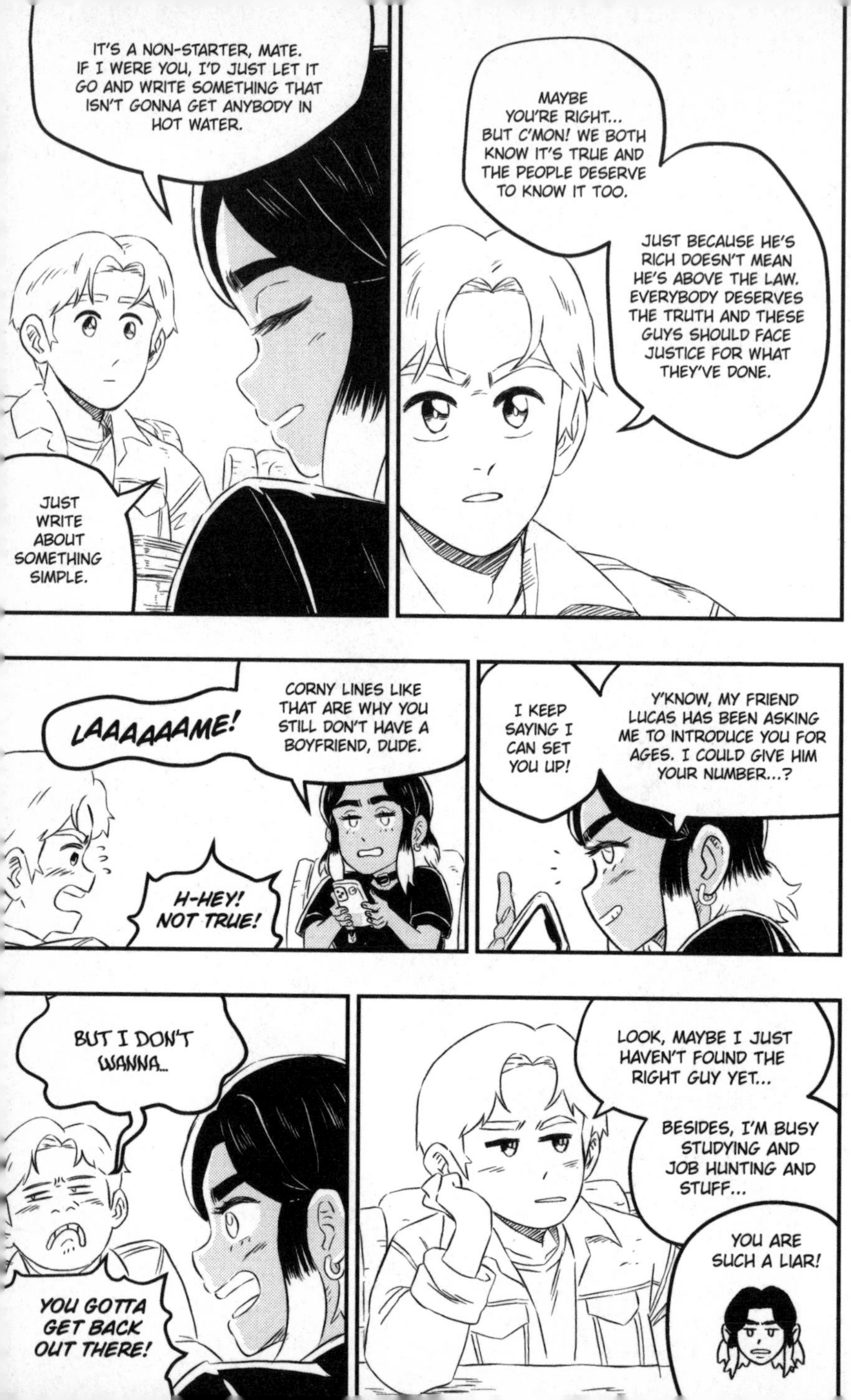
IT'S A NON-STARTER, MATE. IF I WERE YOU, I'D JUST LET IT GO AND WRITE SOMETHING THAT ISN'T GONNA GET ANYBODY IN HOT WATER.
JUST WRITE ABOUT SOMETHING SIMPLE.
MAYBE YOU'RE RIGHT... BUT C'MON! WE BOTH KNOW IT'S TRUE AND THE PEOPLE DESERVE TO KNOW IT TOO.
JUST BECAUSE HE'S RICH DOESN'T MEAN HE'S ABOVE THE LAW. EVERYBODY DESERVES THE TRUTH AND THESE GUYS SHOULD FACE JUSTICE FOR WHAT THEY'VE DONE.
LAAAAAAME!
CORNY LINES LIKE THAT ARE WHY YOU STILL DON'T HAVE A BOYFRIEND, DUDE.
H-HEY! NOT TRUE!
I KEEP SAYING I CAN SET YOU UP!
Y'KNOW, MY FRIEND LUCAS HAS BEEN ASKING ME TO INTRODUCE YOU FOR AGES. I COULD GIVE HIM YOUR NUMBER...?
BUT I DON'T WANNA...
YOU GOTTA GET BACK OUT THERE!
LOOK, MAYBE I JUST HAVEN'T FOUND THE RIGHT GUY YET...
BESIDES, I'M BUSY STUDYING AND JOB HUNTING AND STUFF...
YOU ARE SUCH A LIAR!

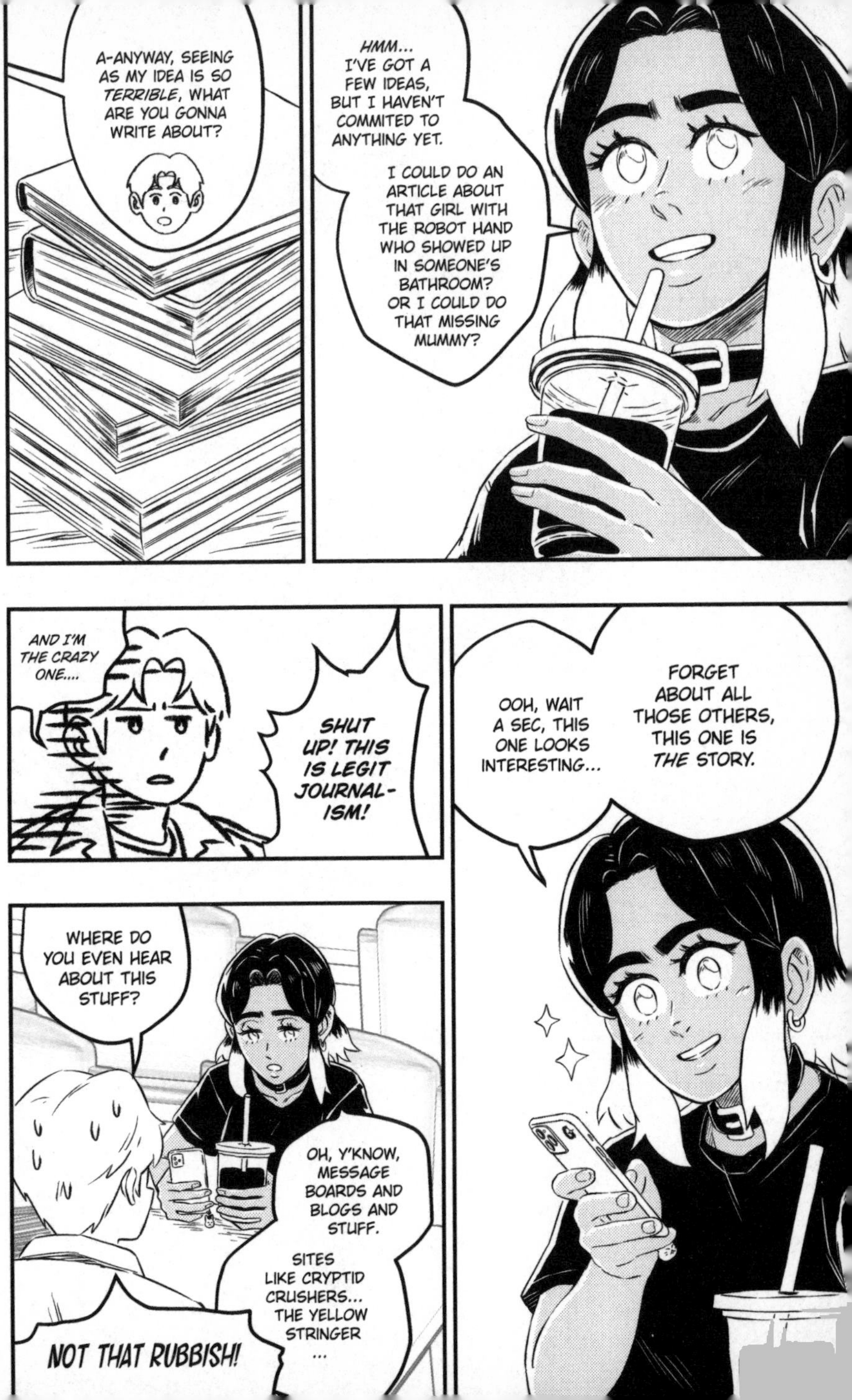
A-ANYWAY, SEEING AS MY IDEA IS SO TERRIBLE, WHAT ARE YOU GONNA WRITE ABOUT?
HMM... I'VE GOT A FEW IDEAS, BUT I HAVEN'T COMMITED TO ANYTHING YET.
I COULD DO AN ARTICLE ABOUT THAT GIRL WITH THE ROBOT HAND WHO SHOWED UP IN SOMEONE'S BATHROOM? OR I COULD DO THAT MISSING MUMMY?
AND I'M THE CRAZY ONE....
SHUT UP! THIS IS LEGIT JOURNAL-ISM!
OOH, WAIT A SEC, THIS ONE LOOKS INTERESTING...
FORGET ABOUT ALL THOSE OTHERS, THIS ONE IS THE STORY.
WHERE DO YOU EVEN HEAR ABOUT THIS STUFF?
OH, Y'KNOW, MESSAGE BOARDS AND BLOGS AND STUFF.
SITES LIKE CRYPTID CRUSHERS... THE YELLOW STRINGER ...
NOT THAT RUBBISH!

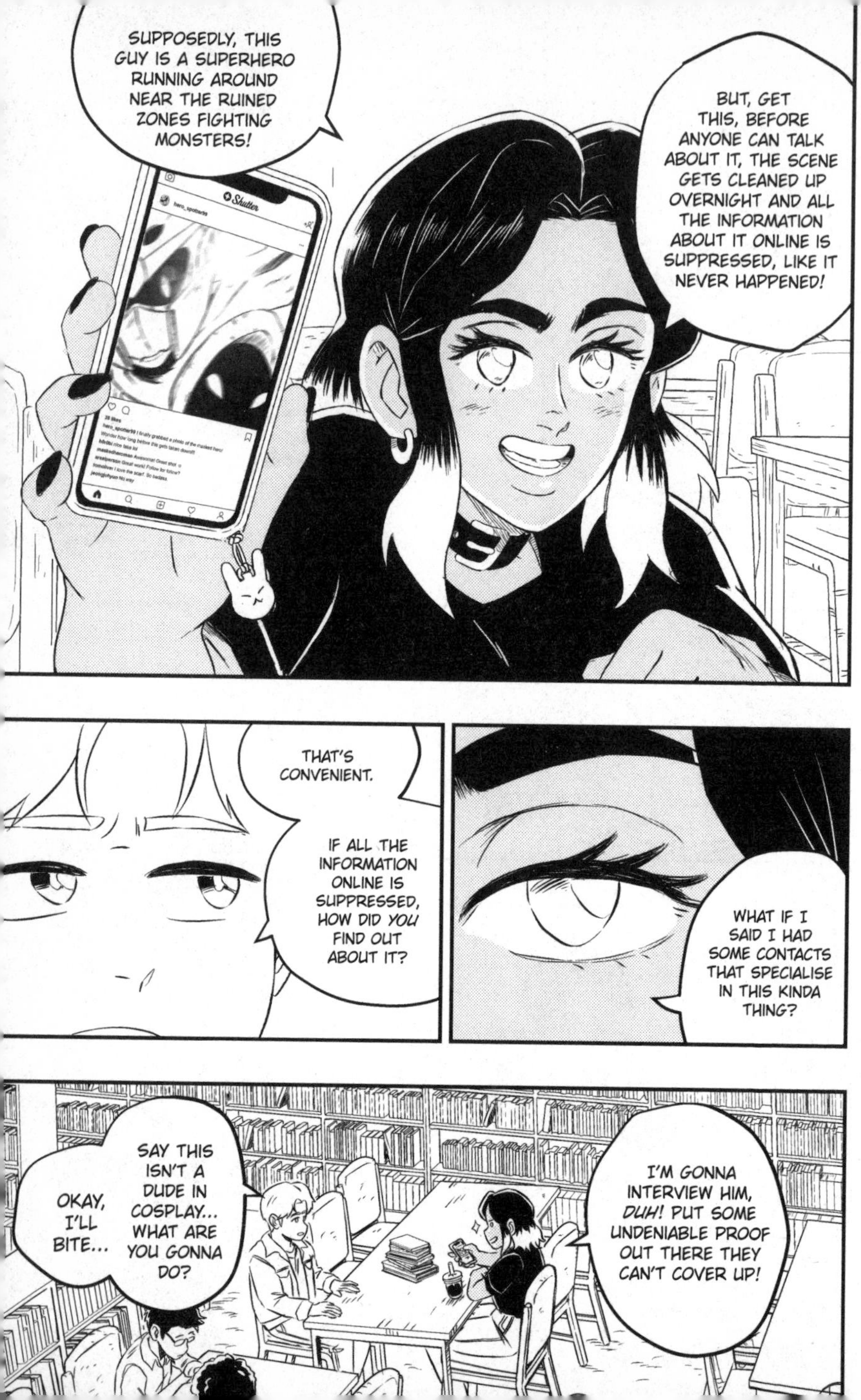
SUPPOSEDLY, THIS GUY IS A SUPERHERO RUNNING AROUND NEAR THE RUINED ZONES FIGHTING MONSTERS!
Shutter
BUT, GET THIS, BEFORE ANYONE CAN TALK ABOUT IT, THE SCENE GETS CLEANED UP OVERNIGHT AND ALL THE INFORMATION ABOUT IT ONLINE IS SUPPRESSED, LIKE IT NEVER HAPPENED!
THAT'S CONVENIENT.
IF ALL THE INFORMATION ONLINE IS SUPPRESSED, HOW DID *YOU* FIND OUT ABOUT IT?
WHAT IF I SAID I HAD SOME CONTACTS THAT SPECIALISE IN THIS KINDA THING?
OKAY, I'LL BITE...
SAY THIS ISN'T A DUDE IN COSPLAY... WHAT ARE YOU GONNA DO?
I'M GONNA INTERVIEW HIM, *DUH*! PUT SOME UNDENIABLE PROOF OUT THERE THEY CAN'T COVER UP!

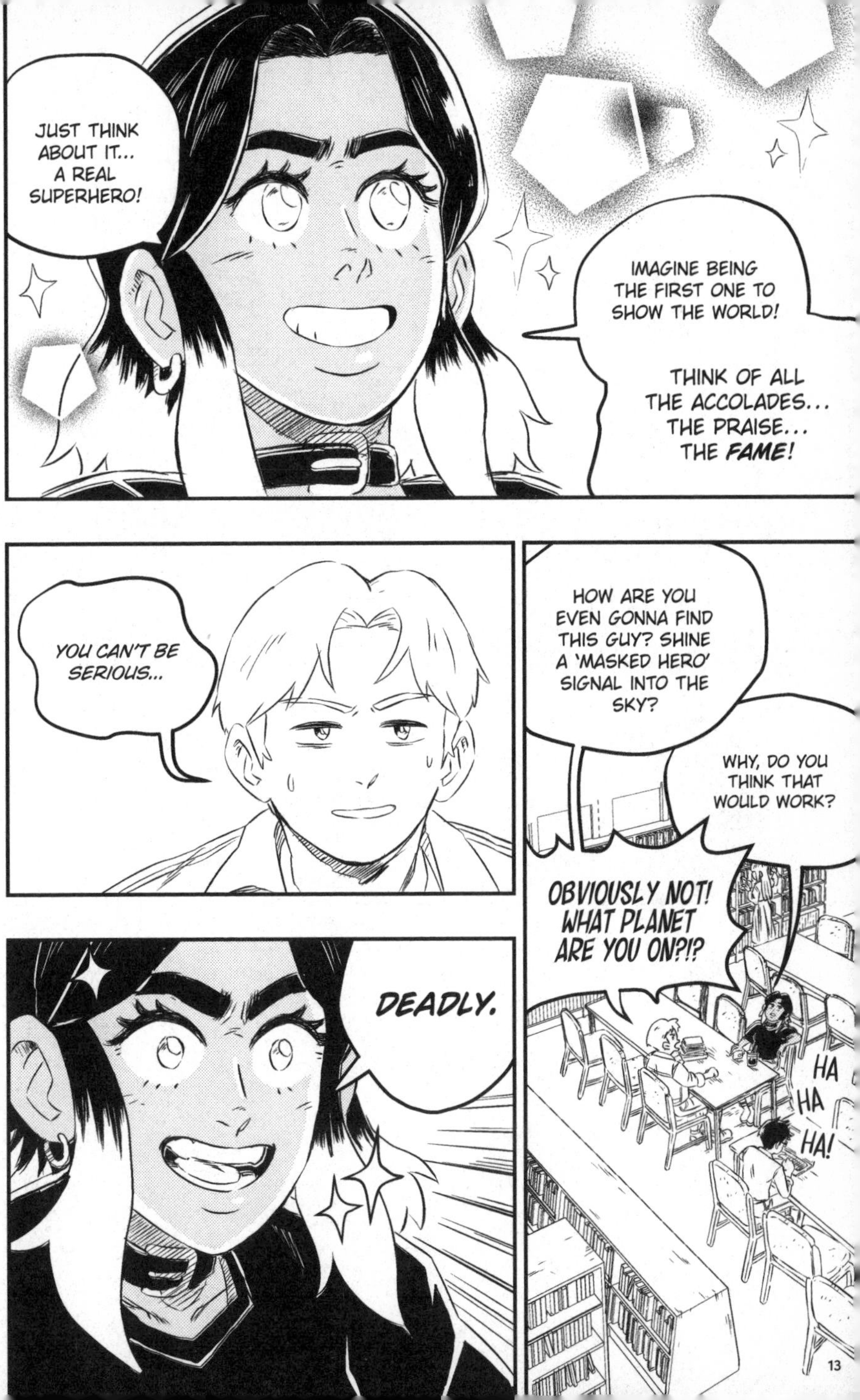
JUST THINK ABOUT IT... A REAL SUPERHERO!
IMAGINE BEING THE FIRST ONE TO SHOW THE WORLD!
THINK OF ALL THE ACCOLADES... THE PRAISE... THE *FAME*!
YOU CAN'T BE SERIOUS...
DEADLY.
HOW ARE YOU EVEN GONNA FIND THIS GUY? SHINE A 'MASKED HERO' SIGNAL INTO THE SKY?
WHY, DO YOU THINK THAT WOULD WORK?
OBVIOUSLY NOT! WHAT PLANET ARE YOU ON?!?
HA HA HA!

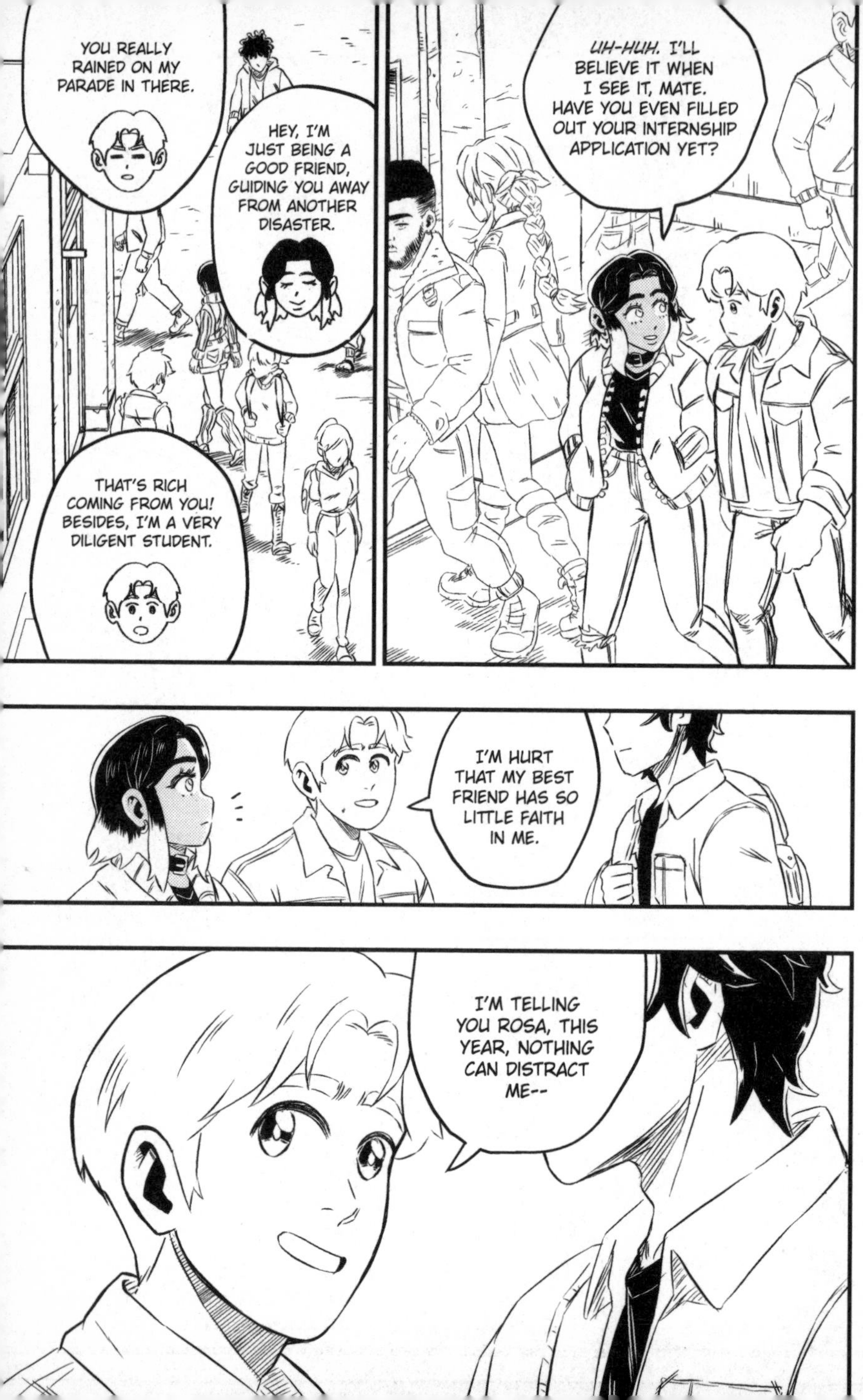
YOU REALLY RAINED ON MY PARADE IN THERE.
HEY, I'M JUST BEING A GOOD FRIEND, GUIDING YOU AWAY FROM ANOTHER DISASTER.
THAT'S RICH COMING FROM YOU! BESIDES, I'M A VERY DILIGENT STUDENT.
UH-HUH. I'LL BELIEVE IT WHEN I SEE IT, MATE. HAVE YOU EVEN FILLED OUT YOUR INTERNSHIP APPLICATION YET?
I'M HURT THAT MY BEST FRIEND HAS SO LITTLE FAITH IN ME.
I'M TELLING YOU ROSA, THIS YEAR, NOTHING CAN DISTRACT ME--

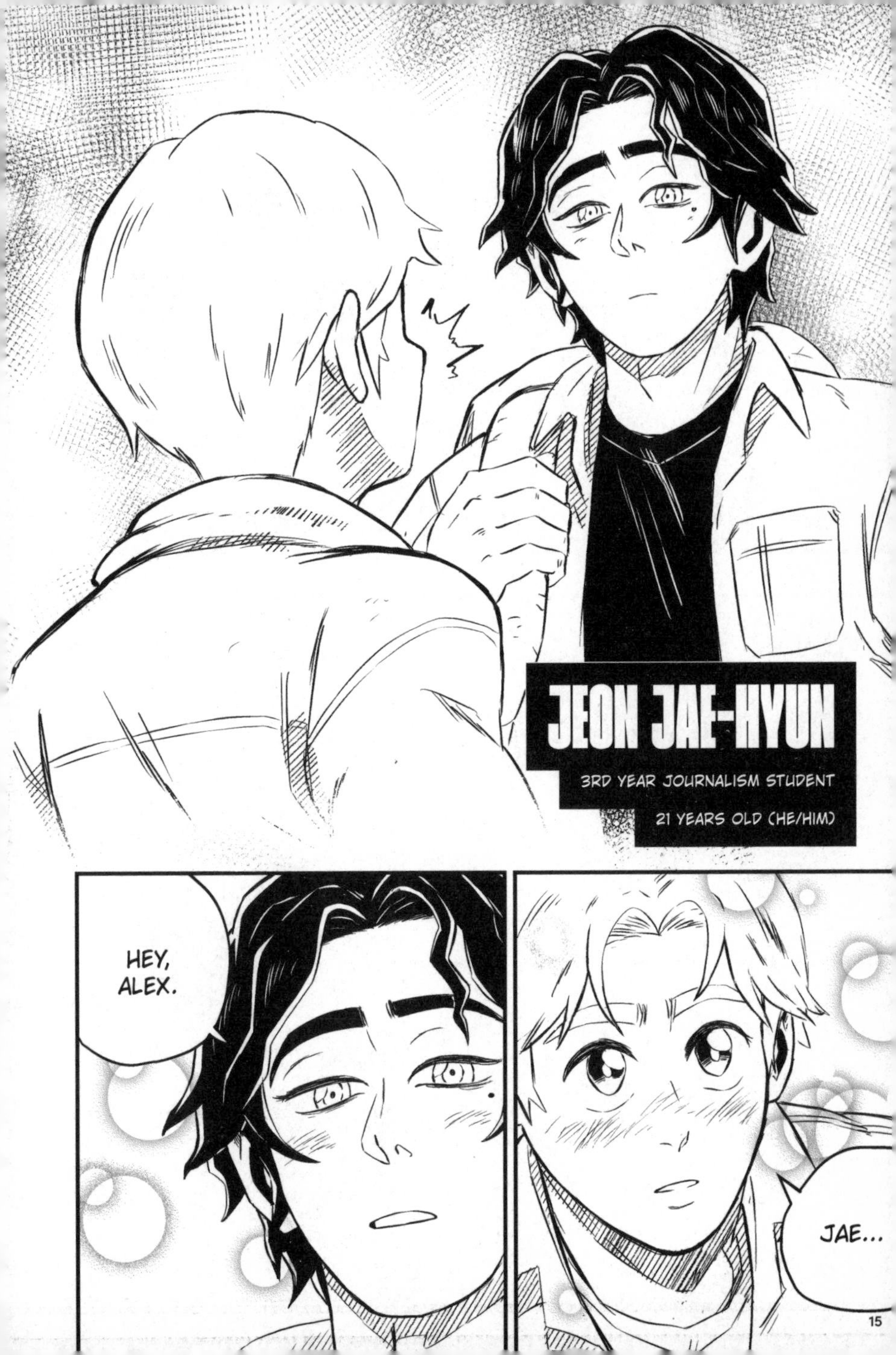
JEON JAE-HYUN
3RD YEAR JOURNALISM STUDENT
21 YEARS OLD (HE/HIM)
HEY, ALEX.
JAE...

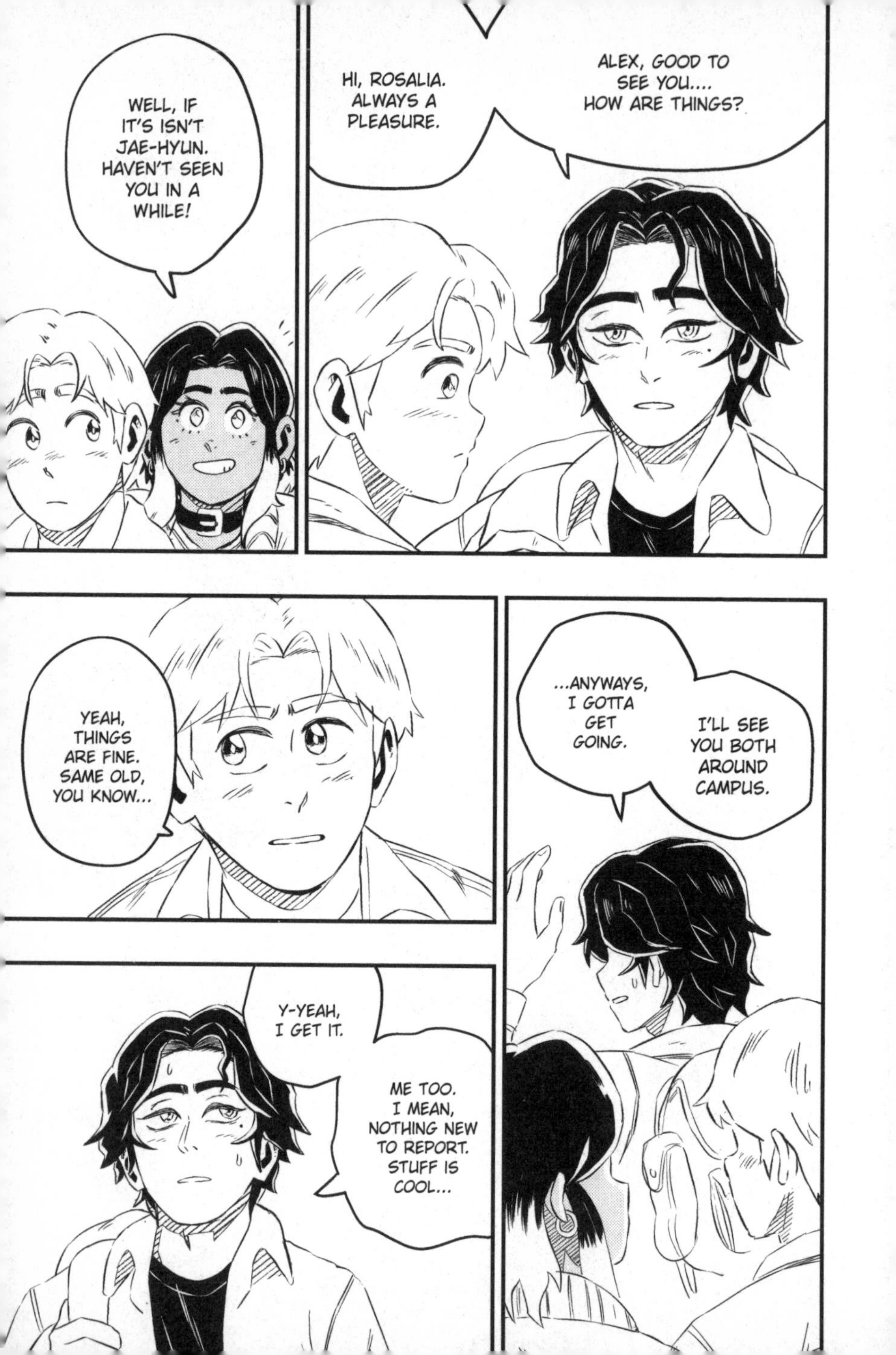
WELL, IF IT'S ISN'T JAE-HYUN. HAVEN'T SEEN YOU IN A WHILE!
HI, ROSALIA. ALWAYS A PLEASURE.
ALEX, GOOD TO SEE YOU.... HOW ARE THINGS?
YEAH, THINGS ARE FINE. SAME OLD, YOU KNOW...
Y-YEAH, I GET IT.
ME TOO. I MEAN, NOTHING NEW TO REPORT. STUFF IS COOL...
...ANYWAYS, I GOTTA GET GOING.
I'LL SEE YOU BOTH AROUND CAMPUS.

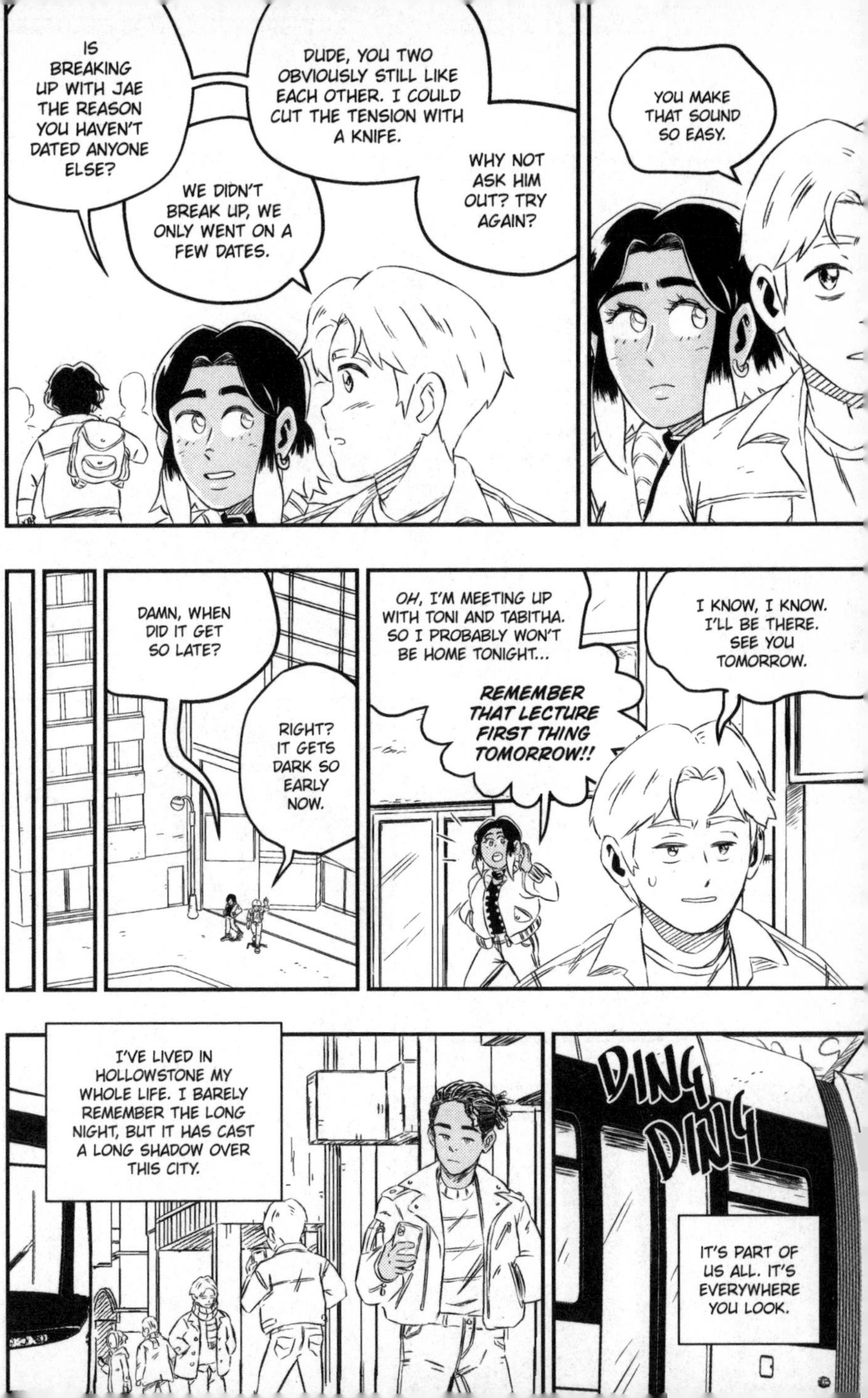
IS BREAKING UP WITH JAE THE REASON YOU HAVEN'T DATED ANYONE ELSE?
DUDE, YOU TWO OBVIOUSLY STILL LIKE EACH OTHER. I COULD CUT THE TENSION WITH A KNIFE.
WE DIDN'T BREAK UP, WE ONLY WENT ON A FEW DATES.
WHY NOT ASK HIM OUT? TRY AGAIN?
YOU MAKE THAT SOUND SO EASY.
DAMN, WHEN DID IT GET SO LATE?
RIGHT? IT GETS DARK SO EARLY NOW.
OH, I'M MEETING UP WITH TONI AND TABITHA. SO I PROBABLY WON'T BE HOME TONIGHT...
REMEMBER THAT LECTURE FIRST THING TOMORROW!!
I KNOW, I KNOW. I'LL BE THERE. SEE YOU TOMORROW.
I'VE LIVED IN HOLLOWSTONE MY WHOLE LIFE. I BARELY REMEMBER THE LONG NIGHT, BUT IT HAS CAST A LONG SHADOW OVER THIS CITY.
DING DING
IT'S PART OF US ALL. IT'S EVERYWHERE YOU LOOK.

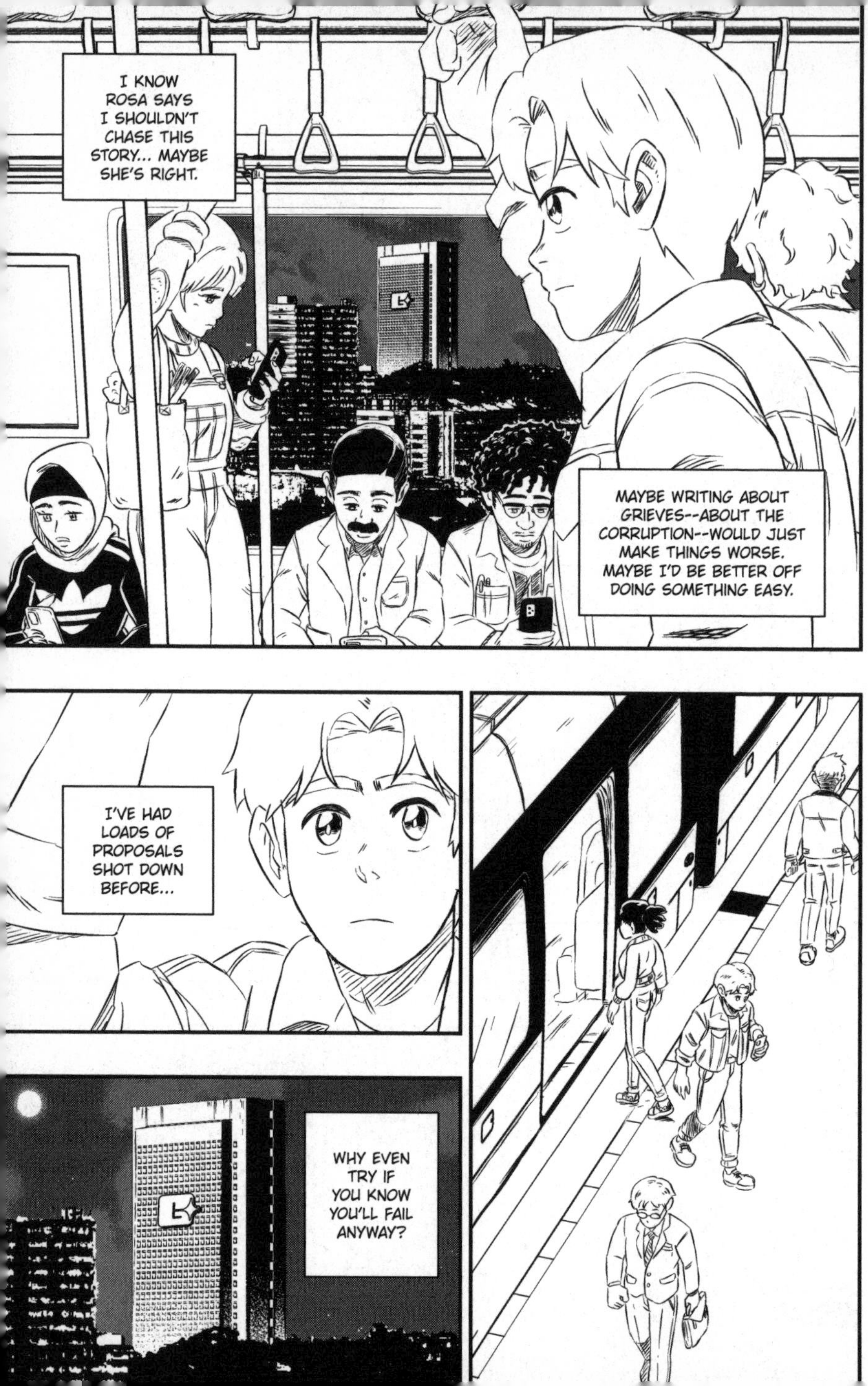
I KNOW ROSA SAYS I SHOULDN'T CHASE THIS STORY... MAYBE SHE'S RIGHT.
MAYBE WRITING ABOUT GRIEVES--ABOUT THE CORRUPTION--WOULD JUST MAKE THINGS WORSE. MAYBE I'D BE BETTER OFF DOING SOMETHING EASY.
I'VE HAD LOADS OF PROPOSALS SHOT DOWN BEFORE...
WHY EVEN TRY IF YOU KNOW YOU'LL FAIL ANYWAY?

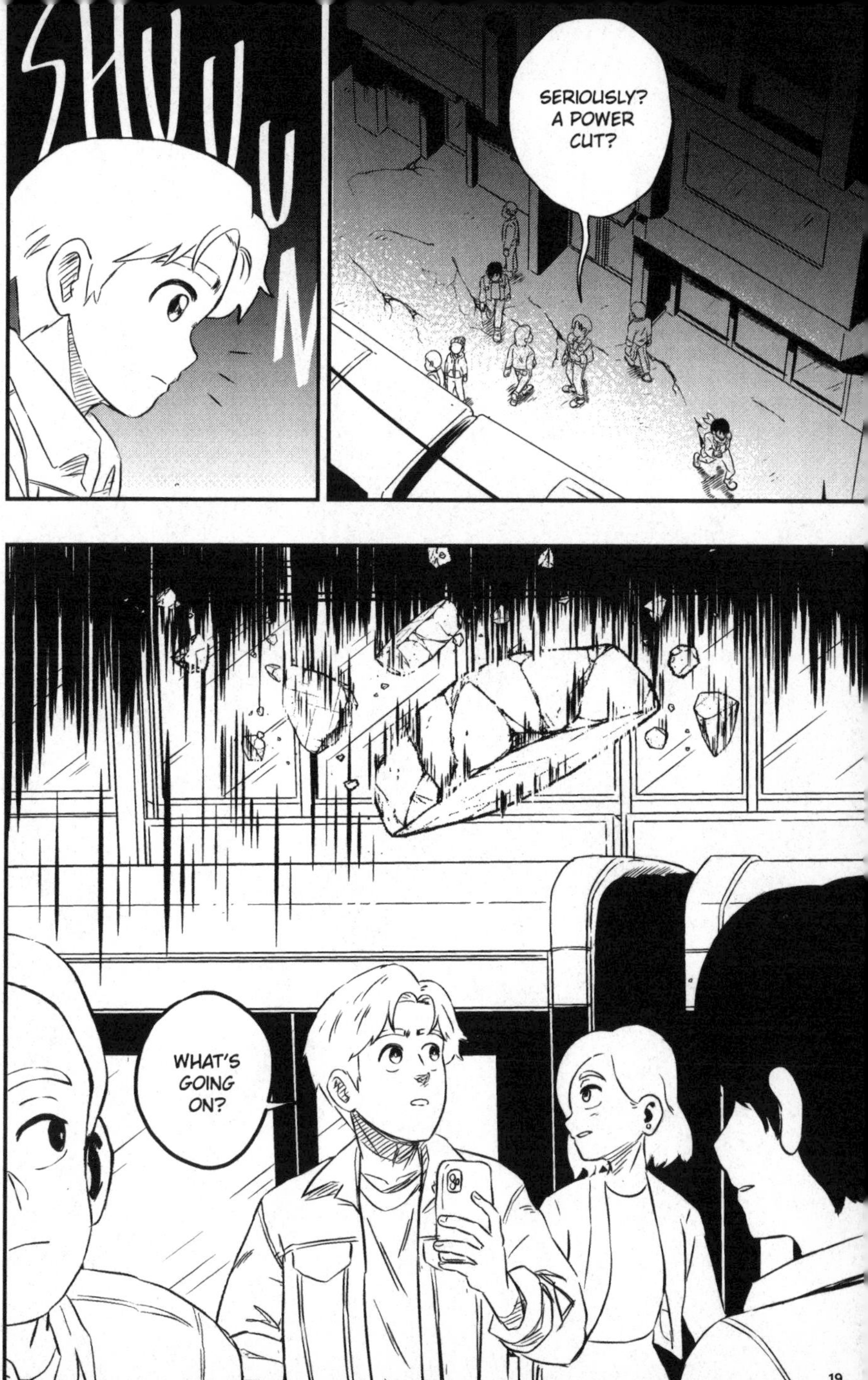
SHUUUN
SERIOUSLY? A POWER CUT?
WHAT'S GOING ON?

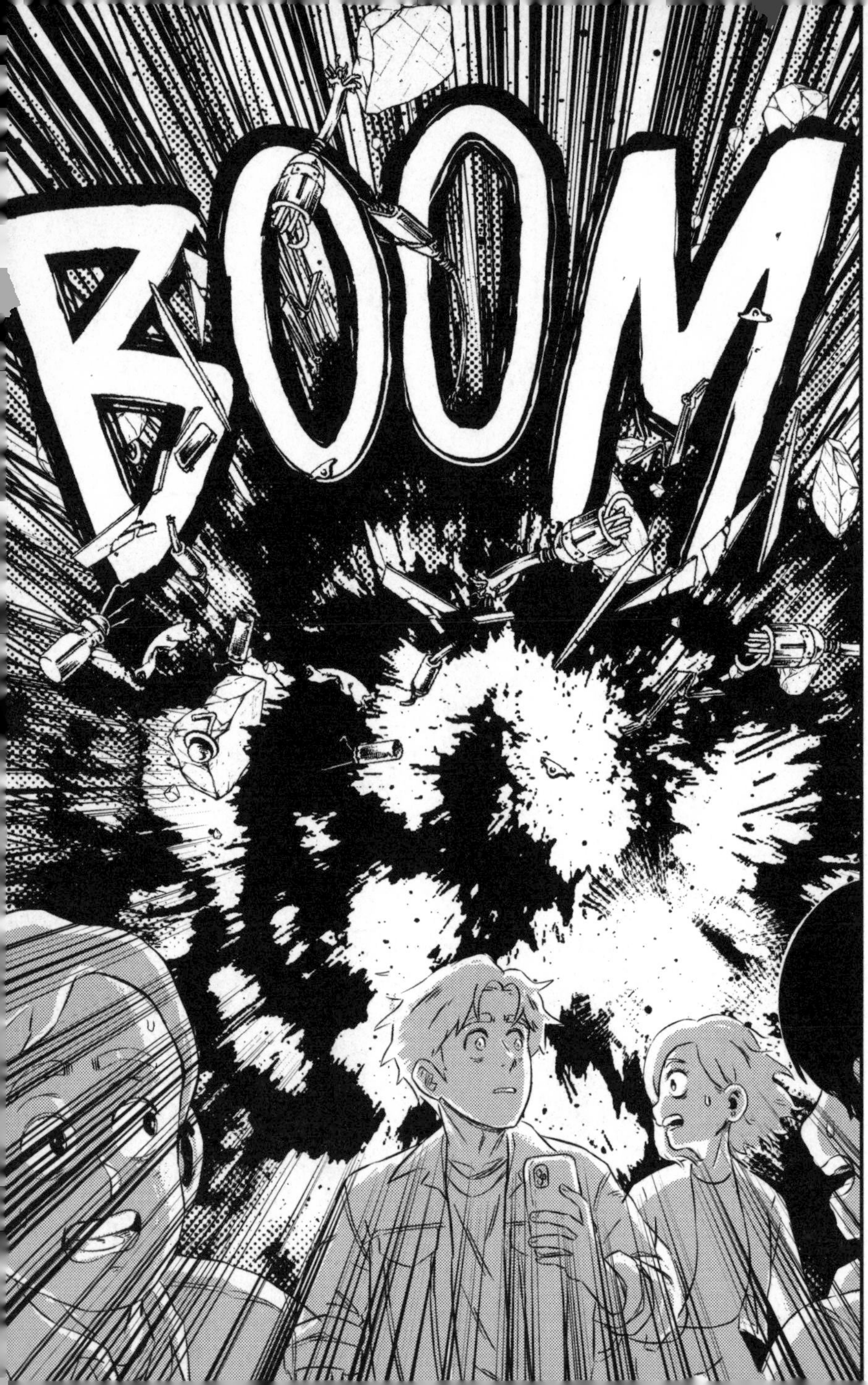
BOOM

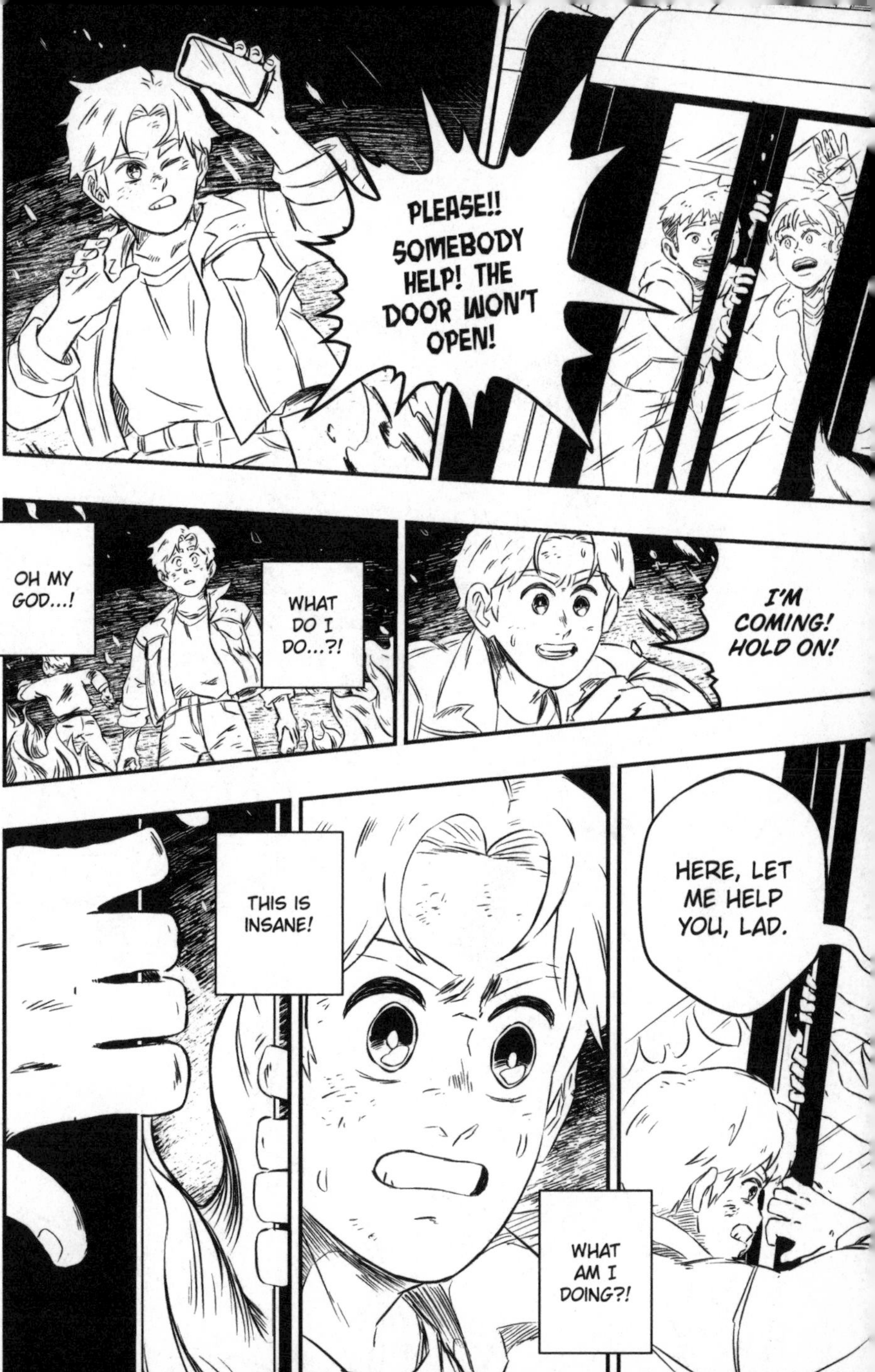
PLEASE!! SOMEBODY HELP! THE DOOR WON'T OPEN!
OH MY GOD...!
WHAT DO I DO...?!
I'M COMING! HOLD ON!
THIS IS INSANE!
HERE, LET ME HELP YOU, LAD.
WHAT AM I DOING?!

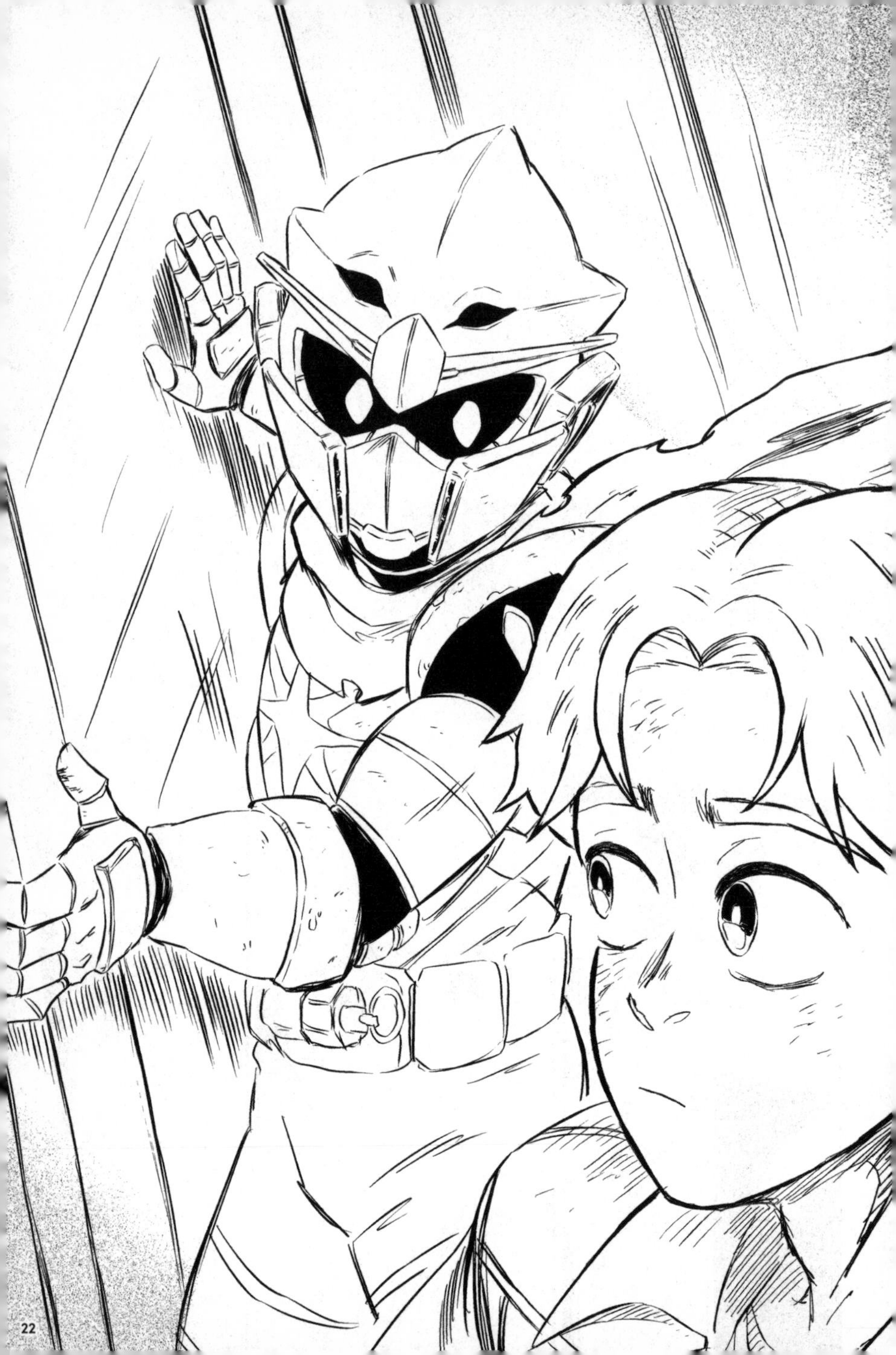

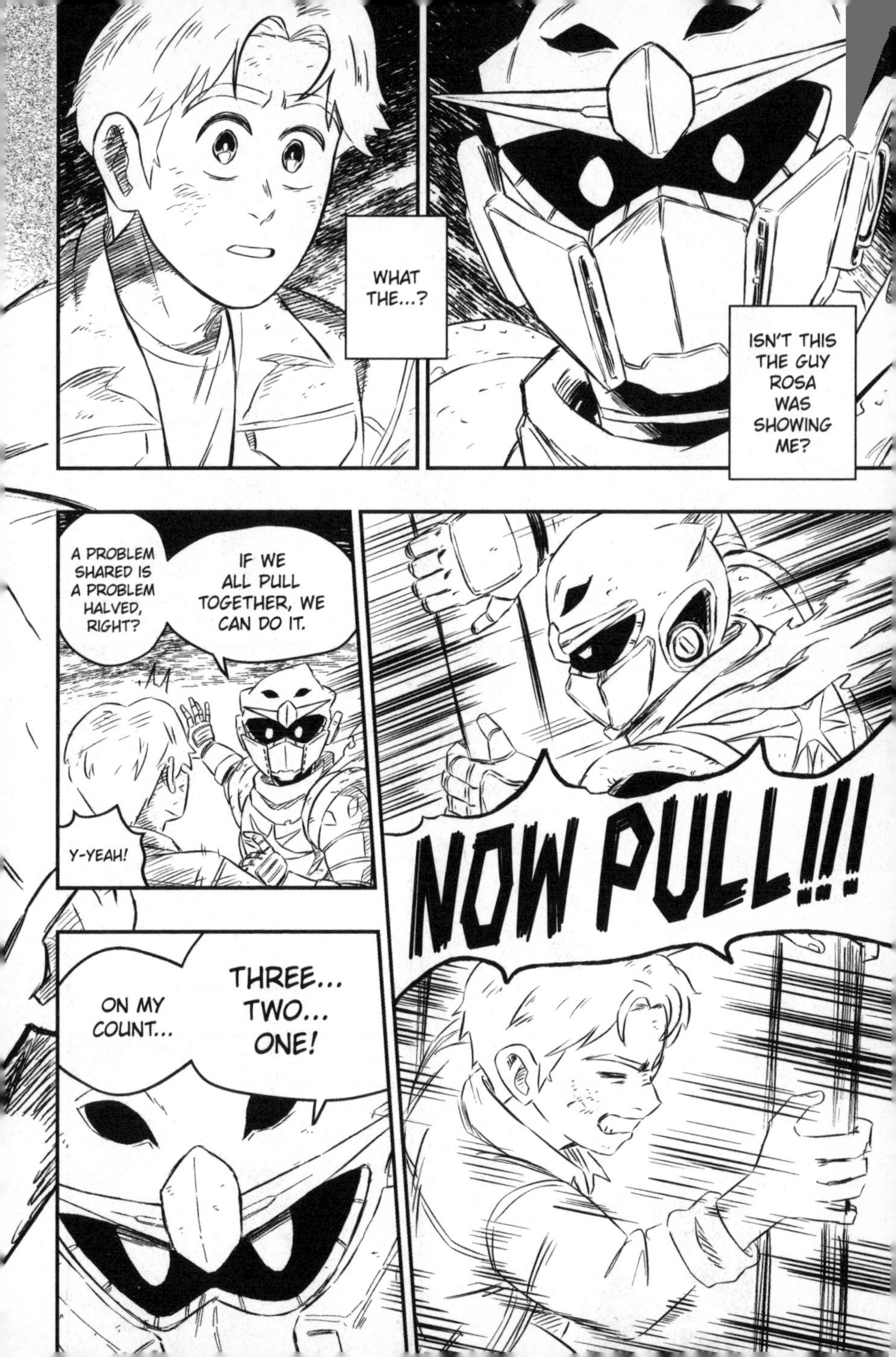
WHAT THE...?
ISN'T THIS THE GUY ROSA WAS SHOWING ME?
IF WE ALL PULL TOGETHER, WE CAN DO IT.
A PROBLEM SHARED IS A PROBLEM HALVED, RIGHT?
Y-YEAH!
ON MY COUNT...
THREE... TWO... ONE!
NOW PULL!!!

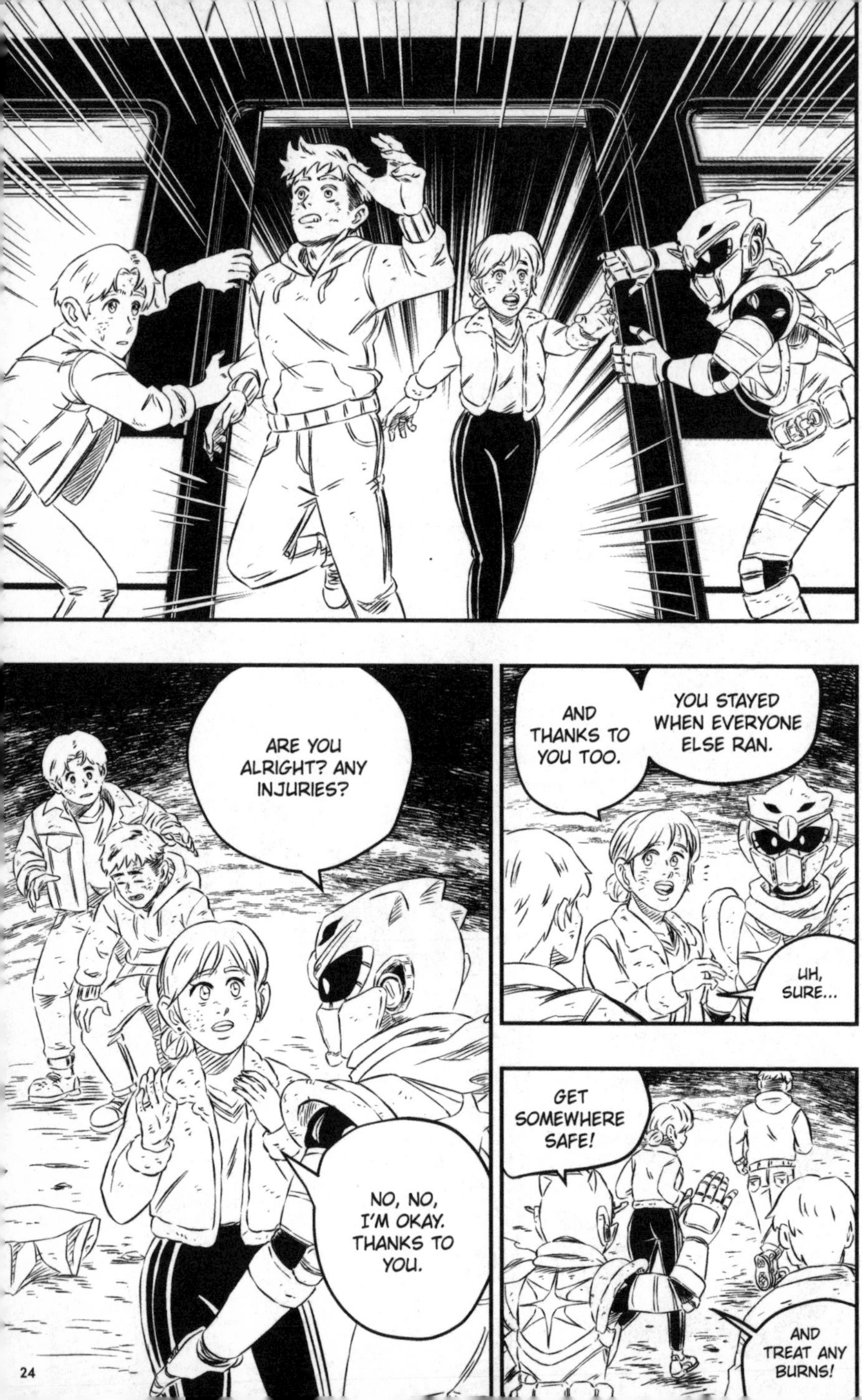

ARE YOU ALRIGHT? ANY INJURIES?
NO, NO, I'M OKAY. THANKS TO YOU.
AND THANKS TO YOU TOO.
YOU STAYED WHEN EVERYONE ELSE RAN.
UH, SURE...
GET SOMEWHERE SAFE!
AND TREAT ANY BURNS!

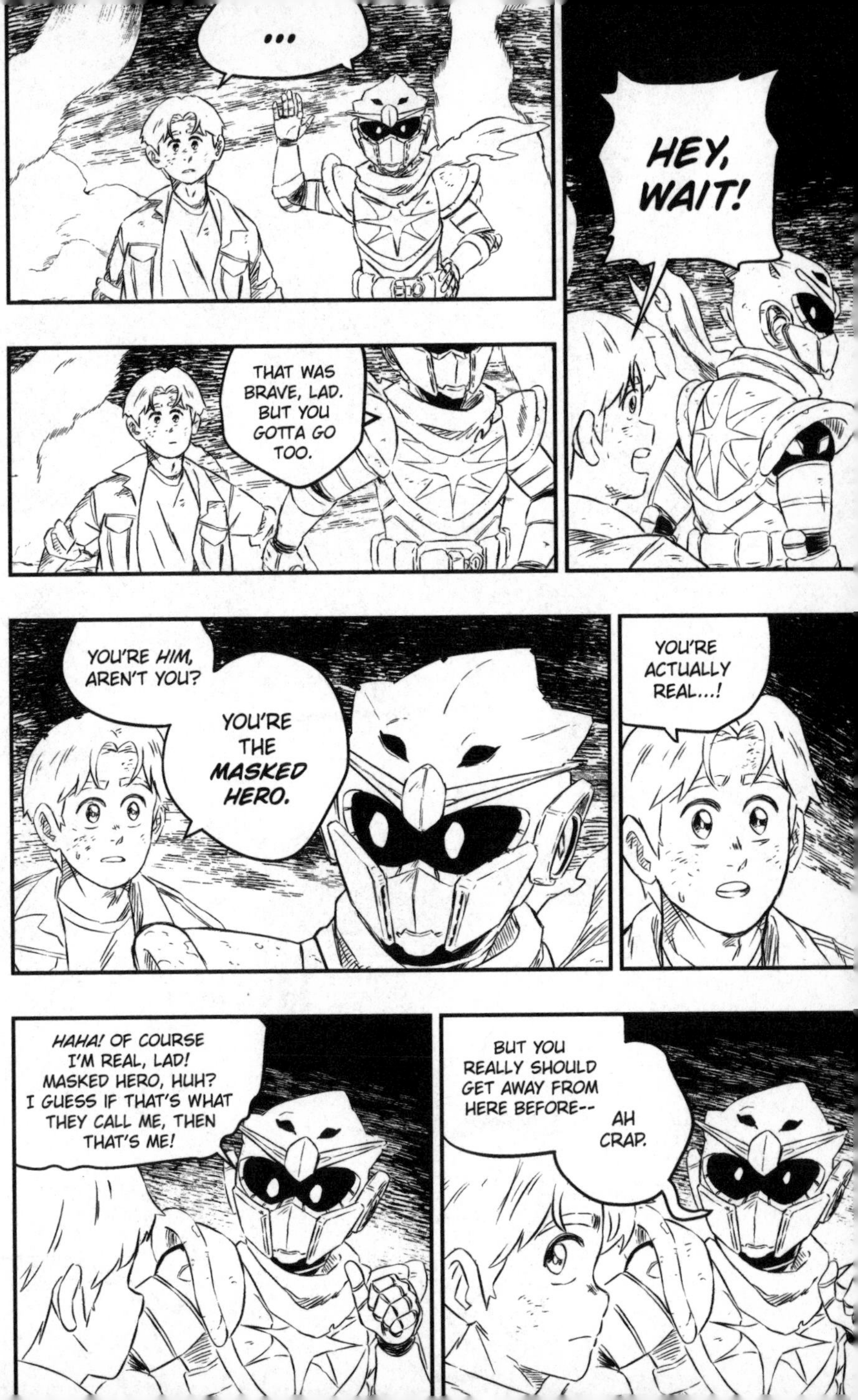
...
HEY, WAIT!
THAT WAS BRAVE, LAD. BUT YOU GOTTA GO TOO.
YOU'RE *HIM*, AREN'T YOU?
YOU'RE THE ***MASKED HERO.***
YOU'RE ACTUALLY REAL...!
HAHA! OF COURSE I'M REAL, LAD! MASKED HERO, HUH? I GUESS IF THAT'S WHAT THEY CALL ME, THEN THAT'S ME!
BUT YOU REALLY SHOULD GET AWAY FROM HERE BEFORE--
AH CRAP.

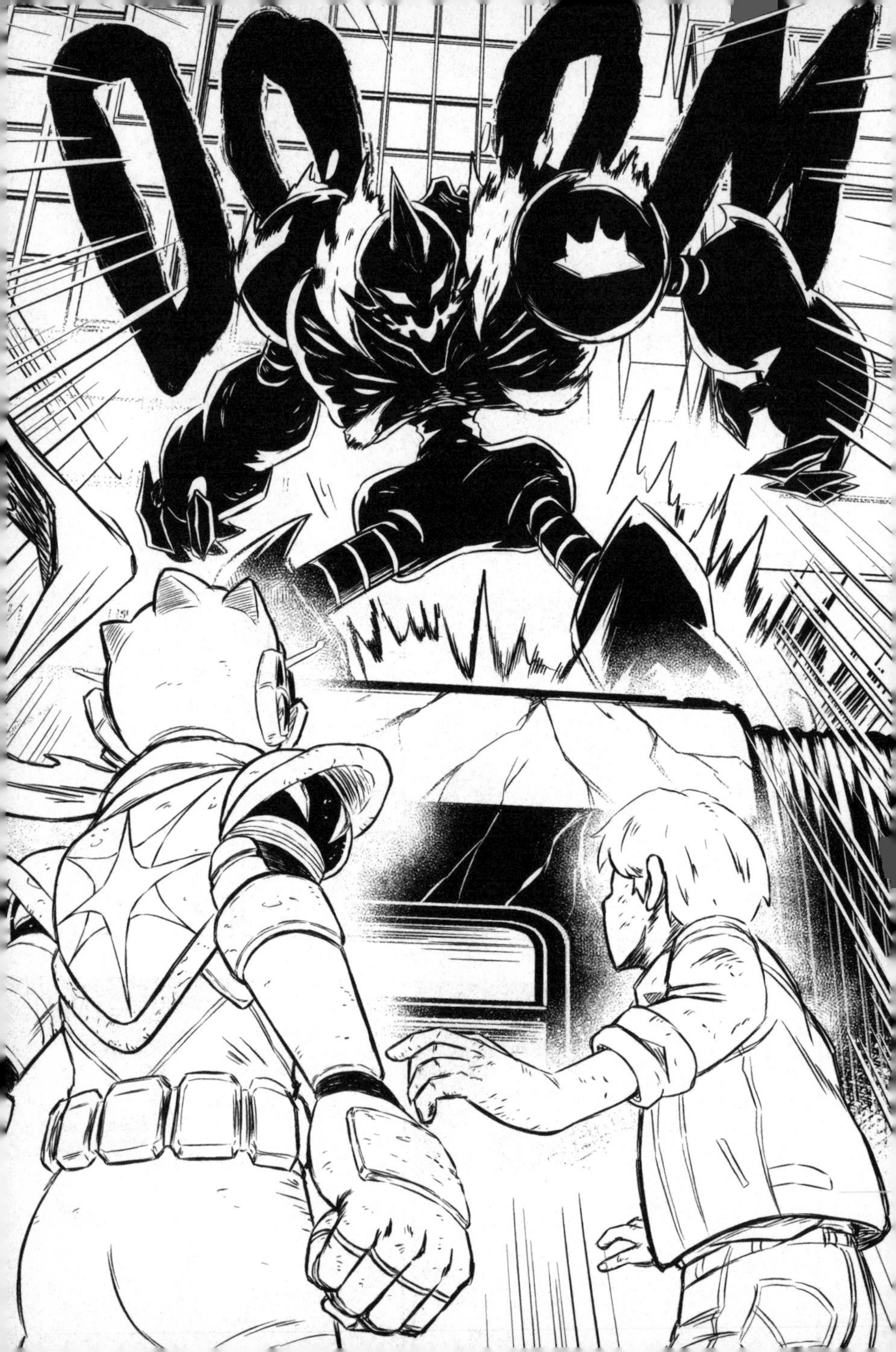
DOOM

HENSHIN!

CHAPTER TWO
KAIJU

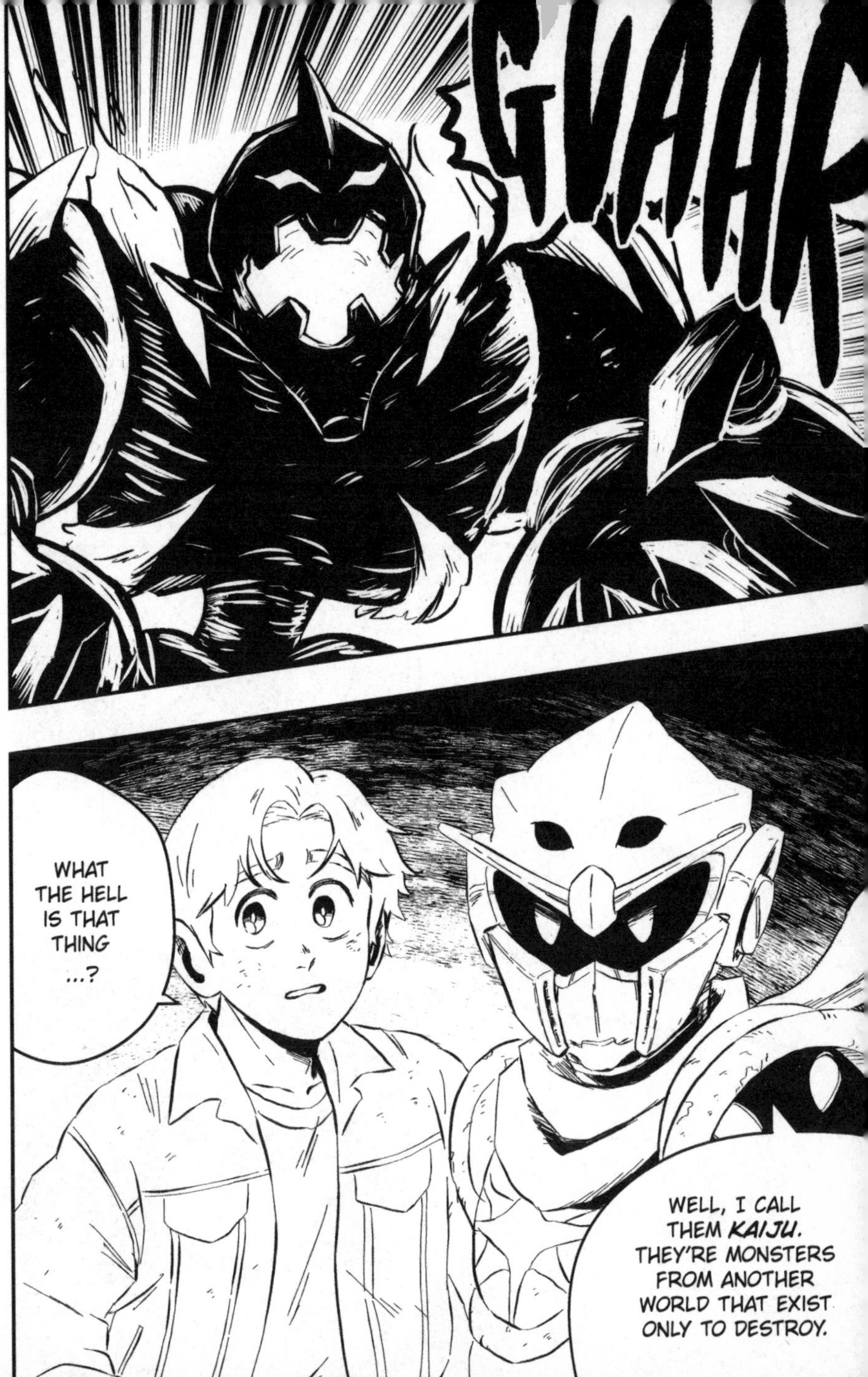
WHAT THE HELL IS THAT THING ...?
WELL, I CALL THEM *KAIJU*. THEY'RE MONSTERS FROM ANOTHER WORLD THAT EXIST ONLY TO DESTROY.

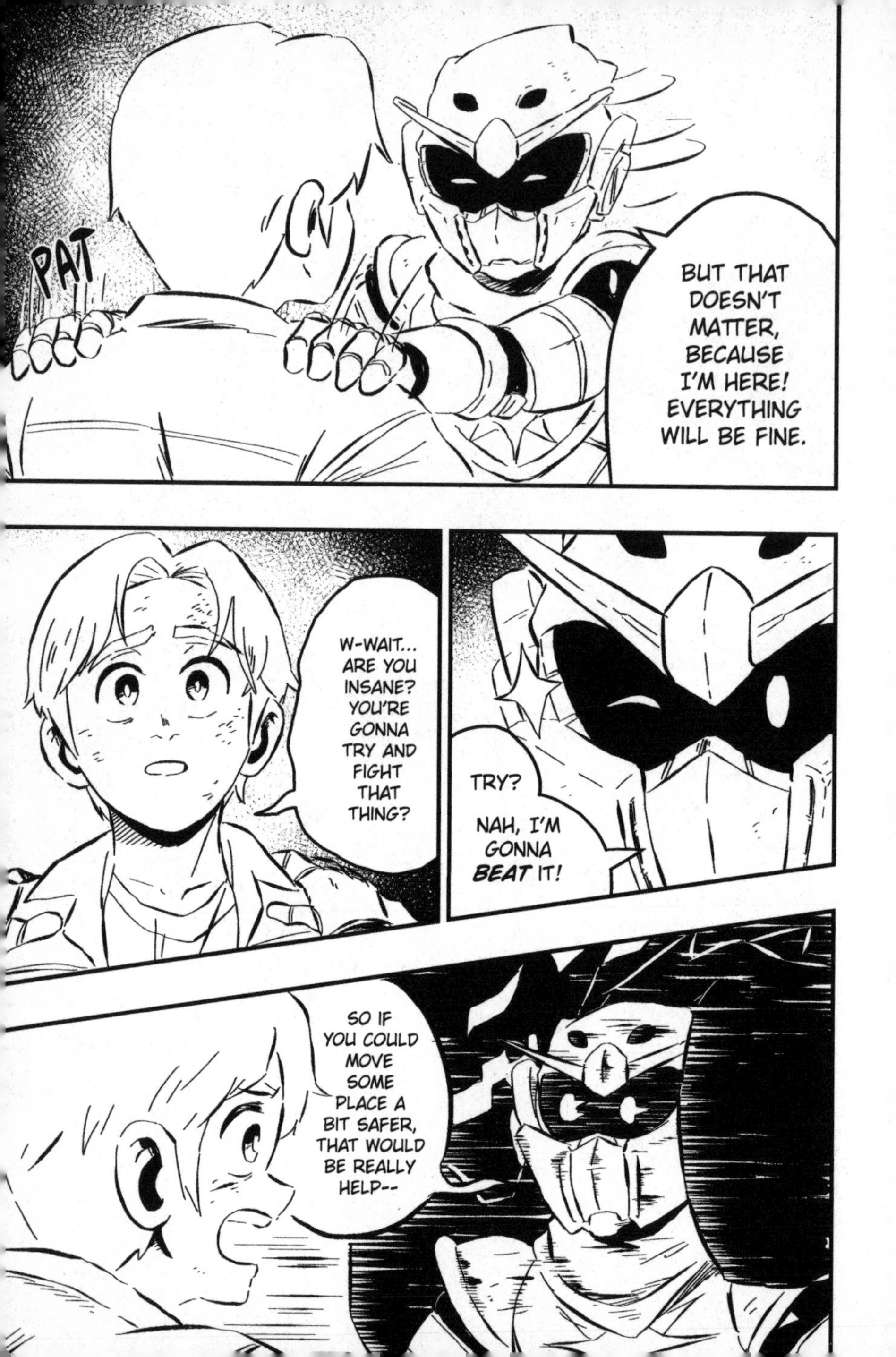
PAT
BUT THAT DOESN'T MATTER, BECAUSE I'M HERE! EVERYTHING WILL BE FINE.
W-WAIT... ARE YOU INSANE? YOU'RE GONNA TRY AND FIGHT THAT THING?
TRY?
NAH, I'M GONNA BEAT IT!
SO IF YOU COULD MOVE SOME PLACE A BIT SAFER, THAT WOULD BE REALLY HELP--

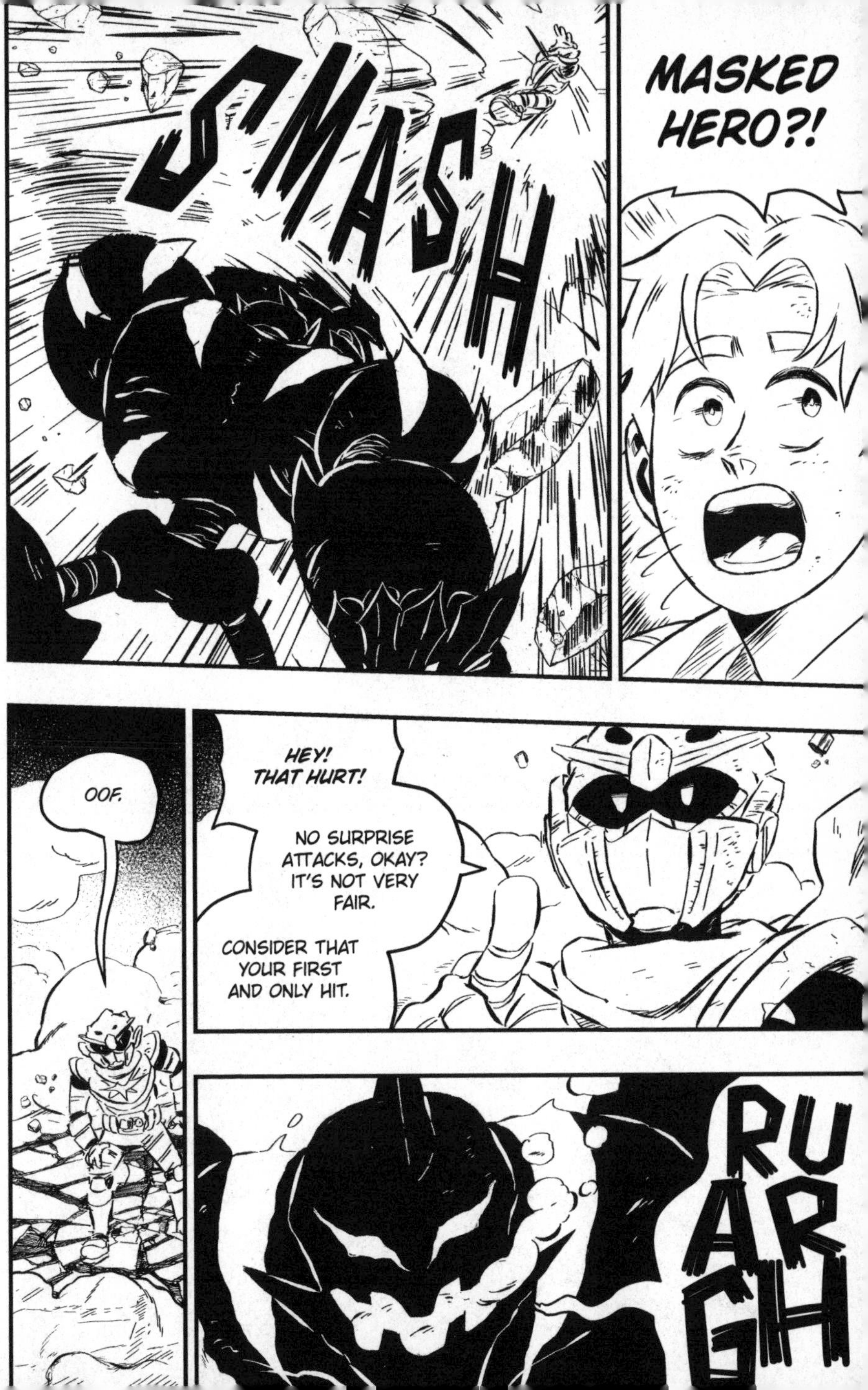
SMASH
MASKED HERO?!
HEY! THAT HURT!
NO SURPRISE ATTACKS, OKAY? IT'S NOT VERY FAIR.
CONSIDER THAT YOUR FIRST AND ONLY HIT.
OOF.
RUARGH

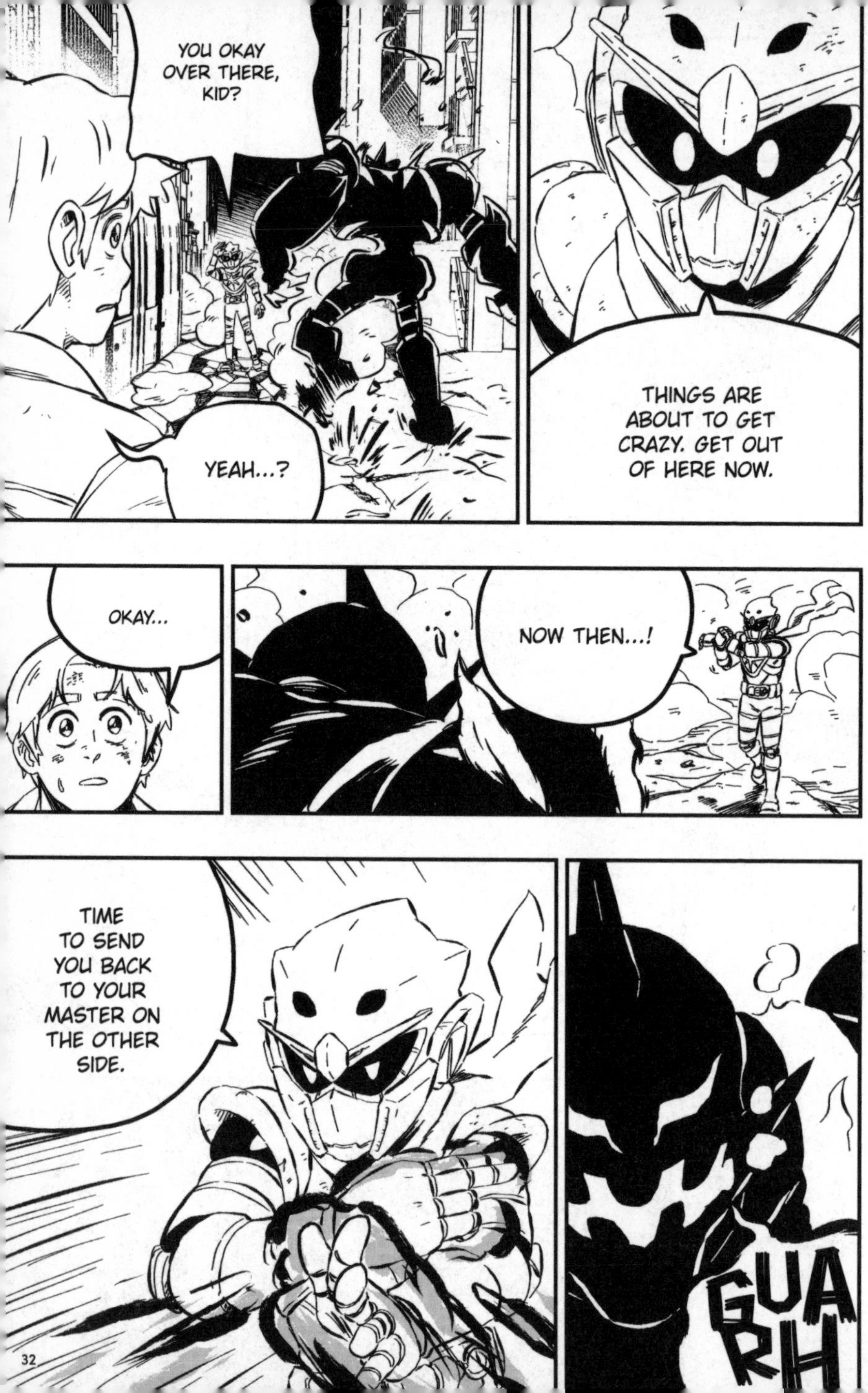
YOU OKAY OVER THERE, KID?
YEAH...?
THINGS ARE ABOUT TO GET CRAZY. GET OUT OF HERE NOW.
OKAY...
NOW THEN...!
TIME TO SEND YOU BACK TO YOUR MASTER ON THE OTHER SIDE.
GUARH

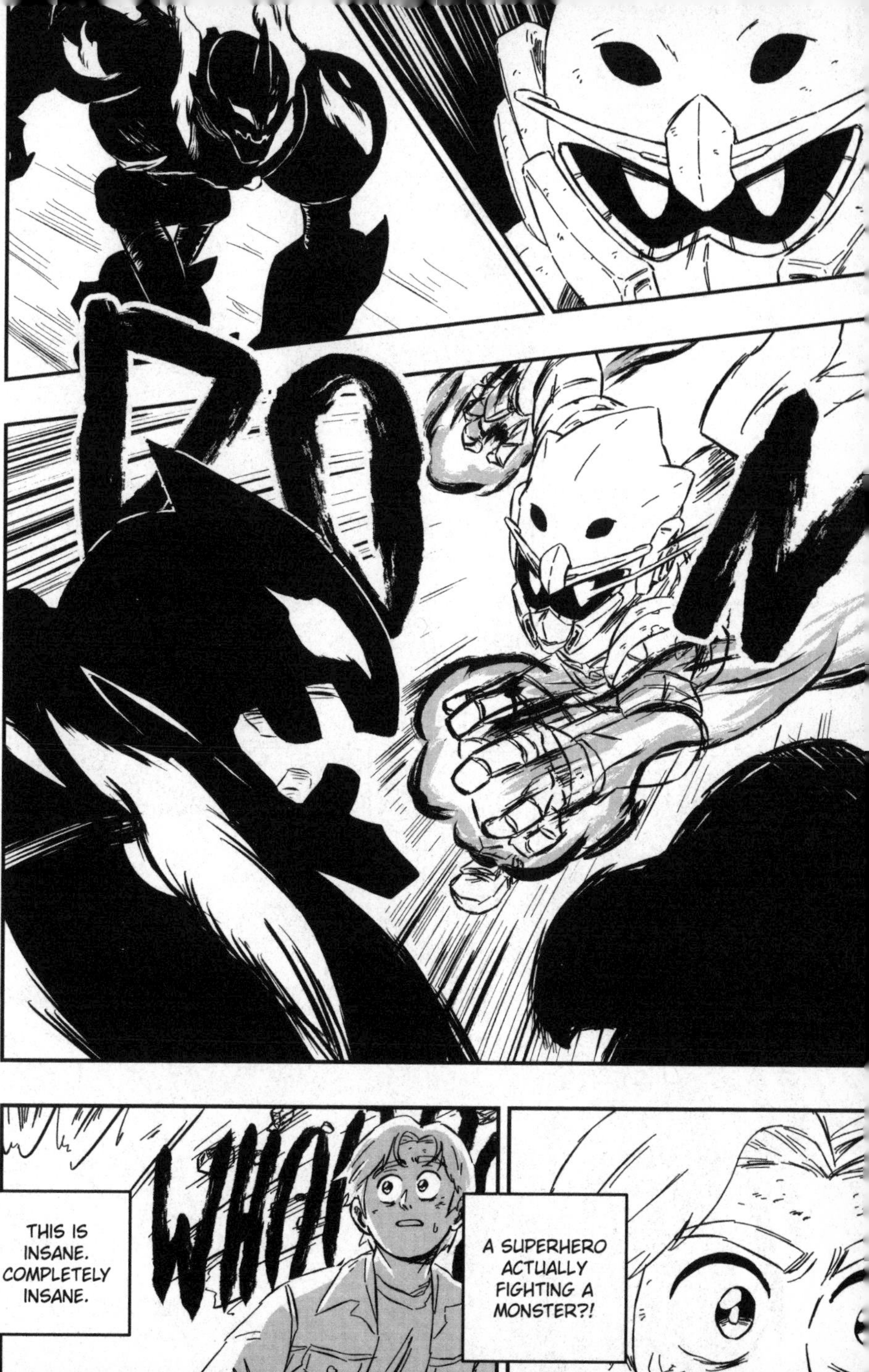
THIS IS INSANE. COMPLETELY INSANE.
A SUPERHERO ACTUALLY FIGHTING A MONSTER?!

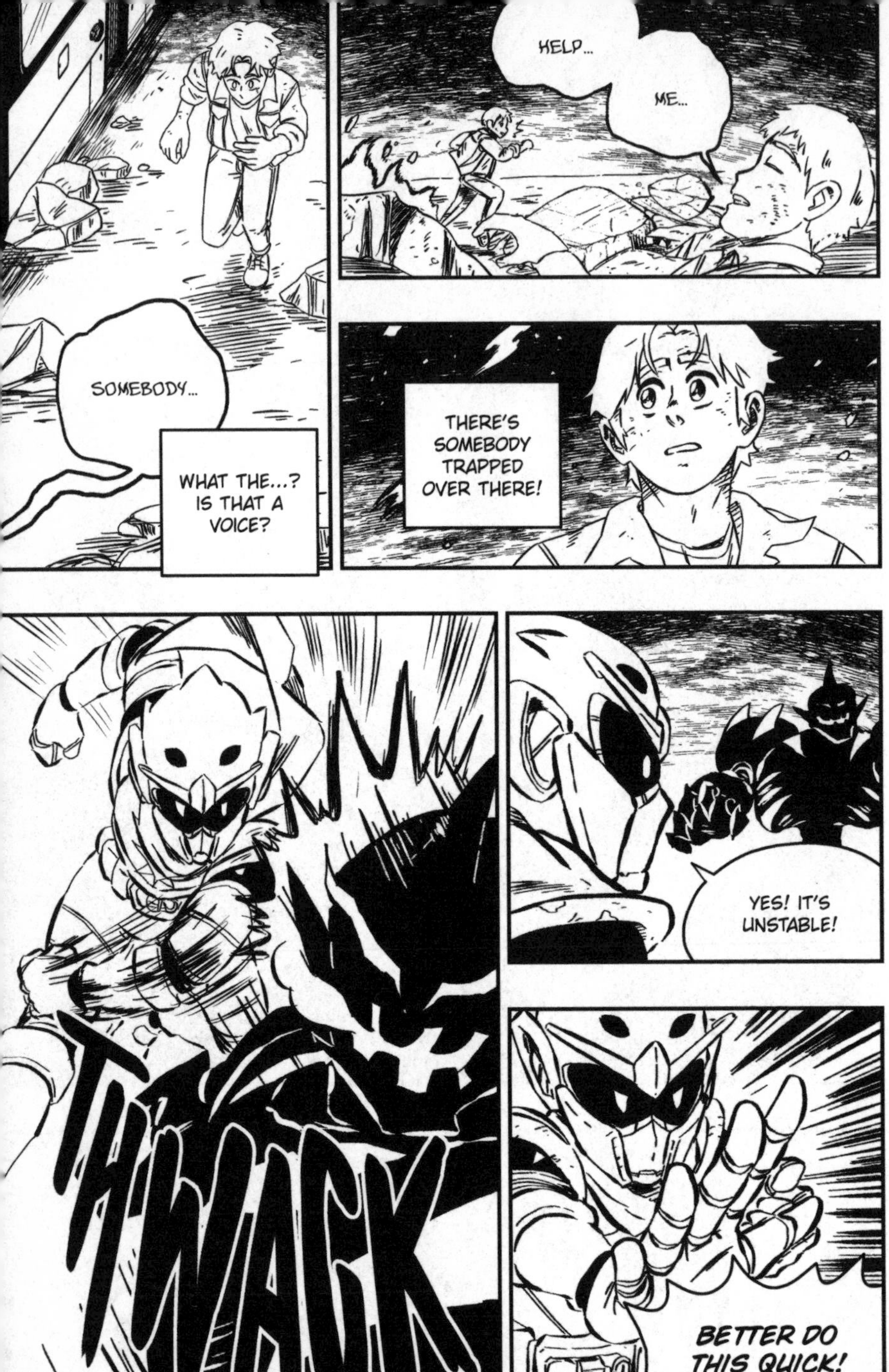

SOMEBODY...
WHAT THE...? IS THAT A VOICE?
HELP...
ME...
THERE'S SOMEBODY TRAPPED OVER THERE!
THWACK
YES! IT'S UNSTABLE!
BETTER DO THIS QUICK!

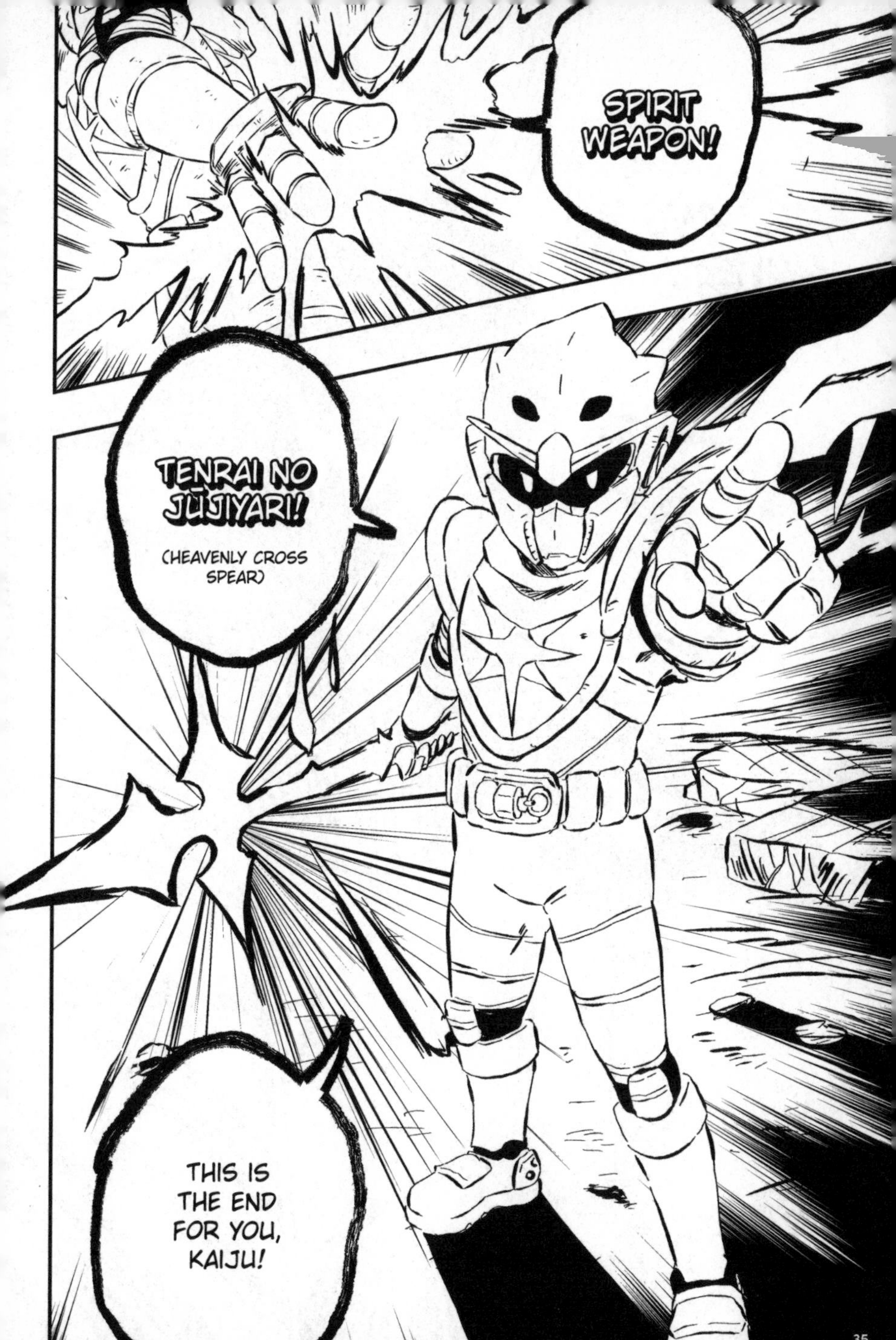

SPIRIT WEAPON!
TENRAI NO JŪJIYARI!
(HEAVENLY CROSS SPEAR)
THIS IS THE END FOR YOU, KAIJU!

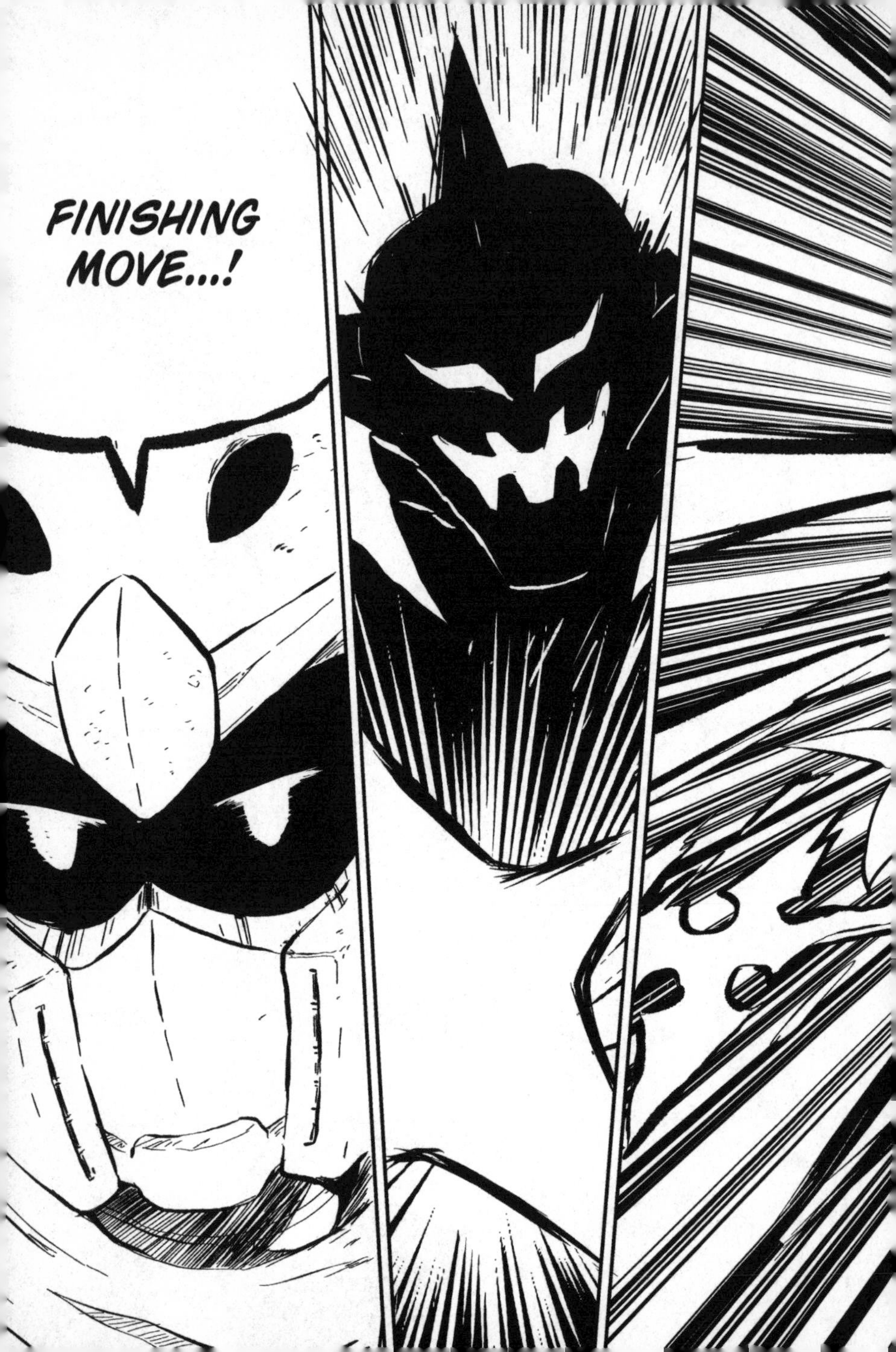
FINISHING MOVE...!

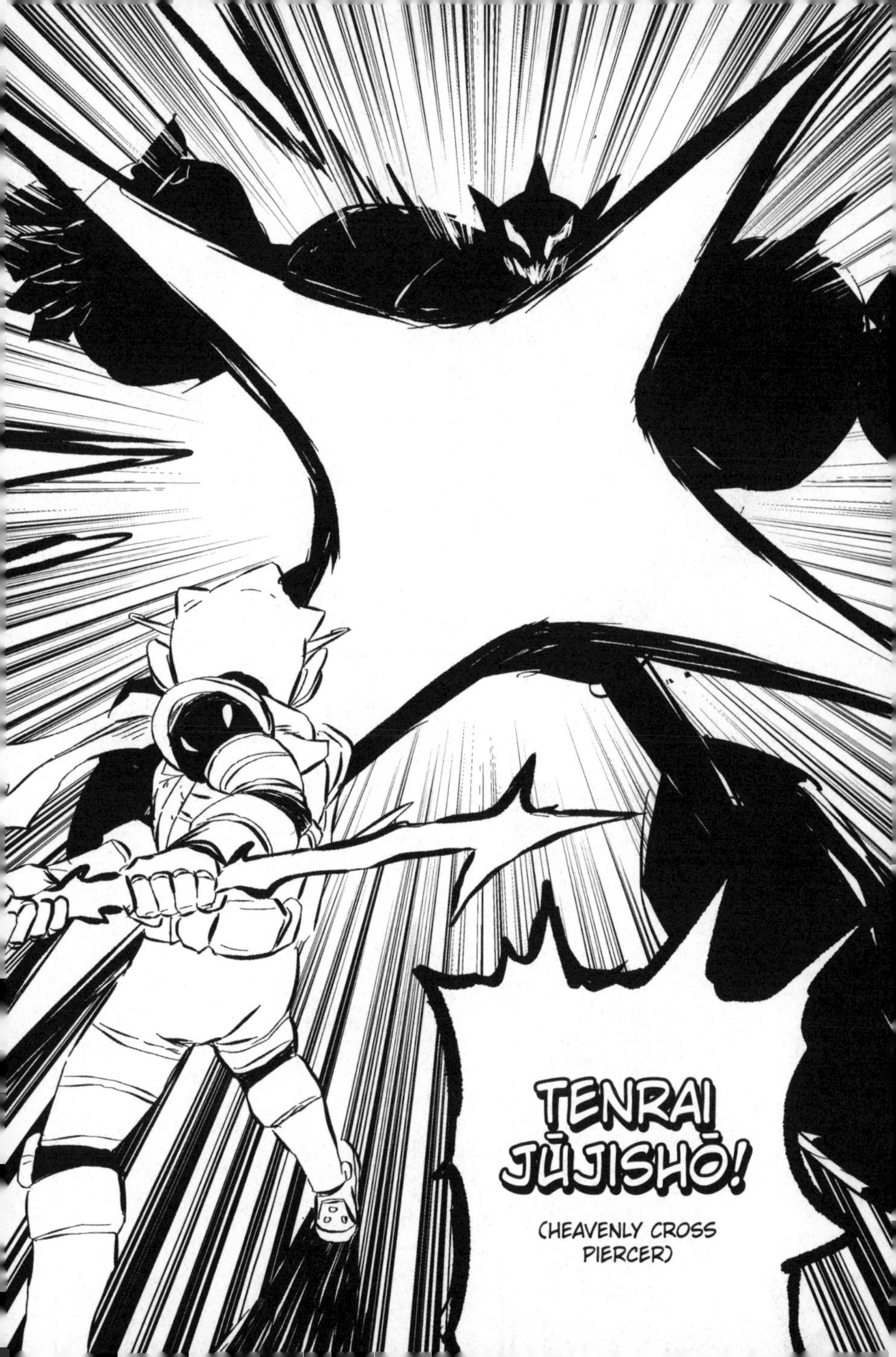
TENRAI JŪJISHŌ!
(HEAVENLY CROSS PIERCER)

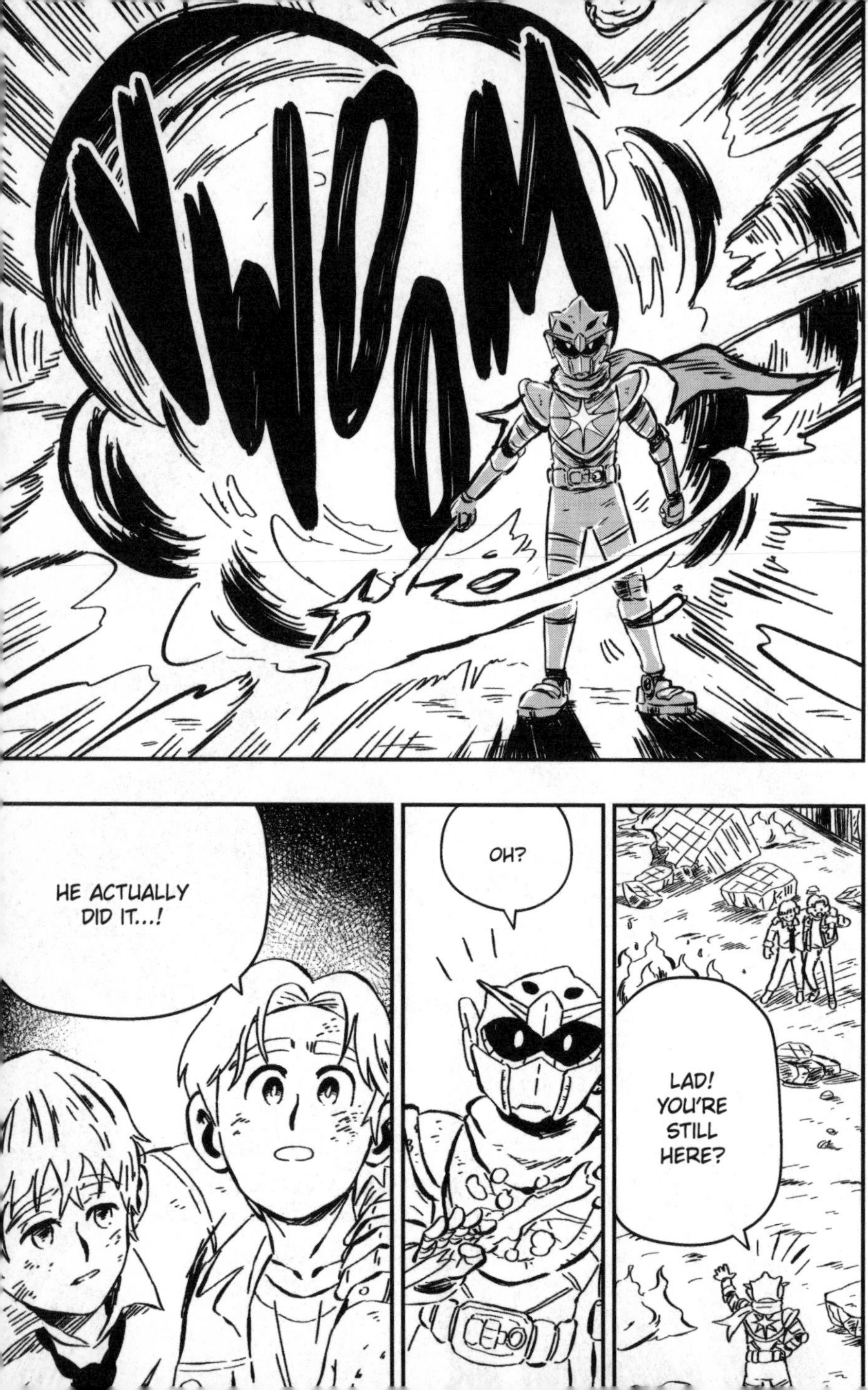
HE ACTUALLY DID IT...!
OH?
LAD! YOU'RE STILL HERE?

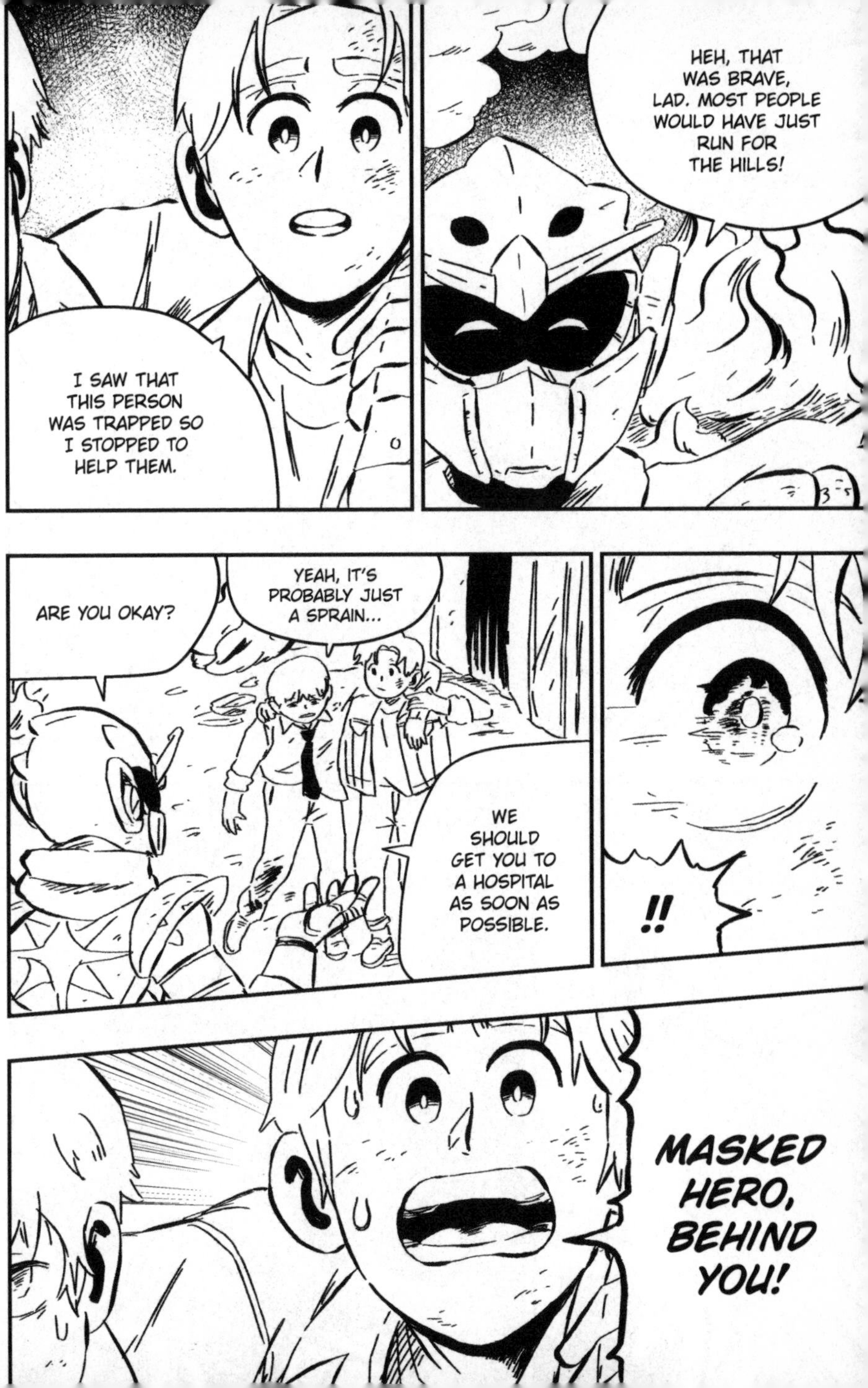
HEH, THAT WAS BRAVE, LAD. MOST PEOPLE WOULD HAVE JUST RUN FOR THE HILLS!
I SAW THAT THIS PERSON WAS TRAPPED SO I STOPPED TO HELP THEM.
ARE YOU OKAY?
YEAH, IT'S PROBABLY JUST A SPRAIN...
WE SHOULD GET YOU TO A HOSPITAL AS SOON AS POSSIBLE.
!!
MASKED HERO, BEHIND YOU!

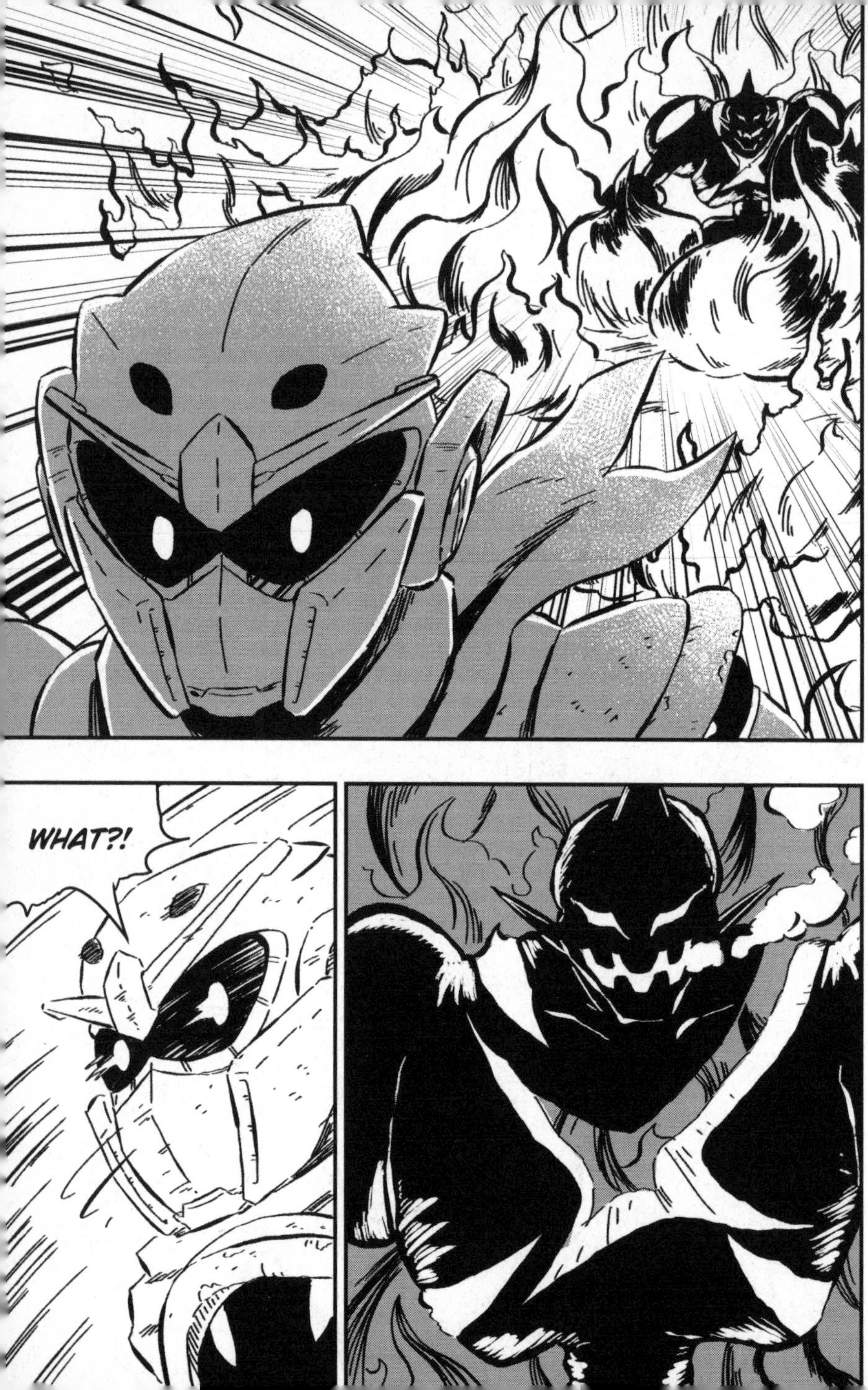
WHAT?!

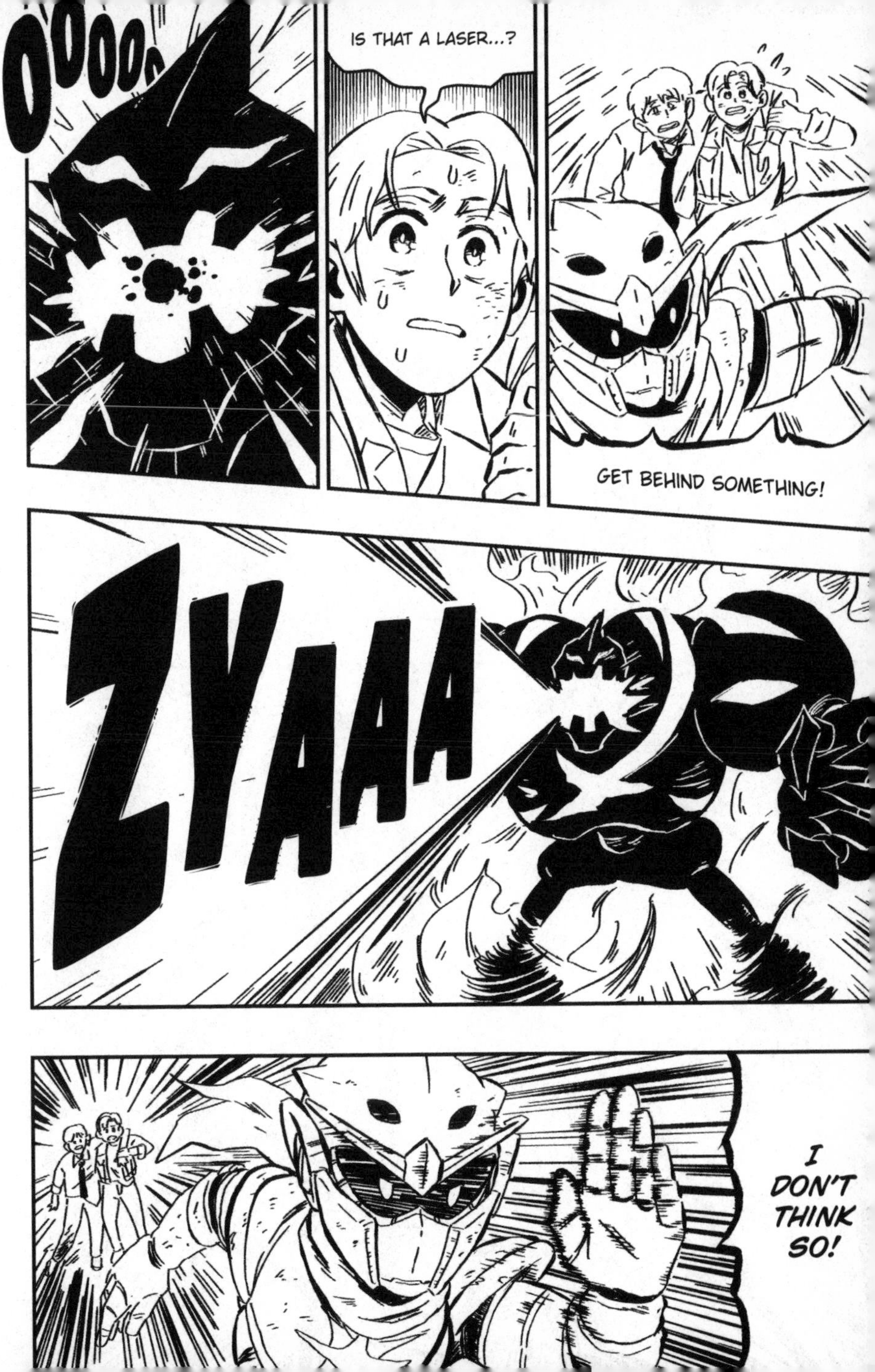
OOOOO
IS THAT A LASER...?
GET BEHIND SOMETHING!
ZYAAA
I DON'T THINK SO!

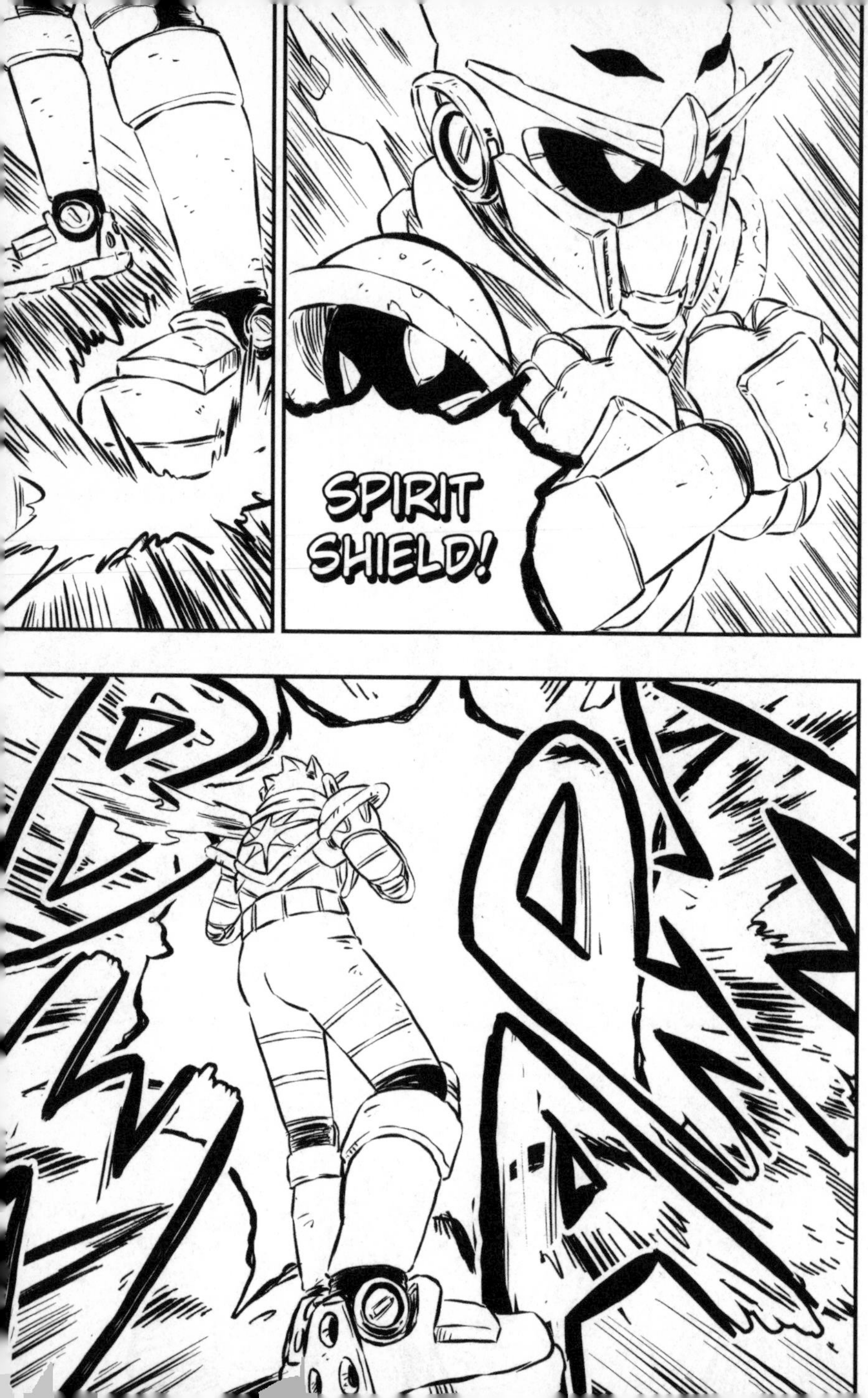
SPIRIT SHIELD!

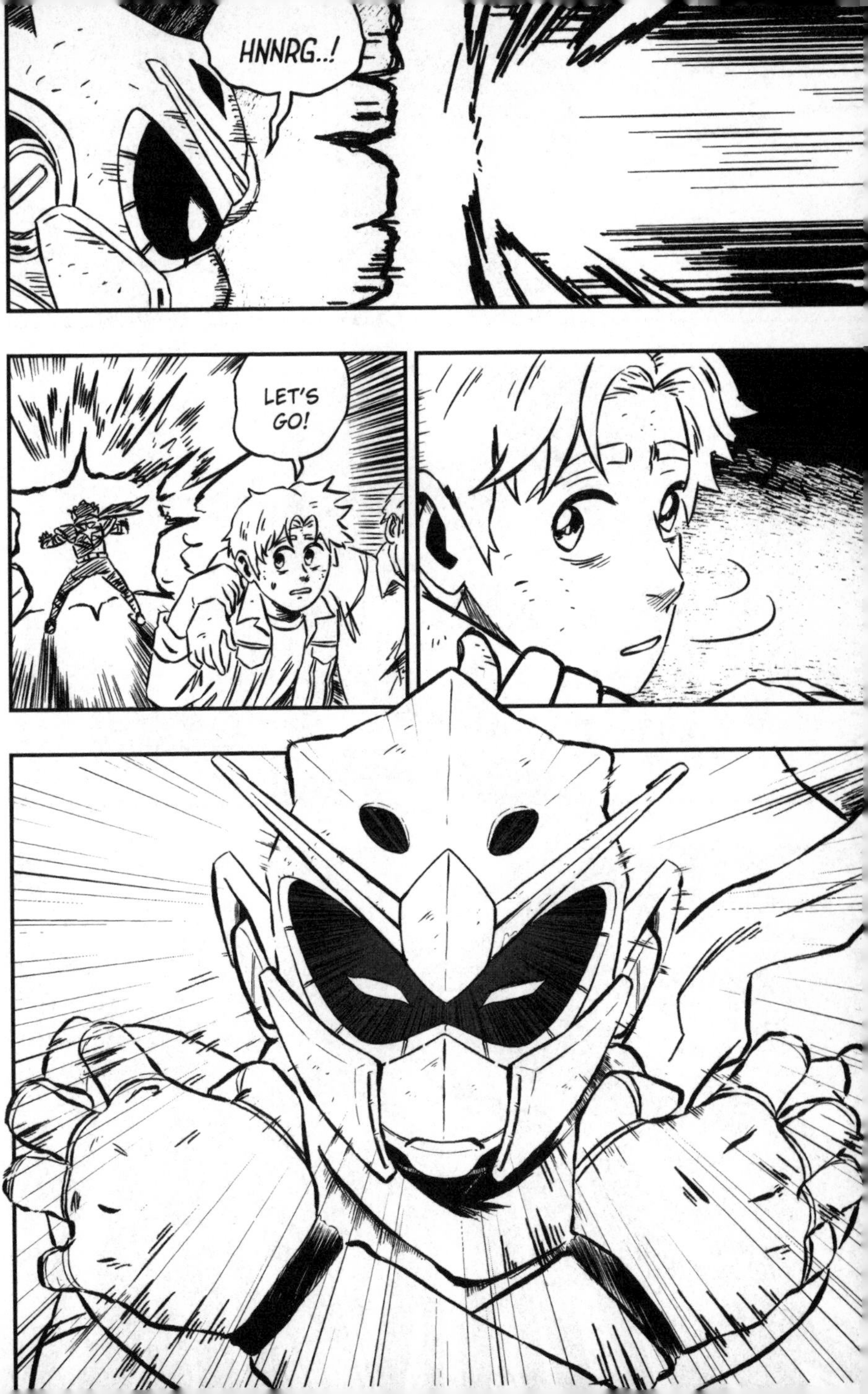
HNNRG..!
LET'S GO!

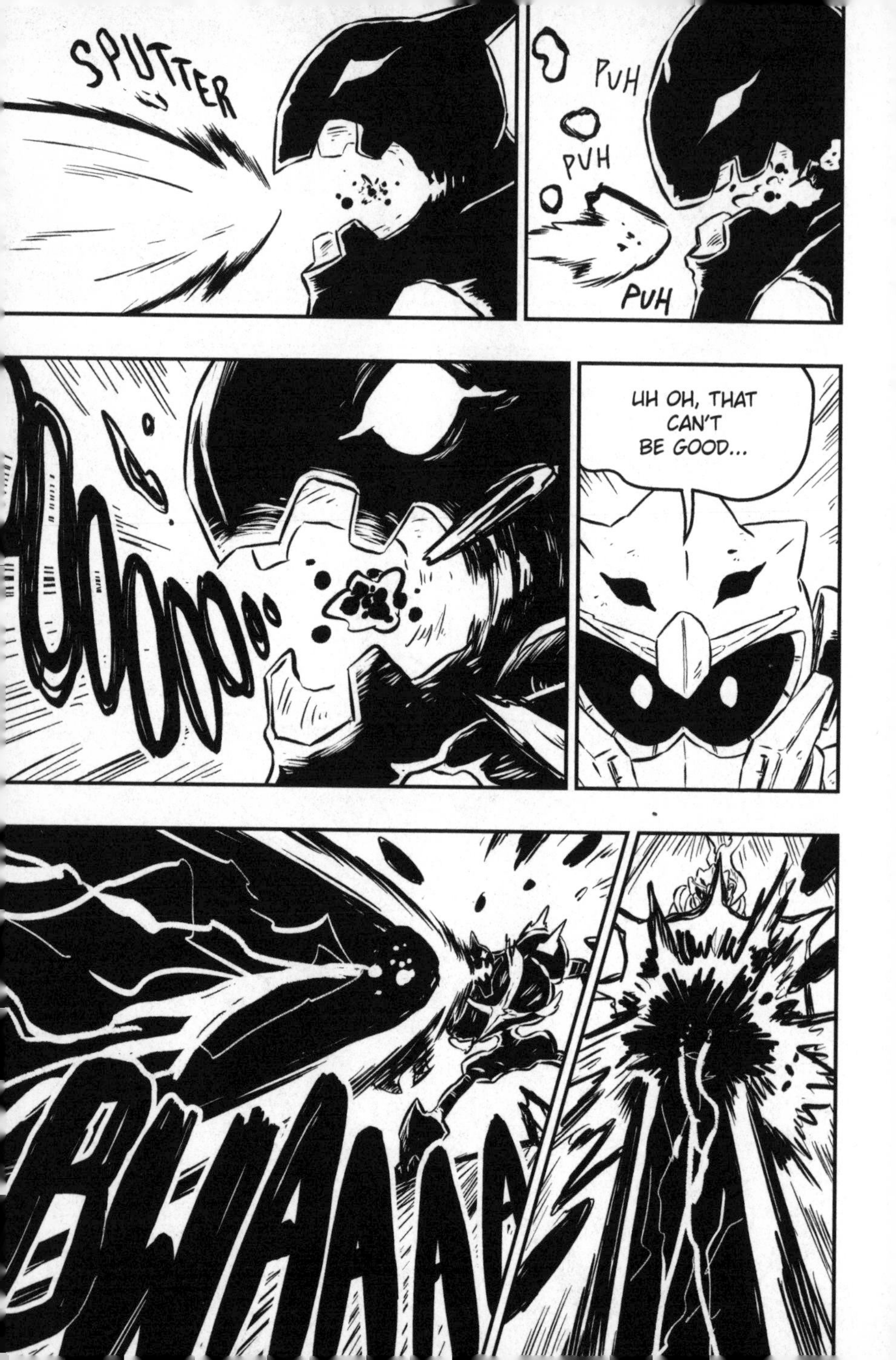
SPUTTER
PUH
PUH
PUH
UH OH, THAT CAN'T BE GOOD...

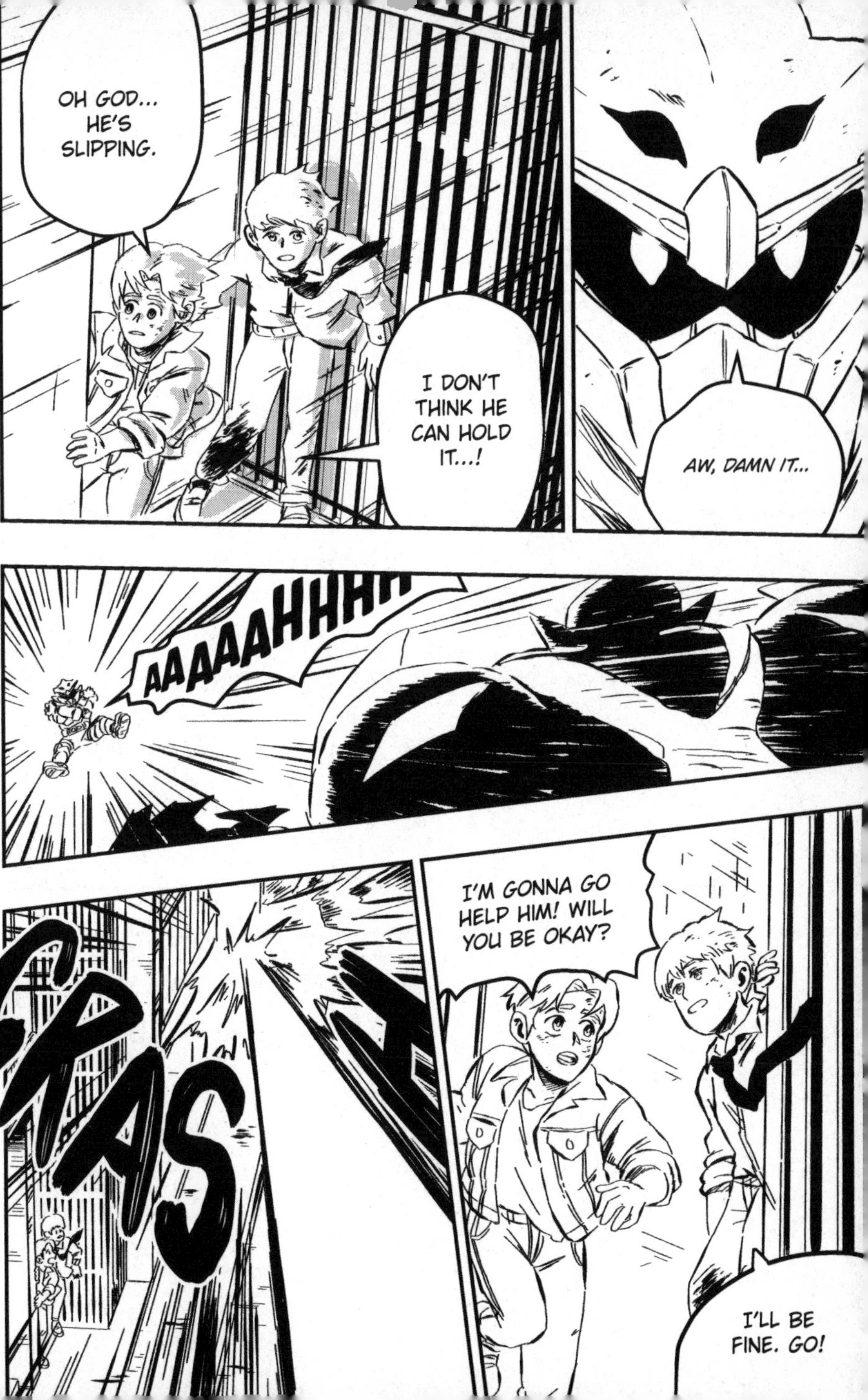
OH GOD... HE'S SLIPPING.
I DON'T THINK HE CAN HOLD IT...!
AW, DAMN IT...
AAAAAHHHH
CRASH
I'M GONNA GO HELP HIM! WILL YOU BE OKAY?
I'LL BE FINE. GO!

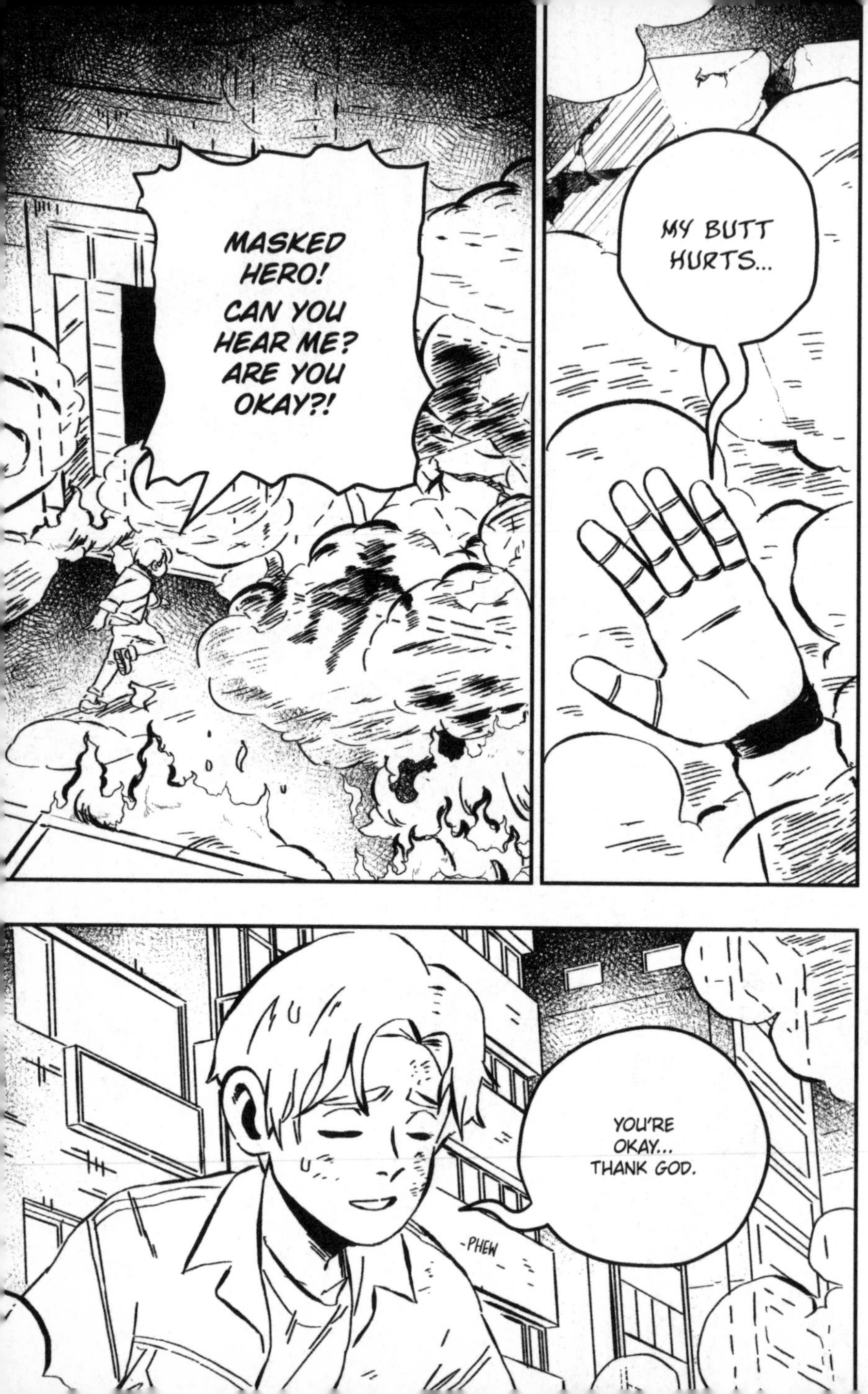
MASKED HERO! CAN YOU HEAR ME? ARE YOU OKAY?!
MY BUTT HURTS...
YOU'RE OKAY... THANK GOD.
-PHEW

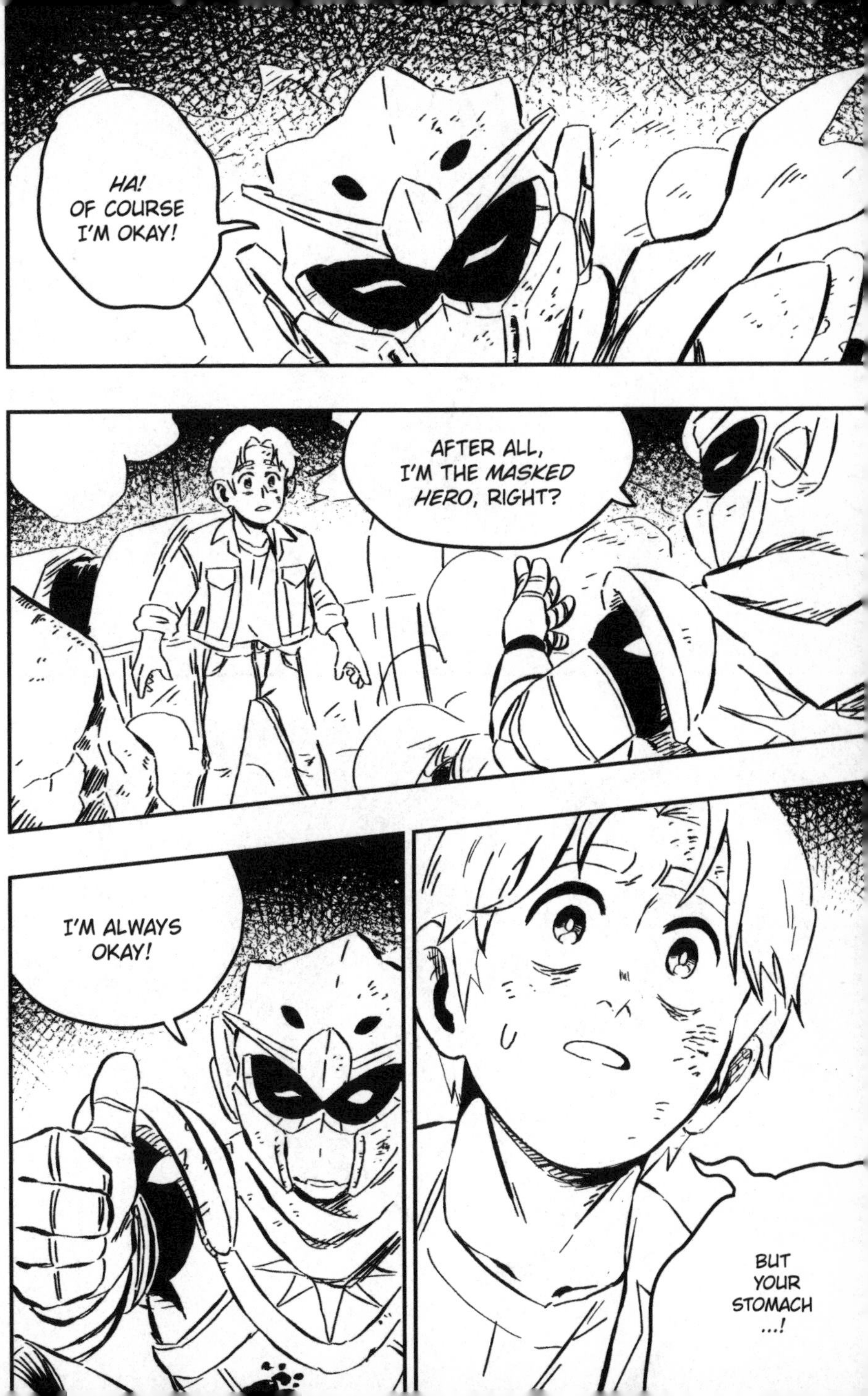
HA! OF COURSE I'M OKAY!
AFTER ALL, I'M THE *MASKED HERO*, RIGHT?
I'M ALWAYS OKAY!
BUT YOUR STOMACH ...!

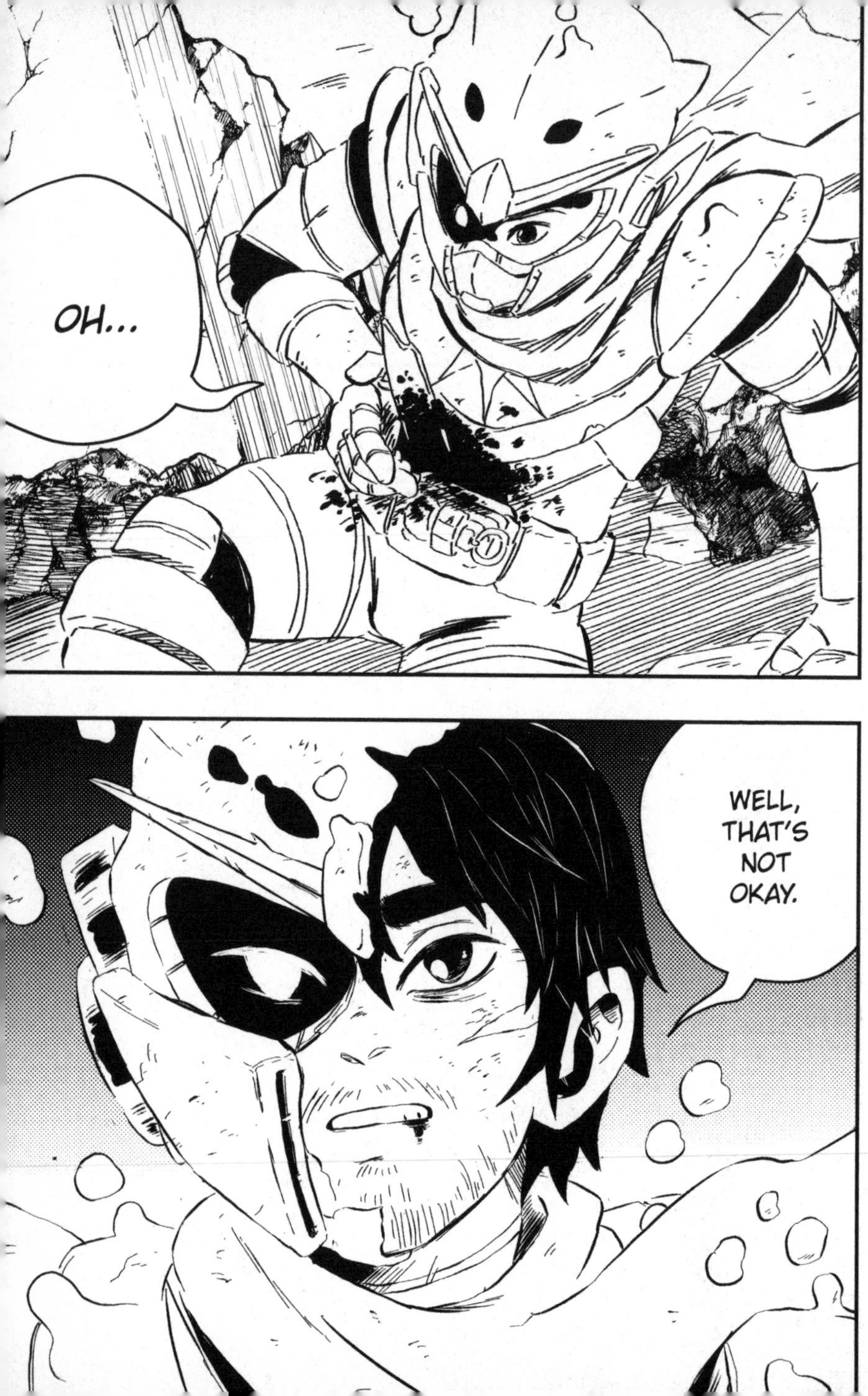
OH...
WELL, THAT'S NOT OKAY.

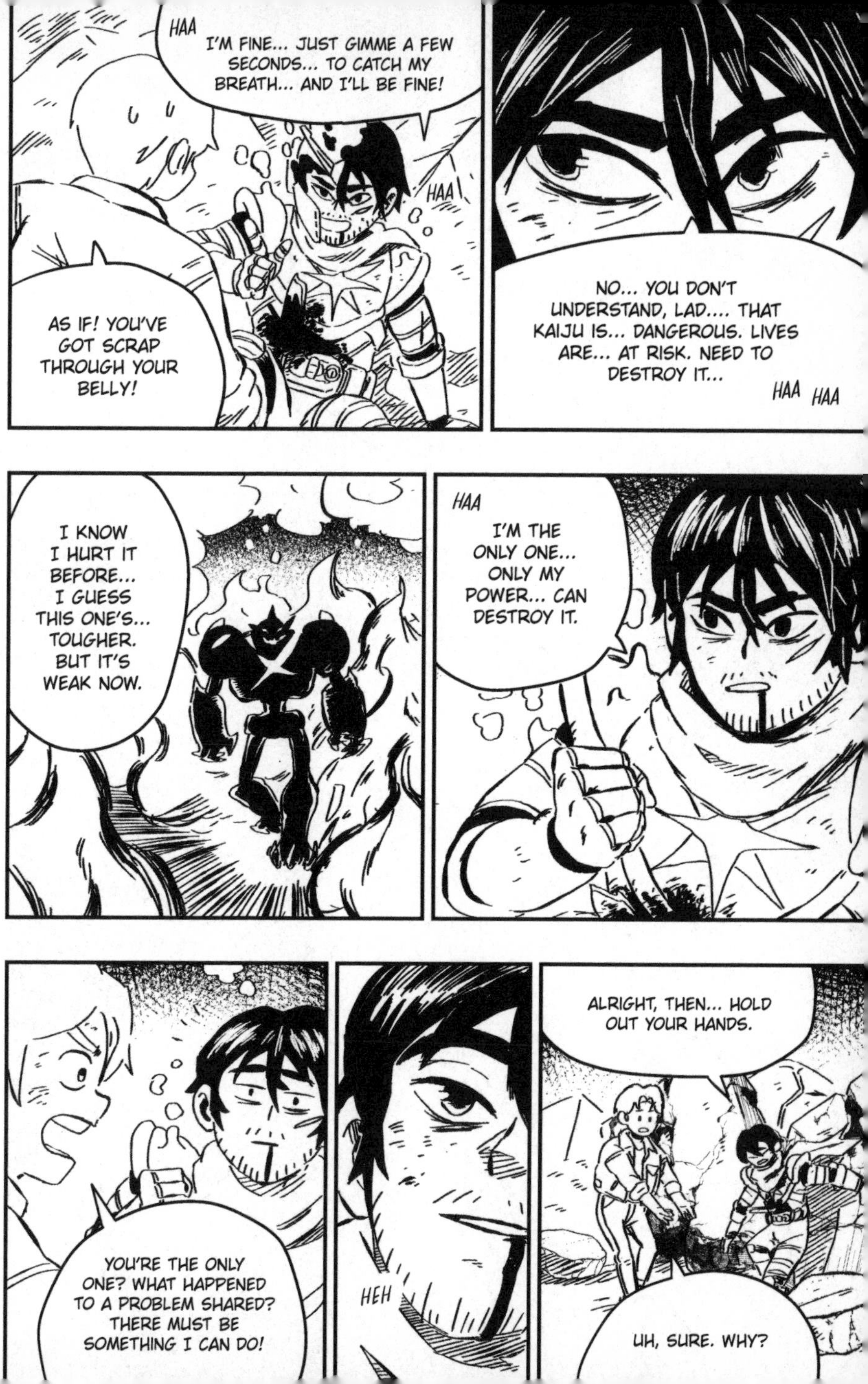
HAA
I'M FINE... JUST GIMME A FEW SECONDS... TO CATCH MY BREATH... AND I'LL BE FINE!
HAA
AS IF! YOU'VE GOT SCRAP THROUGH YOUR BELLY!
NO... YOU DON'T UNDERSTAND, LAD.... THAT KAIJU IS... DANGEROUS. LIVES ARE... AT RISK. NEED TO DESTROY IT...
HAA HAA
I KNOW I HURT IT BEFORE... I GUESS THIS ONE'S... TOUGHER. BUT IT'S WEAK NOW.
HAA
I'M THE ONLY ONE... ONLY MY POWER... CAN DESTROY IT.
YOU'RE THE ONLY ONE? WHAT HAPPENED TO A PROBLEM SHARED? THERE MUST BE SOMETHING I CAN DO!
HEH
ALRIGHT, THEN... HOLD OUT YOUR HANDS.
UH, SURE. WHY?

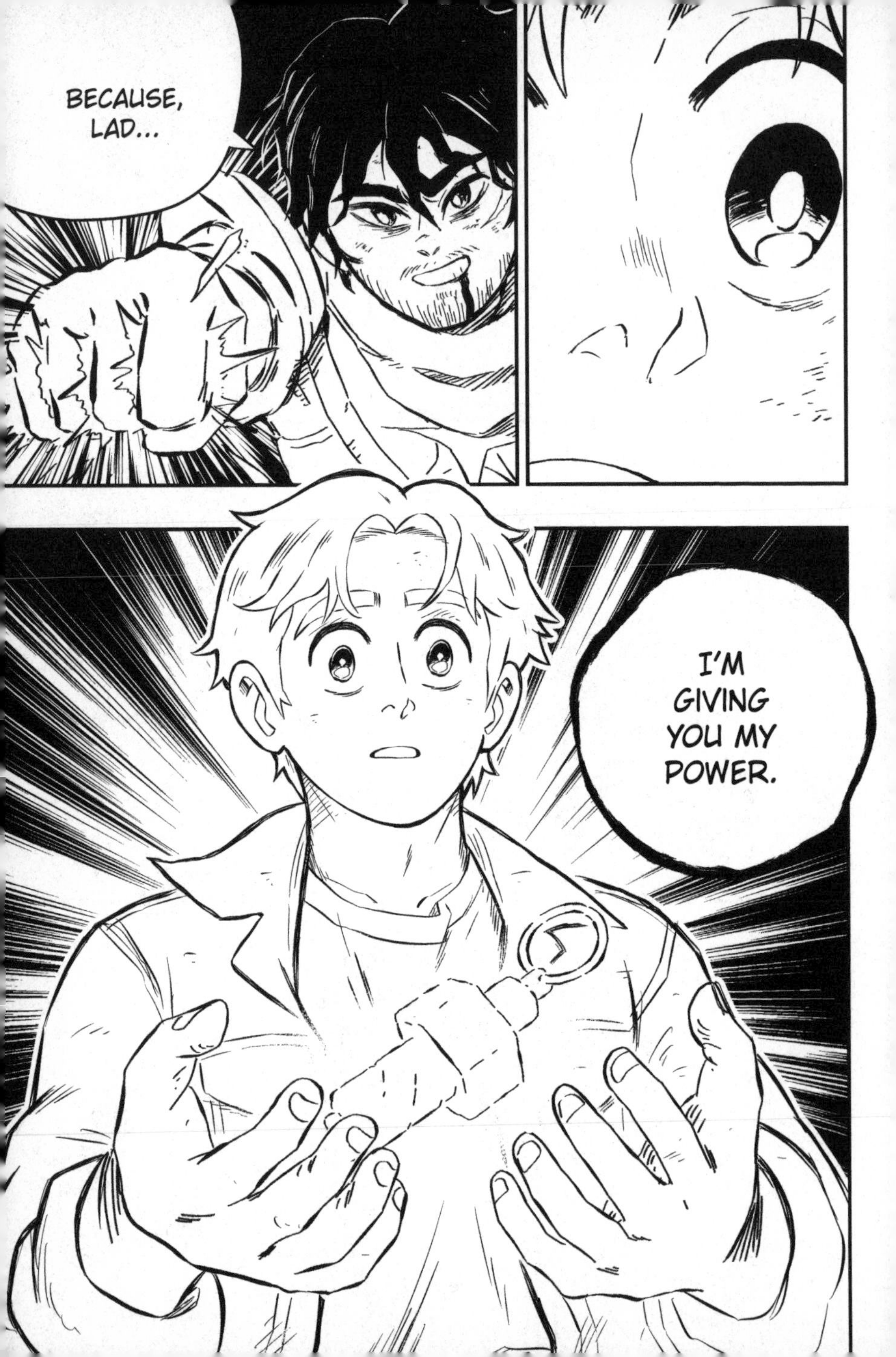
BECAUSE, LAD...
I'M GIVING YOU MY POWER.

CHAPTER THREE

PHOENIX RISING

YOU'RE GIVING ME YOUR POWER ...?

WELL... PART OF IT. THAT WILL GIVE YOU THE ABILITY TO FIGHT BACK.

IT WILL ALLOW YOU TO HENSHIN. TO BECOME... A HERO.

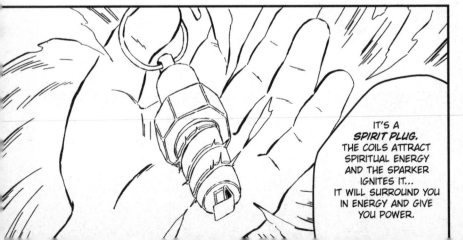

IT'S A *SPIRIT PLUG.* THE COILS ATTRACT SPIRITUAL ENERGY AND THE SPARKER IGNITES IT... IT WILL SURROUND YOU IN ENERGY AND GIVE YOU POWER.

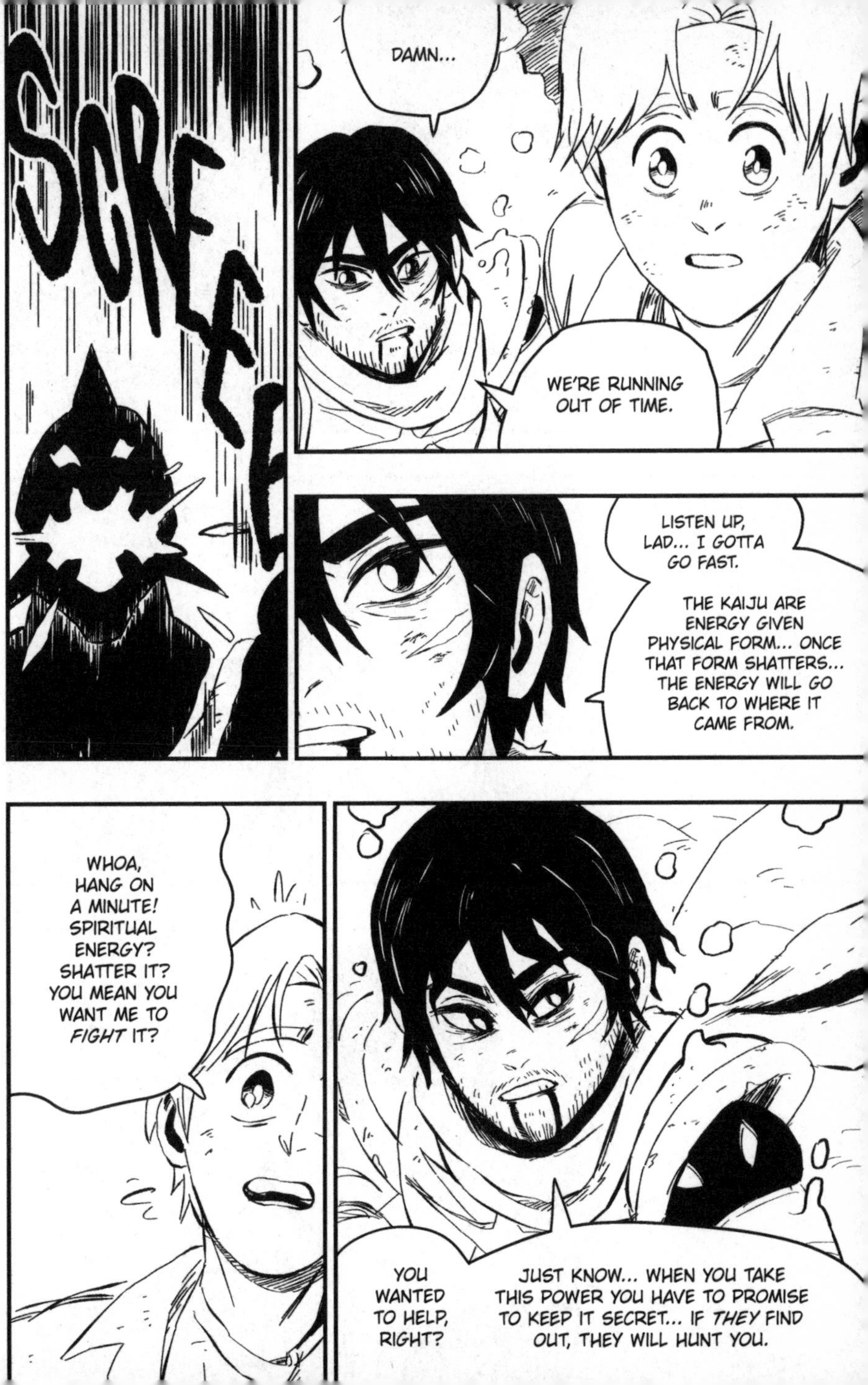
SCREEEE
DAMN...
WE'RE RUNNING OUT OF TIME.
LISTEN UP, LAD... I GOTTA GO FAST.
THE KAIJU ARE ENERGY GIVEN PHYSICAL FORM... ONCE THAT FORM SHATTERS... THE ENERGY WILL GO BACK TO WHERE IT CAME FROM.
WHOA, HANG ON A MINUTE! SPIRITUAL ENERGY? SHATTER IT? YOU MEAN YOU WANT ME TO *FIGHT* IT?
YOU WANTED TO HELP, RIGHT?
JUST KNOW... WHEN YOU TAKE THIS POWER YOU HAVE TO PROMISE TO KEEP IT SECRET... IF *THEY* FIND OUT, THEY WILL HUNT YOU.

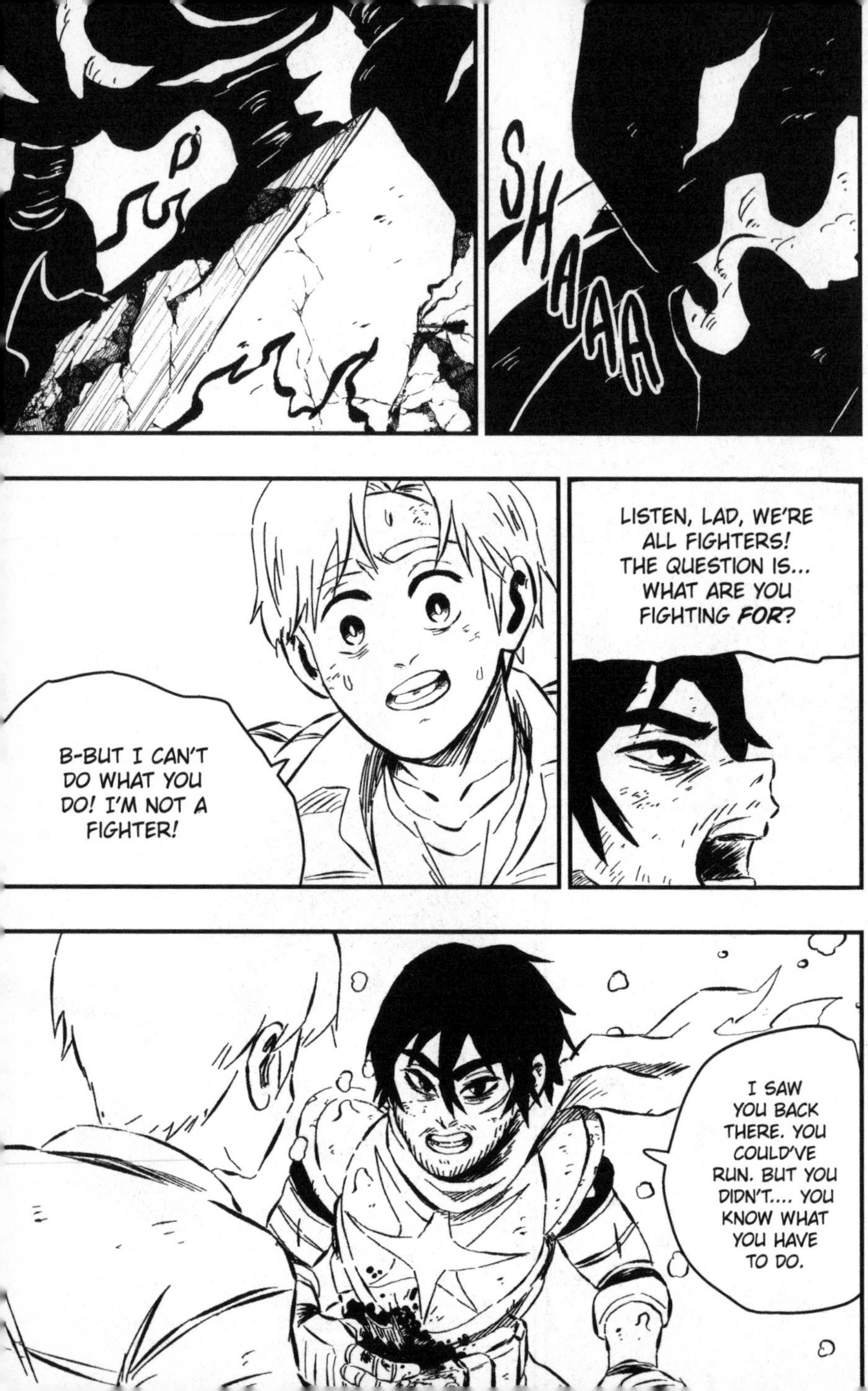
SHAAAA
LISTEN, LAD, WE'RE ALL FIGHTERS! THE QUESTION IS... WHAT ARE YOU FIGHTING *FOR*?
B-BUT I CAN'T DO WHAT YOU DO! I'M NOT A FIGHTER!
I SAW YOU BACK THERE. YOU COULD'VE RUN. BUT YOU DIDN'T.... YOU KNOW WHAT YOU HAVE TO DO.

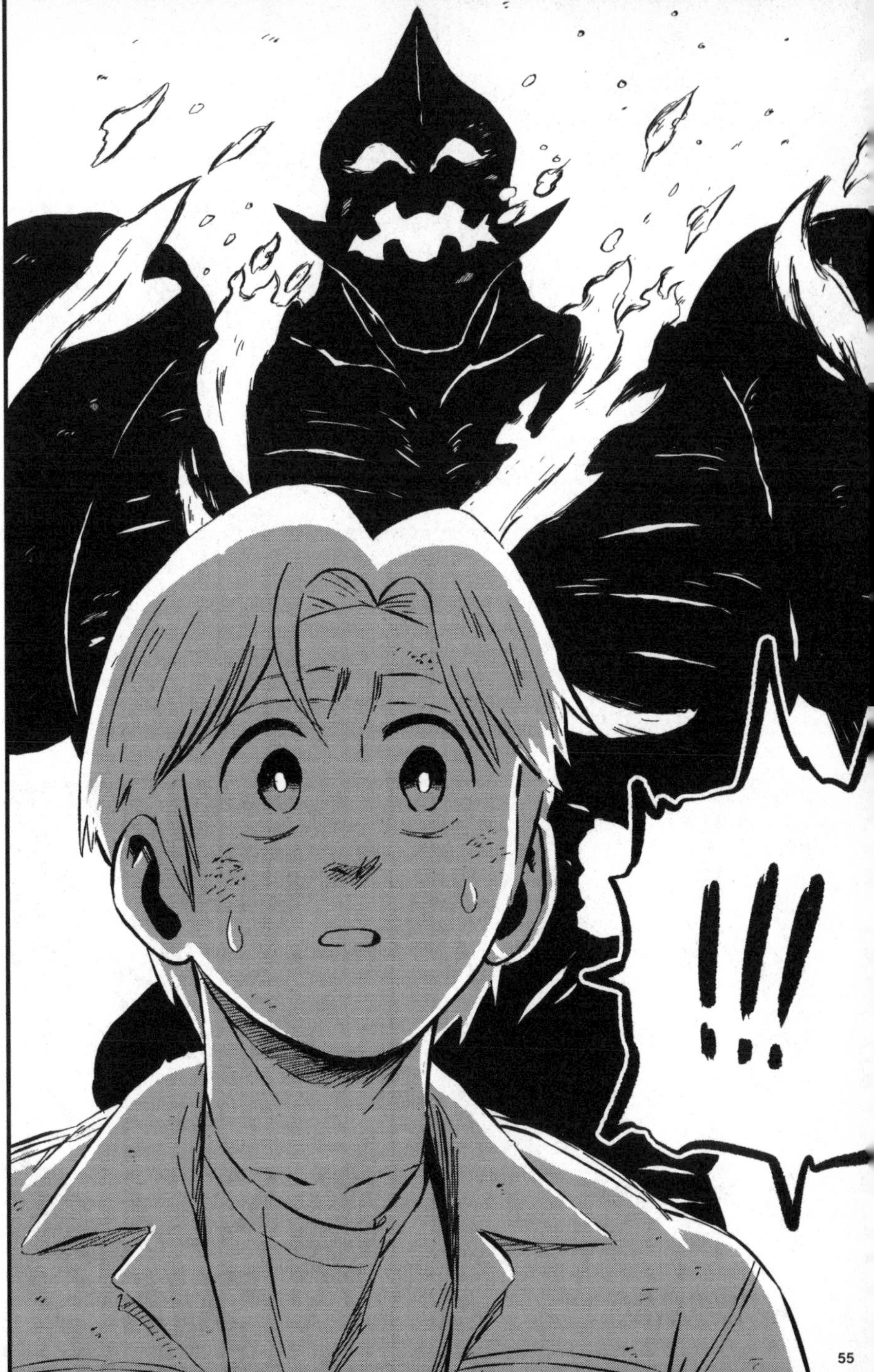
!!!

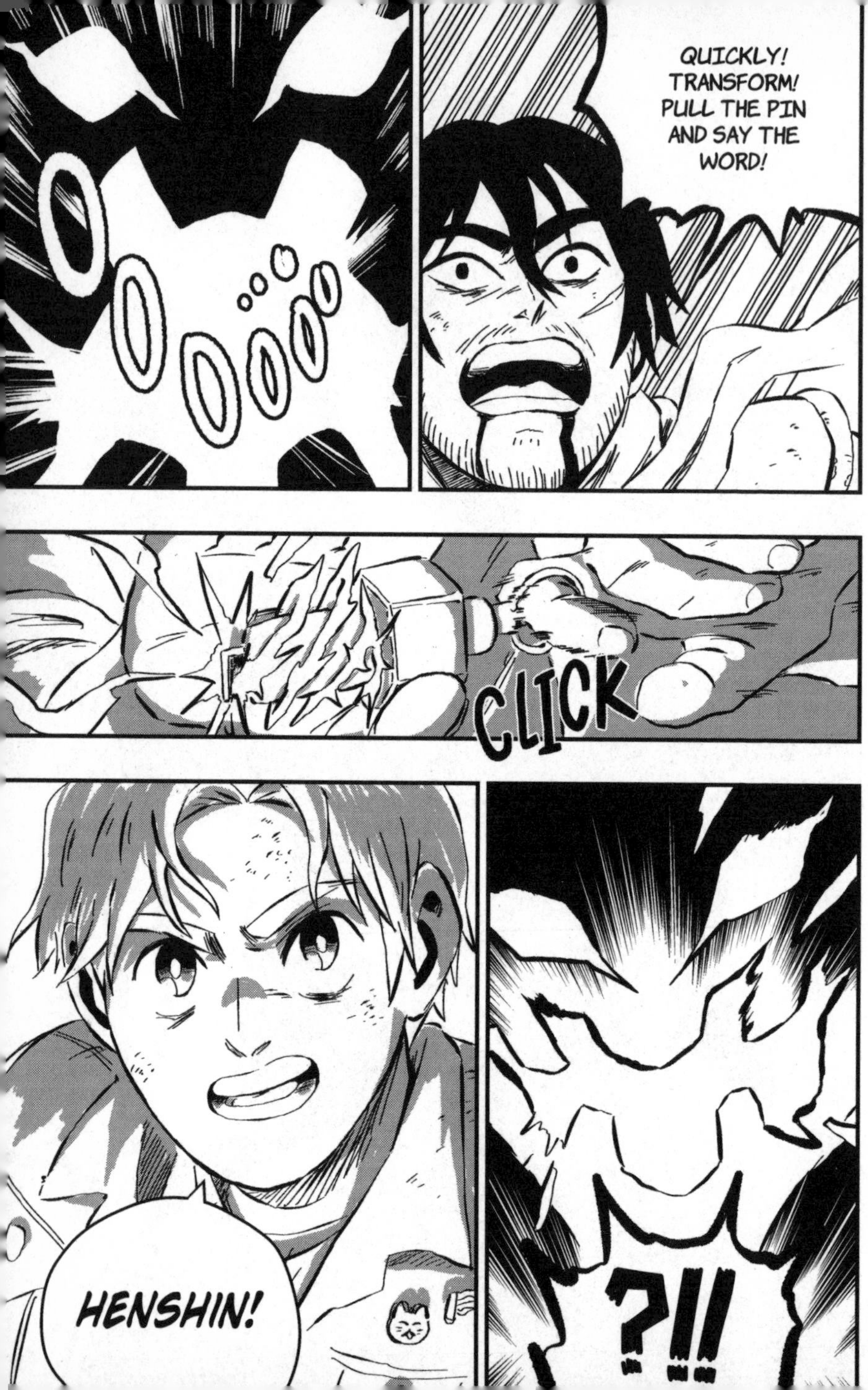
QUICKLY! TRANSFORM! PULL THE PIN AND SAY THE WORD!
CLICK
?!!
HENSHIN!

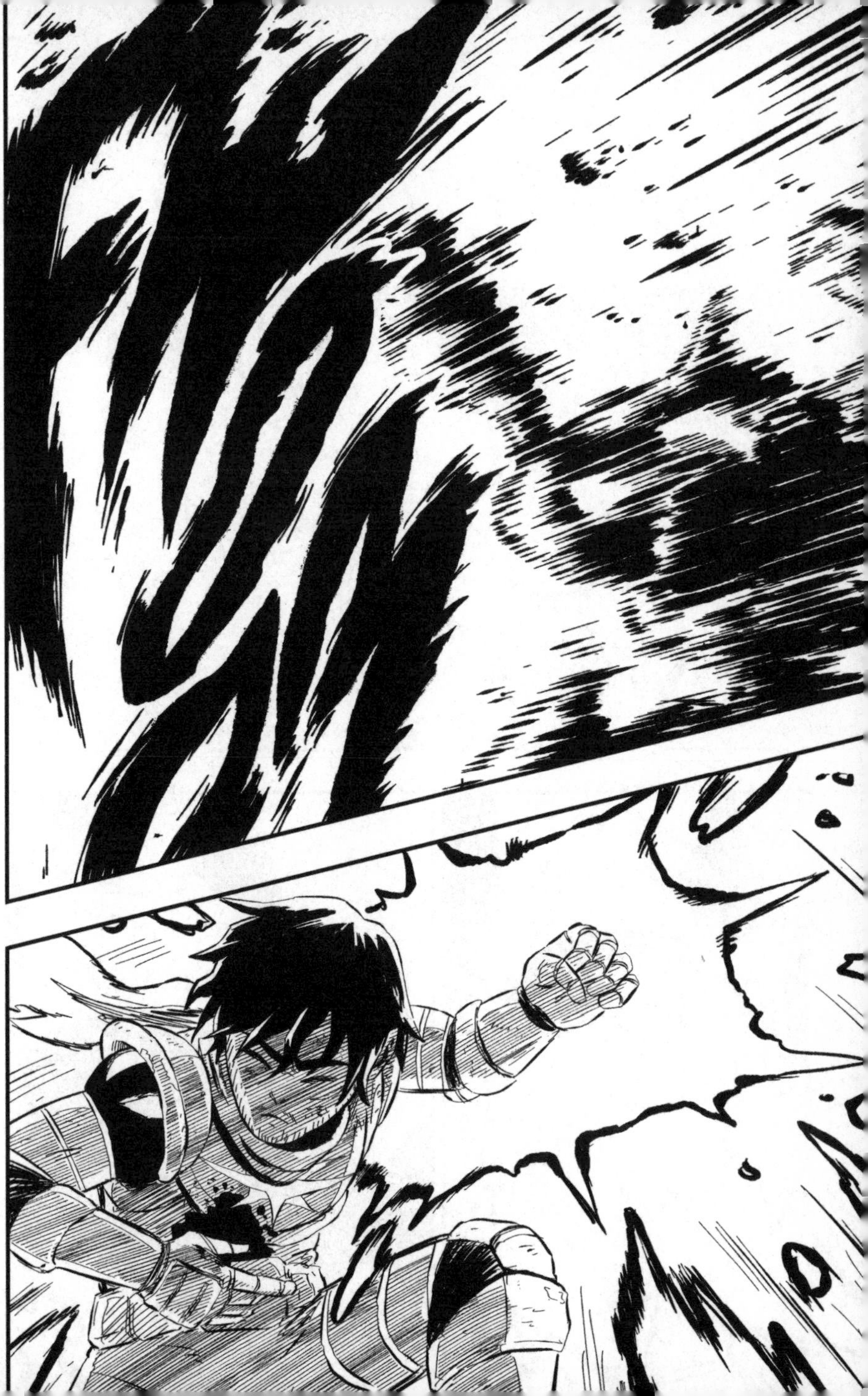

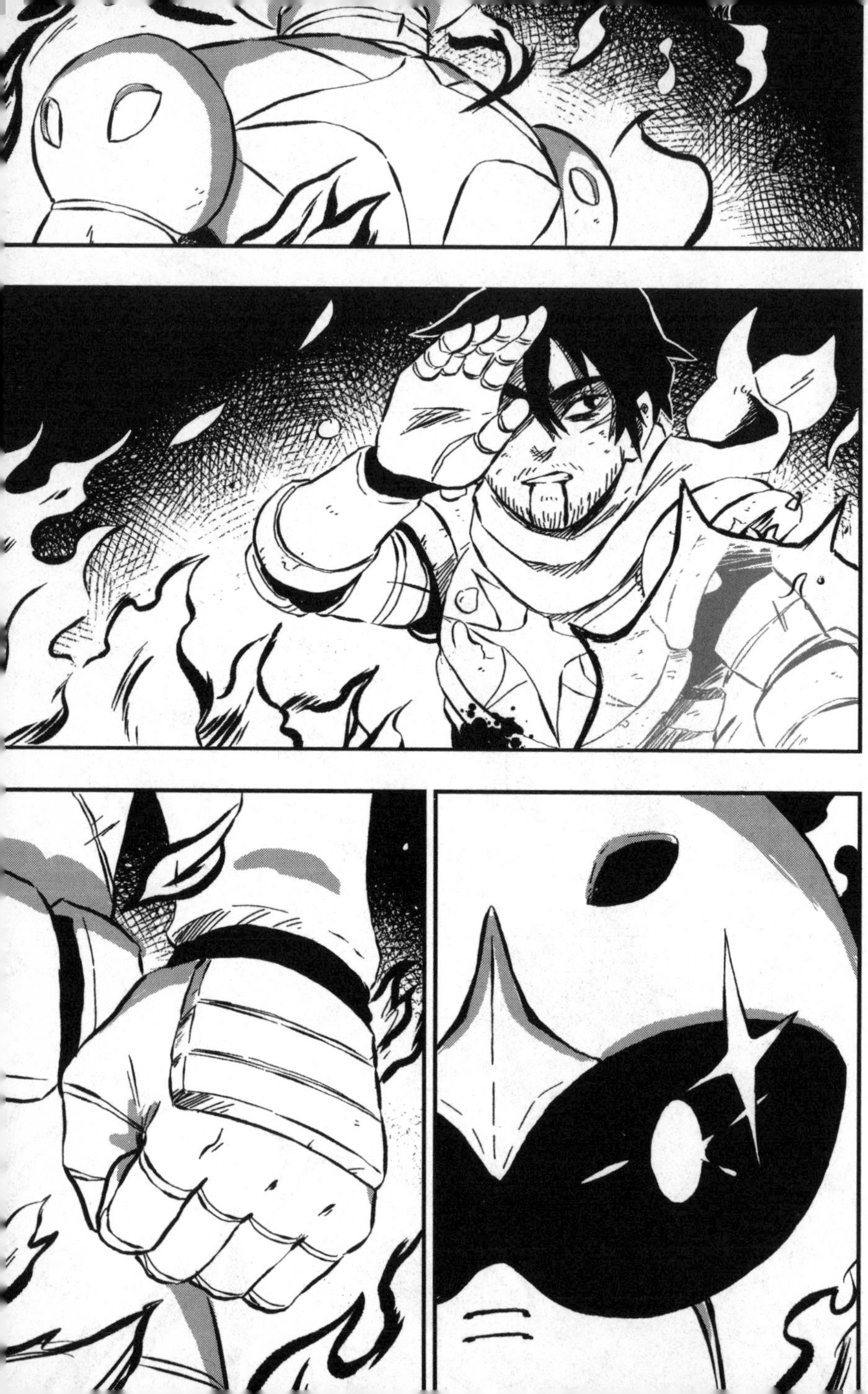

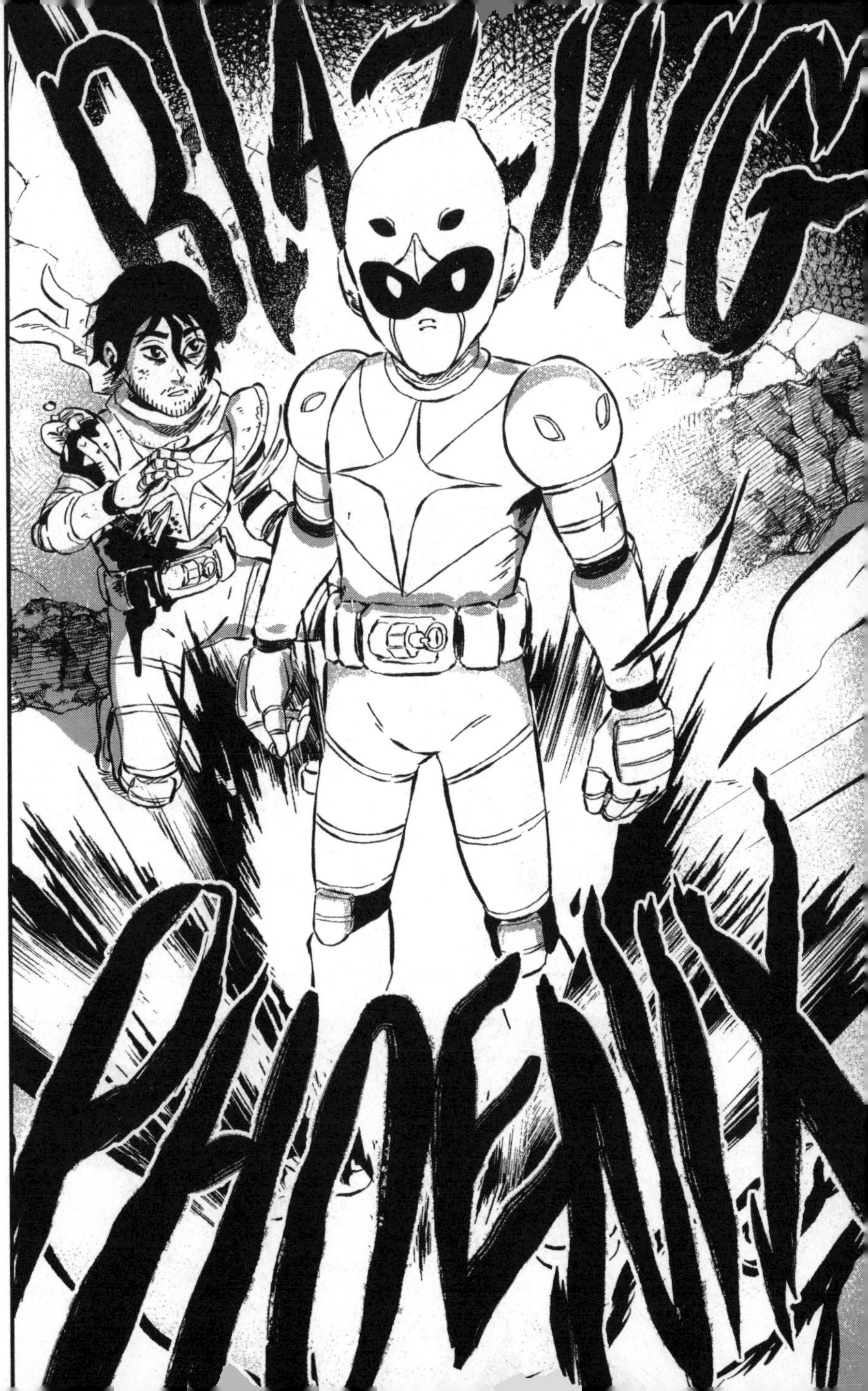
BLAZING
PHOENIX

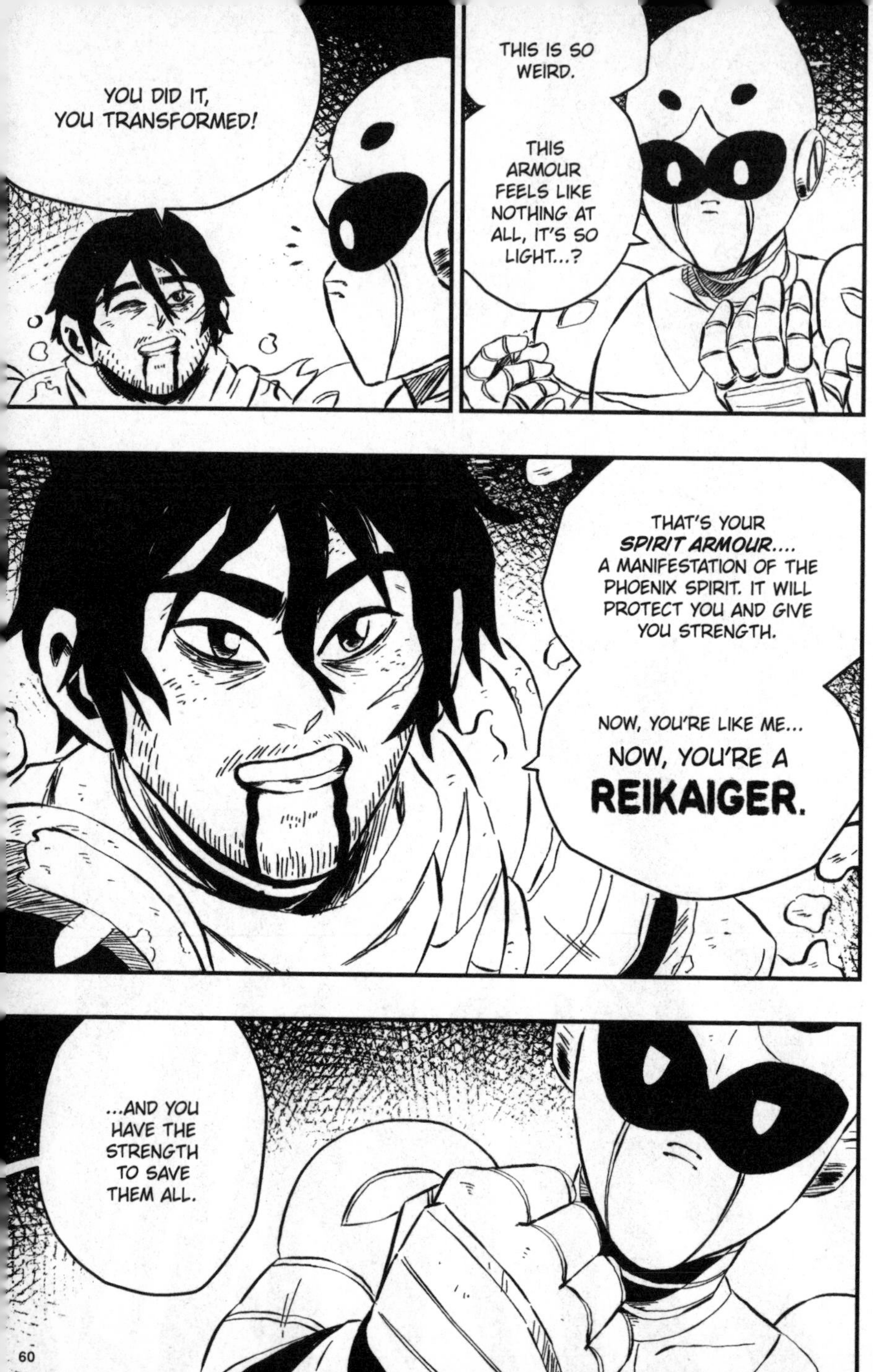
YOU DID IT, YOU TRANSFORMED!
THIS IS SO WEIRD.
THIS ARMOUR FEELS LIKE NOTHING AT ALL, IT'S SO LIGHT...?
THAT'S YOUR *SPIRIT ARMOUR*.... A MANIFESTATION OF THE PHOENIX SPIRIT. IT WILL PROTECT YOU AND GIVE YOU STRENGTH.
NOW, YOU'RE LIKE ME... NOW, YOU'RE A **REIKAIGER**.
...AND YOU HAVE THE STRENGTH TO SAVE THEM ALL.

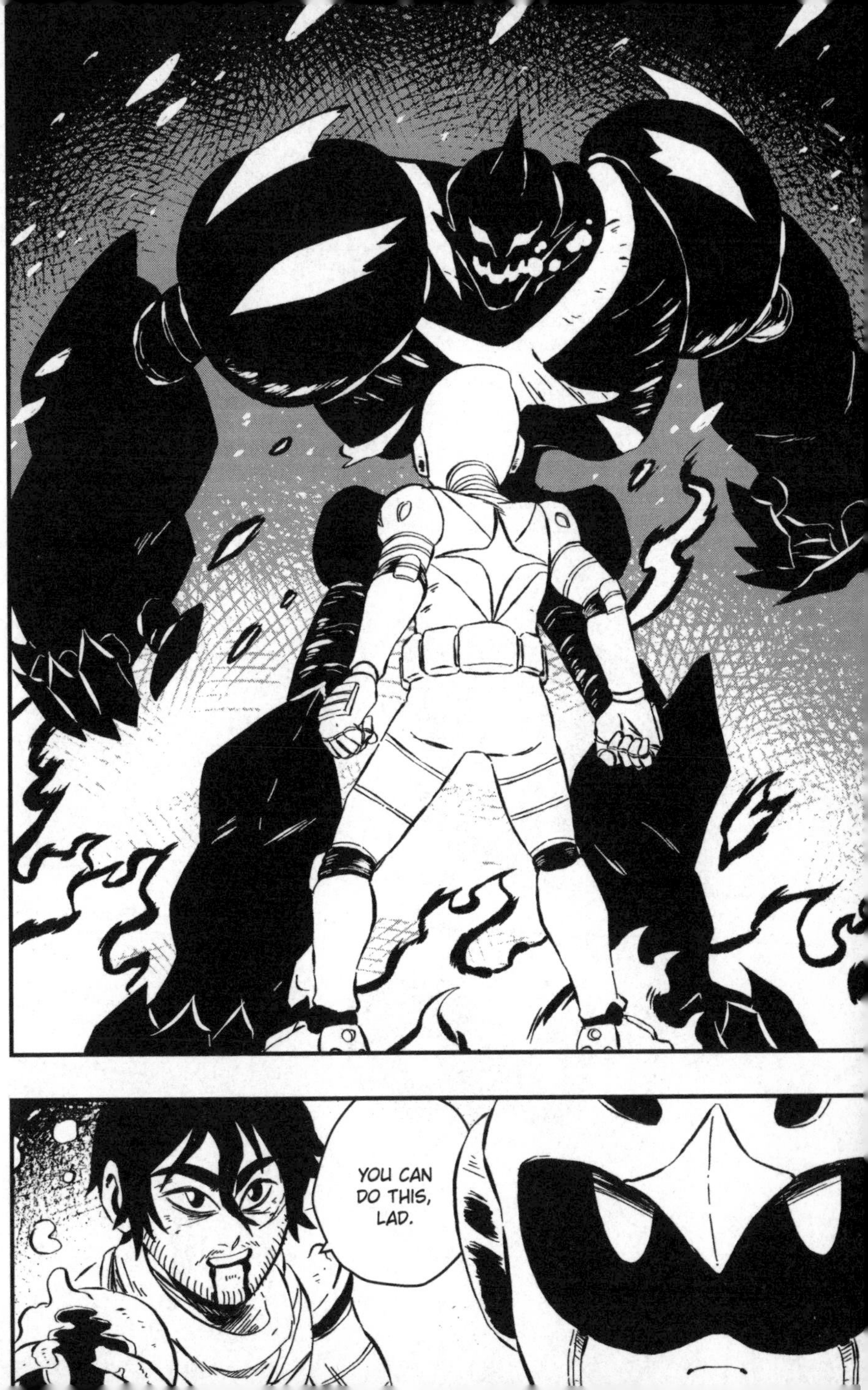
YOU CAN DO THIS, LAD.

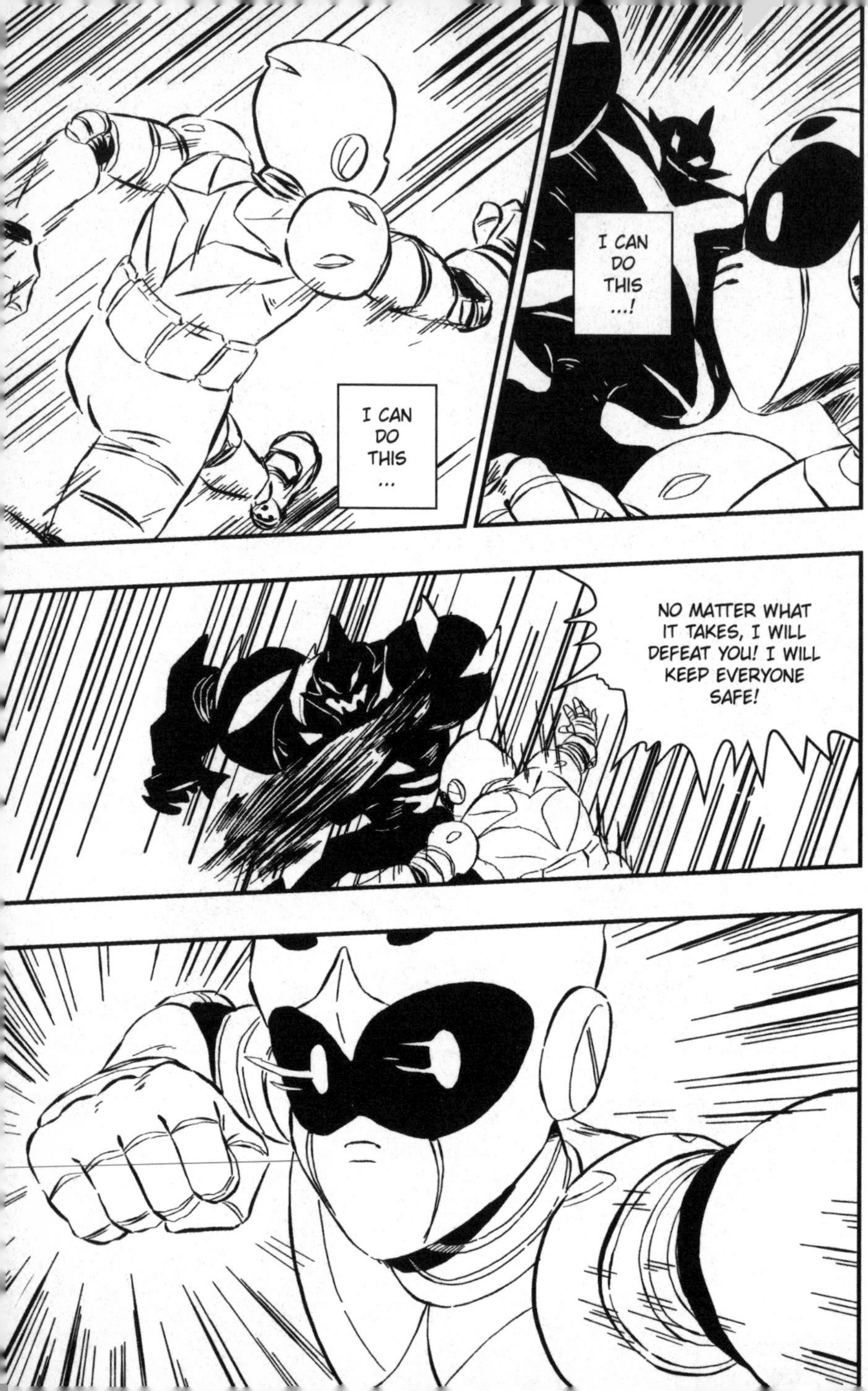
I CAN DO THIS ...!
I CAN DO THIS ...
NO MATTER WHAT IT TAKES, I WILL DEFEAT YOU! I WILL KEEP EVERYONE SAFE!

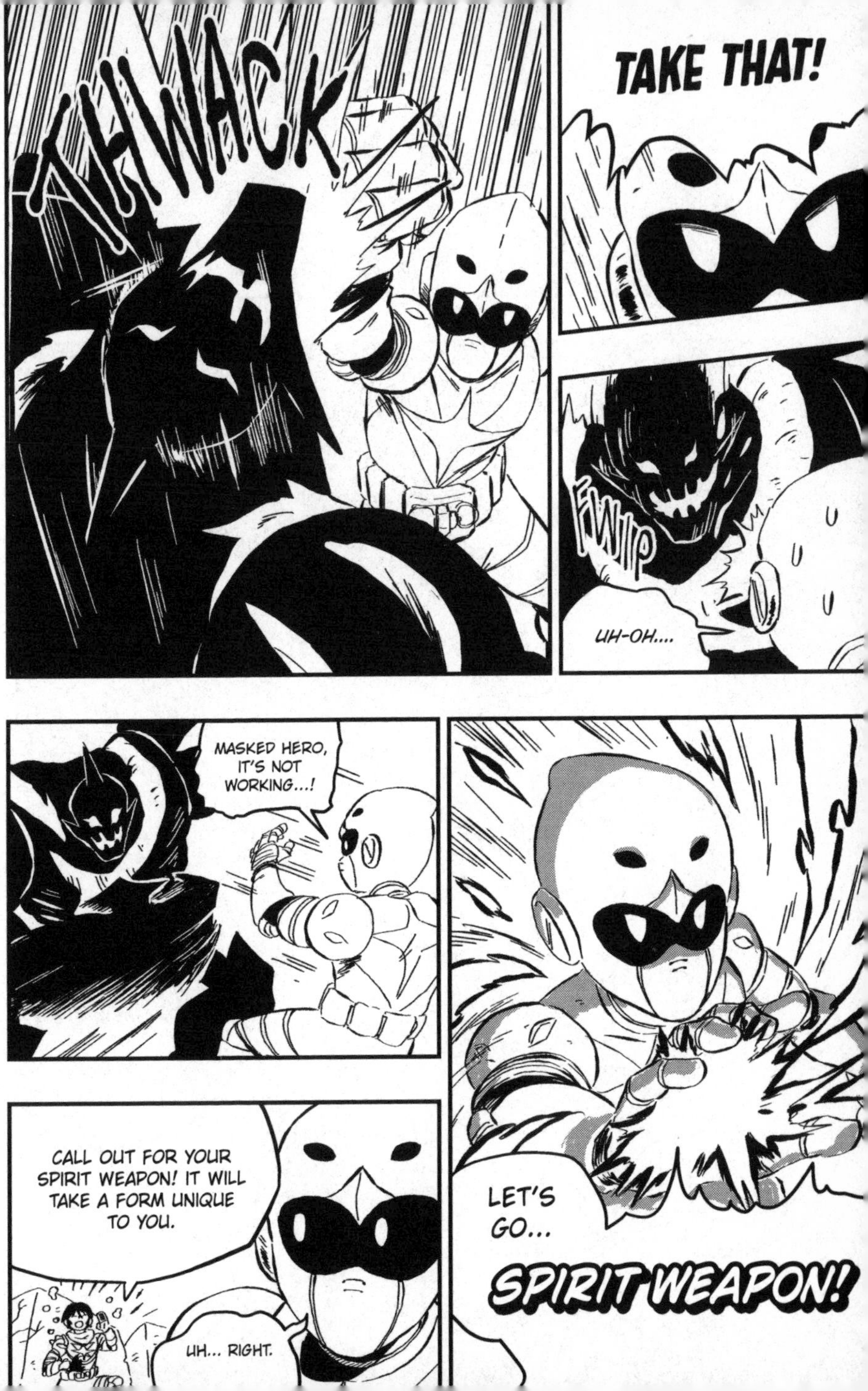
THWACK
TAKE THAT!
FWIP
UH-OH....
MASKED HERO, IT'S NOT WORKING...!
CALL OUT FOR YOUR SPIRIT WEAPON! IT WILL TAKE A FORM UNIQUE TO YOU.
UH... RIGHT.
LET'S GO...
SPIRIT WEAPON!

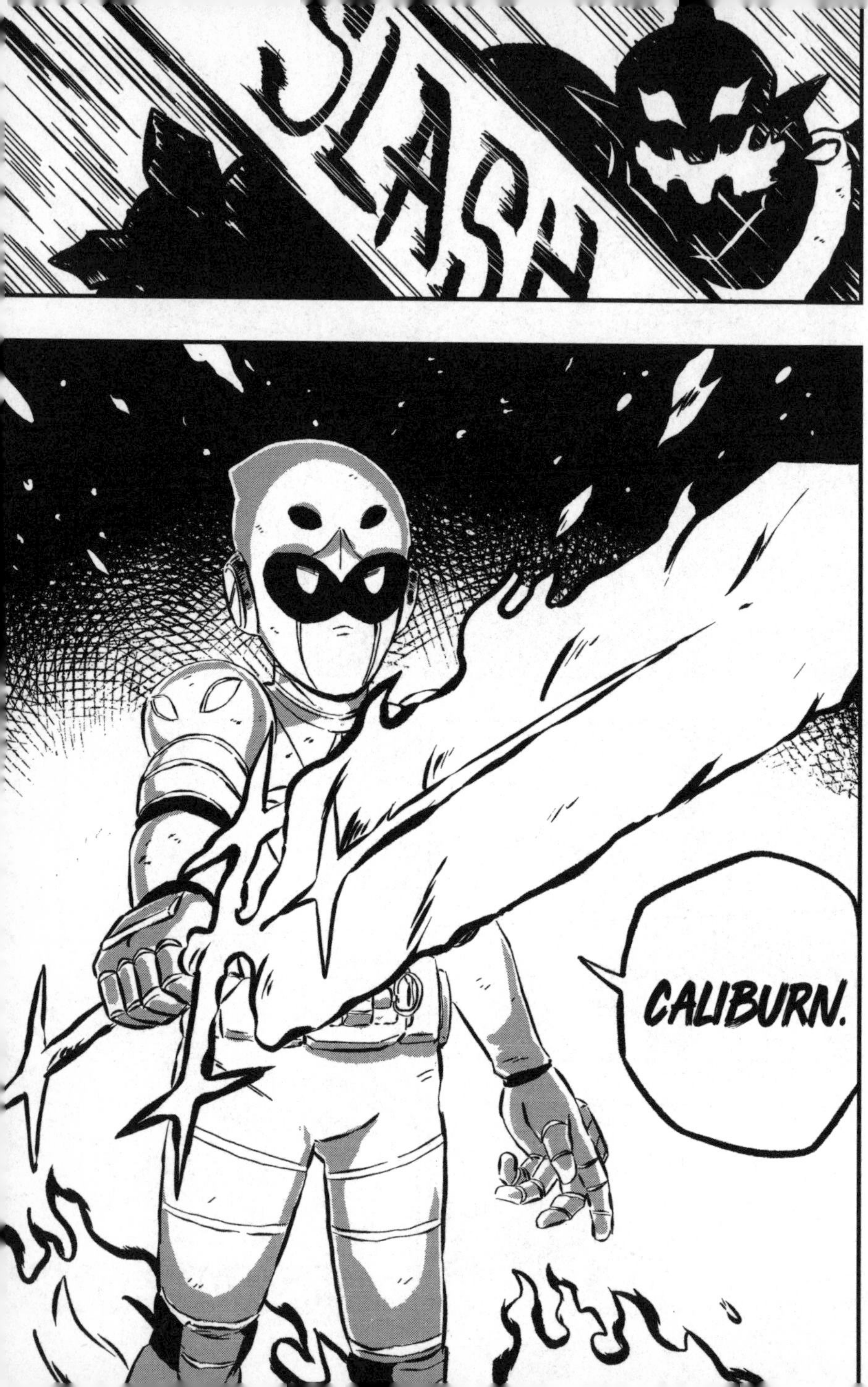
SLASH
CALIBURN.

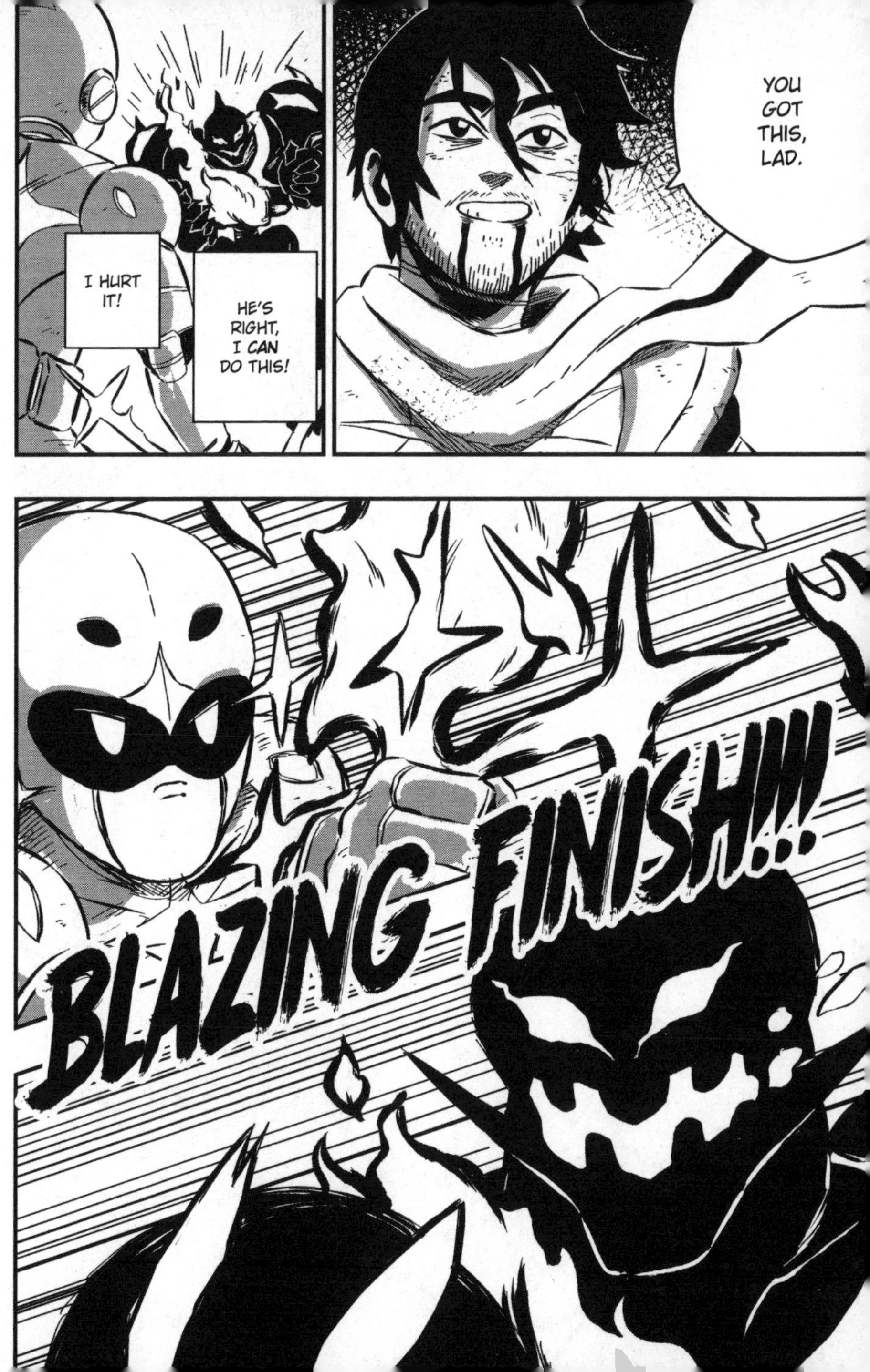
I HURT IT!
HE'S RIGHT, I CAN DO THIS!
YOU GOT THIS, LAD.
BLAZING FINISH!!!

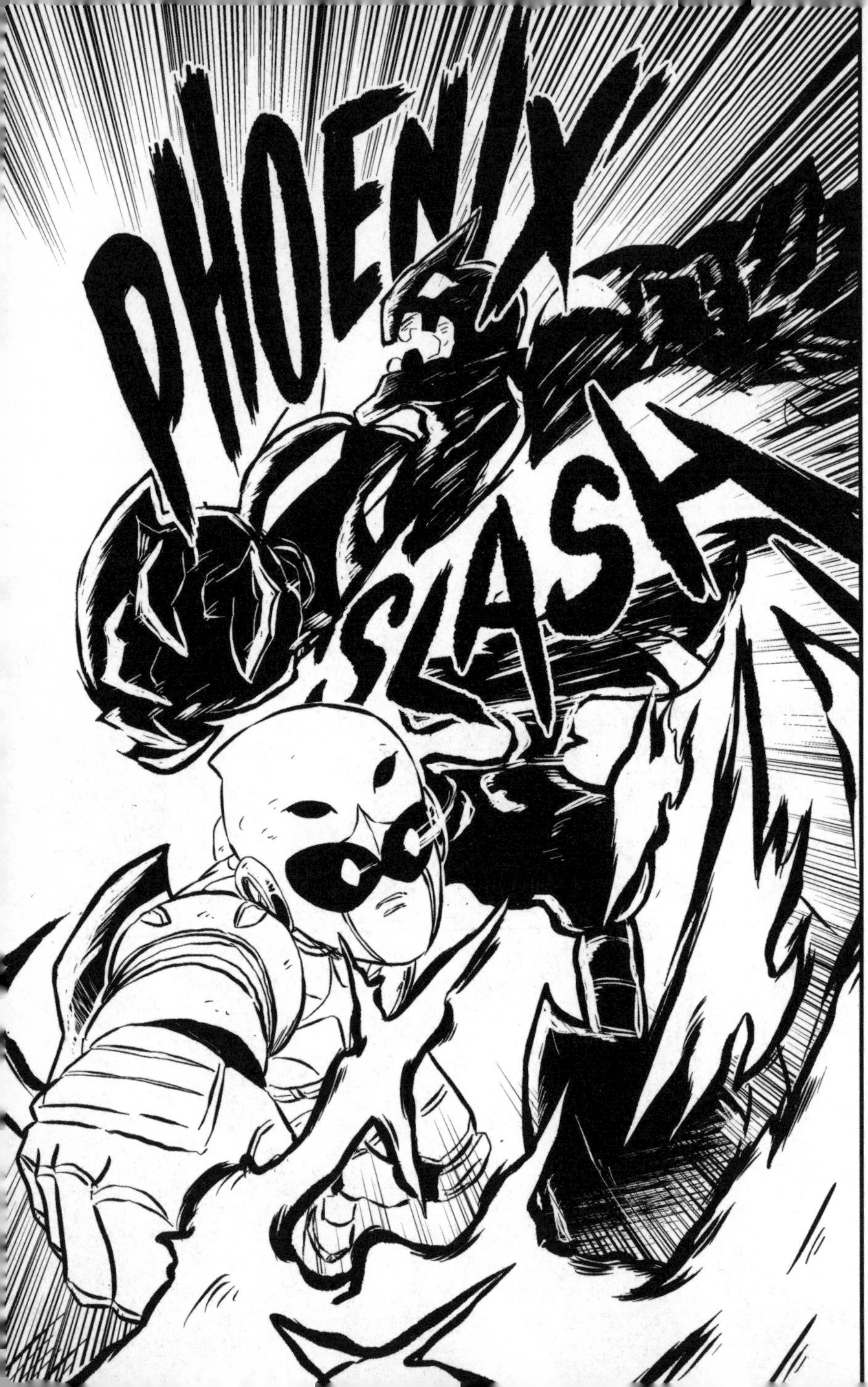
PHOENIX
SLASH

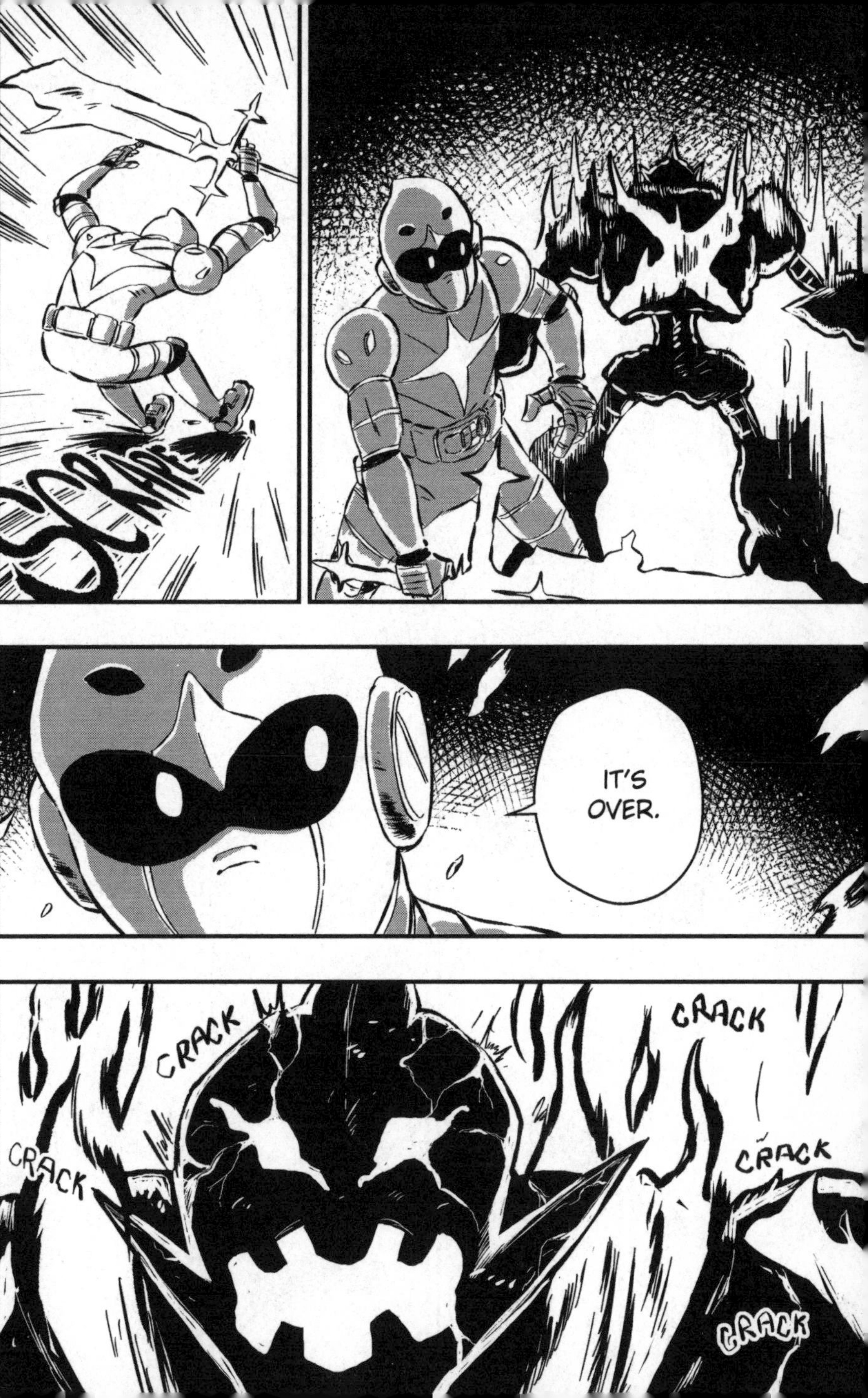
SCRAPE
IT'S OVER.
CRACK
CRACK
CRACK
CRACK
CRACK
CRACK

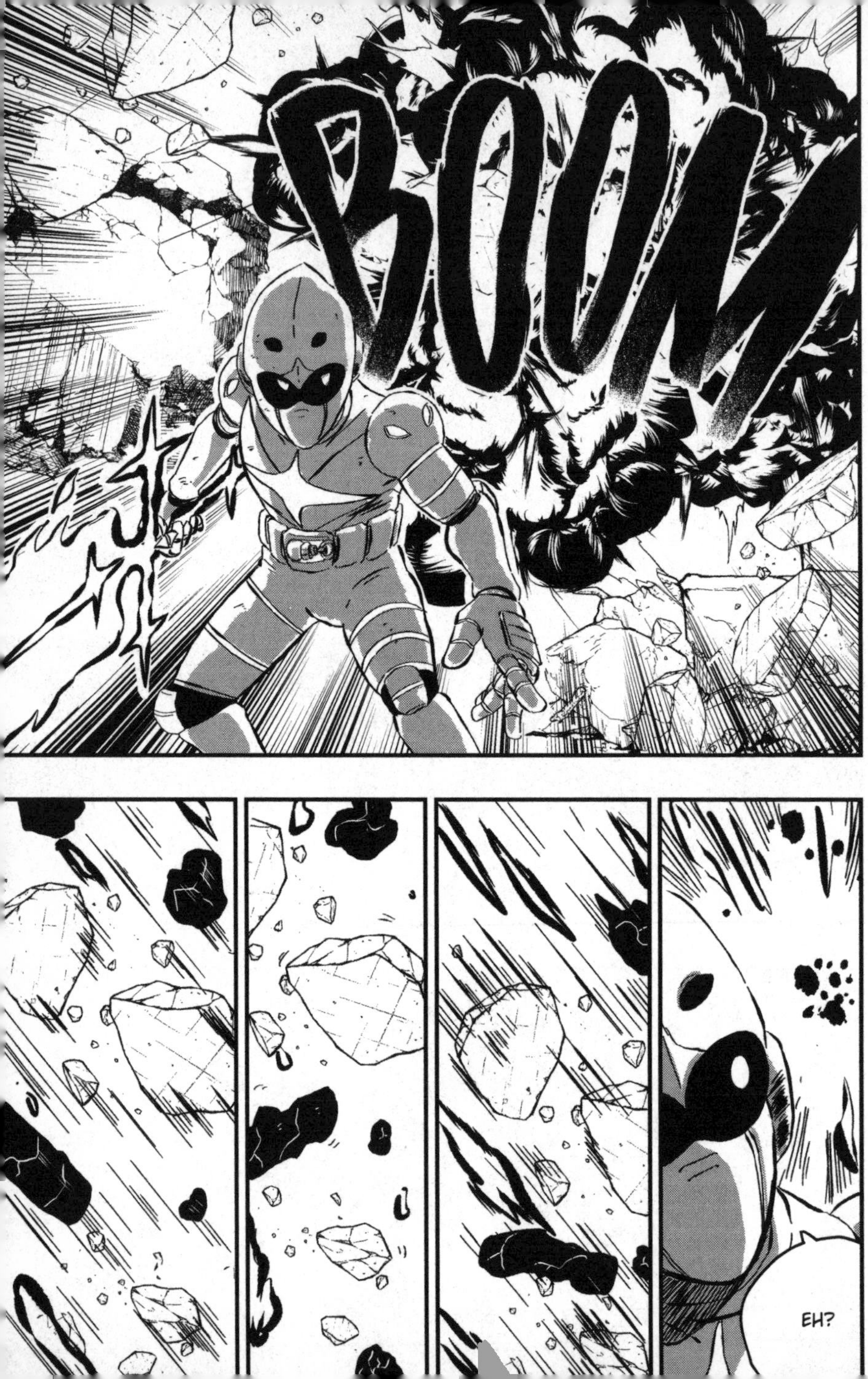
BOOM
EH?

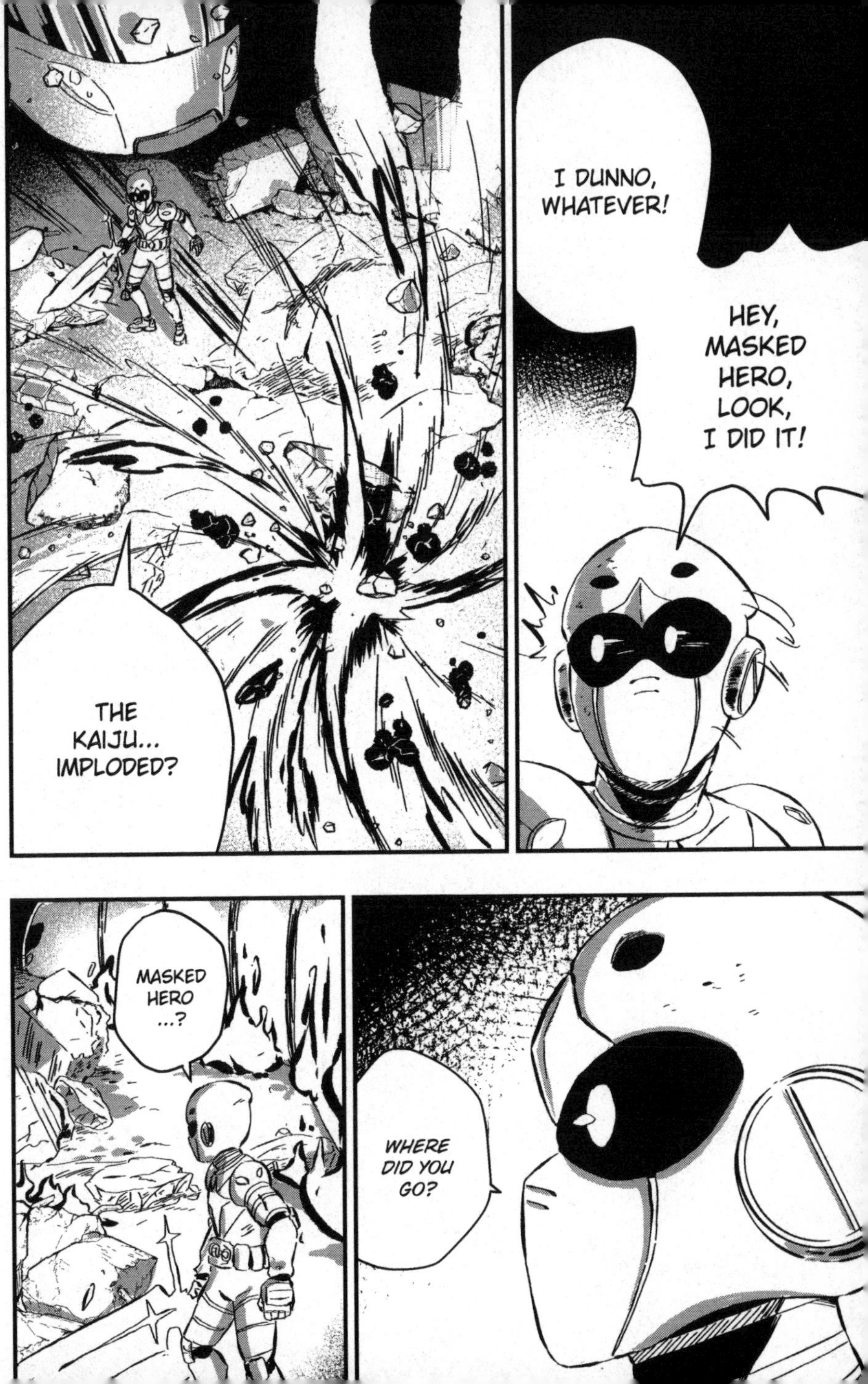
THE KAIJU... IMPLODED?
I DUNNO, WHATEVER!
HEY, MASKED HERO, LOOK, I DID IT!
MASKED HERO ...?
WHERE DID YOU GO?

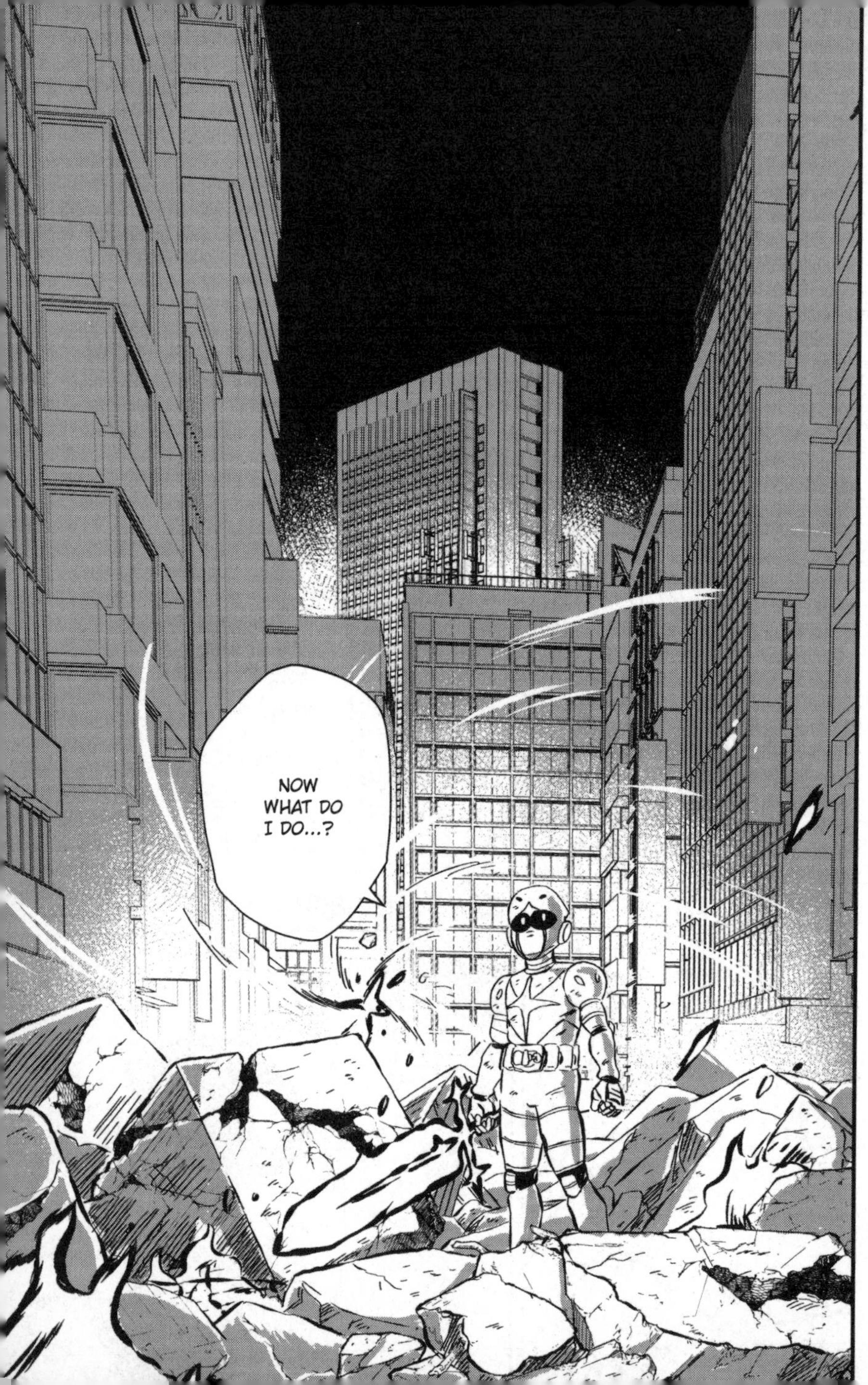
NOW WHAT DO I DO...?

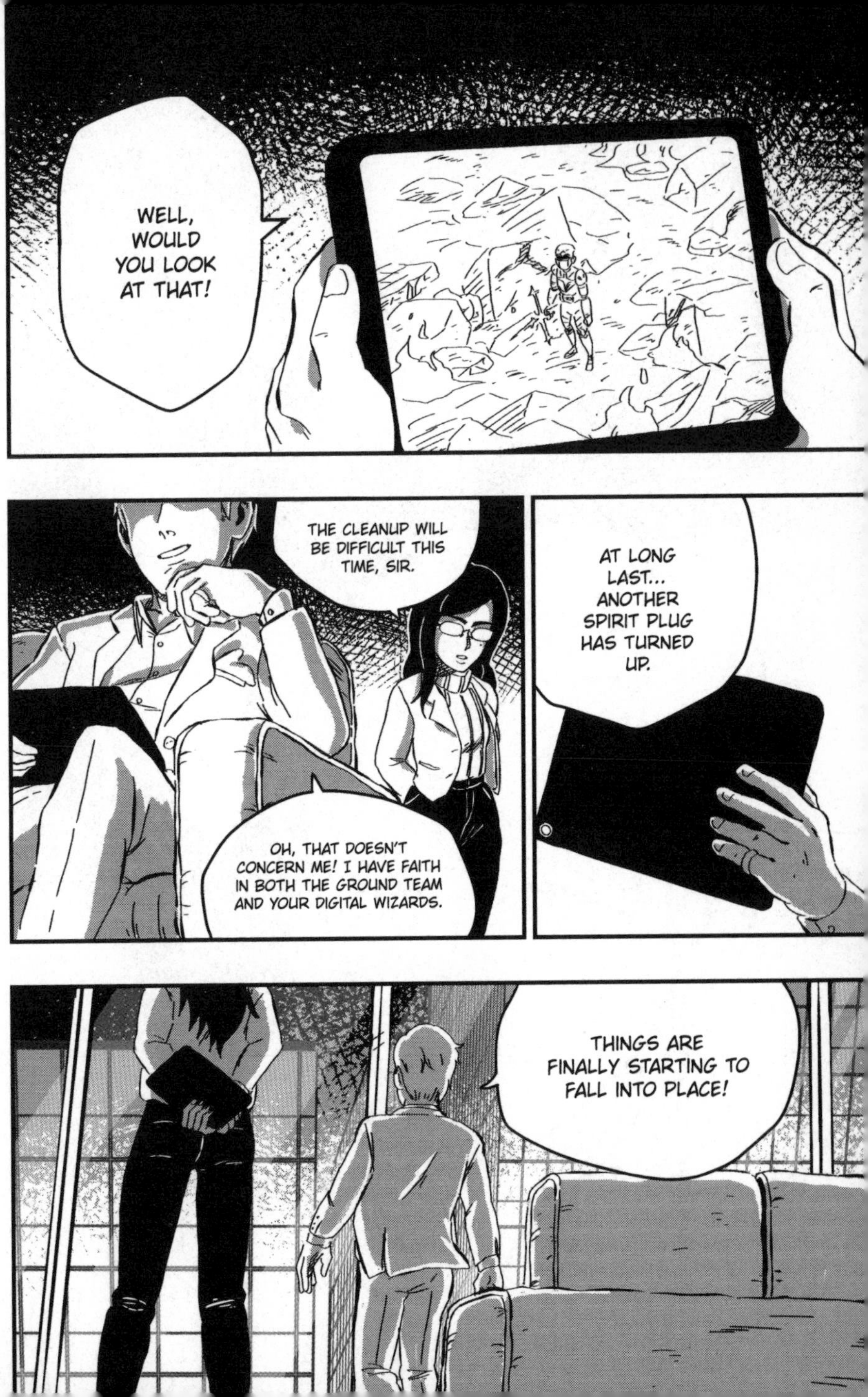
WELL, WOULD YOU LOOK AT THAT!
THE CLEANUP WILL BE DIFFICULT THIS TIME, SIR.
OH, THAT DOESN'T CONCERN ME! I HAVE FAITH IN BOTH THE GROUND TEAM AND YOUR DIGITAL WIZARDS.
AT LONG LAST... ANOTHER SPIRIT PLUG HAS TURNED UP.
THINGS ARE FINALLY STARTING TO FALL INTO PLACE!

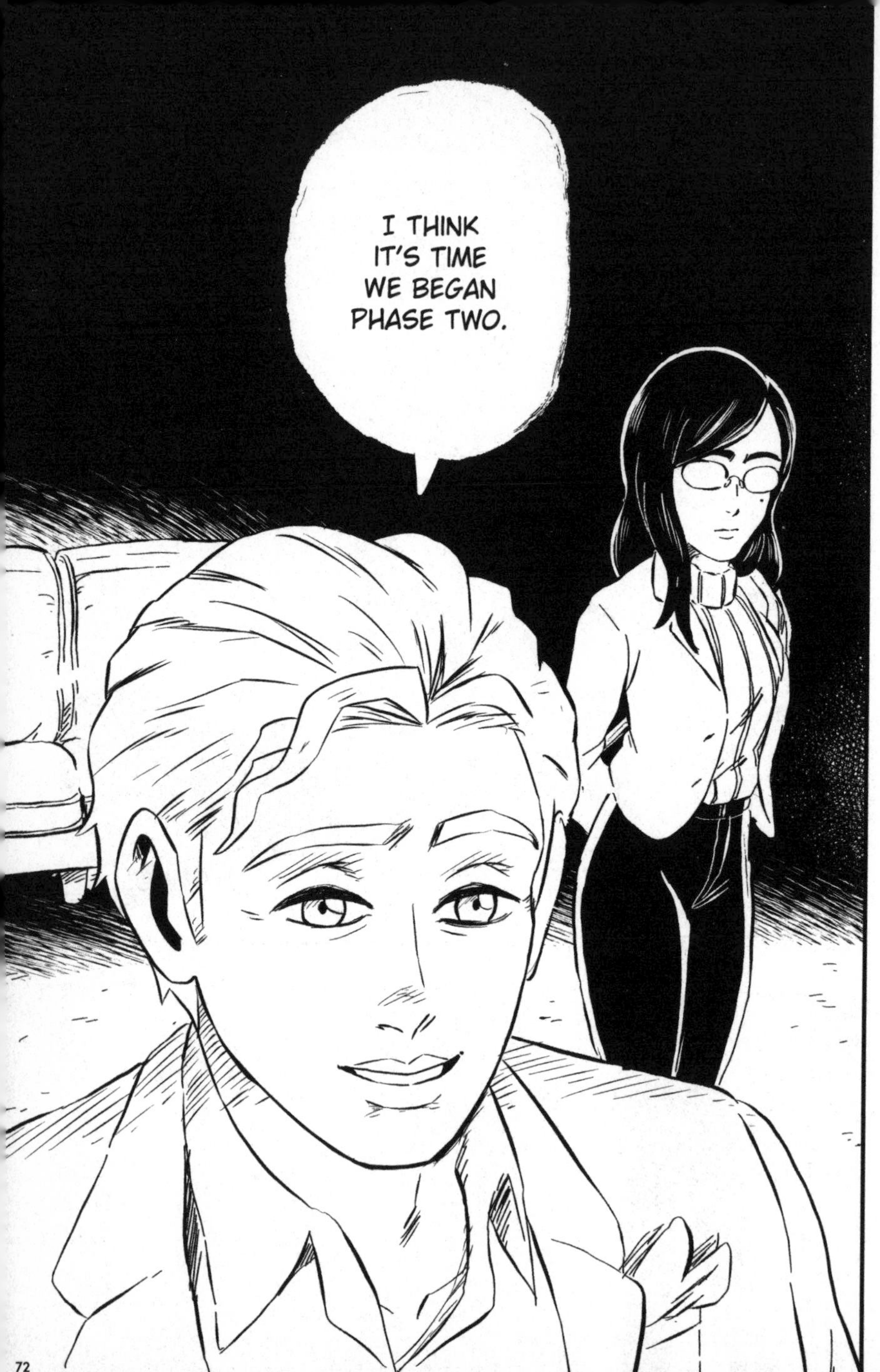
I THINK IT'S TIME WE BEGAN PHASE TWO.

CHAPTER FOUR

MY RESOLVE

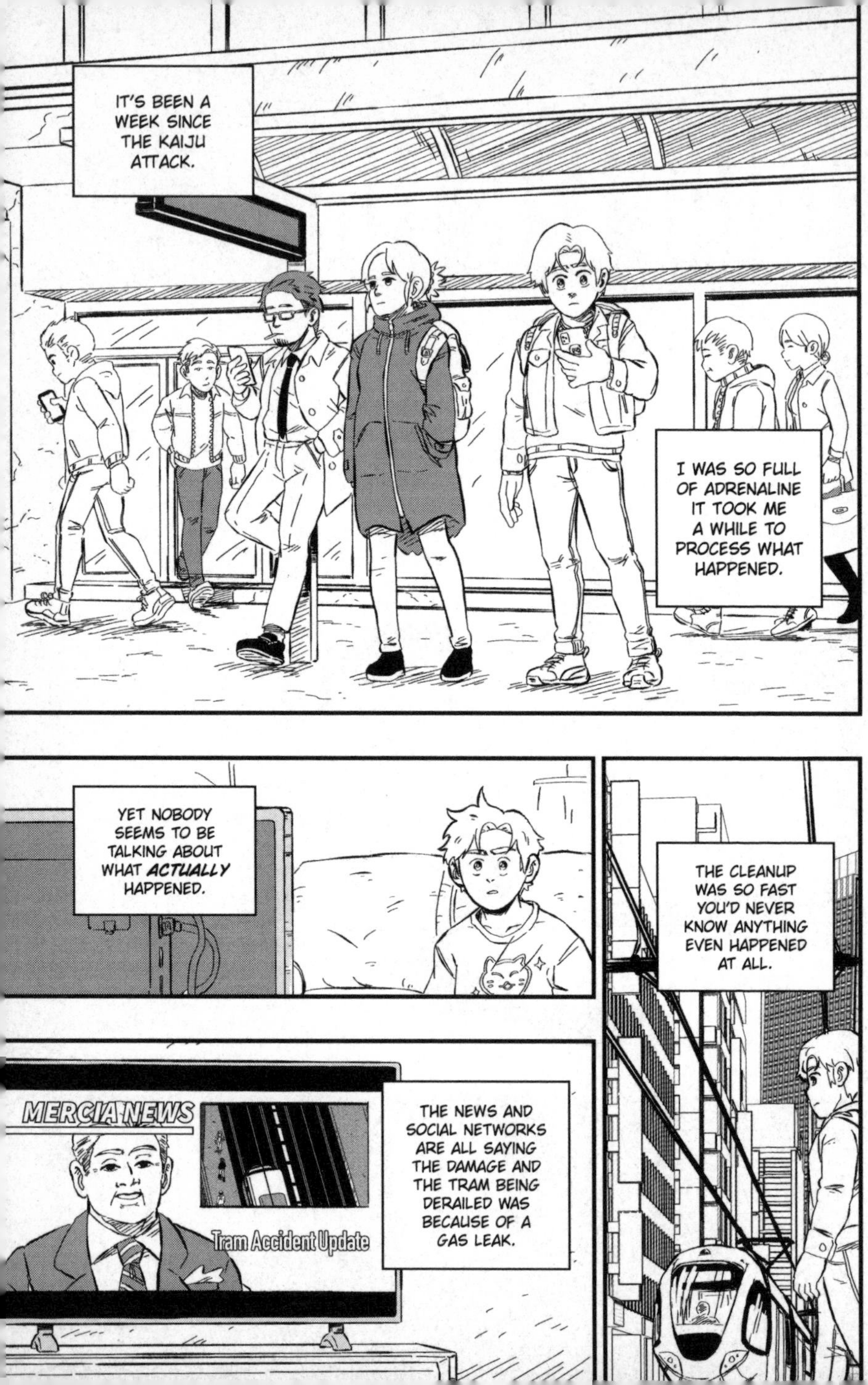
IT'S BEEN A WEEK SINCE THE KAIJU ATTACK.
I WAS SO FULL OF ADRENALINE IT TOOK ME A WHILE TO PROCESS WHAT HAPPENED.
YET NOBODY SEEMS TO BE TALKING ABOUT WHAT ACTUALLY HAPPENED.
THE CLEANUP WAS SO FAST YOU'D NEVER KNOW ANYTHING EVEN HAPPENED AT ALL.
MERCIA NEWS
Tram Accident Update
THE NEWS AND SOCIAL NETWORKS ARE ALL SAYING THE DAMAGE AND THE TRAM BEING DERAILED WAS BECAUSE OF A GAS LEAK.

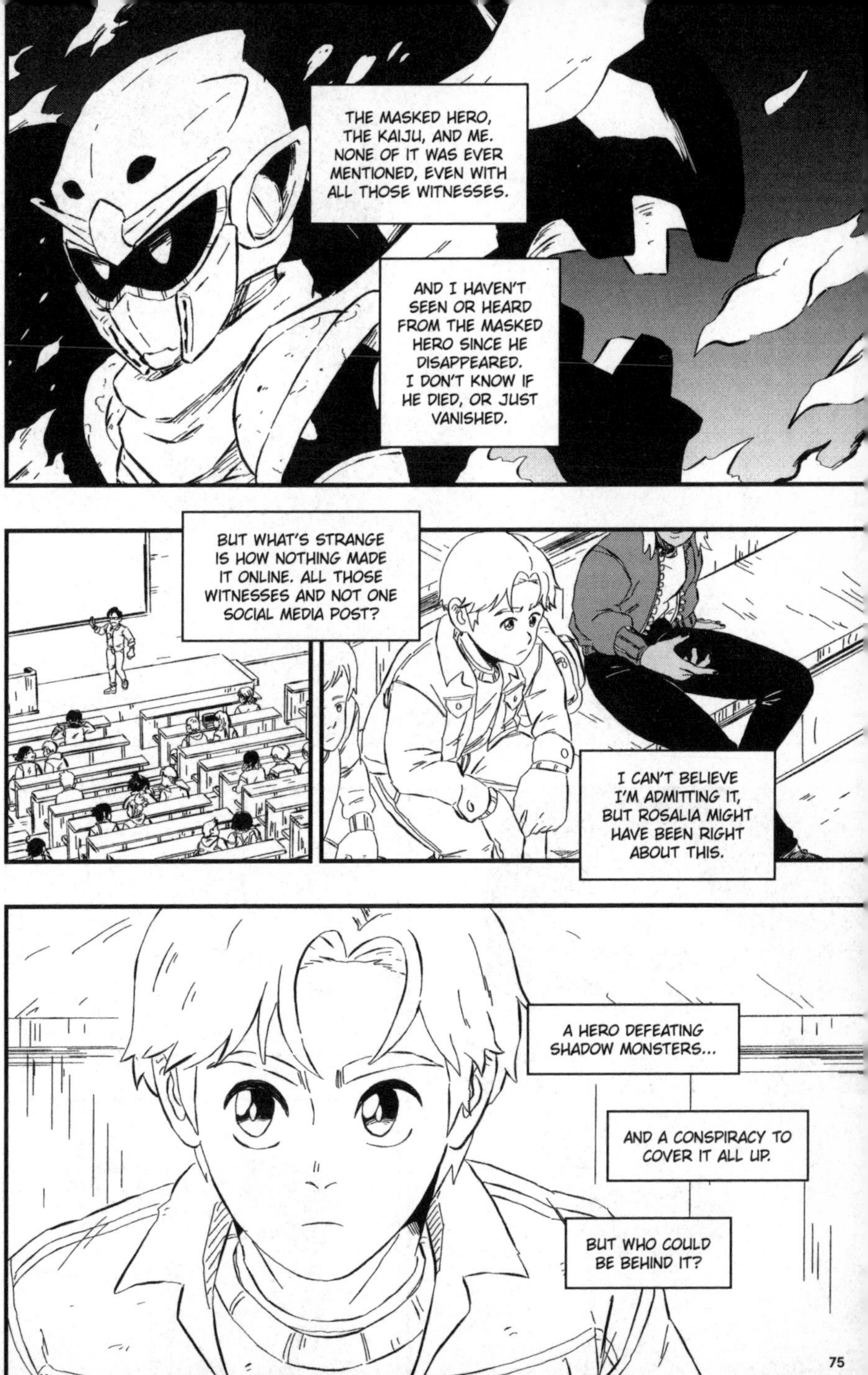
THE MASKED HERO, THE KAIJU, AND ME. NONE OF IT WAS EVER MENTIONED, EVEN WITH ALL THOSE WITNESSES.
AND I HAVEN'T SEEN OR HEARD FROM THE MASKED HERO SINCE HE DISAPPEARED. I DON'T KNOW IF HE DIED, OR JUST VANISHED.
BUT WHAT'S STRANGE IS HOW NOTHING MADE IT ONLINE. ALL THOSE WITNESSES AND NOT ONE SOCIAL MEDIA POST?
I CAN'T BELIEVE I'M ADMITTING IT, BUT ROSALIA MIGHT HAVE BEEN RIGHT ABOUT THIS.
A HERO DEFEATING SHADOW MONSTERS...
AND A CONSPIRACY TO COVER IT ALL UP.
BUT WHO COULD BE BEHIND IT?

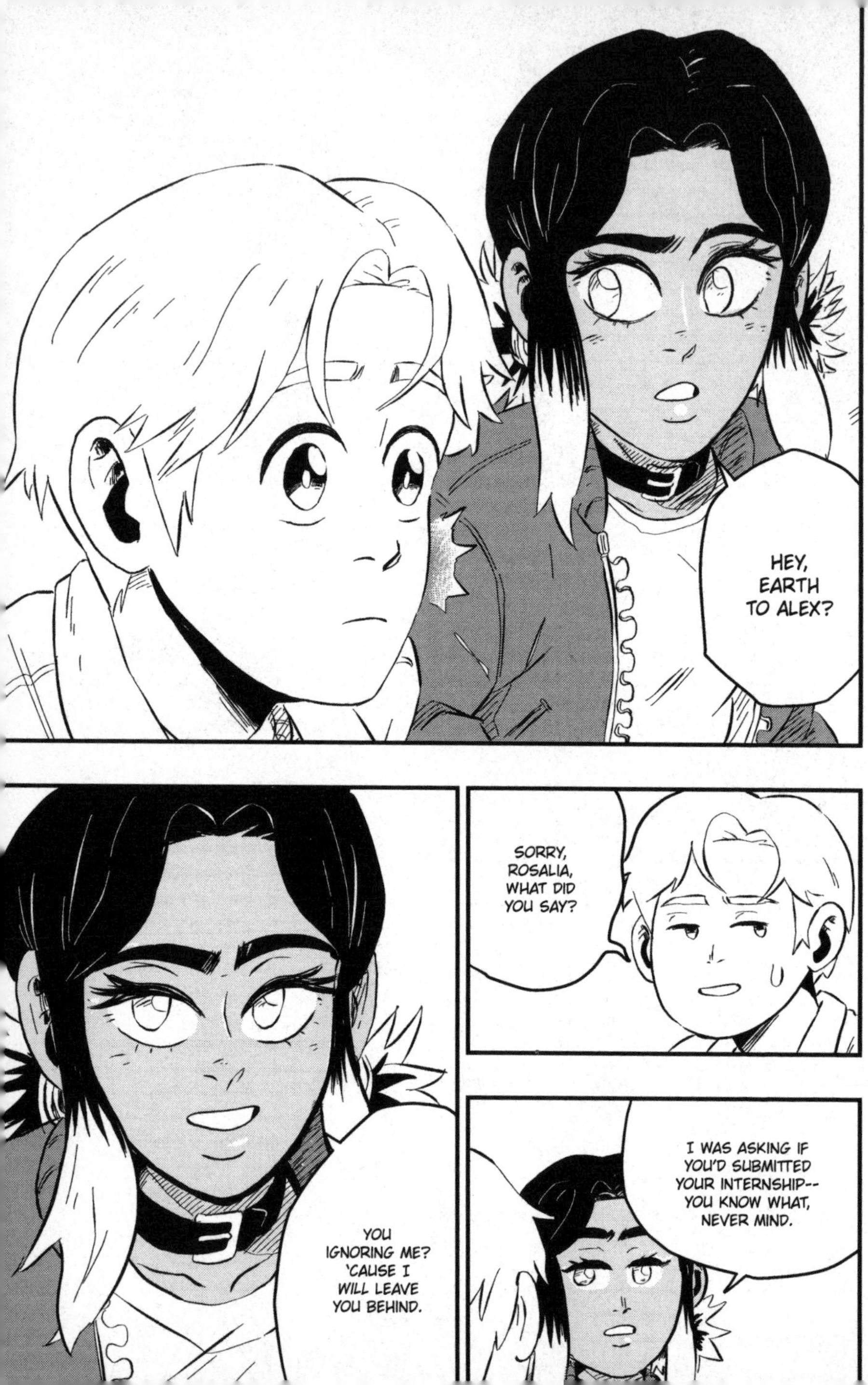
HEY, EARTH TO ALEX?
YOU IGNORING ME? 'CAUSE I WILL LEAVE YOU BEHIND.
SORRY, ROSALIA, WHAT DID YOU SAY?
I WAS ASKING IF YOU'D SUBMITTED YOUR INTERNSHIP-- YOU KNOW WHAT, NEVER MIND.

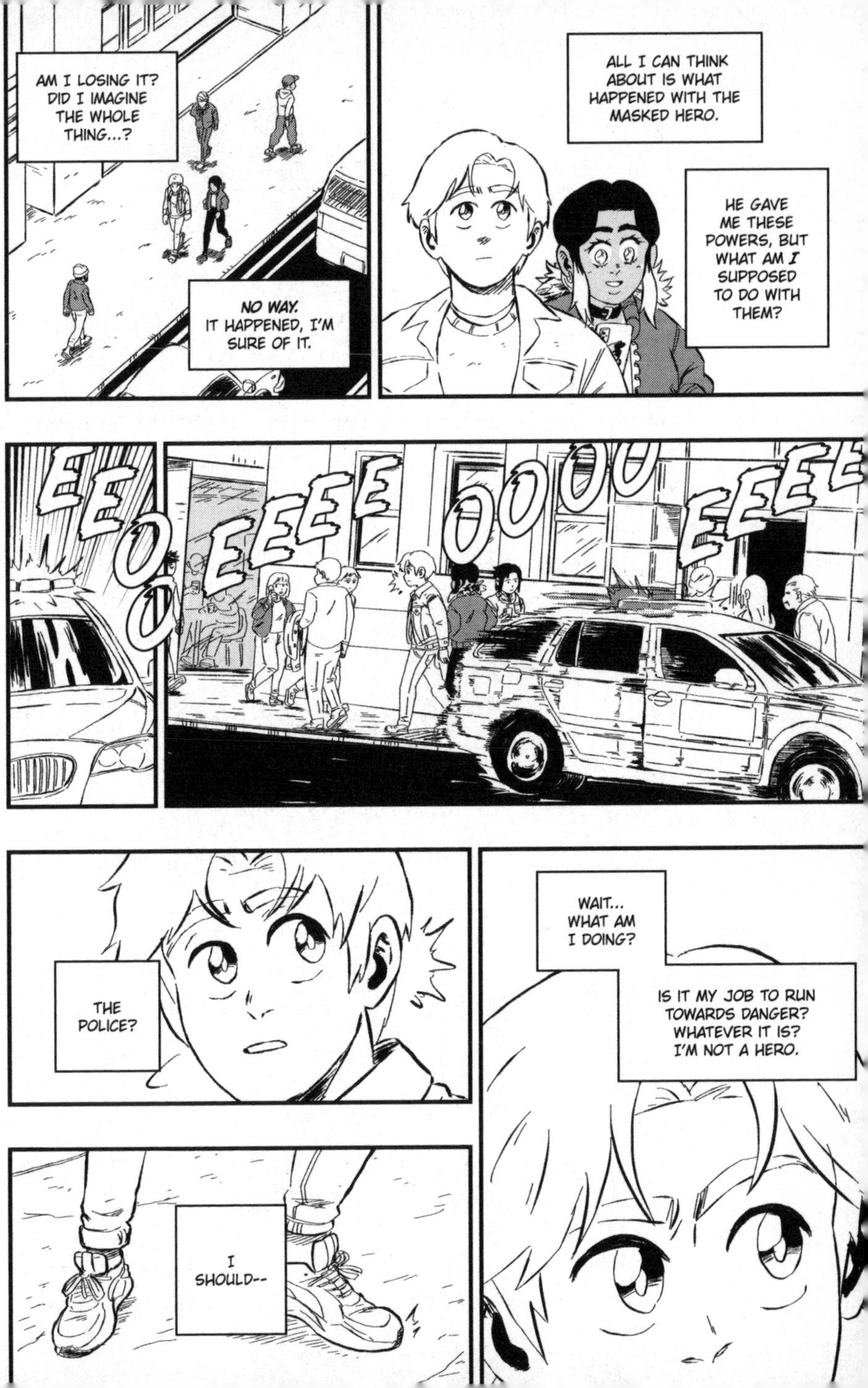
AM I LOSING IT? DID I IMAGINE THE WHOLE THING...?
NO WAY. IT HAPPENED, I'M SURE OF IT.
ALL I CAN THINK ABOUT IS WHAT HAPPENED WITH THE MASKED HERO.
HE GAVE ME THESE POWERS, BUT WHAT AM I SUPPOSED TO DO WITH THEM?
EEOO EEEE OOOO EEEE
THE POLICE?
WAIT... WHAT AM I DOING?
IS IT MY JOB TO RUN TOWARDS DANGER? WHATEVER IT IS? I'M NOT A HERO.
I SHOULD--

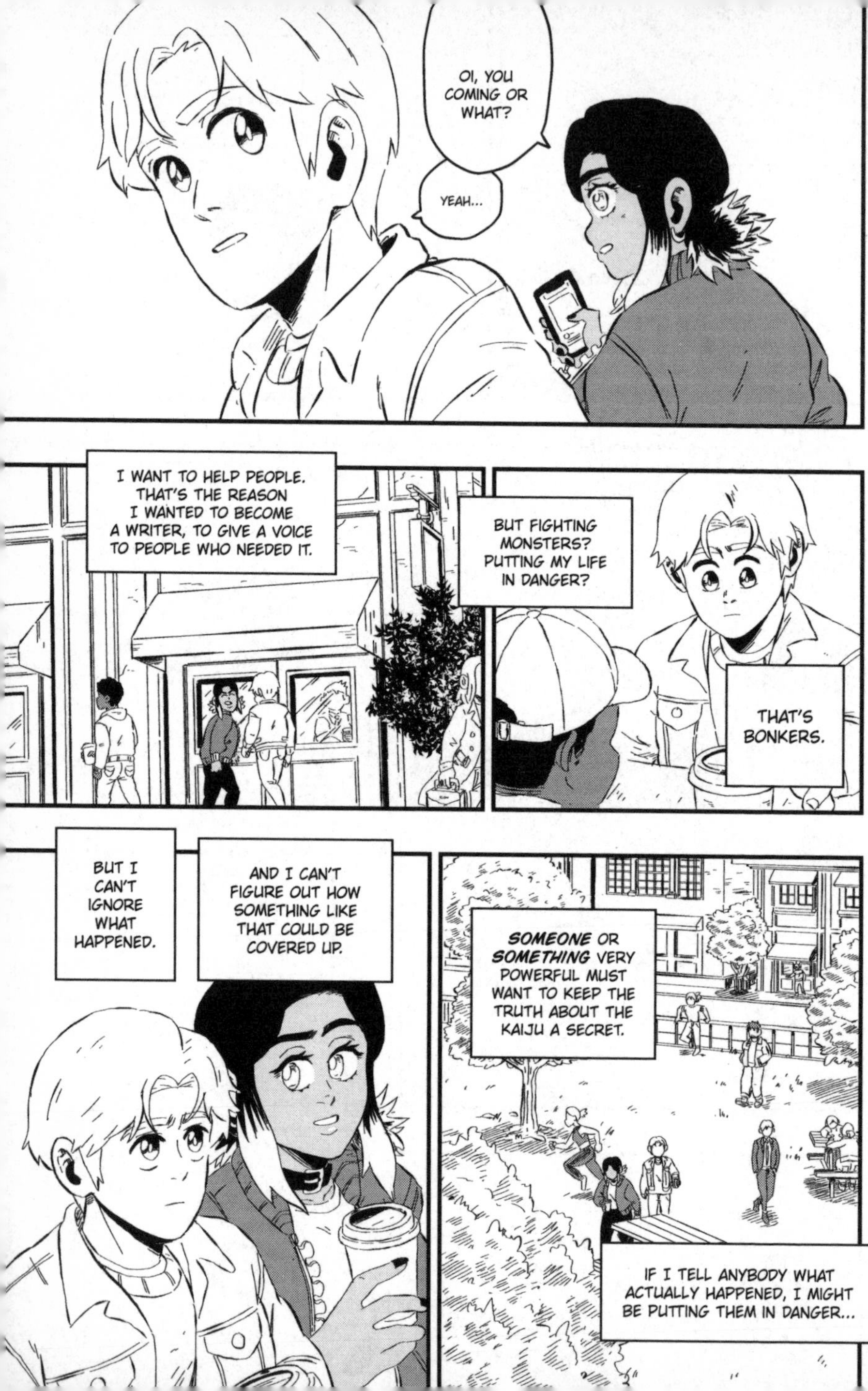

OI, YOU COMING OR WHAT?
YEAH...
I WANT TO HELP PEOPLE. THAT'S THE REASON I WANTED TO BECOME A WRITER, TO GIVE A VOICE TO PEOPLE WHO NEEDED IT.
BUT FIGHTING MONSTERS? PUTTING MY LIFE IN DANGER?
THAT'S BONKERS.
BUT I CAN'T IGNORE WHAT HAPPENED.
AND I CAN'T FIGURE OUT HOW SOMETHING LIKE THAT COULD BE COVERED UP.
SOMEONE OR ***SOMETHING*** VERY POWERFUL MUST WANT TO KEEP THE TRUTH ABOUT THE KAIJU A SECRET.
IF I TELL ANYBODY WHAT ACTUALLY HAPPENED, I MIGHT BE PUTTING THEM IN DANGER...

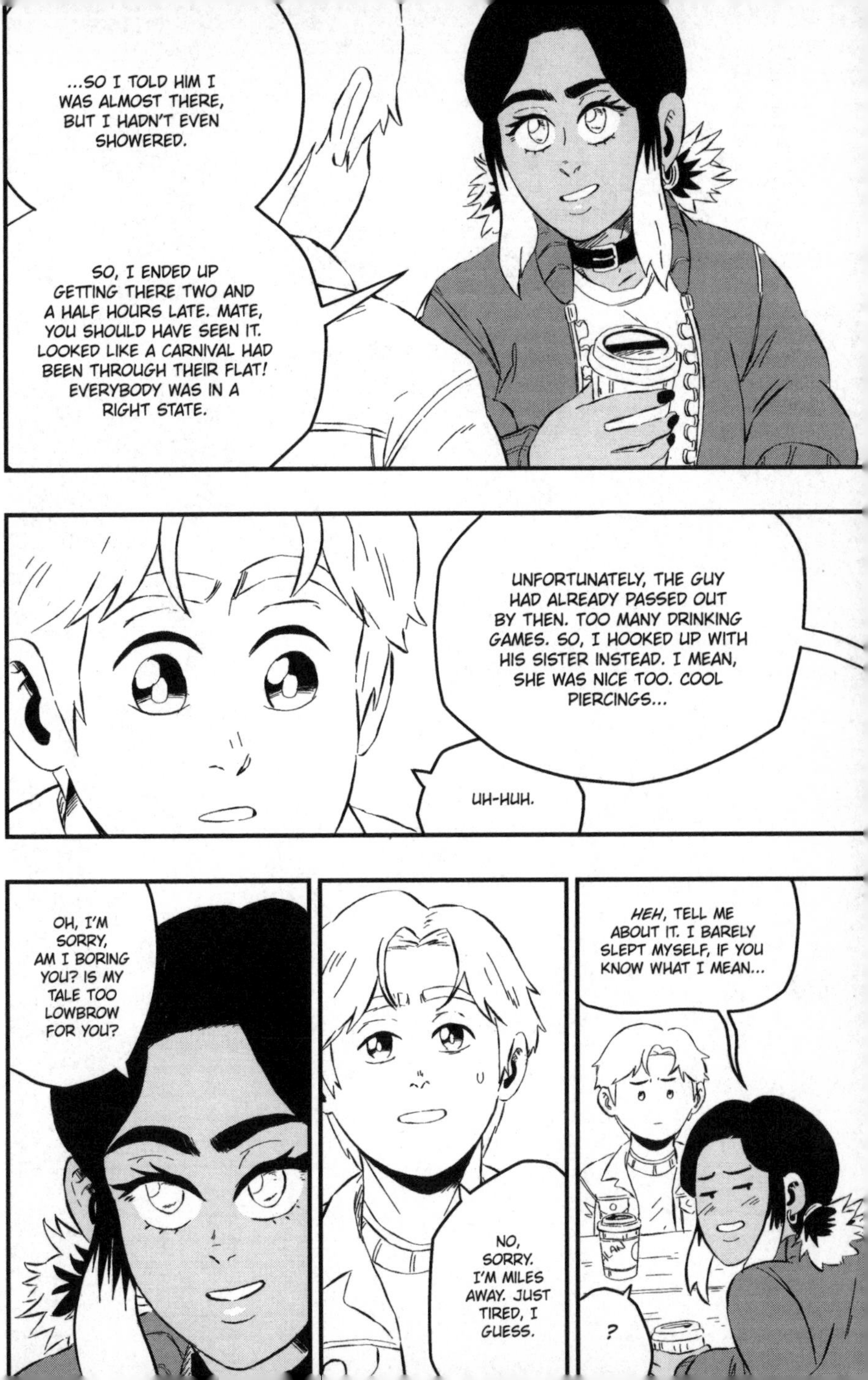
...SO I TOLD HIM I WAS ALMOST THERE, BUT I HADN'T EVEN SHOWERED.
SO, I ENDED UP GETTING THERE TWO AND A HALF HOURS LATE. MATE, YOU SHOULD HAVE SEEN IT. LOOKED LIKE A CARNIVAL HAD BEEN THROUGH THEIR FLAT! EVERYBODY WAS IN A RIGHT STATE.
UNFORTUNATELY, THE GUY HAD ALREADY PASSED OUT BY THEN. TOO MANY DRINKING GAMES. SO, I HOOKED UP WITH HIS SISTER INSTEAD. I MEAN, SHE WAS NICE TOO. COOL PIERCINGS...
UH-HUH.
OH, I'M SORRY, AM I BORING YOU? IS MY TALE TOO LOWBROW FOR YOU?
NO, SORRY. I'M MILES AWAY. JUST TIRED, I GUESS.
HEH, TELL ME ABOUT IT. I BARELY SLEPT MYSELF, IF YOU KNOW WHAT I MEAN...
?

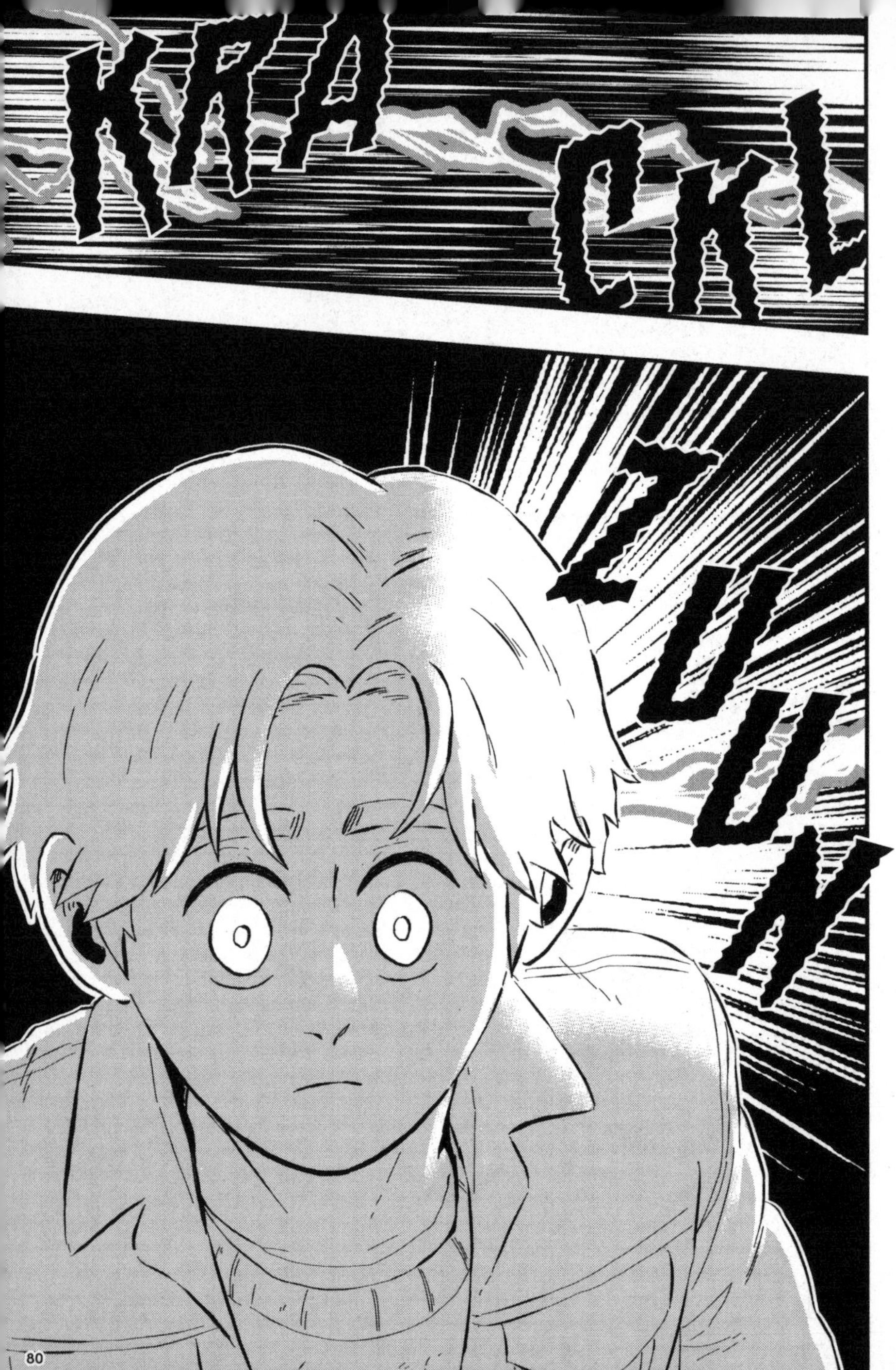
KRA-CKL
ZUUM

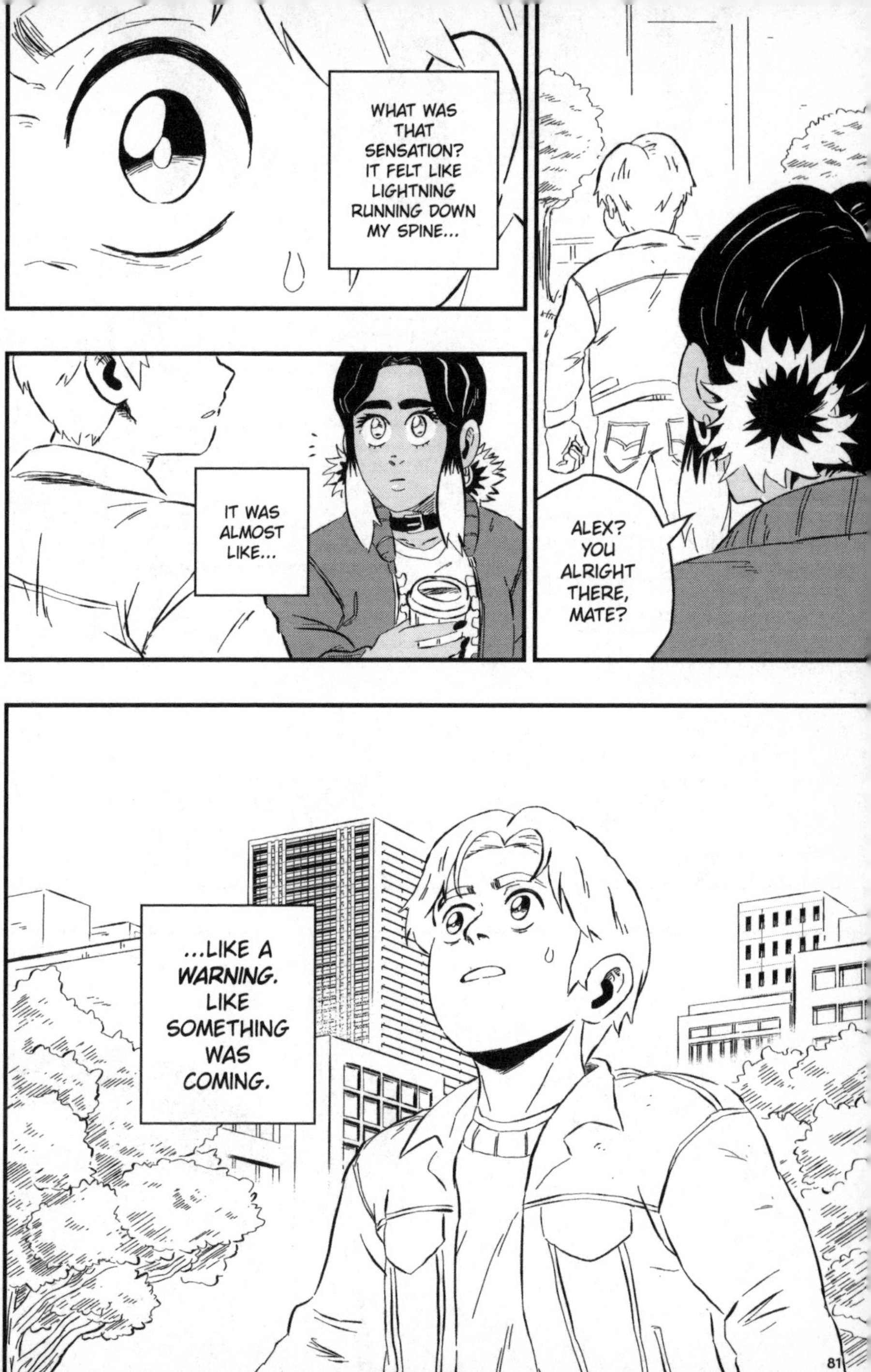
WHAT WAS THAT SENSATION? IT FELT LIKE LIGHTNING RUNNING DOWN MY SPINE...
ALEX? YOU ALRIGHT THERE, MATE?
IT WAS ALMOST LIKE...
...LIKE A WARNING. LIKE SOMETHING WAS COMING.

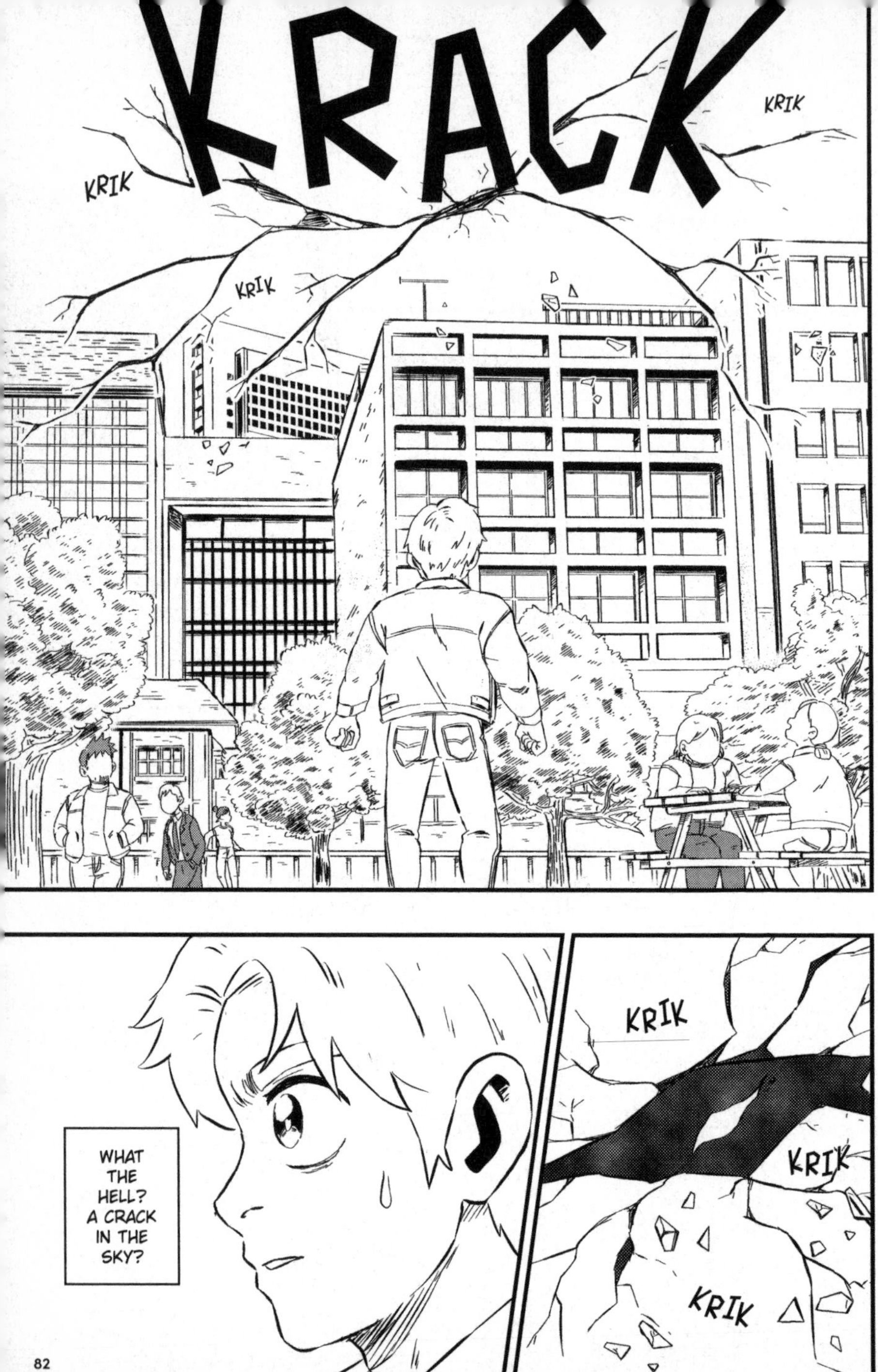
KRACK
KRIK
KRIK
KRIK
WHAT THE HELL? A CRACK IN THE SKY?
KRIK
KRIK
KRIK

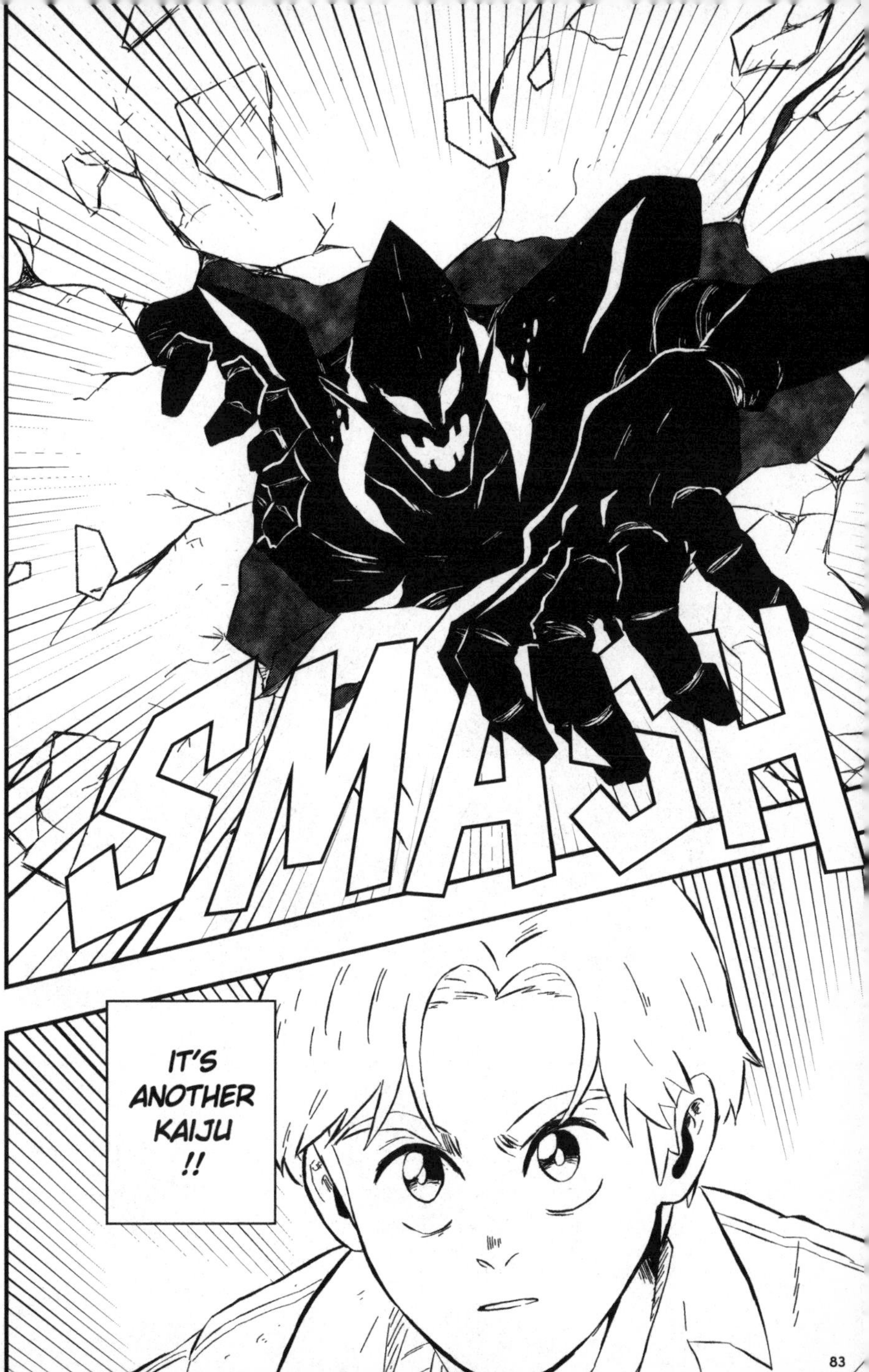
SMASH
IT'S ANOTHER KAIJU !!

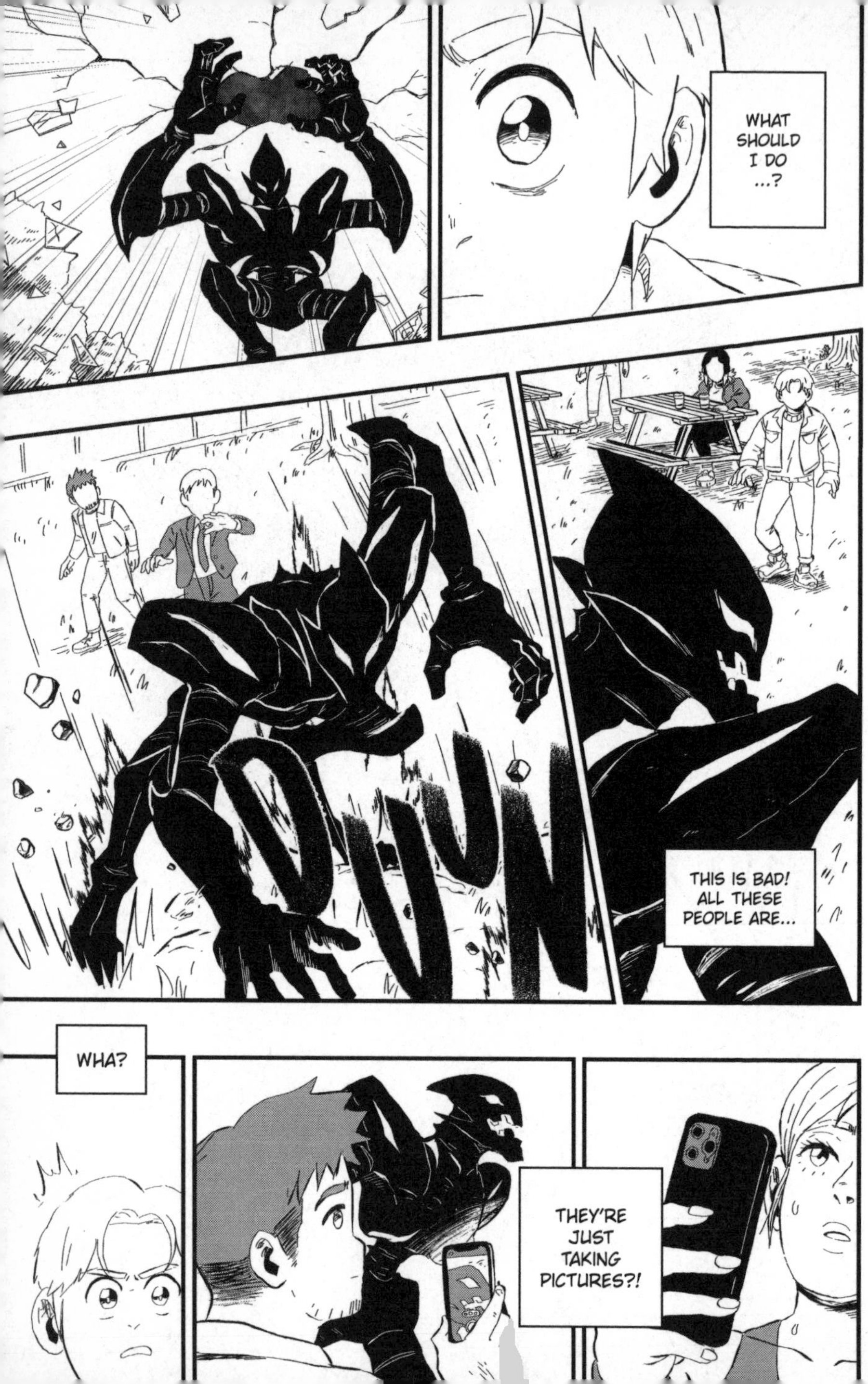

WHAT SHOULD I DO ...?
DOUN
THIS IS BAD! ALL THESE PEOPLE ARE...
WHA?
THEY'RE JUST TAKING PICTURES?!

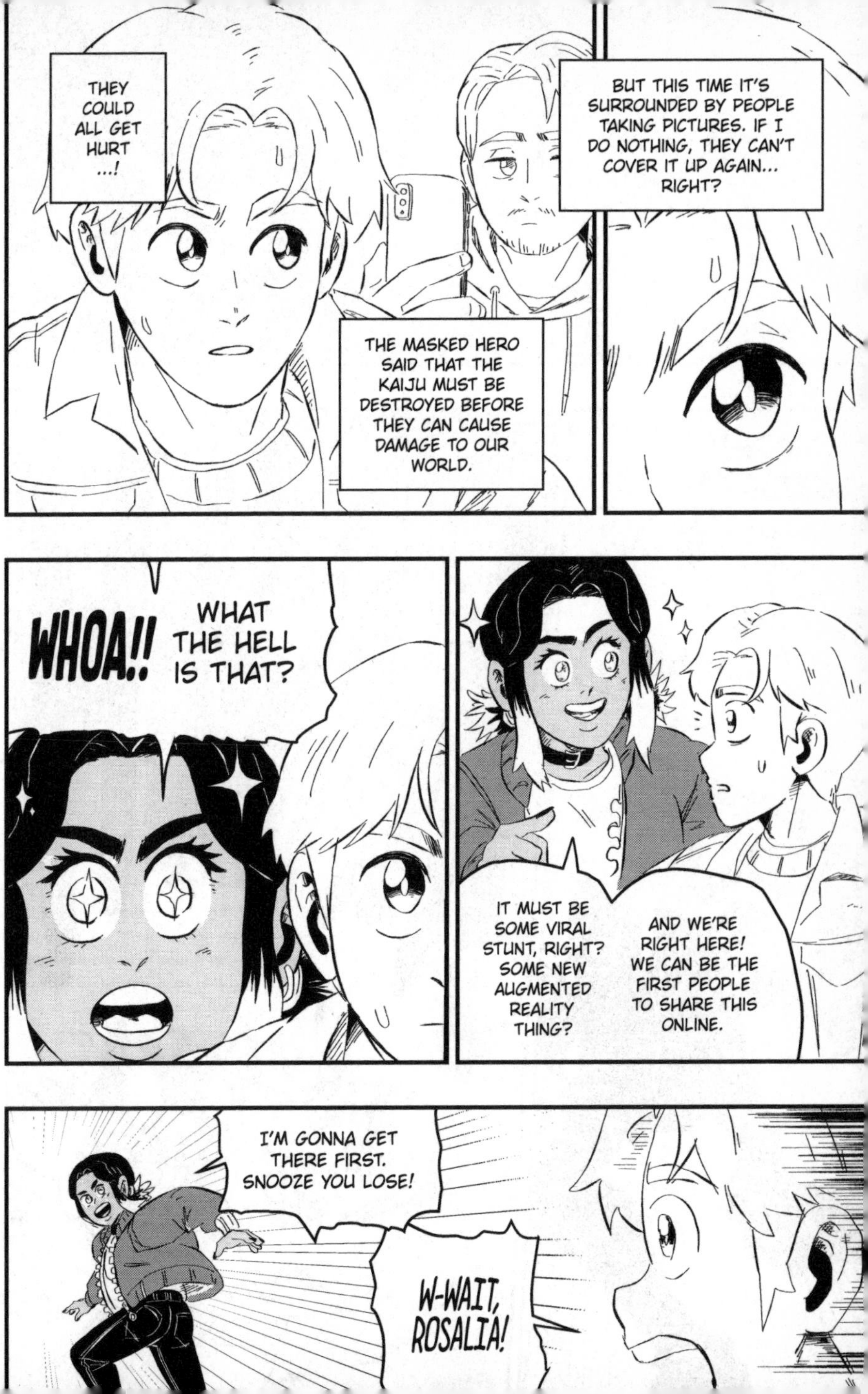
THEY COULD ALL GET HURT ...!
THE MASKED HERO SAID THAT THE KAIJU MUST BE DESTROYED BEFORE THEY CAN CAUSE DAMAGE TO OUR WORLD.
BUT THIS TIME IT'S SURROUNDED BY PEOPLE TAKING PICTURES. IF I DO NOTHING, THEY CAN'T COVER IT UP AGAIN... RIGHT?
WHOA!!
WHAT THE HELL IS THAT?
IT MUST BE SOME VIRAL STUNT, RIGHT? SOME NEW AUGMENTED REALITY THING?
AND WE'RE RIGHT HERE! WE CAN BE THE FIRST PEOPLE TO SHARE THIS ONLINE.
I'M GONNA GET THERE FIRST. SNOOZE YOU LOSE!
W-WAIT, ROSALIA!

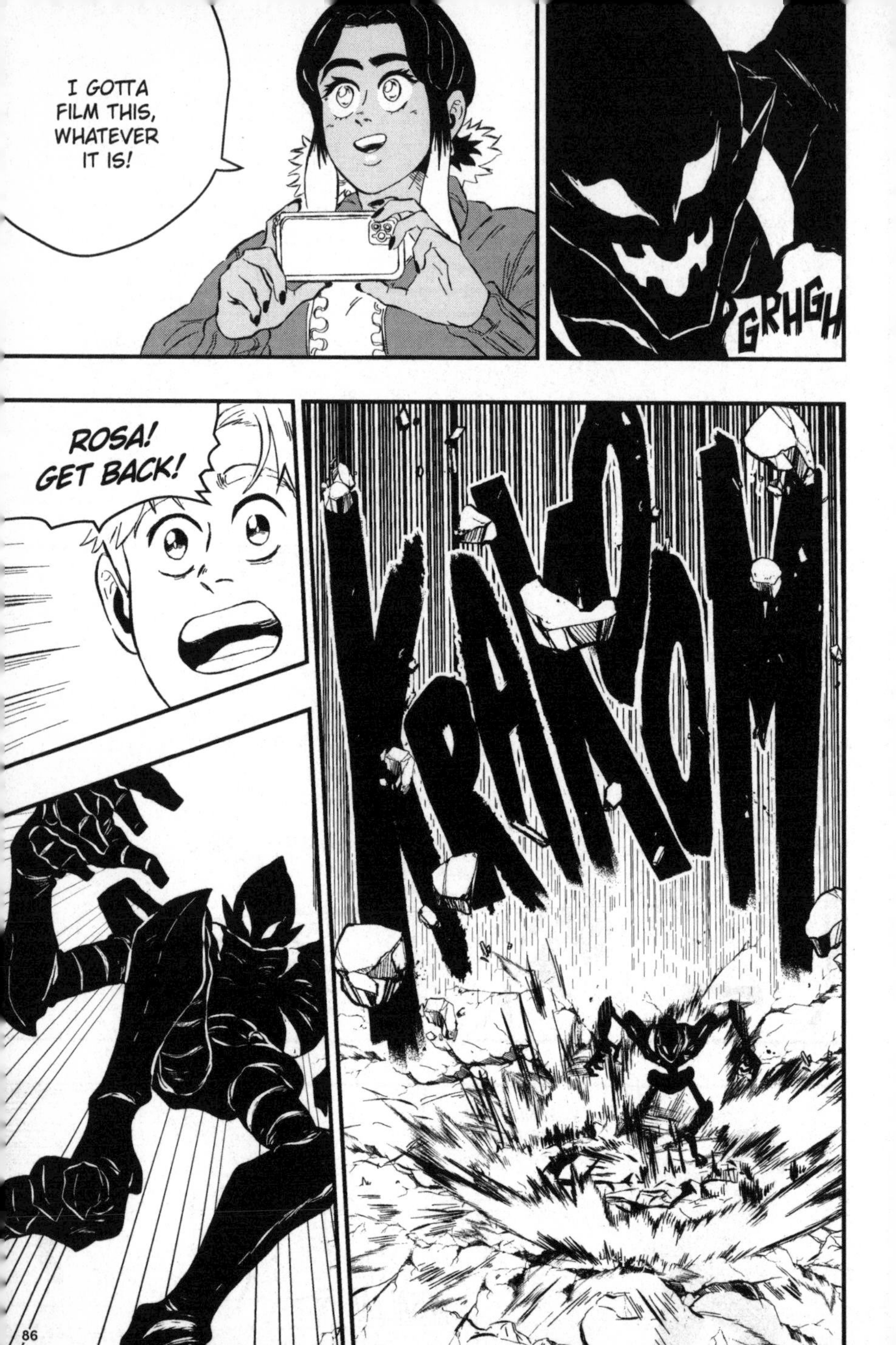
I GOTTA FILM THIS, WHATEVER IT IS!
GRHGH
ROSA! GET BACK!
KRAKOM

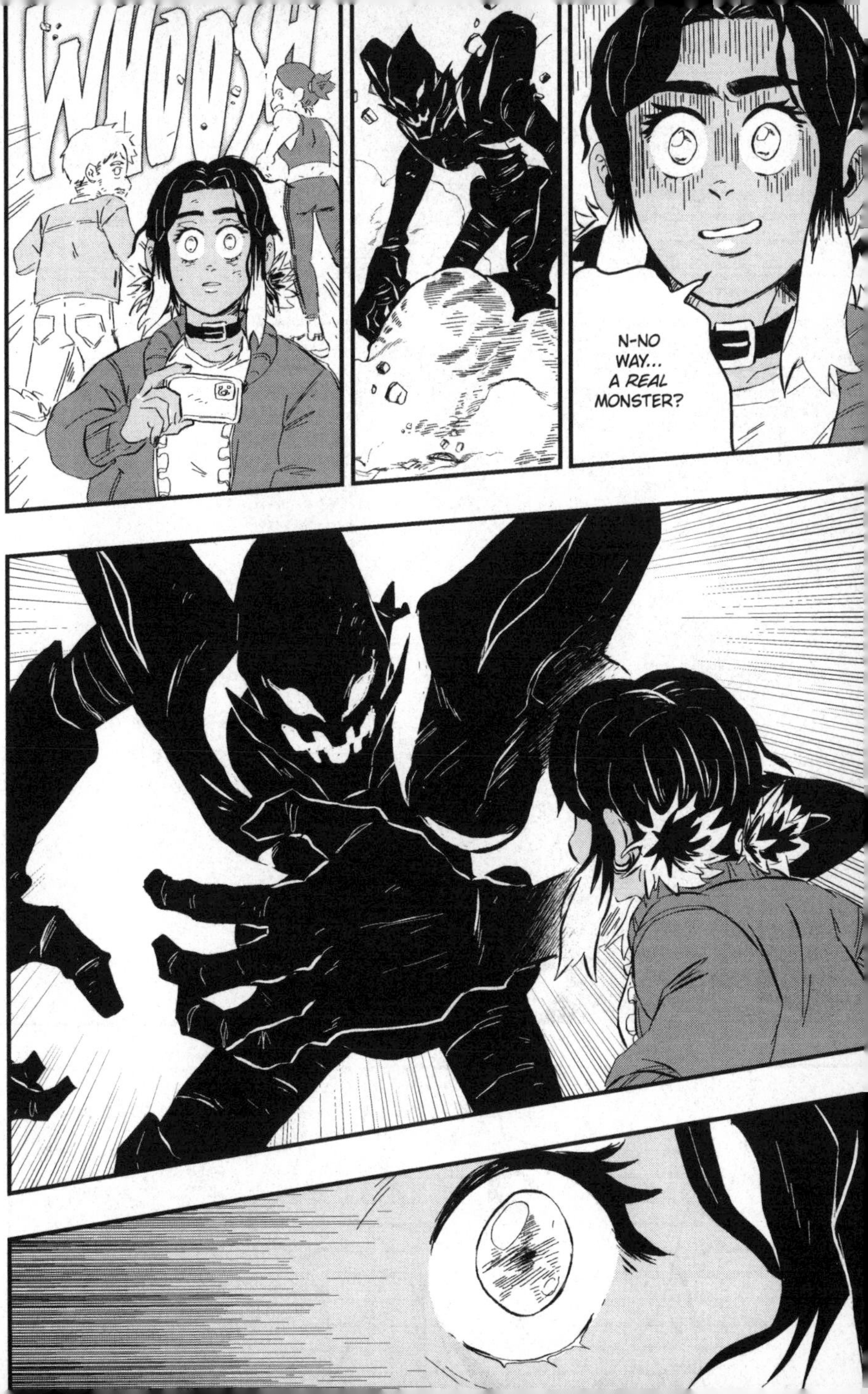
WHOOSH
N-NO WAY... A *REAL* MONSTER?

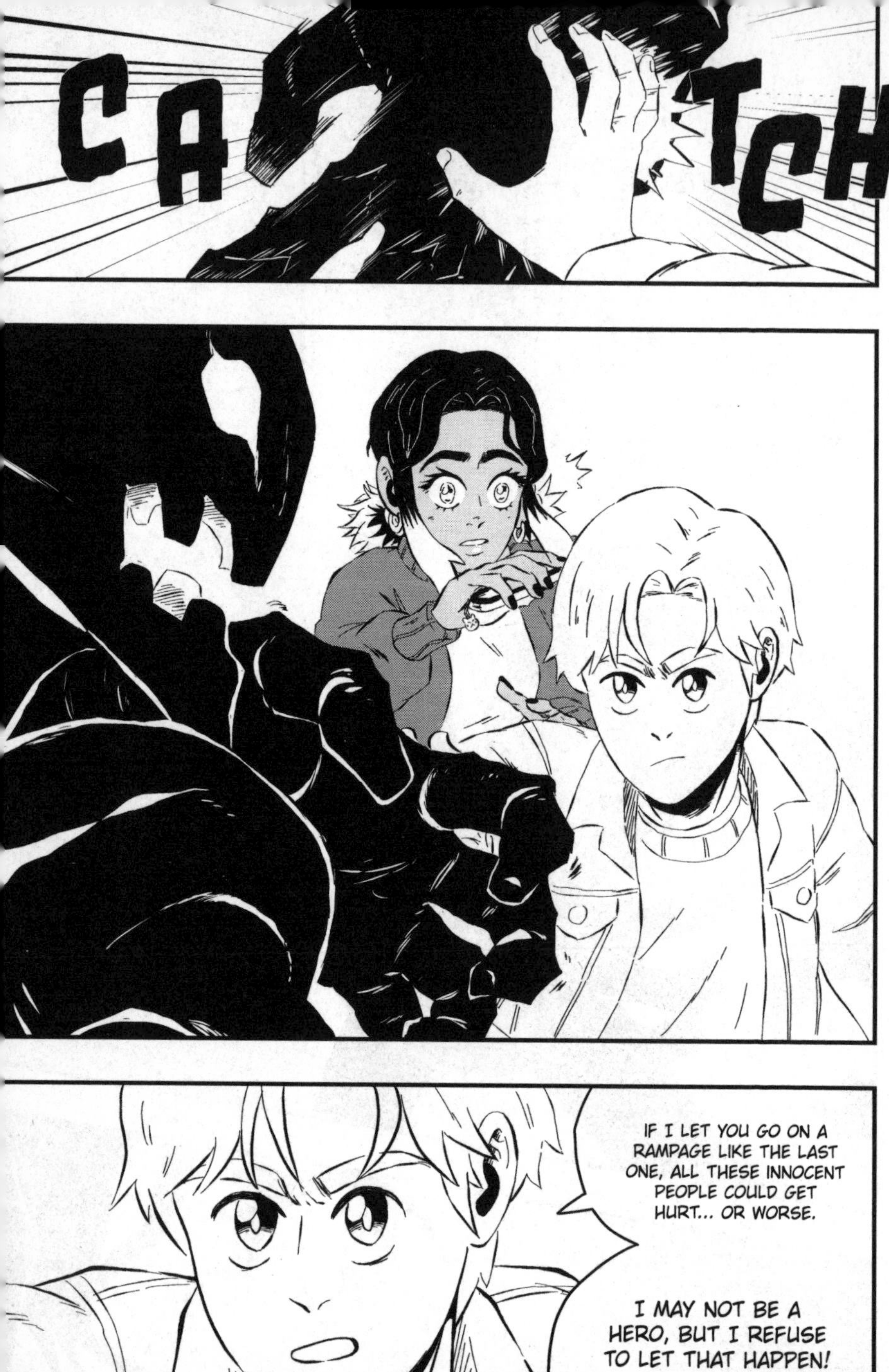
CATCH
IF I LET YOU GO ON A RAMPAGE LIKE THE LAST ONE, ALL THESE INNOCENT PEOPLE COULD GET HURT... OR WORSE.
I MAY NOT BE A HERO, BUT I REFUSE TO LET THAT HAPPEN!

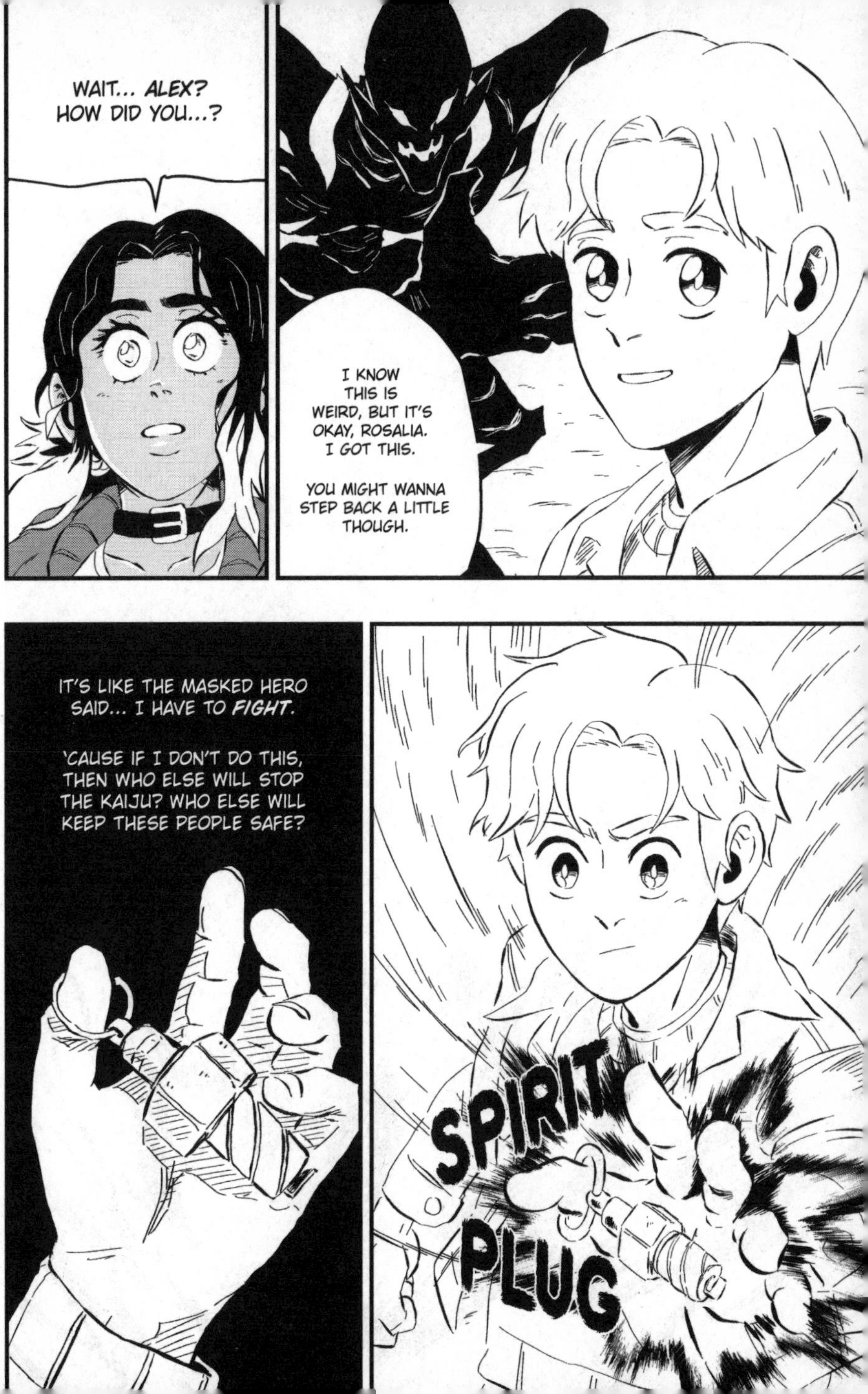
WAIT... *ALEX?* HOW DID YOU...?
I KNOW THIS IS WEIRD, BUT IT'S OKAY, ROSALIA. I GOT THIS.
YOU MIGHT WANNA STEP BACK A LITTLE THOUGH.
IT'S LIKE THE MASKED HERO SAID... I HAVE TO *FIGHT*.
'CAUSE IF I DON'T DO THIS, THEN WHO ELSE WILL STOP THE KAIJU? WHO ELSE WILL KEEP THESE PEOPLE SAFE?
SPIRIT PLUG

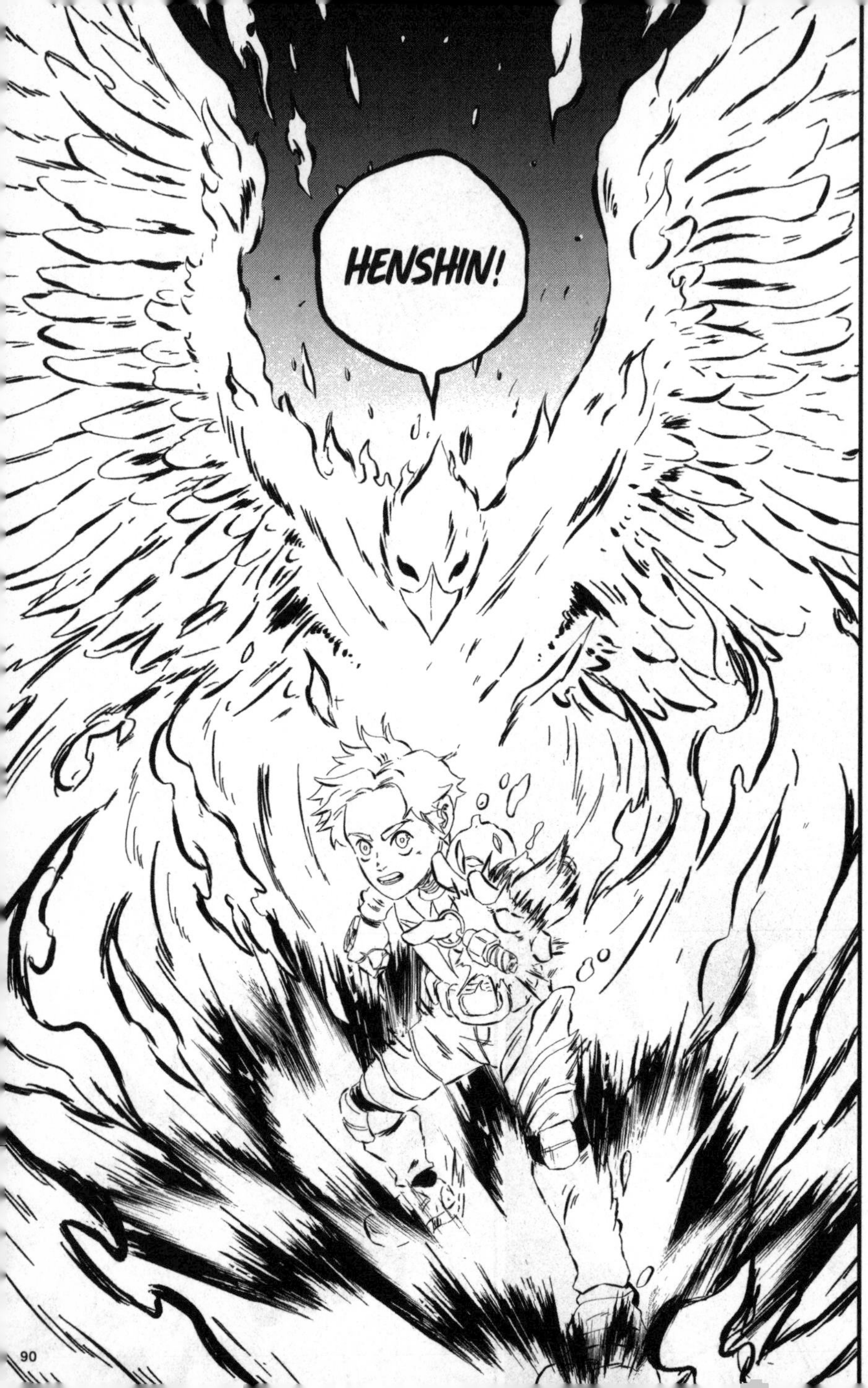
HENSHIN!

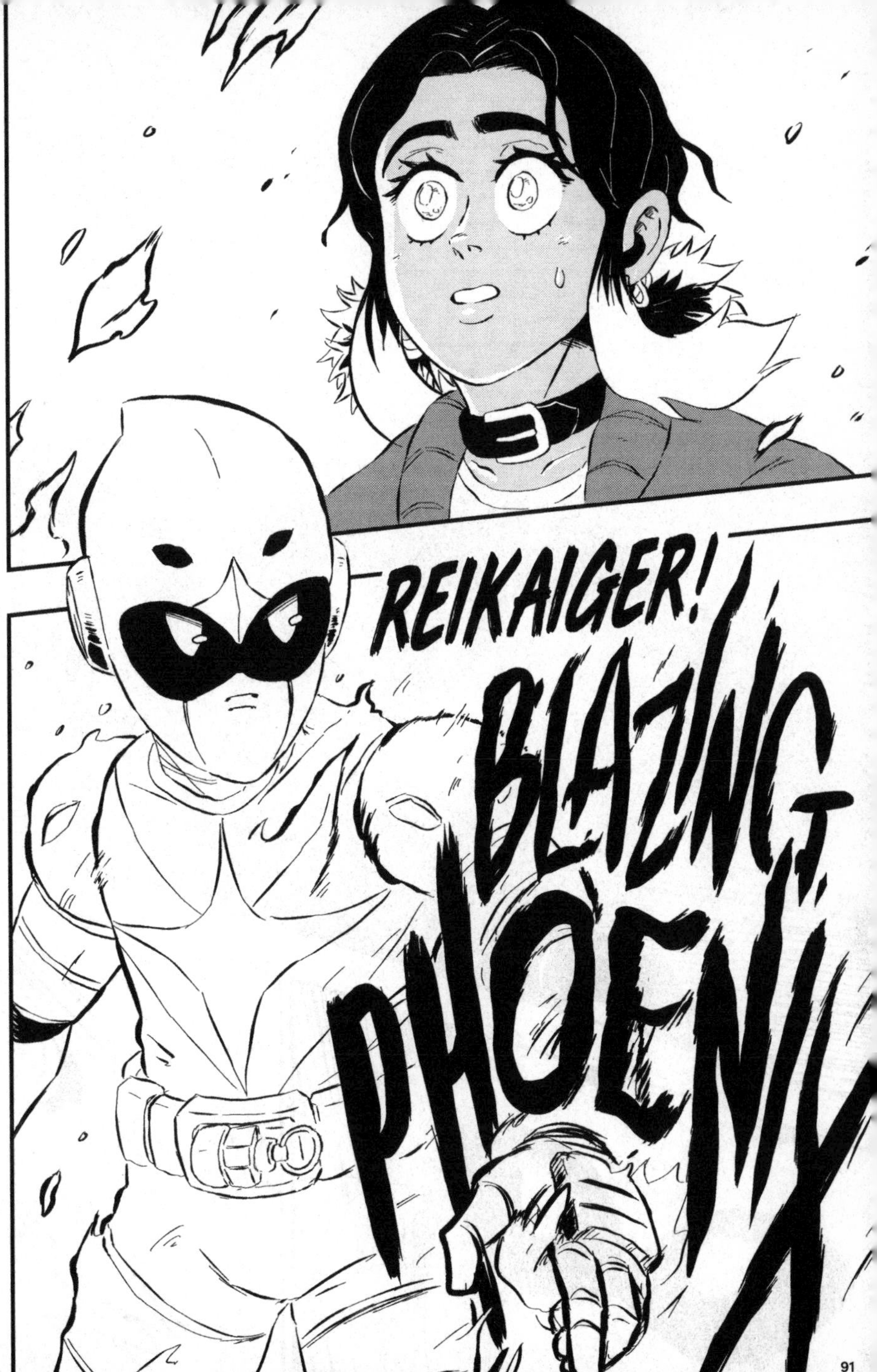
REIKAIGER!
BLAZING PHOENIX

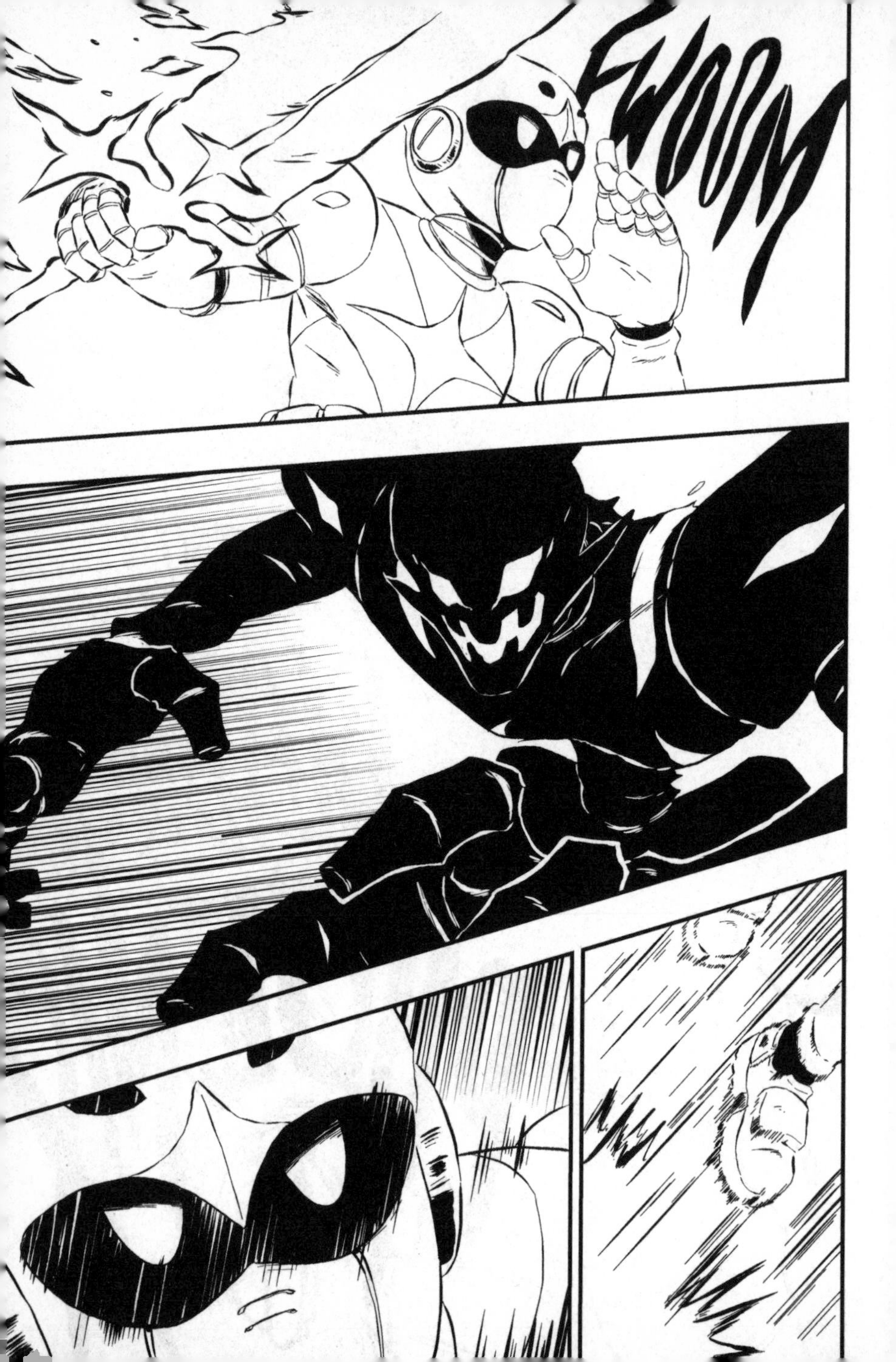
FWOOM

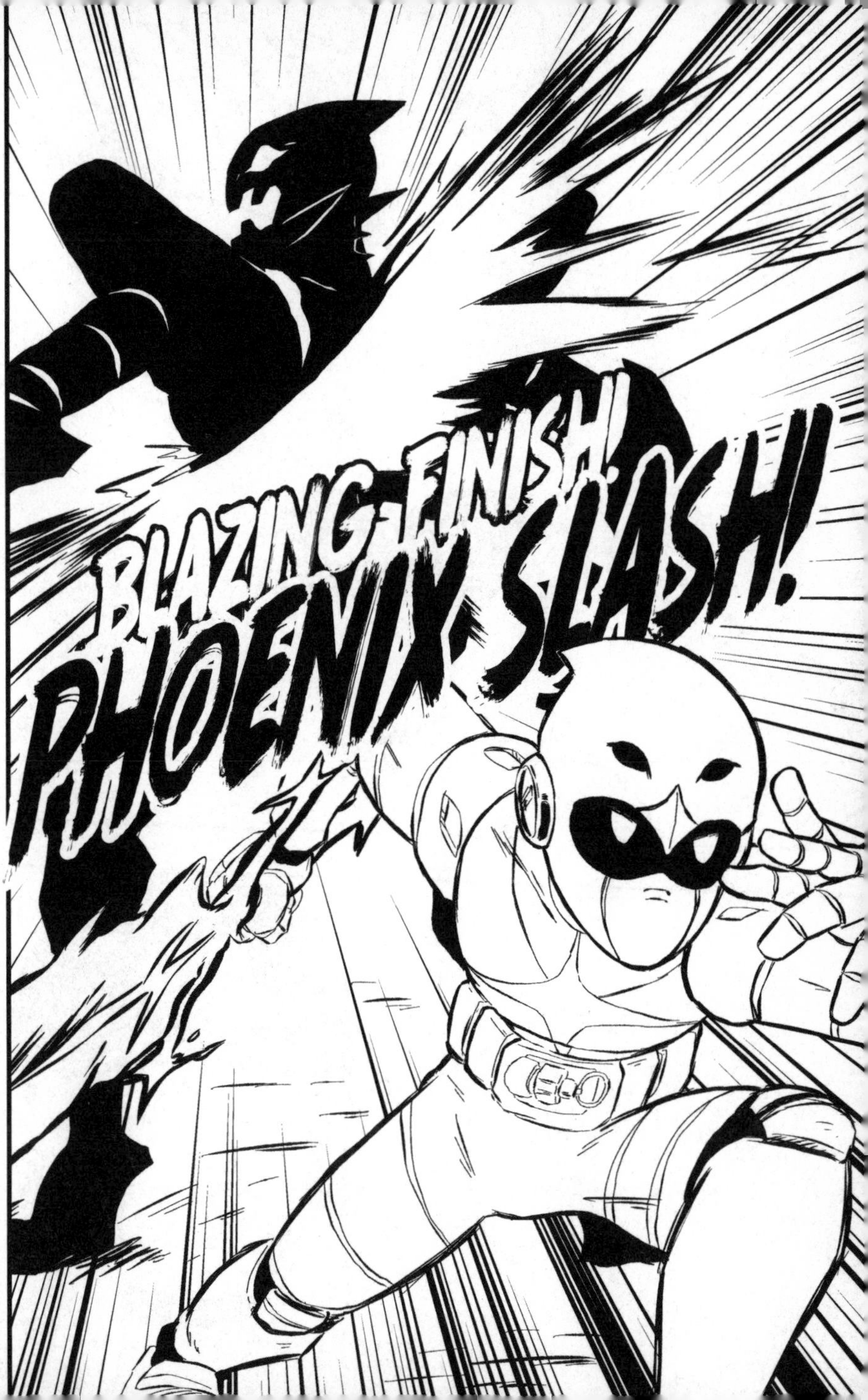
BLAZING FINISH!
PHOENIX SLASH!

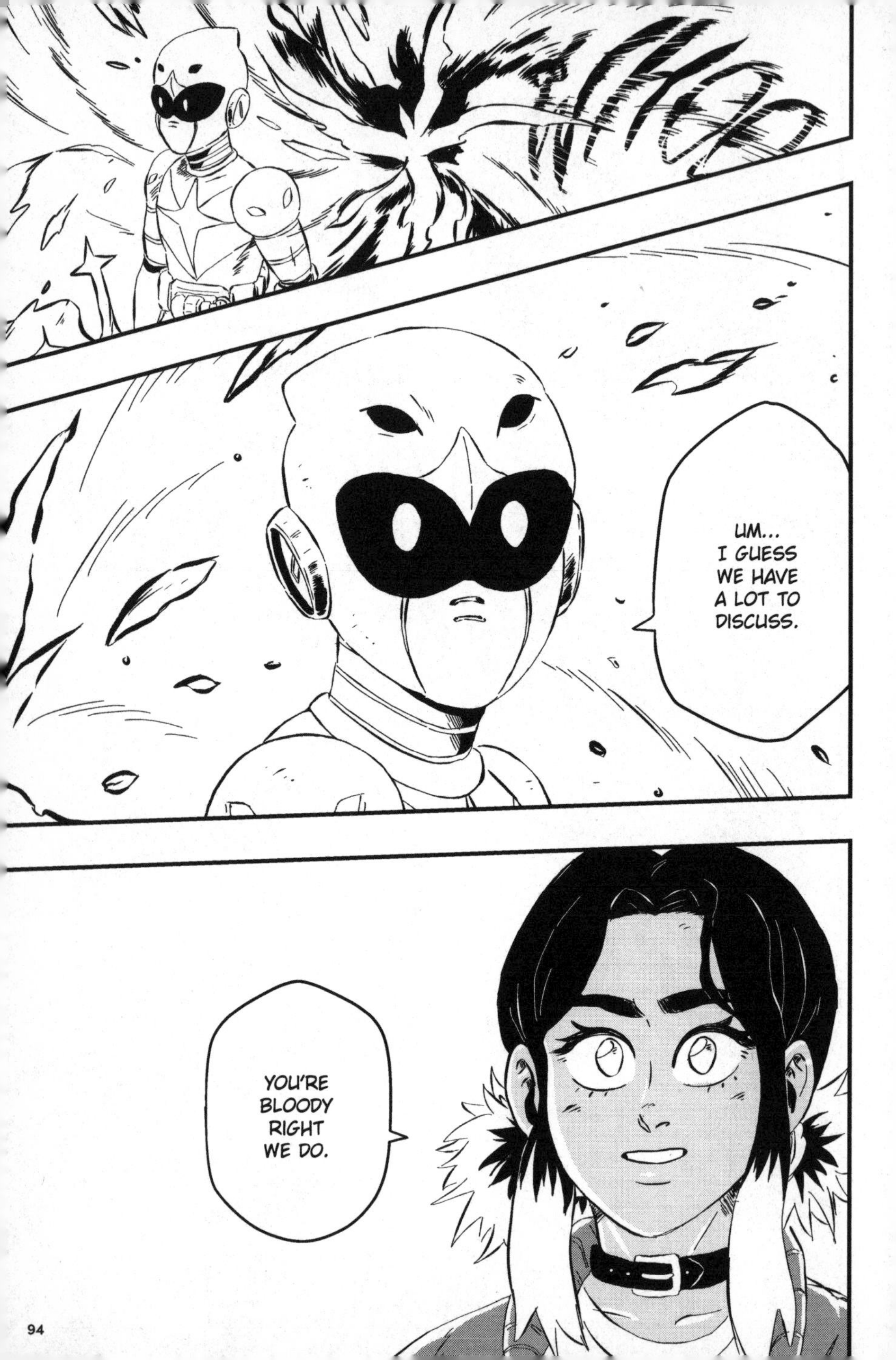
UM... I GUESS WE HAVE A LOT TO DISCUSS.
YOU'RE BLOODY RIGHT WE DO.

CHAPTER FIVE PLACEMENT

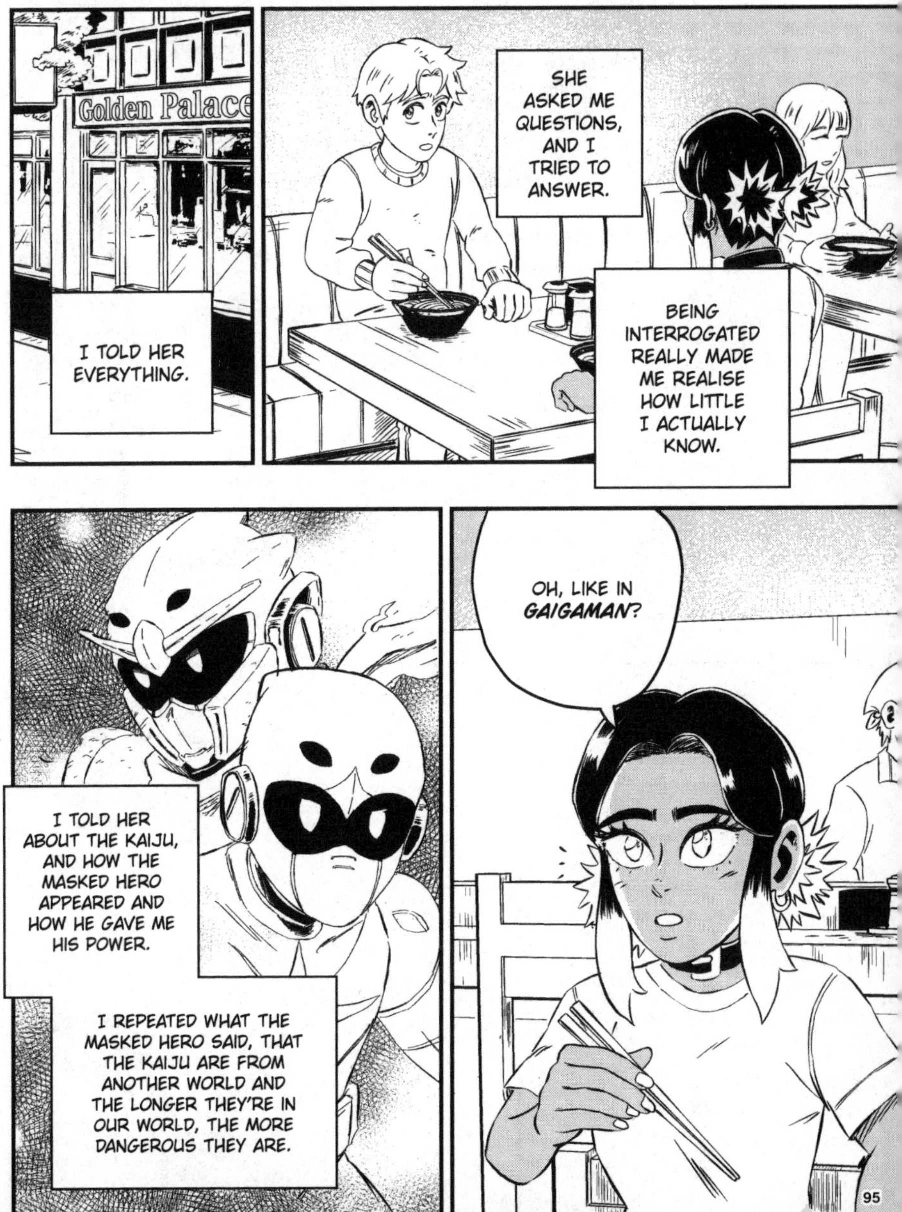
Golden Palace
I TOLD HER EVERYTHING.
SHE ASKED ME QUESTIONS, AND I TRIED TO ANSWER.
BEING INTERROGATED REALLY MADE ME REALISE HOW LITTLE I ACTUALLY KNOW.
I TOLD HER ABOUT THE KAIJU, AND HOW THE MASKED HERO APPEARED AND HOW HE GAVE ME HIS POWER.
I REPEATED WHAT THE MASKED HERO SAID, THAT THE KAIJU ARE FROM ANOTHER WORLD AND THE LONGER THEY'RE IN OUR WORLD, THE MORE DANGEROUS THEY ARE.
OH, LIKE IN *GAIGAMAN*?

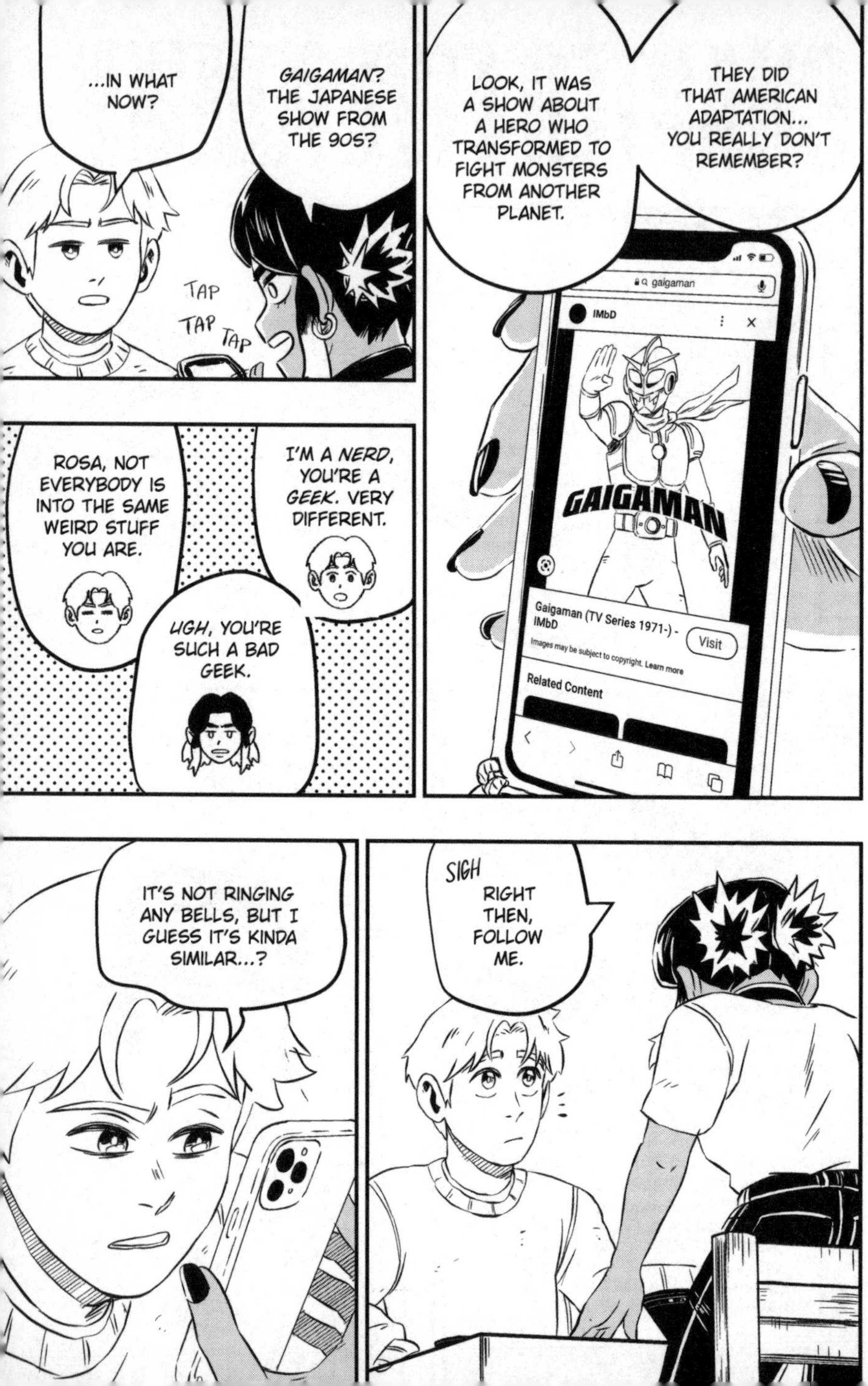
...IN WHAT NOW?
GAIGAMAN? THE JAPANESE SHOW FROM THE 90S?
TAP
TAP
TAP
LOOK, IT WAS A SHOW ABOUT A HERO WHO TRANSFORMED TO FIGHT MONSTERS FROM ANOTHER PLANET.
THEY DID THAT AMERICAN ADAPTATION... YOU REALLY DON'T REMEMBER?
gaigaman
IMbD
GAIGAMAN
Gaigaman (TV Series 1971-) - IMbD
Visit
Images may be subject to copyright. Learn more
Related Content
ROSA, NOT EVERYBODY IS INTO THE SAME WEIRD STUFF YOU ARE.
I'M A NERD, YOU'RE A GEEK. VERY DIFFERENT.
UGH, YOU'RE SUCH A BAD GEEK.
IT'S NOT RINGING ANY BELLS, BUT I GUESS IT'S KINDA SIMILAR...?
SIGH
RIGHT THEN, FOLLOW ME.

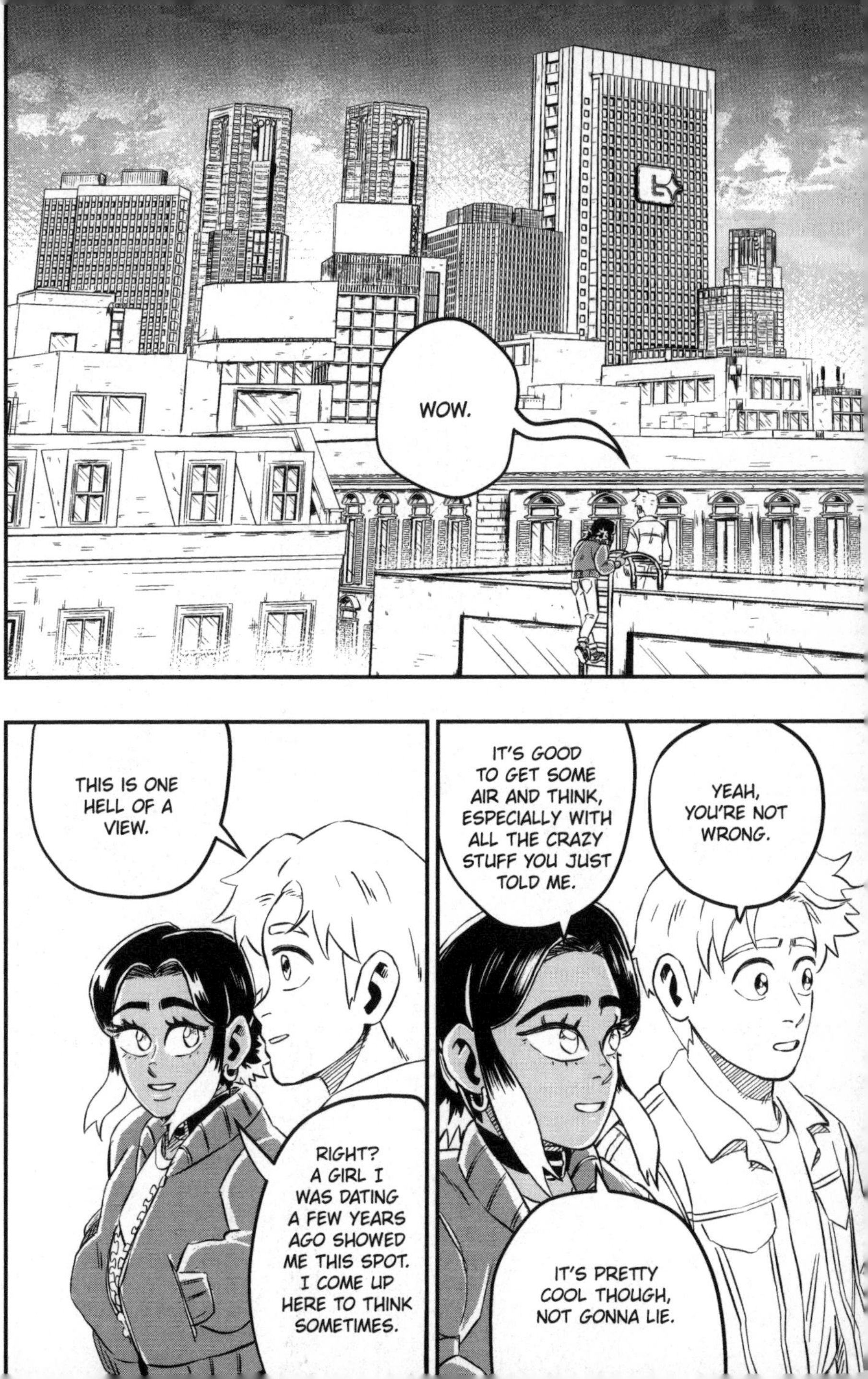
WOW.
THIS IS ONE HELL OF A VIEW.
RIGHT? A GIRL I WAS DATING A FEW YEARS AGO SHOWED ME THIS SPOT. I COME UP HERE TO THINK SOMETIMES.
IT'S GOOD TO GET SOME AIR AND THINK, ESPECIALLY WITH ALL THE CRAZY STUFF YOU JUST TOLD ME.
YEAH, YOU'RE NOT WRONG.
IT'S PRETTY COOL THOUGH, NOT GONNA LIE.

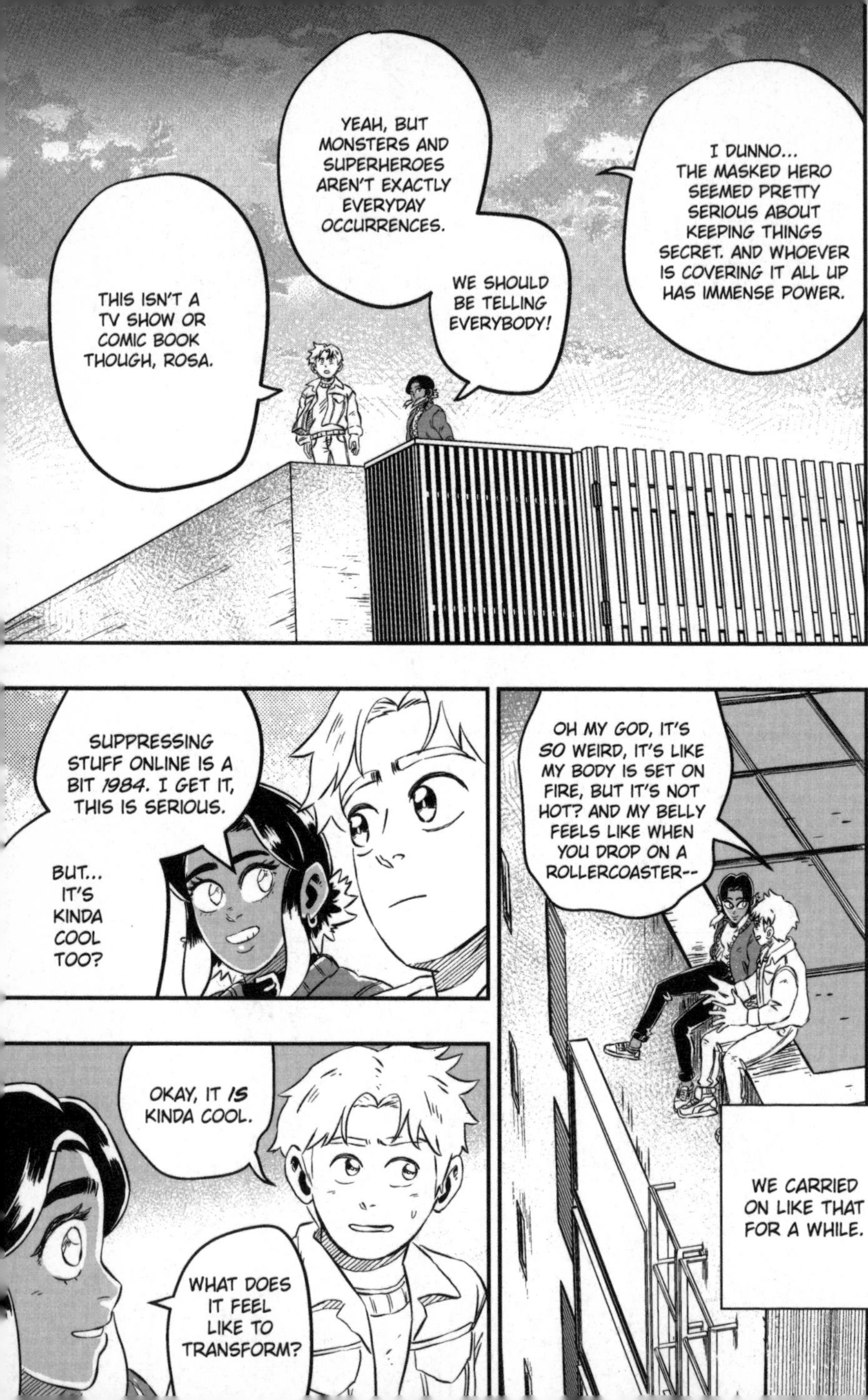

THIS ISN'T A TV SHOW OR COMIC BOOK THOUGH, ROSA.
YEAH, BUT MONSTERS AND SUPERHEROES AREN'T EXACTLY EVERYDAY OCCURRENCES.
WE SHOULD BE TELLING EVERYBODY!
I DUNNO... THE MASKED HERO SEEMED PRETTY SERIOUS ABOUT KEEPING THINGS SECRET. AND WHOEVER IS COVERING IT ALL UP HAS IMMENSE POWER.
SUPPRESSING STUFF ONLINE IS A BIT *1984*. I GET IT, THIS IS SERIOUS.
BUT... IT'S KINDA COOL TOO?
OKAY, IT *IS* KINDA COOL.
WHAT DOES IT FEEL LIKE TO TRANSFORM?
OH MY GOD, IT'S *SO* WEIRD, IT'S LIKE MY BODY IS SET ON FIRE, BUT IT'S NOT HOT? AND MY BELLY FEELS LIKE WHEN YOU DROP ON A ROLLERCOASTER--
WE CARRIED ON LIKE THAT FOR A WHILE.

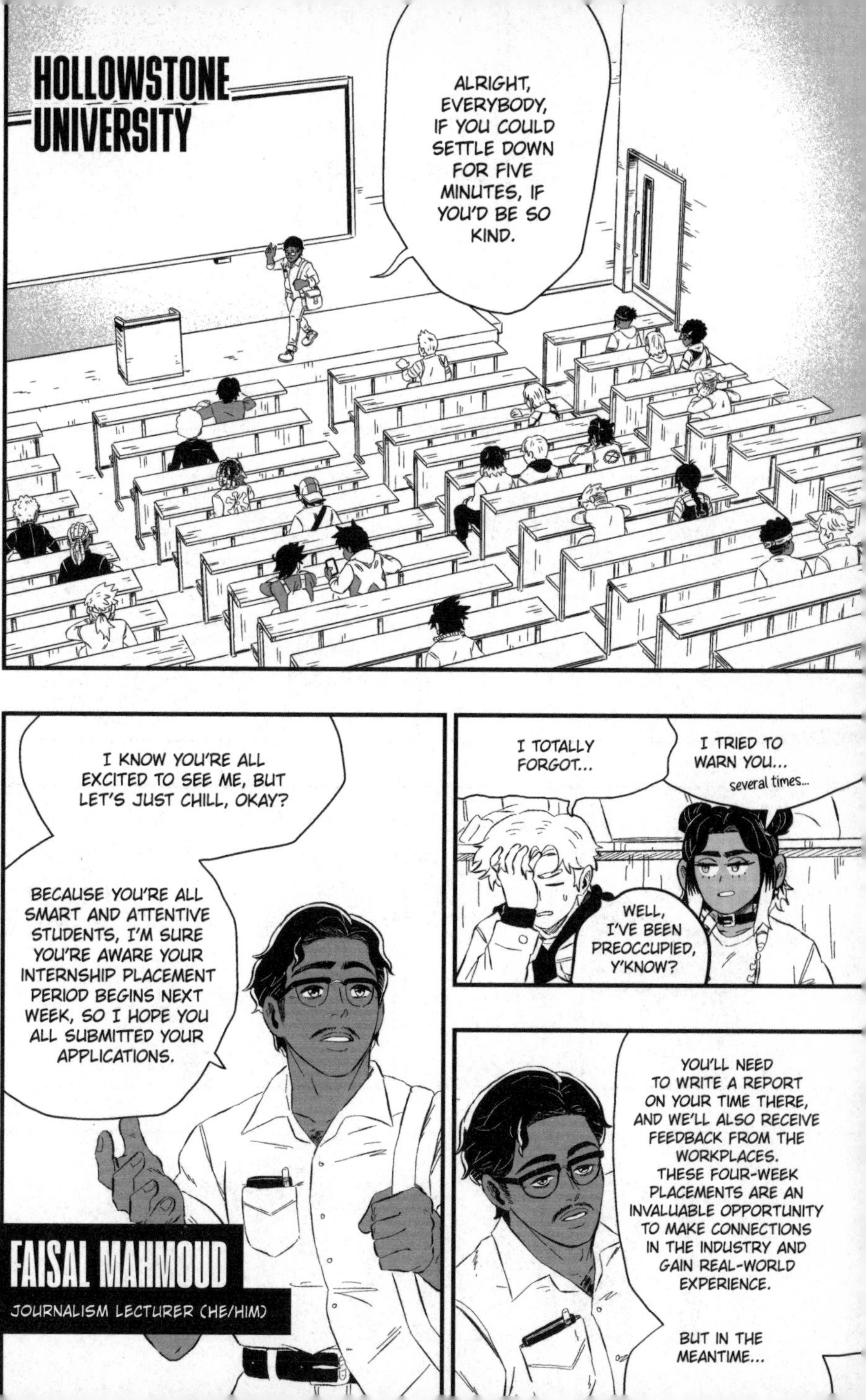
HOLLOWSTONE UNIVERSITY
ALRIGHT, EVERYBODY, IF YOU COULD SETTLE DOWN FOR FIVE MINUTES, IF YOU'D BE SO KIND.
I KNOW YOU'RE ALL EXCITED TO SEE ME, BUT LET'S JUST CHILL, OKAY?
BECAUSE YOU'RE ALL SMART AND ATTENTIVE STUDENTS, I'M SURE YOU'RE AWARE YOUR INTERNSHIP PLACEMENT PERIOD BEGINS NEXT WEEK, SO I HOPE YOU ALL SUBMITTED YOUR APPLICATIONS.
FAISAL MAHMOUD
JOURNALISM LECTURER (HE/HIM)
I TOTALLY FORGOT...
I TRIED TO WARN YOU... several times...
WELL, I'VE BEEN PREOCCUPIED, Y'KNOW?
YOU'LL NEED TO WRITE A REPORT ON YOUR TIME THERE, AND WE'LL ALSO RECEIVE FEEDBACK FROM THE WORKPLACES. THESE FOUR-WEEK PLACEMENTS ARE AN INVALUABLE OPPORTUNITY TO MAKE CONNECTIONS IN THE INDUSTRY AND GAIN REAL-WORLD EXPERIENCE.
BUT IN THE MEANTIME...

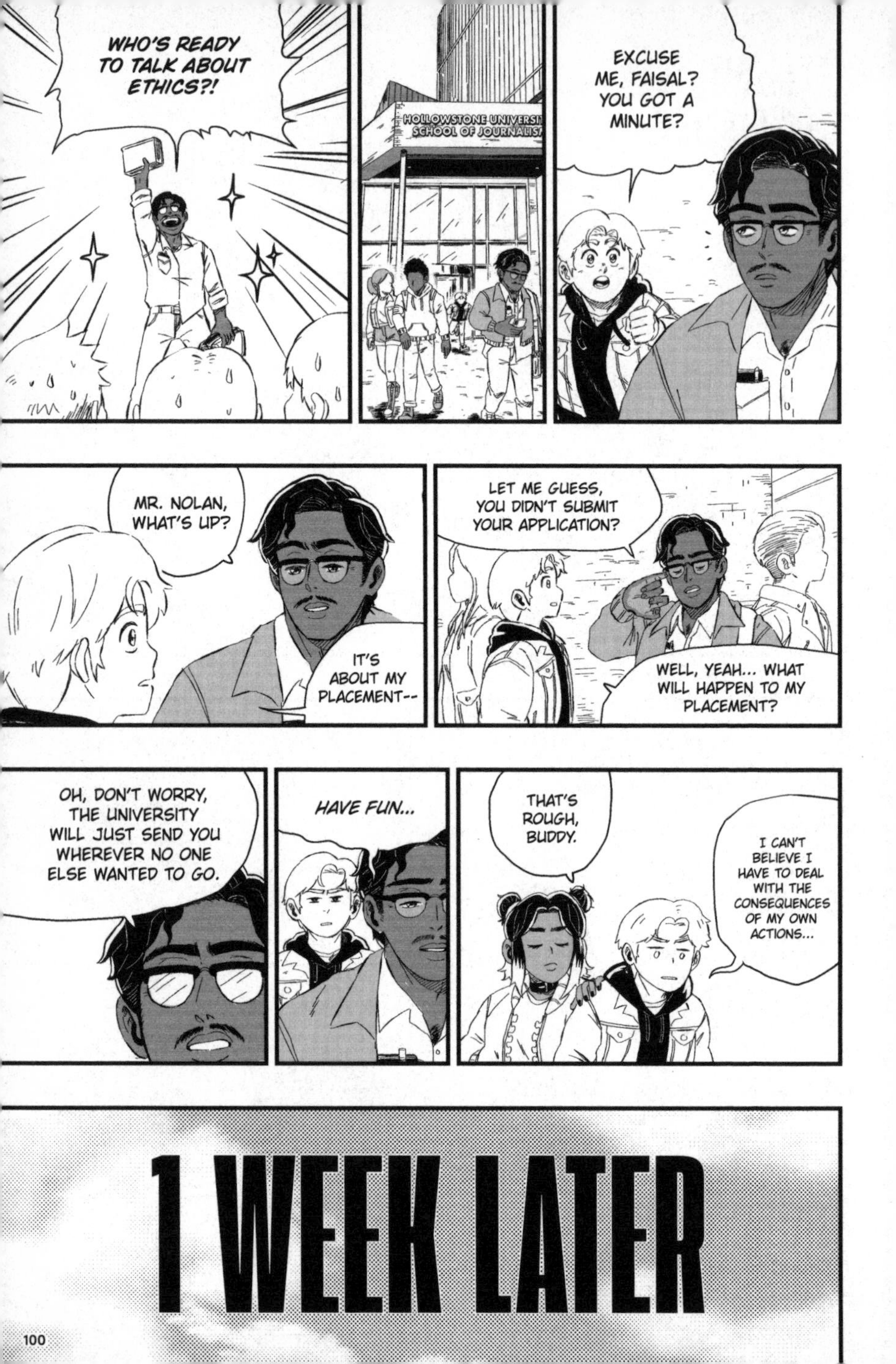
WHO'S READY TO TALK ABOUT ETHICS?!
HOLLOWSTONE UNIVERSITY SCHOOL OF JOURNALISM
EXCUSE ME, FAISAL? YOU GOT A MINUTE?
MR. NOLAN, WHAT'S UP?
IT'S ABOUT MY PLACEMENT--
LET ME GUESS, YOU DIDN'T SUBMIT YOUR APPLICATION?
WELL, YEAH... WHAT WILL HAPPEN TO MY PLACEMENT?
OH, DON'T WORRY, THE UNIVERSITY WILL JUST SEND YOU WHEREVER NO ONE ELSE WANTED TO GO.
HAVE FUN...
THAT'S ROUGH, BUDDY.
I CAN'T BELIEVE I HAVE TO DEAL WITH THE CONSEQUENCES OF MY OWN ACTIONS...
1 WEEK LATER

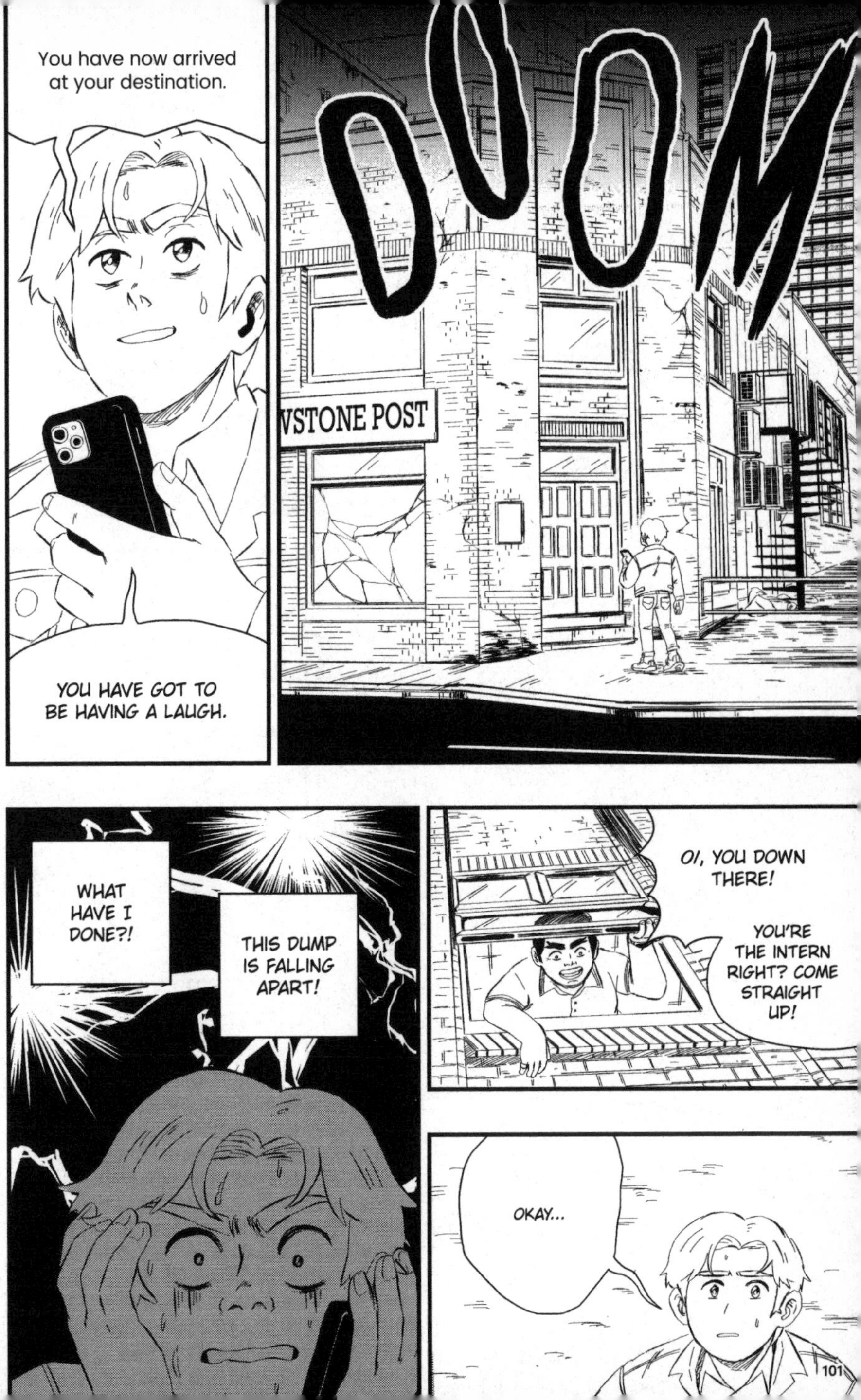
You have now arrived at your destination.
YOU HAVE GOT TO BE HAVING A LAUGH.
DOOOM
VSTONE POST
WHAT HAVE I DONE?!
THIS DUMP IS FALLING APART!
OI, YOU DOWN THERE!
YOU'RE THE INTERN RIGHT? COME STRAIGHT UP!
OKAY...

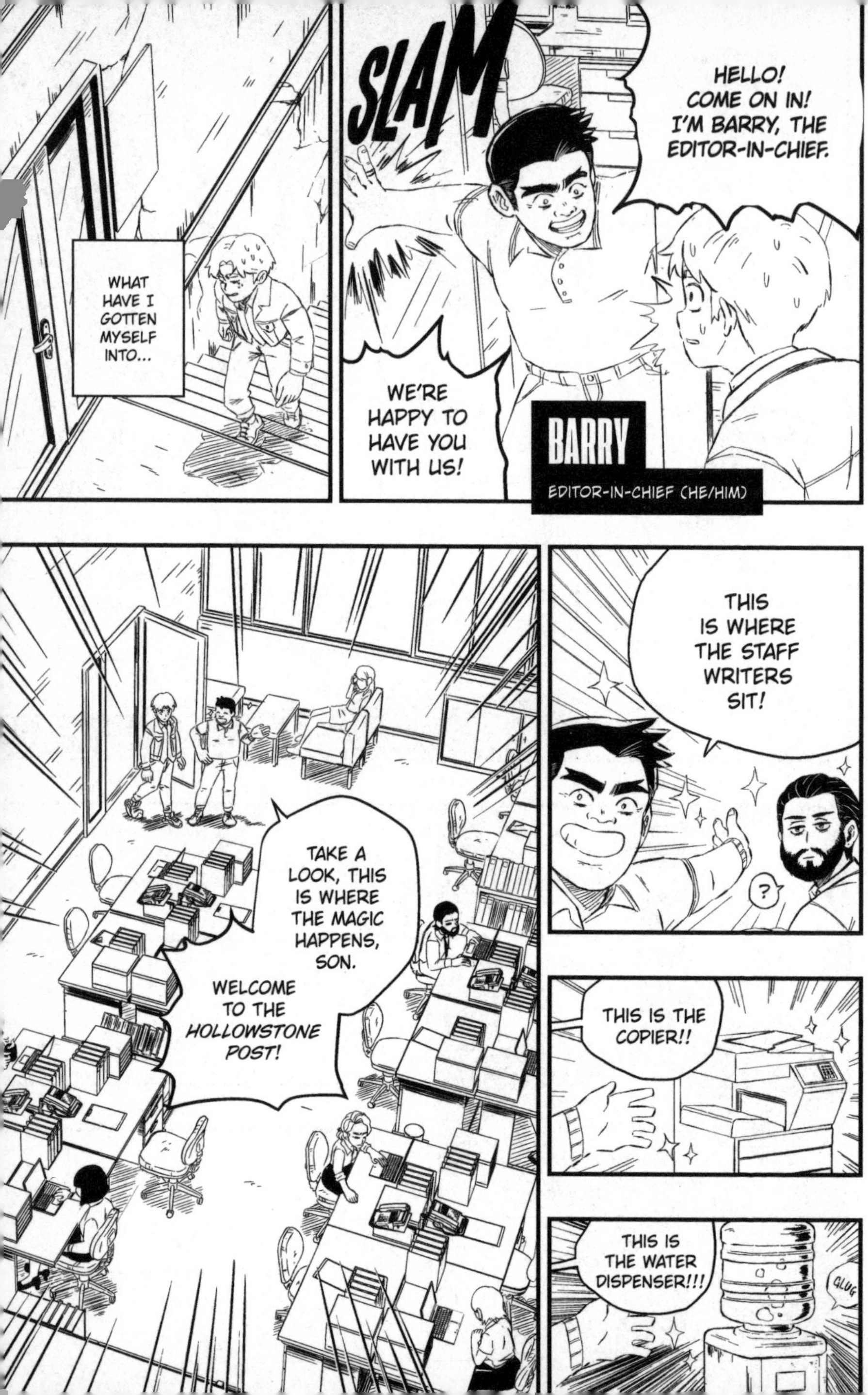
WHAT HAVE I GOTTEN MYSELF INTO...
SLAM
HELLO! COME ON IN! I'M BARRY, THE EDITOR-IN-CHIEF.
WE'RE HAPPY TO HAVE YOU WITH US!
BARRY
EDITOR-IN-CHIEF (HE/HIM)
TAKE A LOOK, THIS IS WHERE THE MAGIC HAPPENS, SON.
WELCOME TO THE *HOLLOWSTONE POST!*
THIS IS WHERE THE STAFF WRITERS SIT!
?
THIS IS THE COPIER!!
THIS IS THE WATER DISPENSER!!!
GLUG

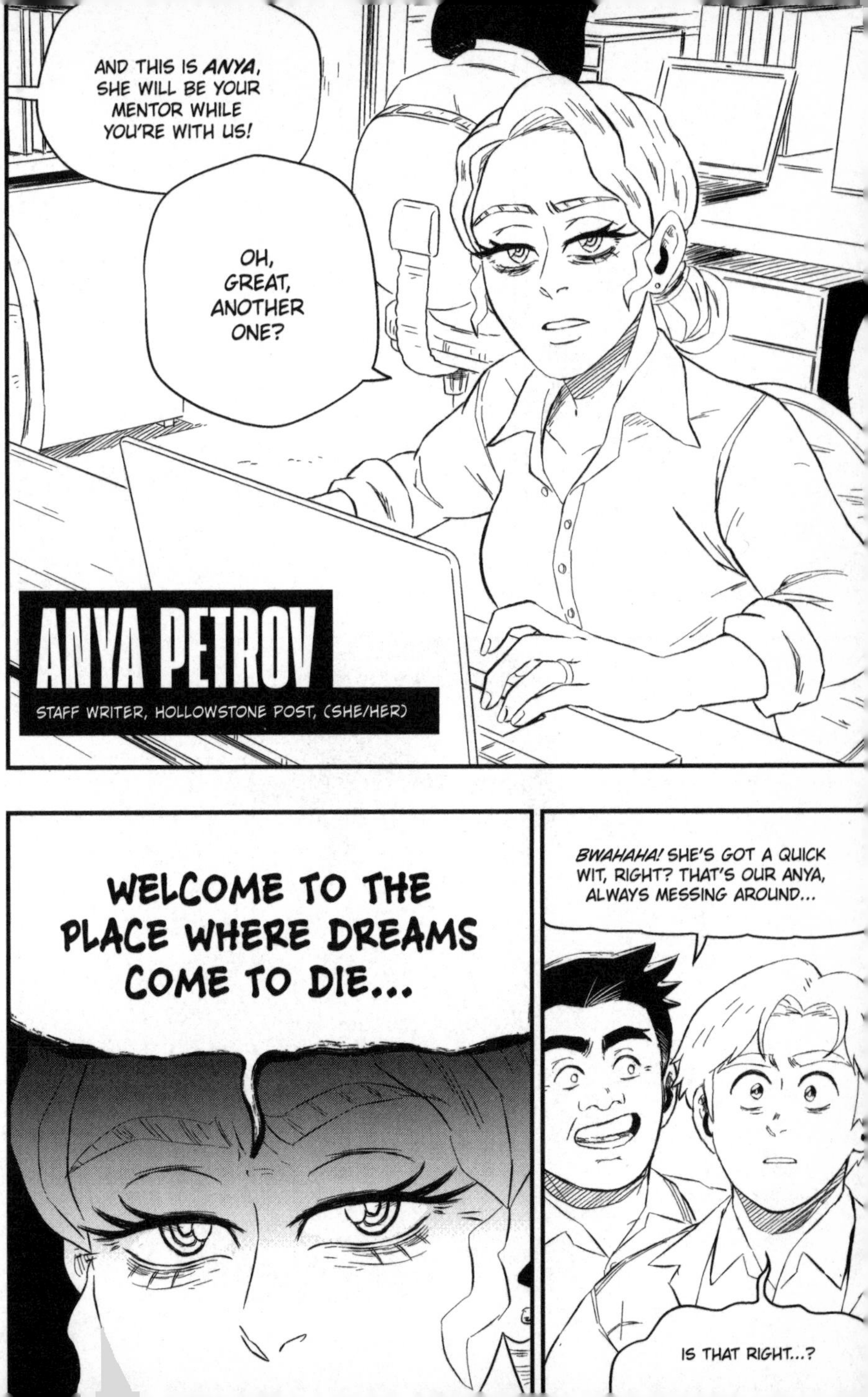
AND THIS IS ANYA, SHE WILL BE YOUR MENTOR WHILE YOU'RE WITH US!
OH, GREAT, ANOTHER ONE?
ANYA PETROV
STAFF WRITER, HOLLOWSTONE POST, (SHE/HER)
WELCOME TO THE PLACE WHERE DREAMS COME TO DIE...
BWAHAHA! SHE'S GOT A QUICK WIT, RIGHT? THAT'S OUR ANYA, ALWAYS MESSING AROUND...
IS THAT RIGHT...?

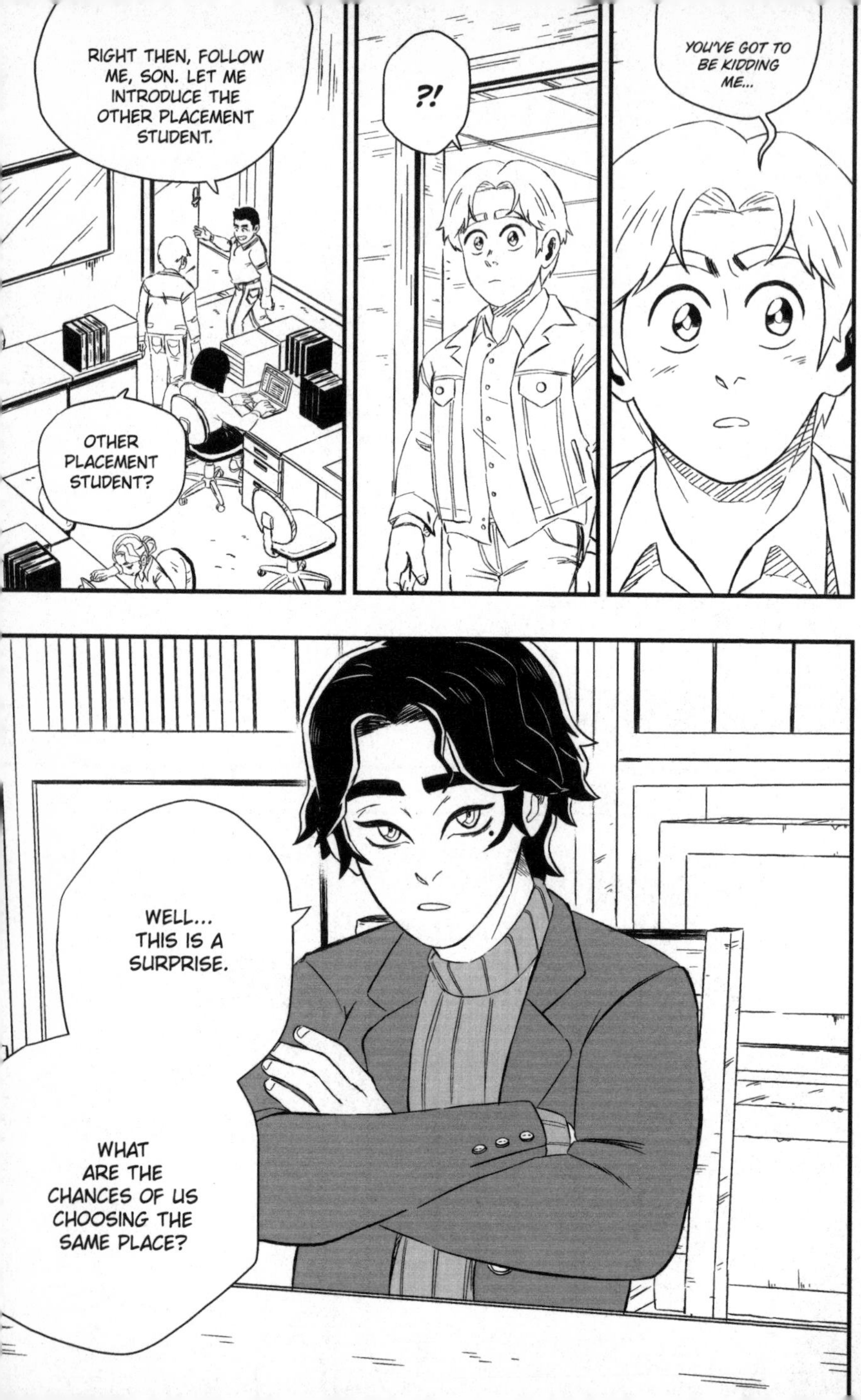
RIGHT THEN, FOLLOW ME, SON. LET ME INTRODUCE THE OTHER PLACEMENT STUDENT.
OTHER PLACEMENT STUDENT?
?!
YOU'VE GOT TO BE KIDDING ME...
WELL... THIS IS A SURPRISE.
WHAT ARE THE CHANCES OF US CHOOSING THE SAME PLACE?

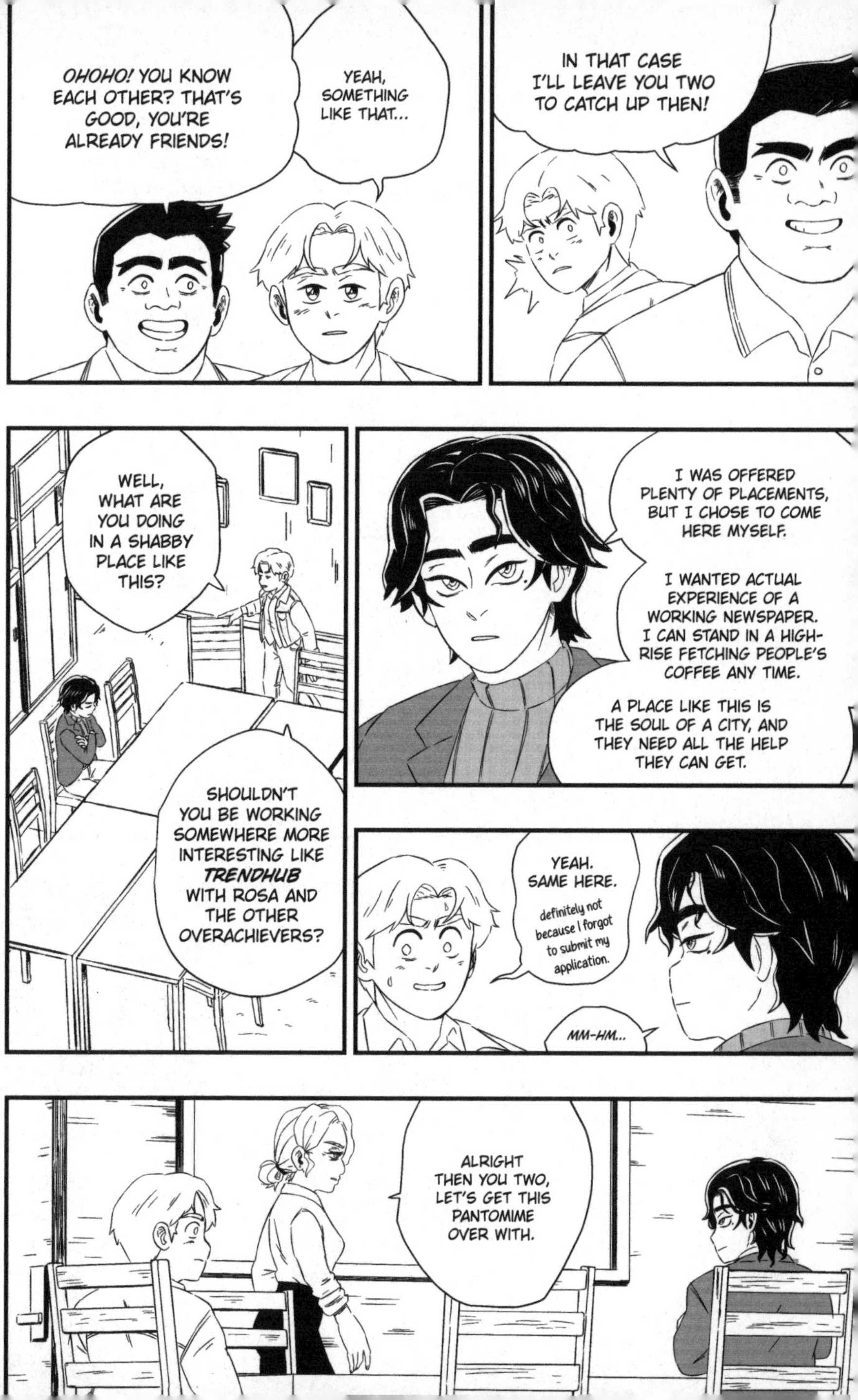
OHOHO! YOU KNOW EACH OTHER? THAT'S GOOD, YOU'RE ALREADY FRIENDS!
YEAH, SOMETHING LIKE THAT...
IN THAT CASE I'LL LEAVE YOU TWO TO CATCH UP THEN!
WELL, WHAT ARE YOU DOING IN A SHABBY PLACE LIKE THIS?
SHOULDN'T YOU BE WORKING SOMEWHERE MORE INTERESTING LIKE ***TRENDHUB*** WITH ROSA AND THE OTHER OVERACHIEVERS?
I WAS OFFERED PLENTY OF PLACEMENTS, BUT I CHOSE TO COME HERE MYSELF.
I WANTED ACTUAL EXPERIENCE OF A WORKING NEWSPAPER. I CAN STAND IN A HIGH-RISE FETCHING PEOPLE'S COFFEE ANY TIME.
A PLACE LIKE THIS IS THE SOUL OF A CITY, AND THEY NEED ALL THE HELP THEY CAN GET.
YEAH. SAME HERE.
definitely not because I forgot to submit my application.
MM-HM...
ALRIGHT THEN YOU TWO, LET'S GET THIS PANTOMIME OVER WITH.

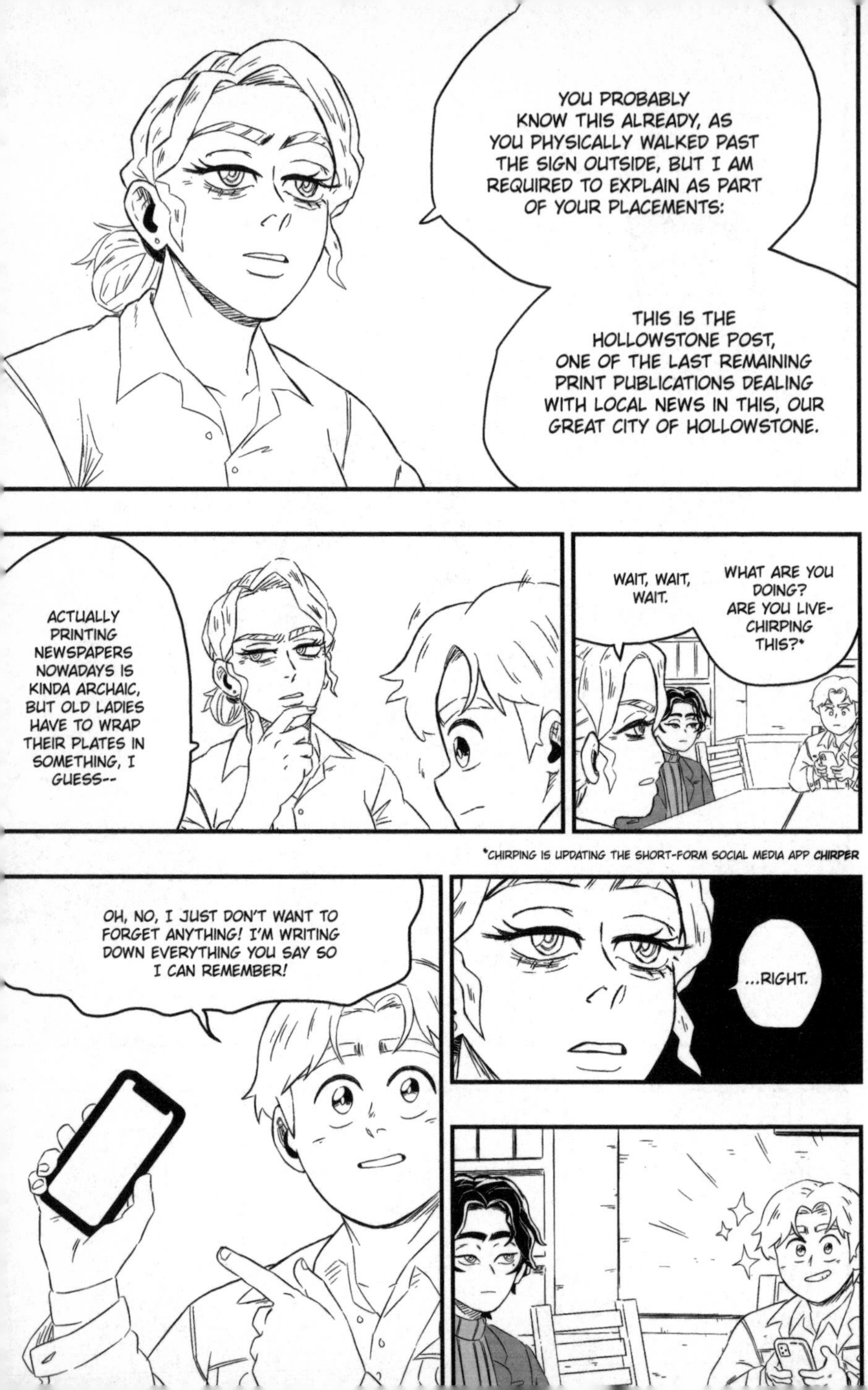

YOU PROBABLY KNOW THIS ALREADY, AS YOU PHYSICALLY WALKED PAST THE SIGN OUTSIDE, BUT I AM REQUIRED TO EXPLAIN AS PART OF YOUR PLACEMENTS:
THIS IS THE HOLLOWSTONE POST, ONE OF THE LAST REMAINING PRINT PUBLICATIONS DEALING WITH LOCAL NEWS IN THIS, OUR GREAT CITY OF HOLLOWSTONE.
ACTUALLY PRINTING NEWSPAPERS NOWADAYS IS KINDA ARCHAIC, BUT OLD LADIES HAVE TO WRAP THEIR PLATES IN SOMETHING, I GUESS--
WAIT, WAIT, WAIT.
WHAT ARE YOU DOING? ARE YOU LIVE-CHIRPING THIS?*
*CHIRPING IS UPDATING THE SHORT-FORM SOCIAL MEDIA APP **CHIRPER**
OH, NO, I JUST DON'T WANT TO FORGET ANYTHING! I'M WRITING DOWN EVERYTHING YOU SAY SO I CAN REMEMBER!
...RIGHT.

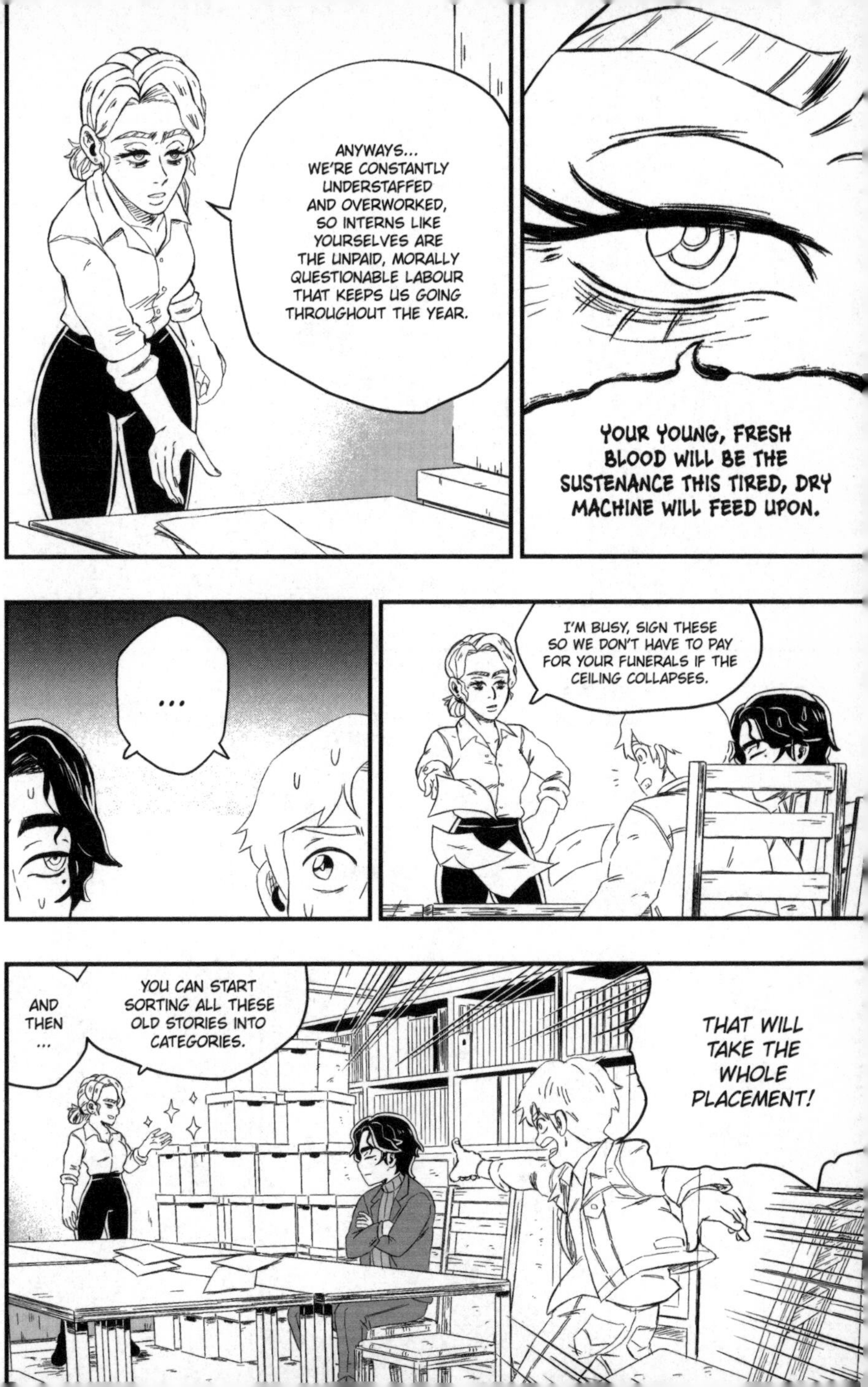
ANYWAYS... WE'RE CONSTANTLY UNDERSTAFFED AND OVERWORKED, SO INTERNS LIKE YOURSELVES ARE THE UNPAID, MORALLY QUESTIONABLE LABOUR THAT KEEPS US GOING THROUGHOUT THE YEAR.
YOUR YOUNG, FRESH BLOOD WILL BE THE SUSTENANCE THIS TIRED, DRY MACHINE WILL FEED UPON.
...
I'M BUSY, SIGN THESE SO WE DON'T HAVE TO PAY FOR YOUR FUNERALS IF THE CEILING COLLAPSES.
AND THEN ...
YOU CAN START SORTING ALL THESE OLD STORIES INTO CATEGORIES.
THAT WILL TAKE THE WHOLE PLACEMENT!

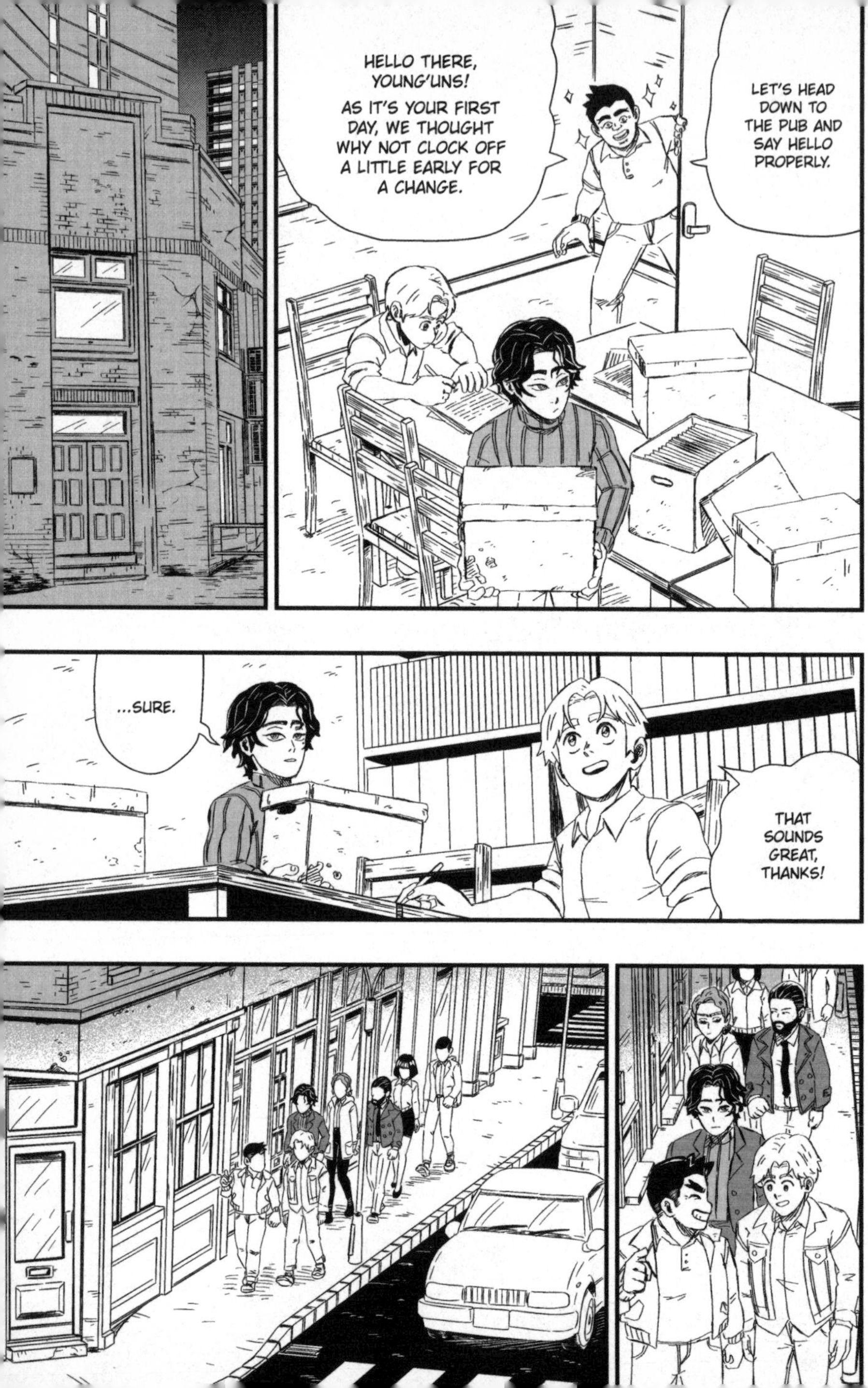
HELLO THERE, YOUNG'UNS!
AS IT'S YOUR FIRST DAY, WE THOUGHT WHY NOT CLOCK OFF A LITTLE EARLY FOR A CHANGE.
LET'S HEAD DOWN TO THE PUB AND SAY HELLO PROPERLY.
...SURE.
THAT SOUNDS GREAT, THANKS!

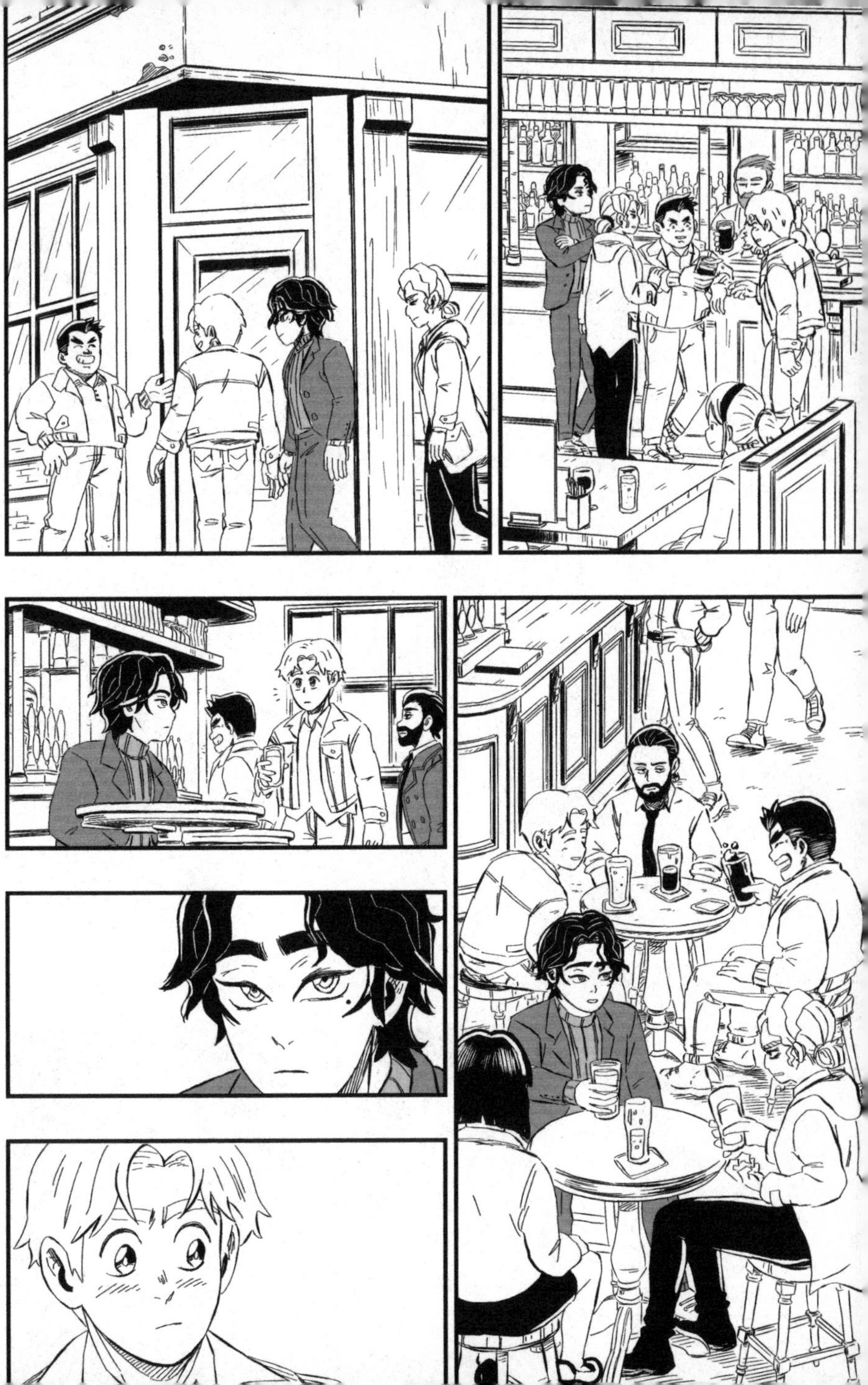

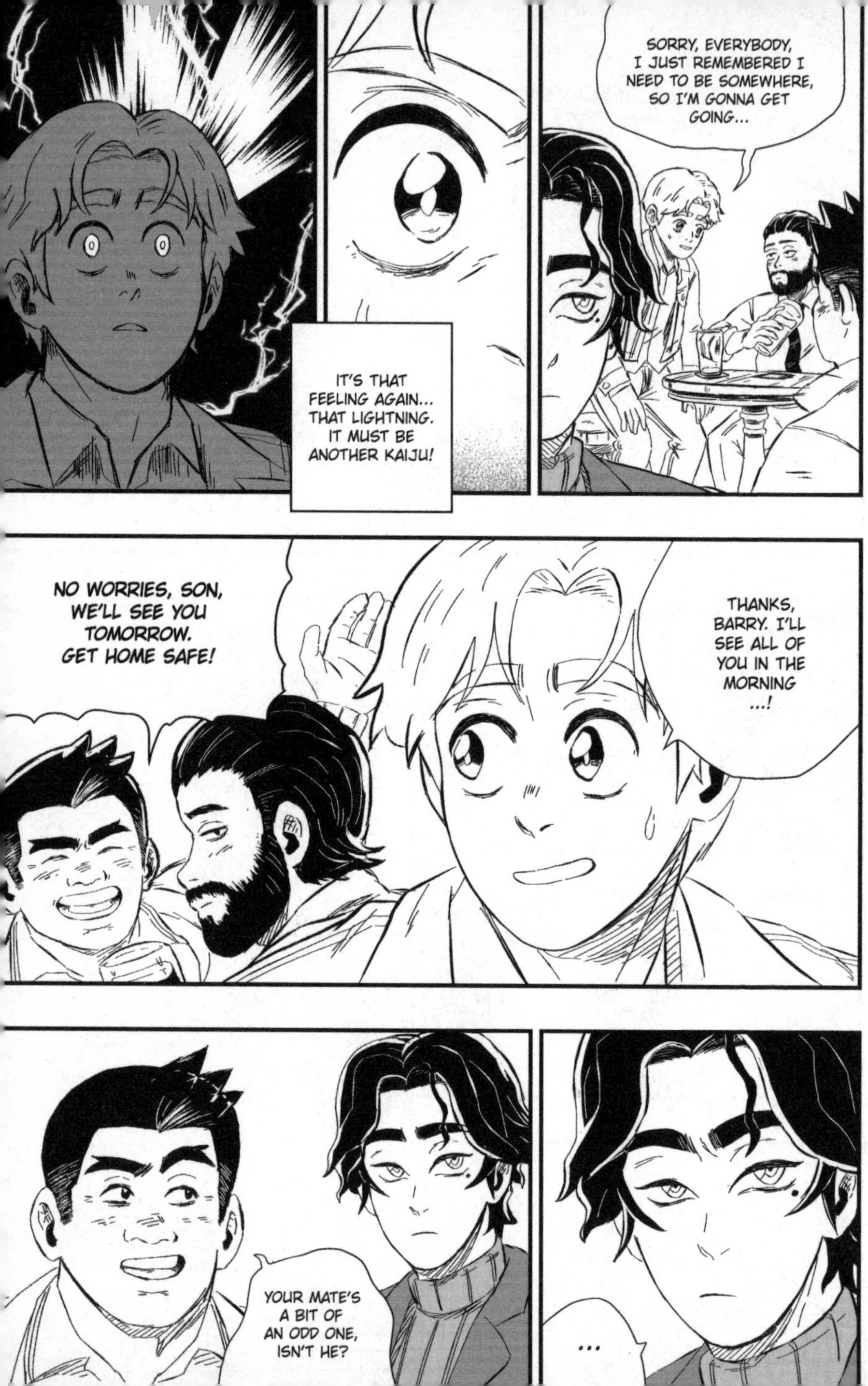
IT'S THAT FEELING AGAIN... THAT LIGHTNING. IT MUST BE ANOTHER KAIJU!
SORRY, EVERYBODY, I JUST REMEMBERED I NEED TO BE SOMEWHERE, SO I'M GONNA GET GOING...
NO WORRIES, SON, WE'LL SEE YOU TOMORROW. GET HOME SAFE!
THANKS, BARRY. I'LL SEE ALL OF YOU IN THE MORNING ...!
YOUR MATE'S A BIT OF AN ODD ONE, ISN'T HE?
...

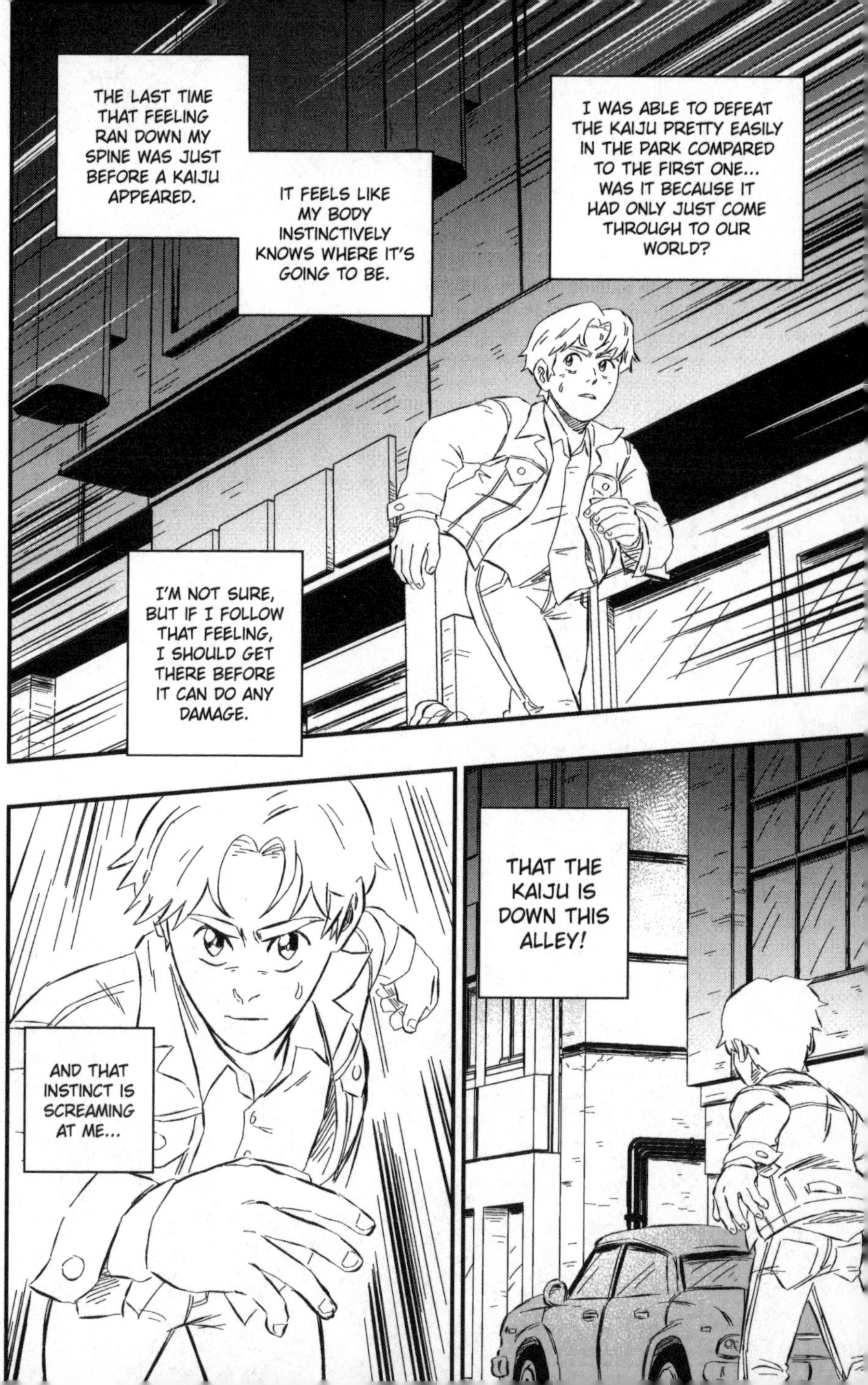
THE LAST TIME THAT FEELING RAN DOWN MY SPINE WAS JUST BEFORE A KAIJU APPEARED.
IT FEELS LIKE MY BODY INSTINCTIVELY KNOWS WHERE IT'S GOING TO BE.
I WAS ABLE TO DEFEAT THE KAIJU PRETTY EASILY IN THE PARK COMPARED TO THE FIRST ONE... WAS IT BECAUSE IT HAD ONLY JUST COME THROUGH TO OUR WORLD?
I'M NOT SURE, BUT IF I FOLLOW THAT FEELING, I SHOULD GET THERE BEFORE IT CAN DO ANY DAMAGE.
AND THAT INSTINCT IS SCREAMING AT ME...
THAT THE KAIJU IS DOWN THIS ALLEY!

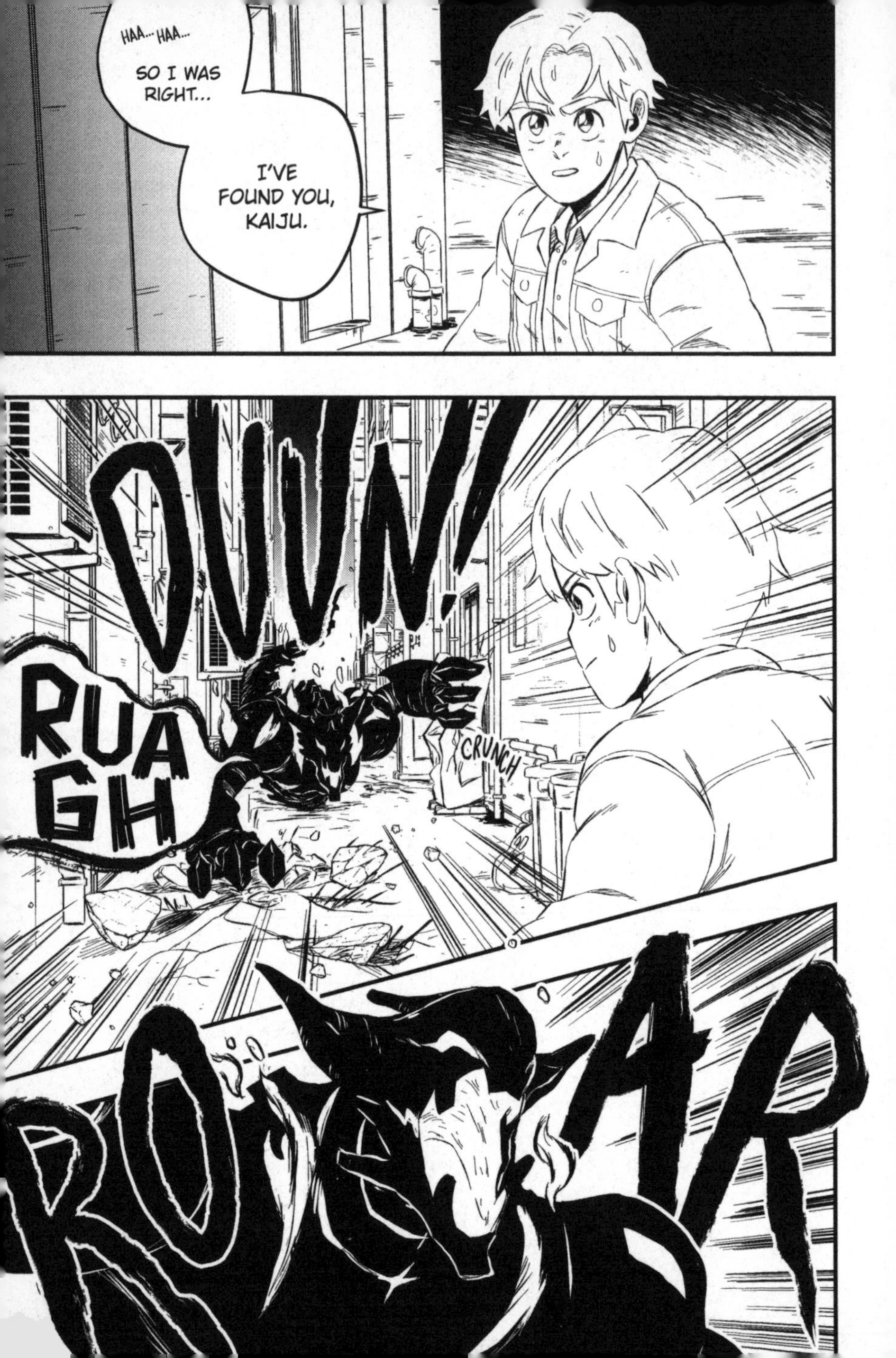
HAA... HAA...
SO I WAS RIGHT...
I'VE FOUND YOU, KAIJU.
DUUN!
RUAGH
CRUNCH
ROAR

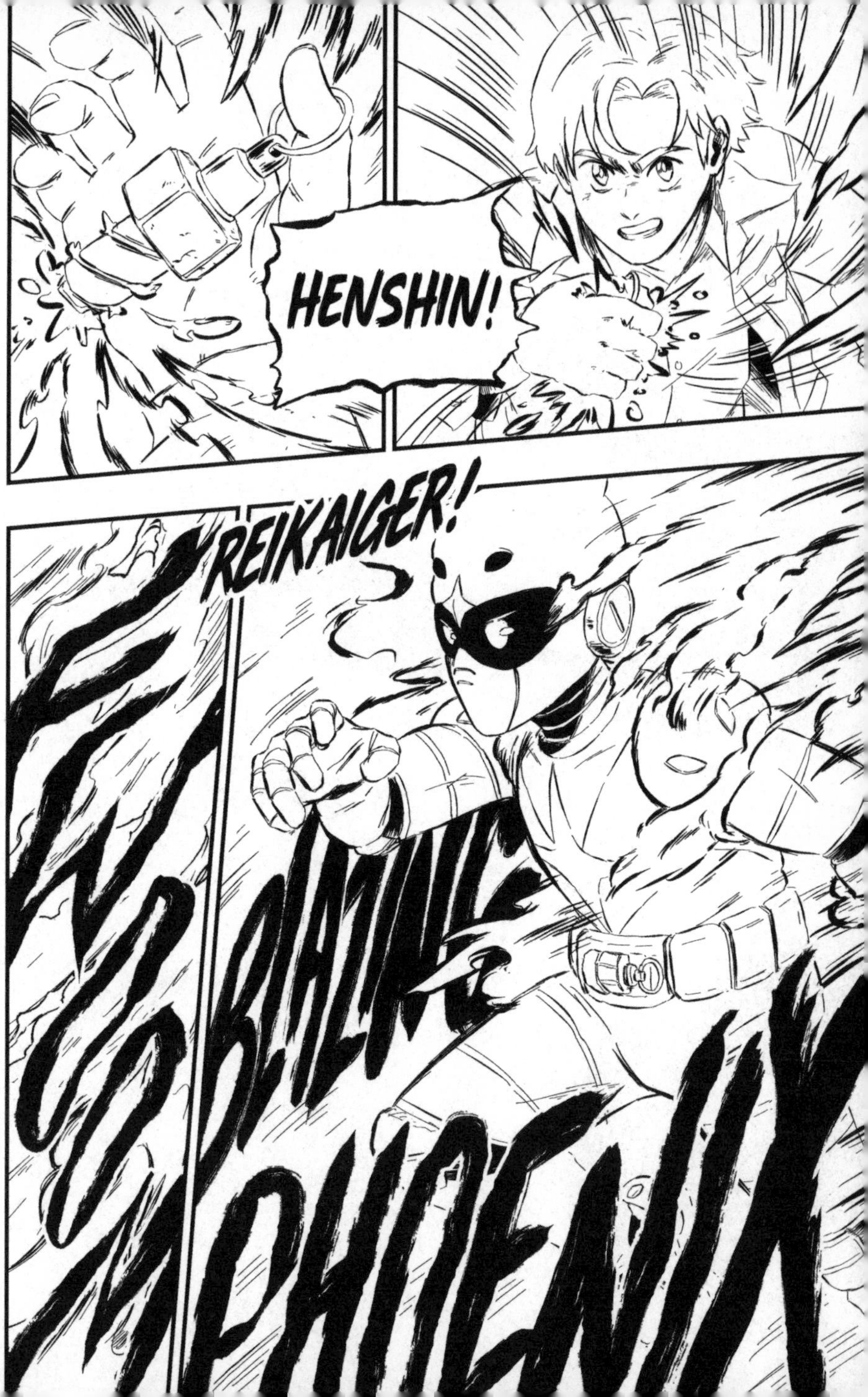
HENSHIN!
REIKAIGER!
BLAZING PHOENIX

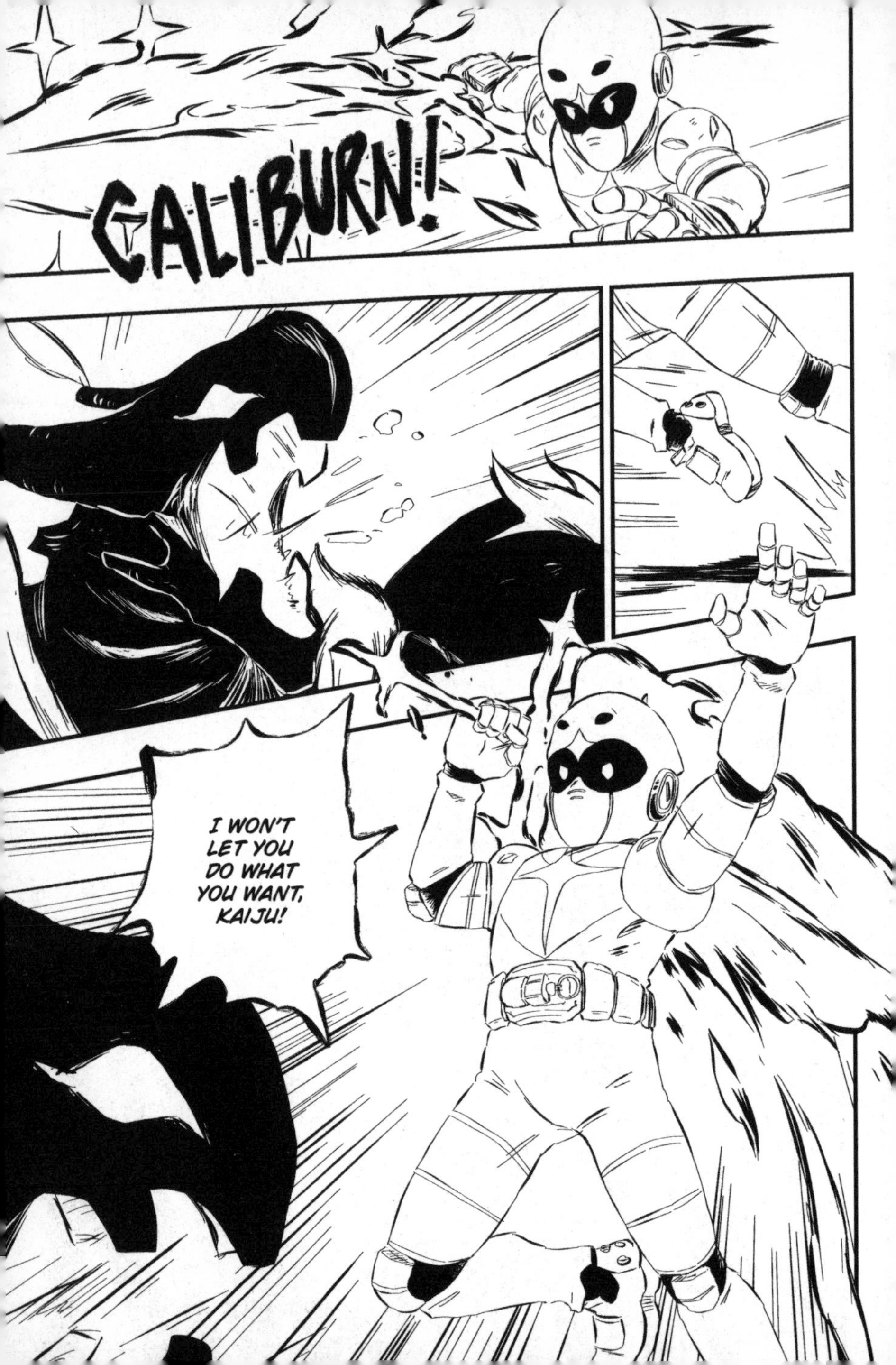
CALIBURN!
I WON'T LET YOU DO WHAT YOU WANT, KAIJU!

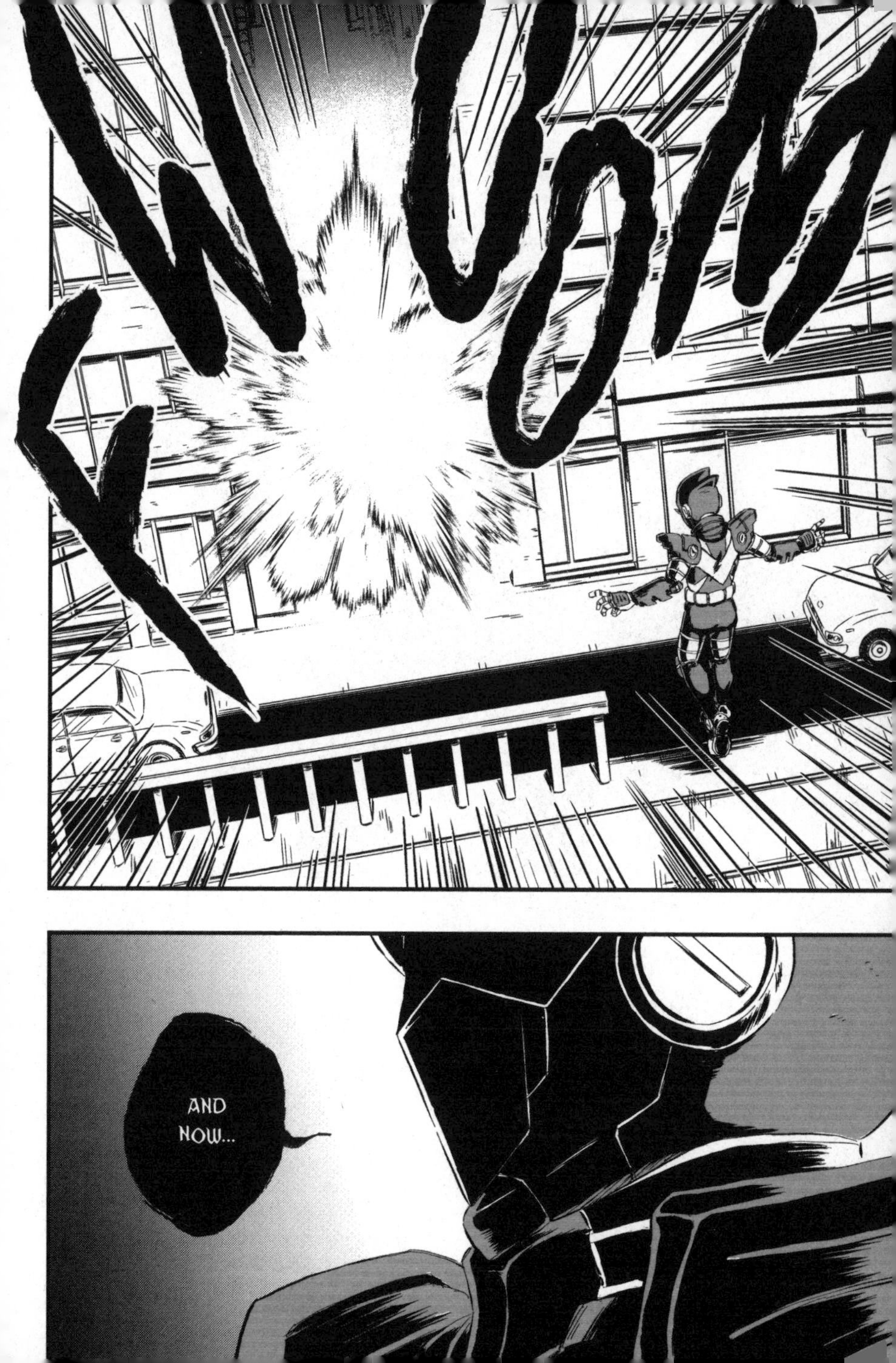
AND NOW...

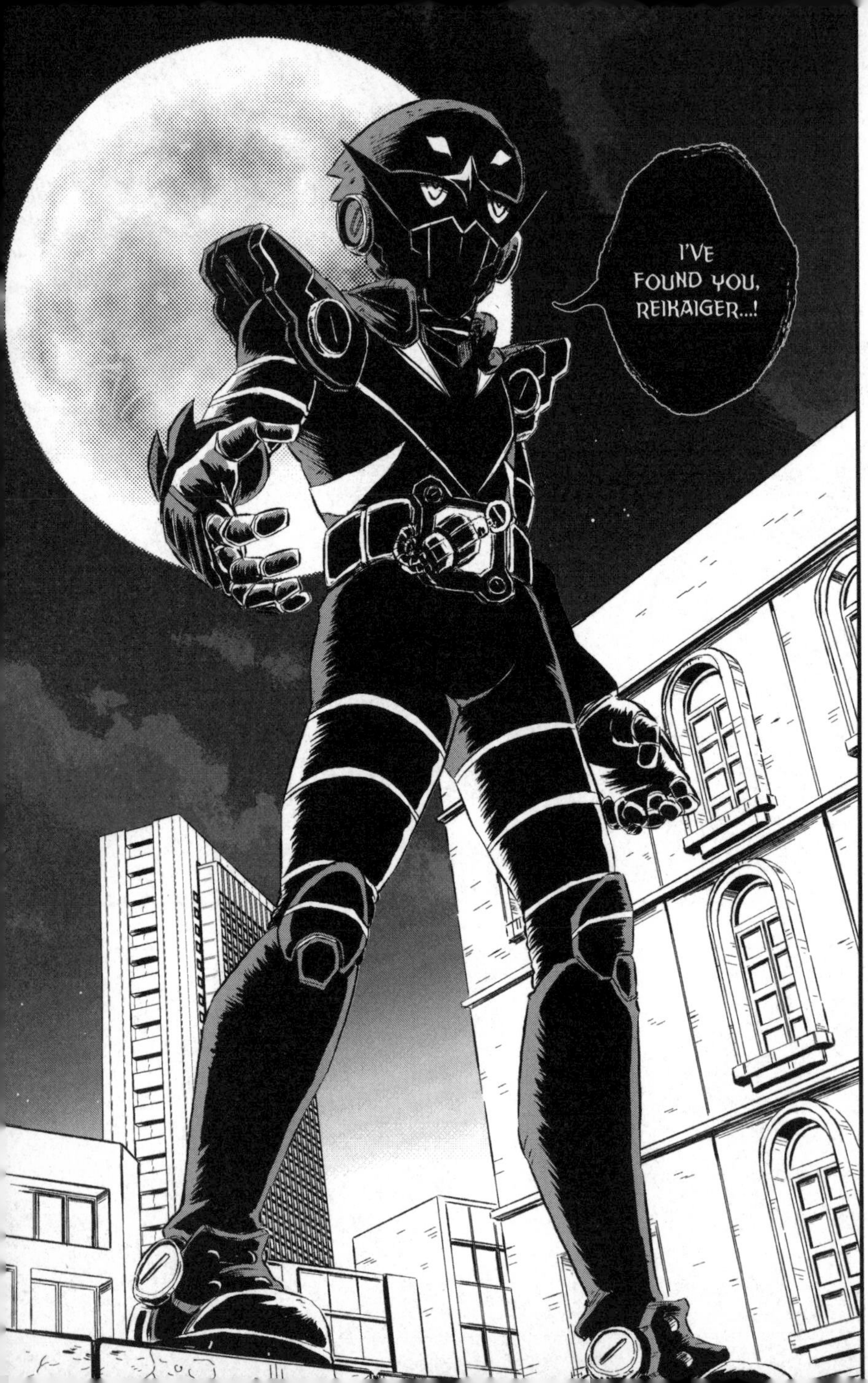
I'VE FOUND YOU, REIKAIGER...!

CHAPTER SIX

OMINOUS

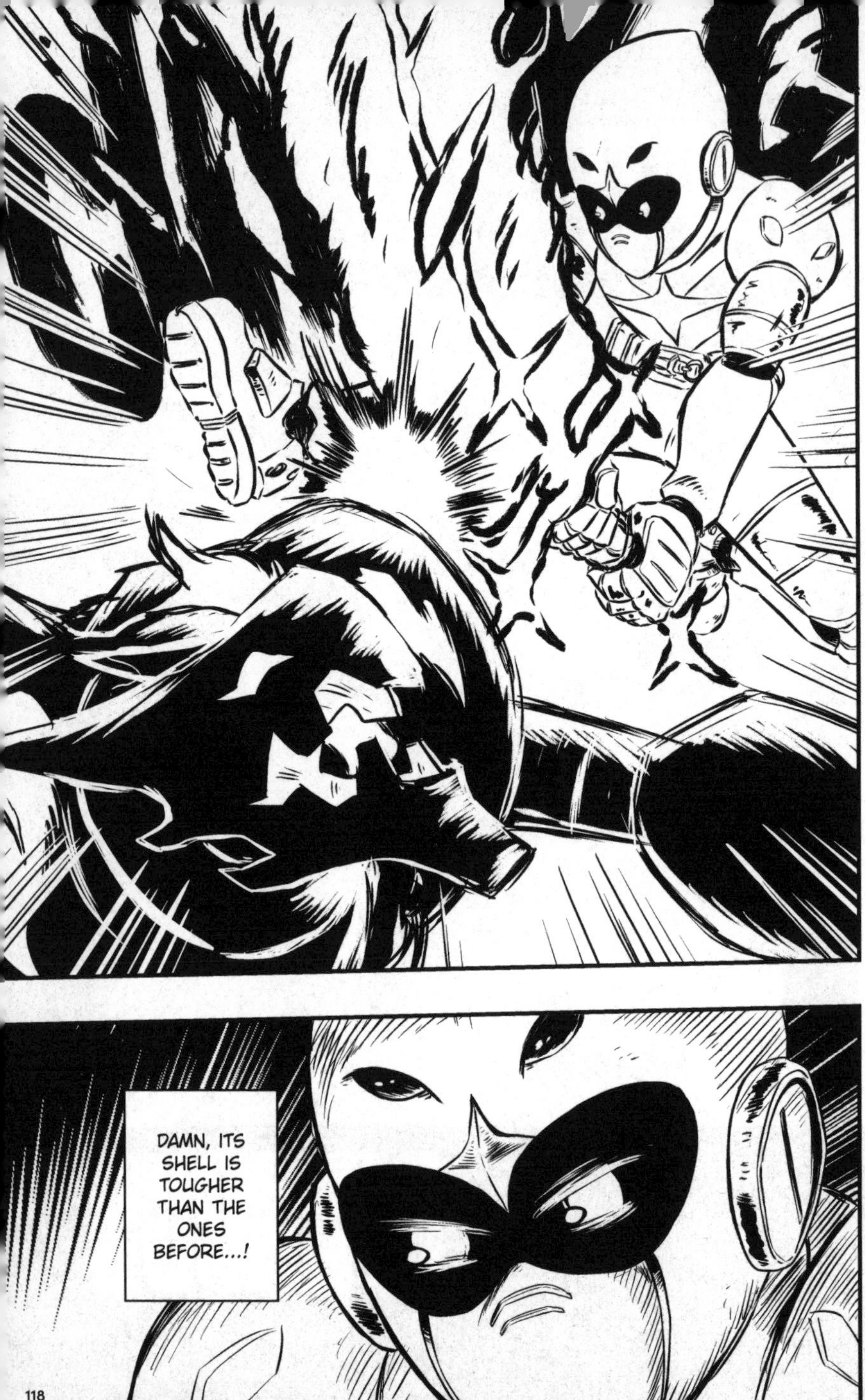
DAMN, ITS SHELL IS TOUGHER THAN THE ONES BEFORE...!

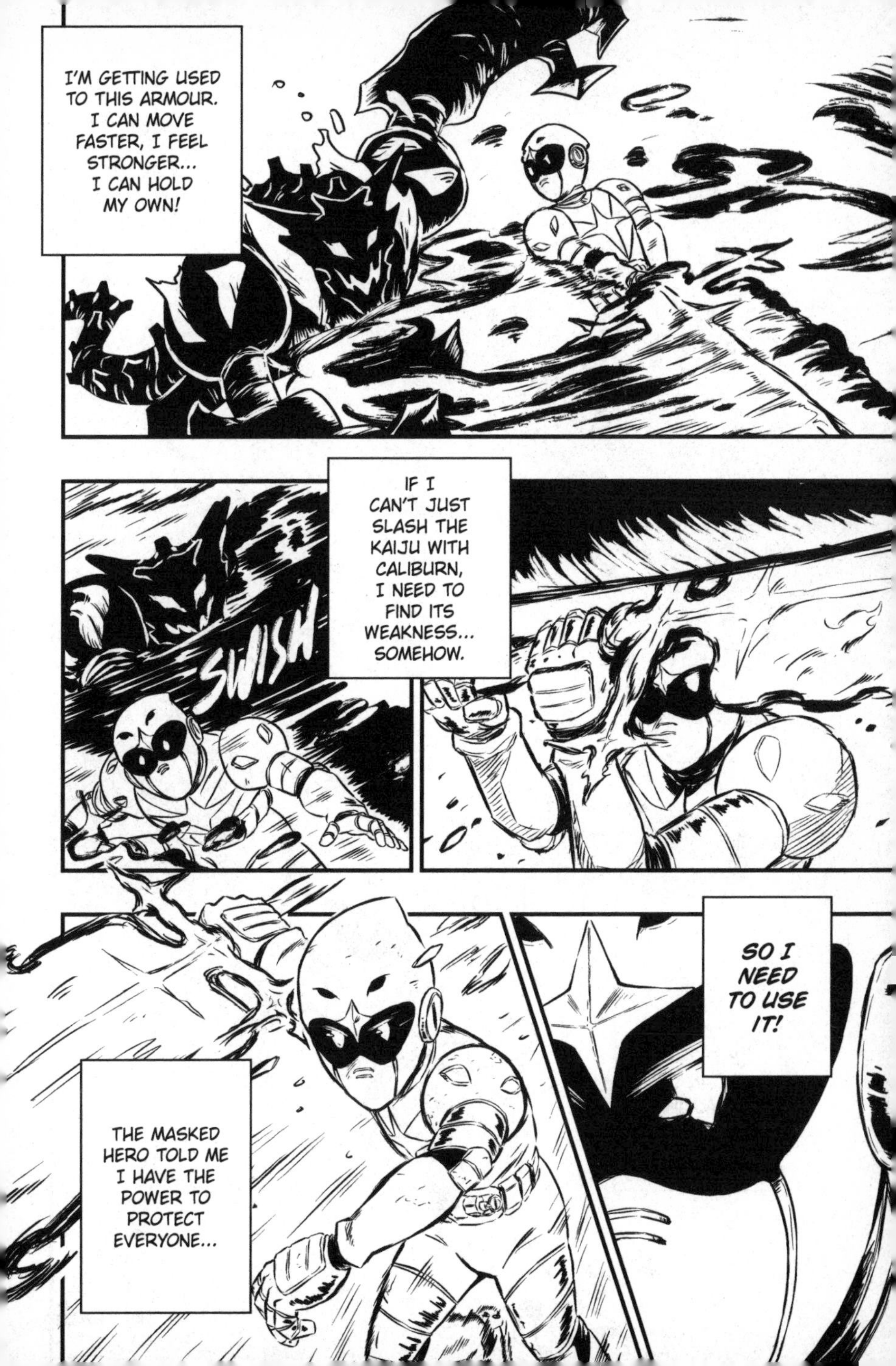
I'M GETTING USED TO THIS ARMOUR. I CAN MOVE FASTER, I FEEL STRONGER... I CAN HOLD MY OWN!
SWISH
IF I CAN'T JUST SLASH THE KAIJU WITH CALIBURN, I NEED TO FIND ITS WEAKNESS... SOMEHOW.
THE MASKED HERO TOLD ME I HAVE THE POWER TO PROTECT EVERYONE...
SO I NEED TO USE IT!

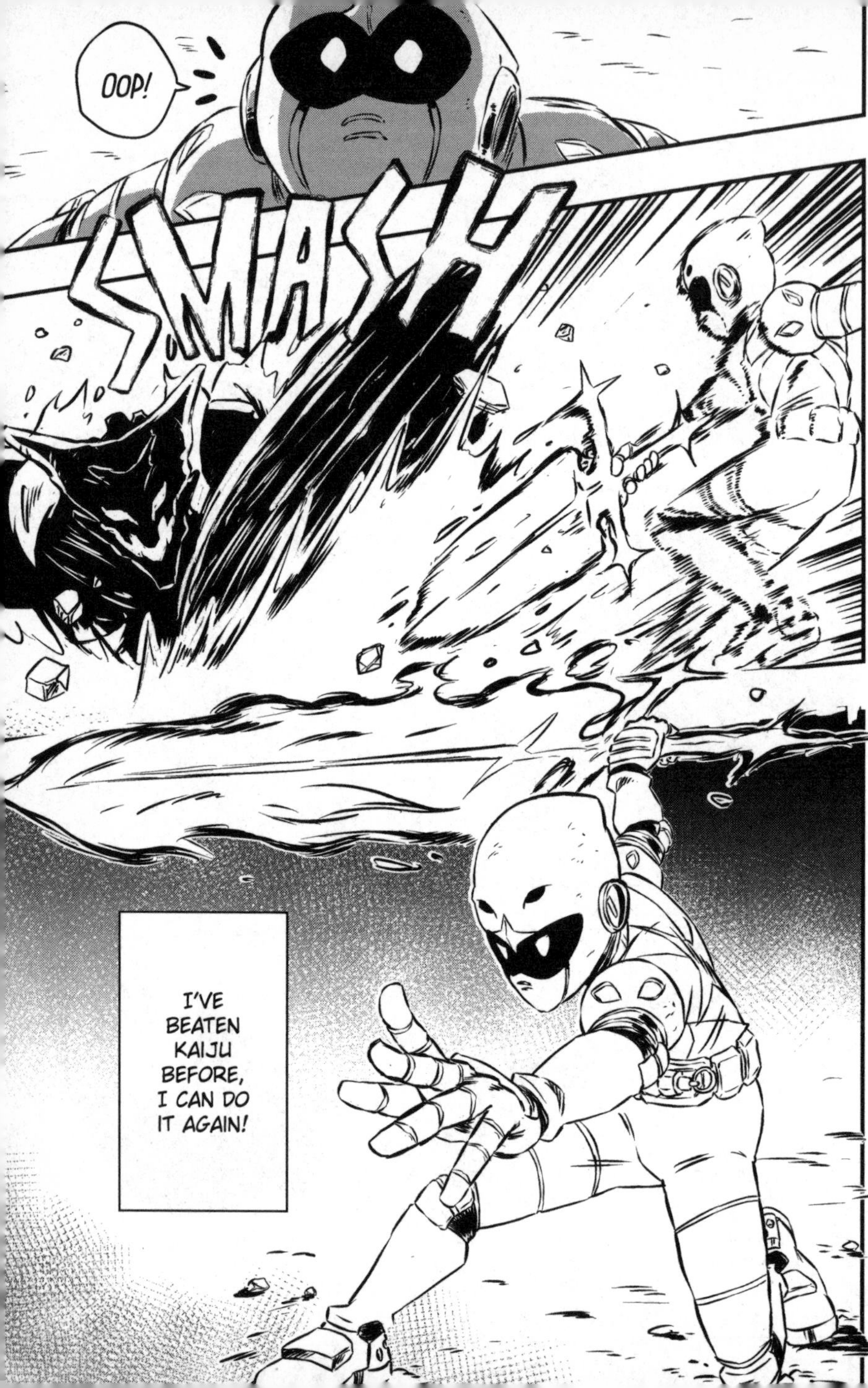
OOP!
SMASH
I'VE BEATEN KAIJU BEFORE, I CAN DO IT AGAIN!

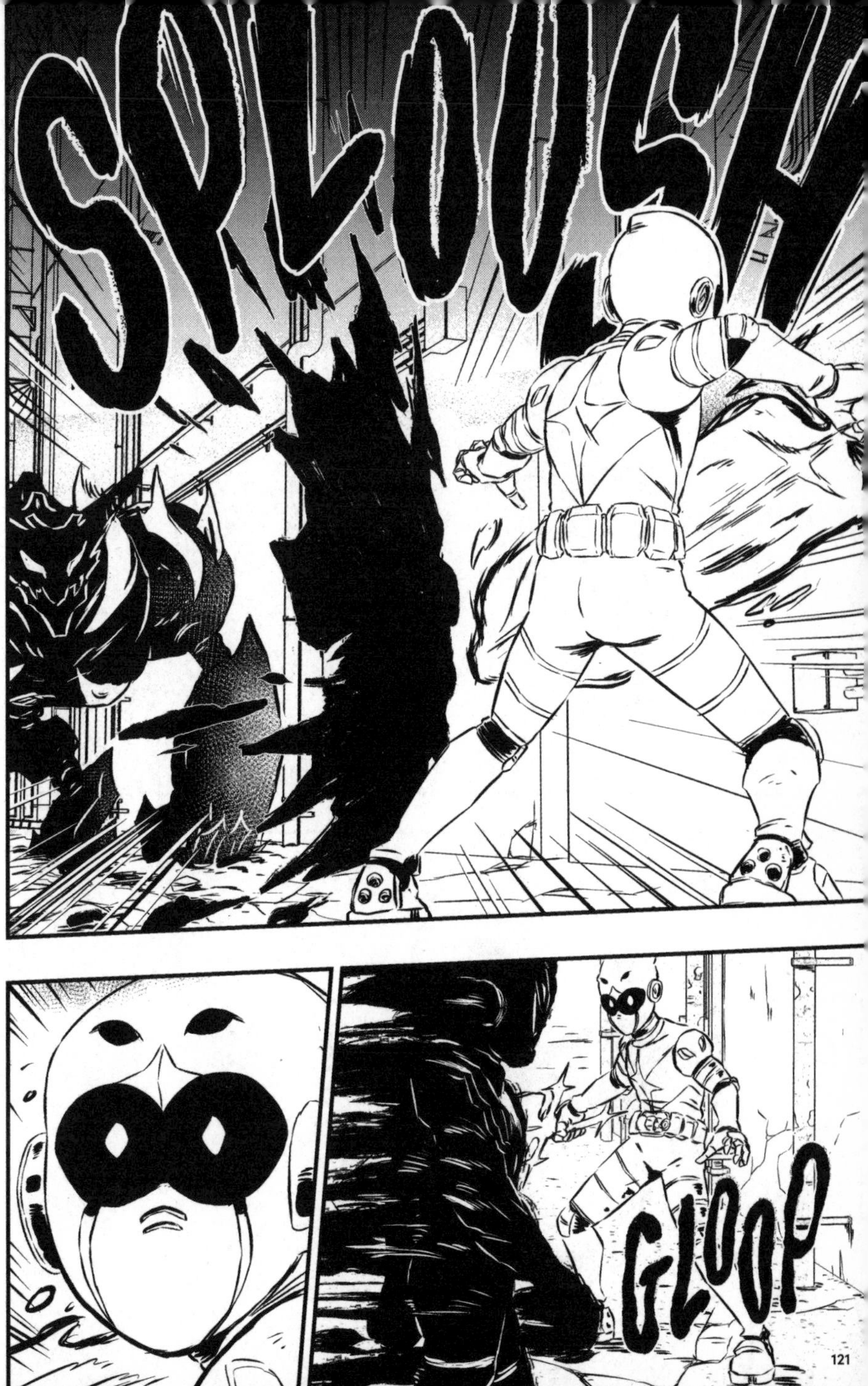
SPLOOSH
GLOOP

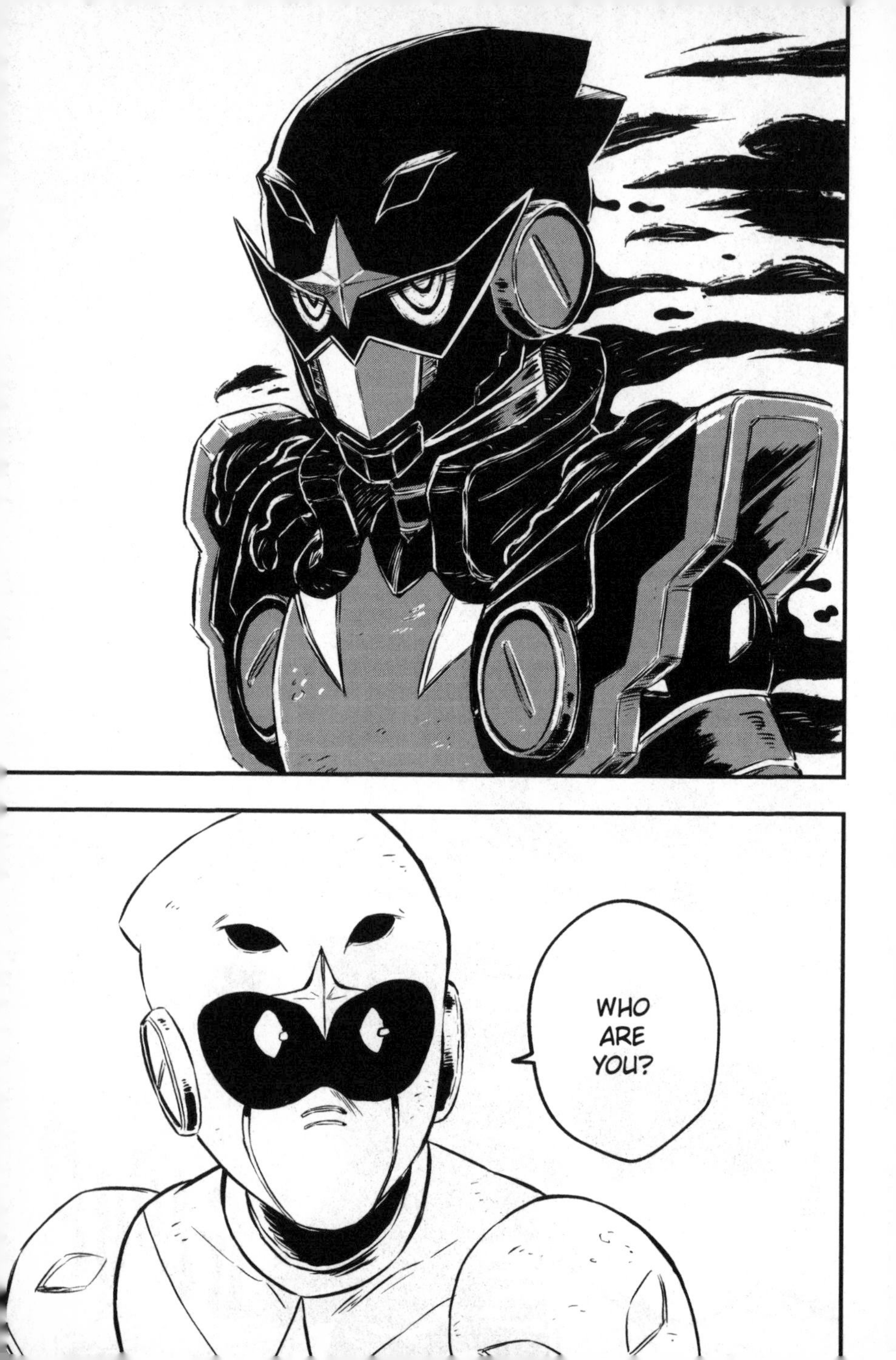
WHO ARE YOU?

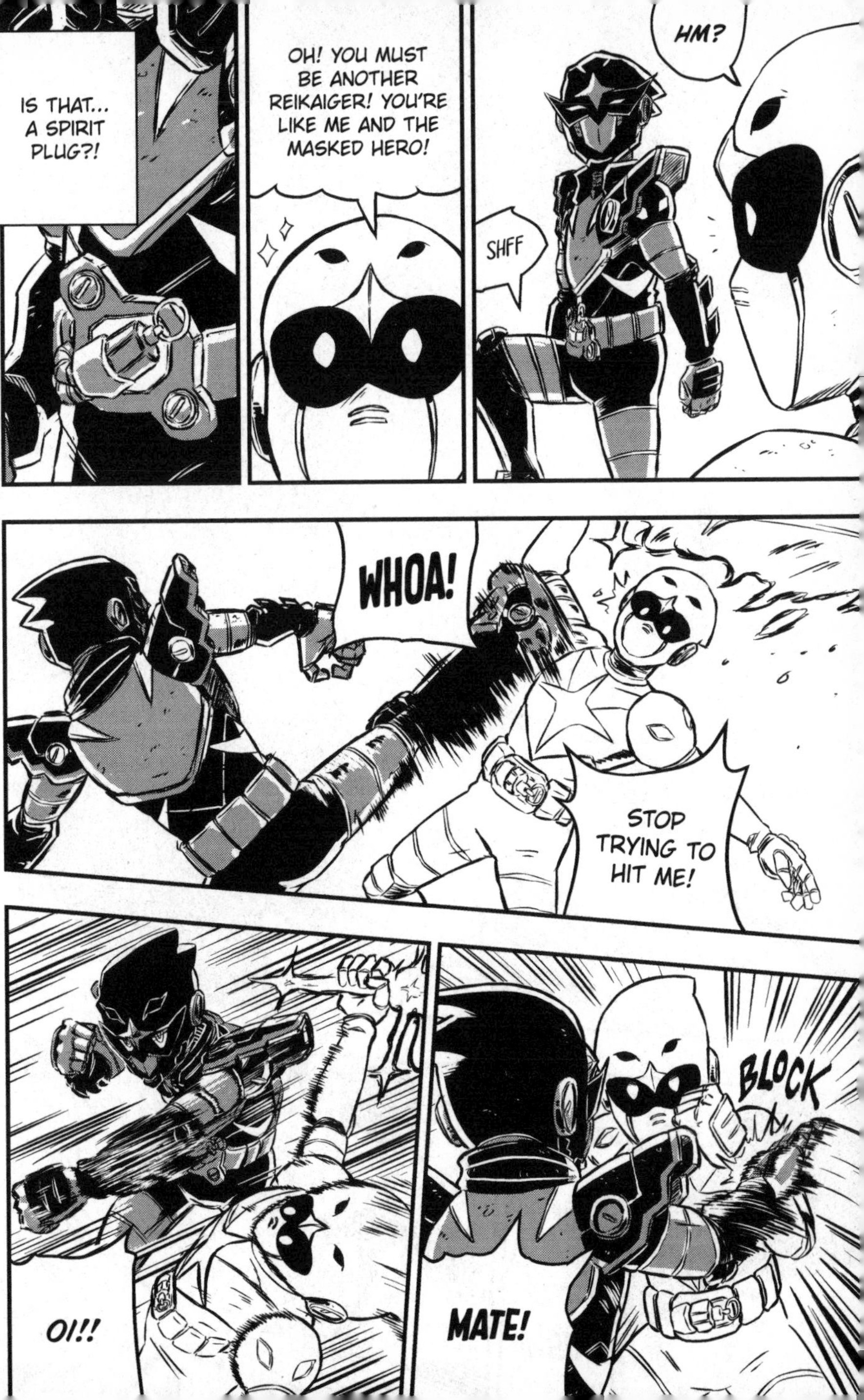
IS THAT... A SPIRIT PLUG?!
OH! YOU MUST BE ANOTHER REIKAIGER! YOU'RE LIKE ME AND THE MASKED HERO!
HM?
SHFF
WHOA!
STOP TRYING TO HIT ME!
OI!!
BLOCK
MATE!

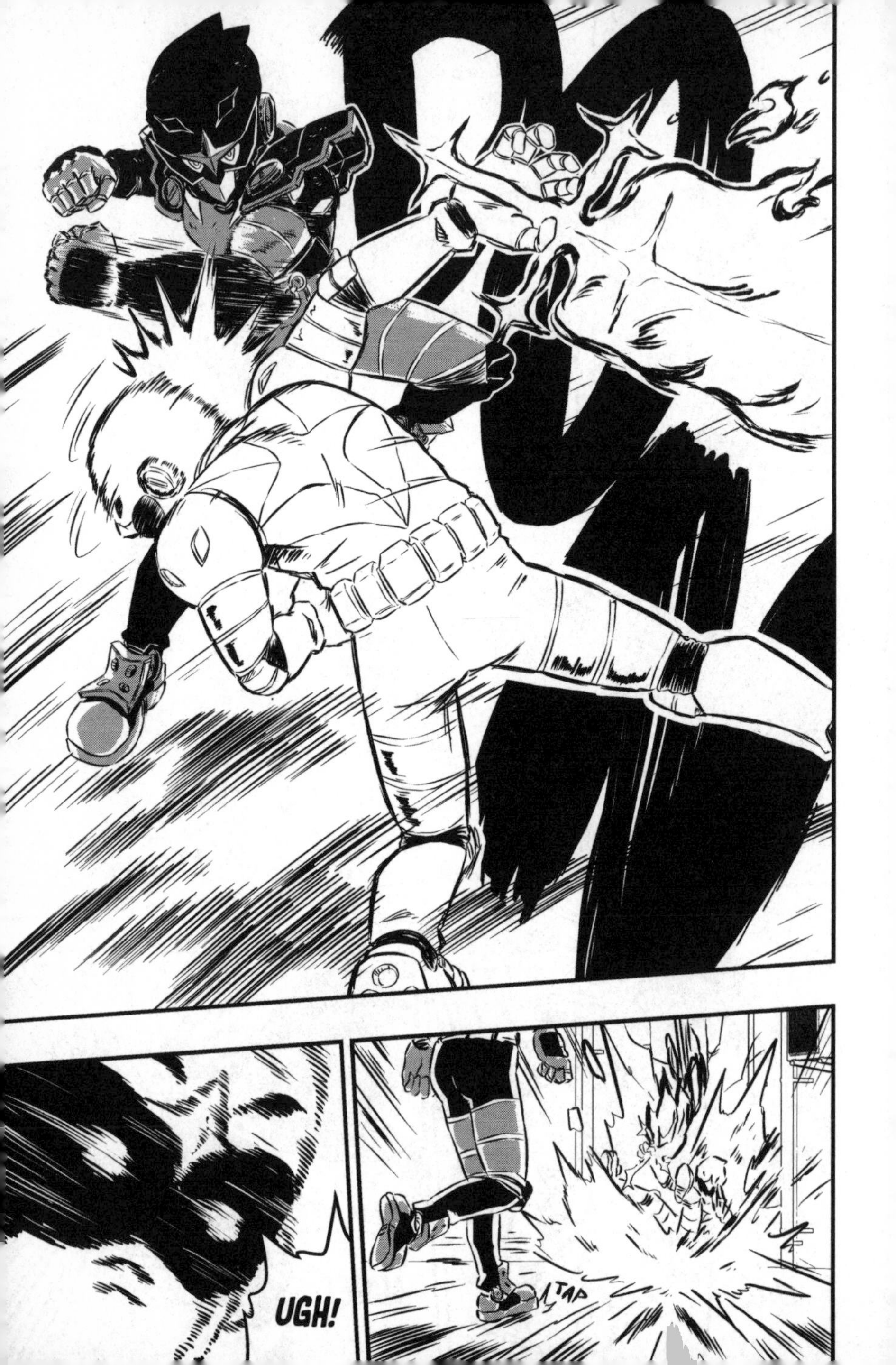
UGH!
TAP

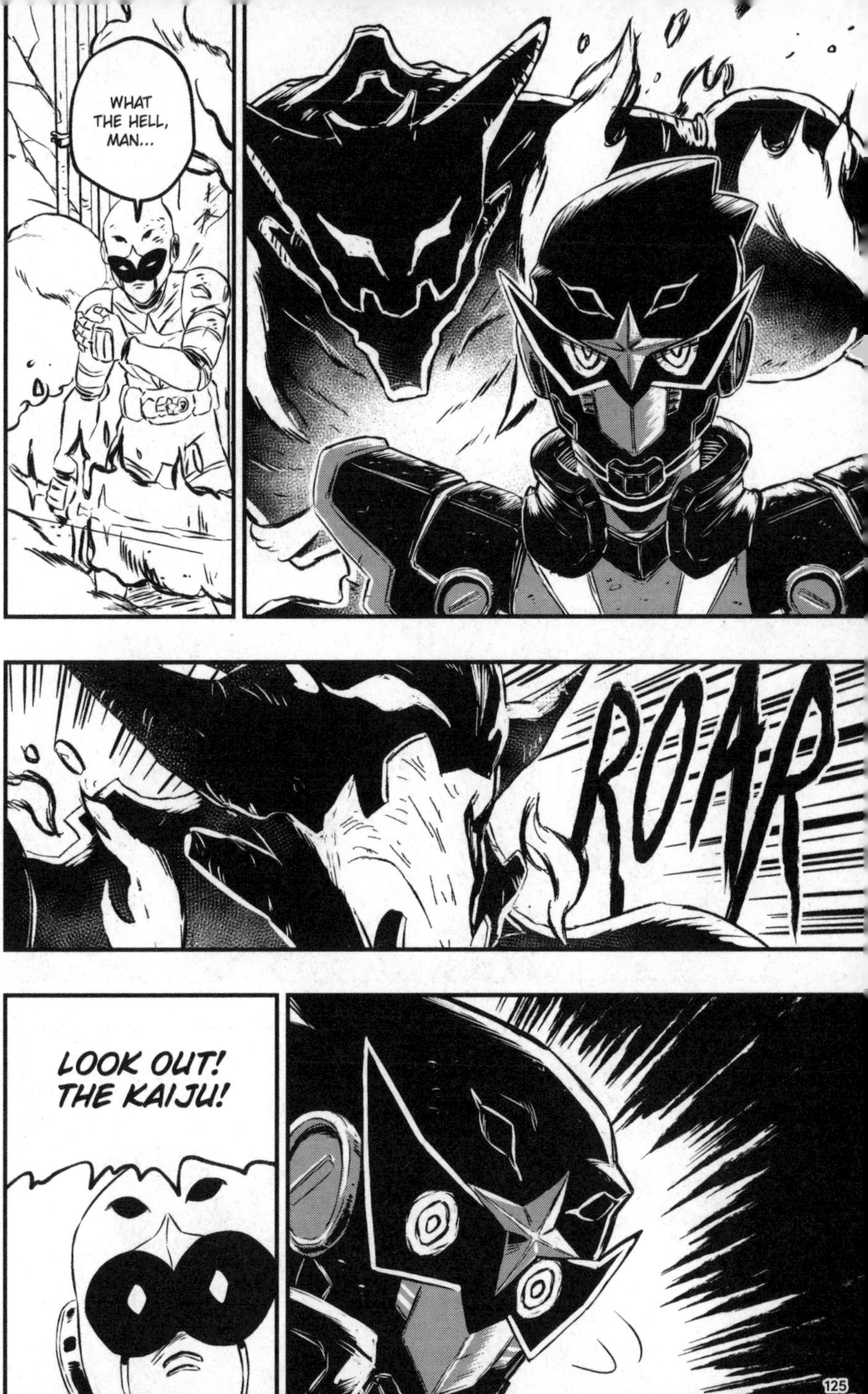
WHAT THE HELL, MAN...
ROAR
LOOK OUT! THE KAIJU!

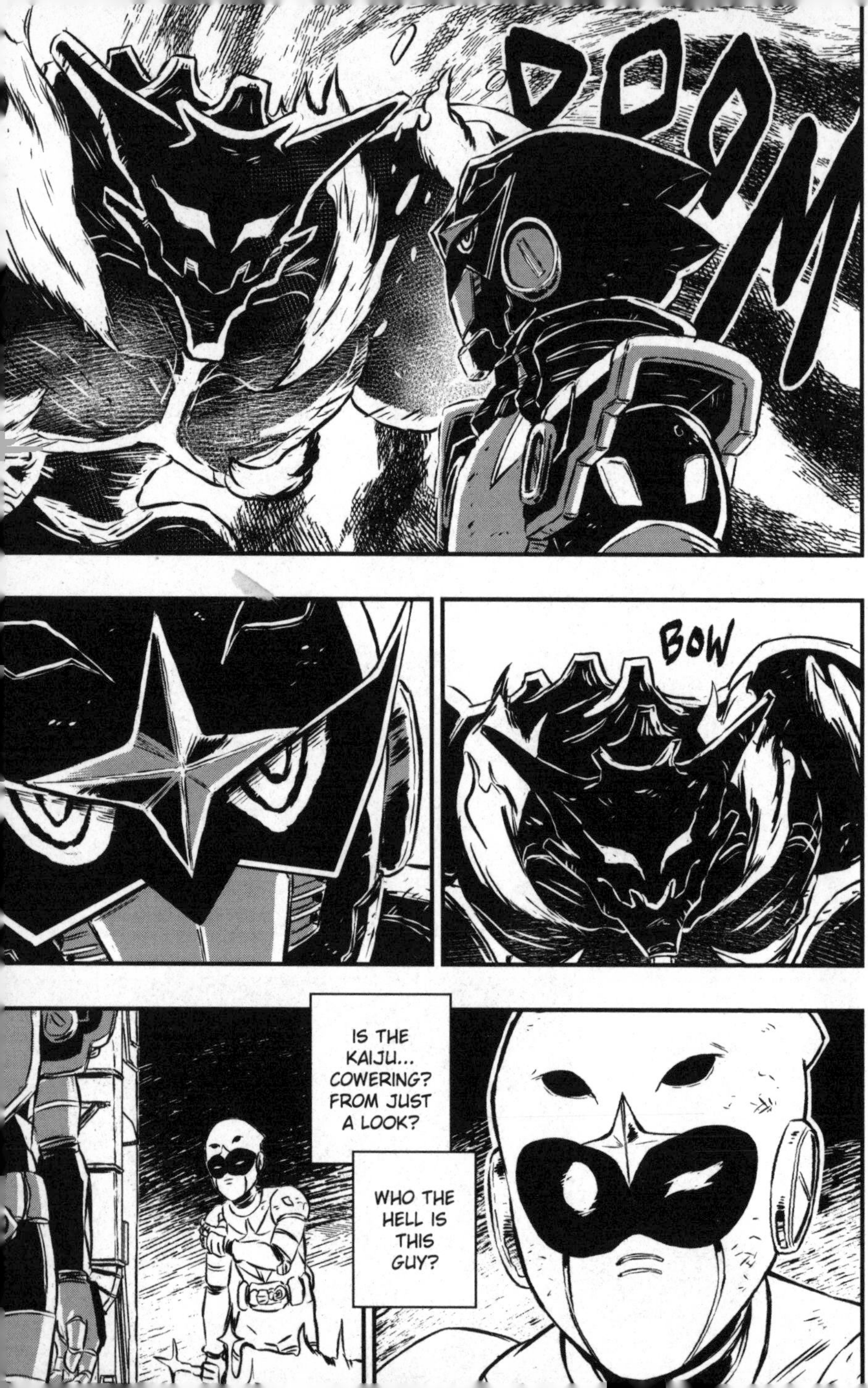
DOOM
BOW
IS THE KAIJU... COWERING? FROM JUST A LOOK?
WHO THE HELL IS THIS GUY?

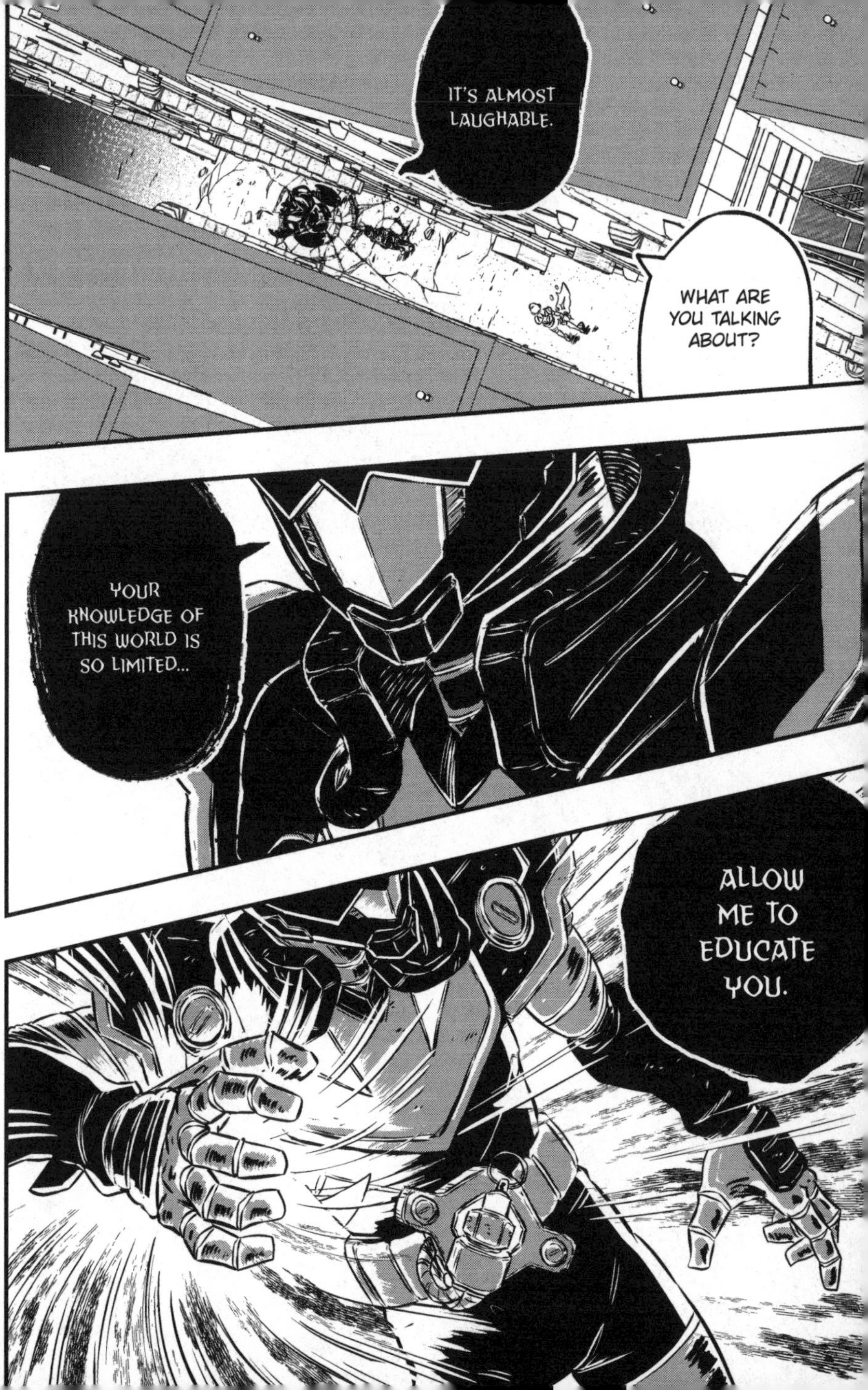

IT'S ALMOST LAUGHABLE.
WHAT ARE YOU TALKING ABOUT?
YOUR KNOWLEDGE OF THIS WORLD IS SO LIMITED...
ALLOW ME TO EDUCATE YOU.

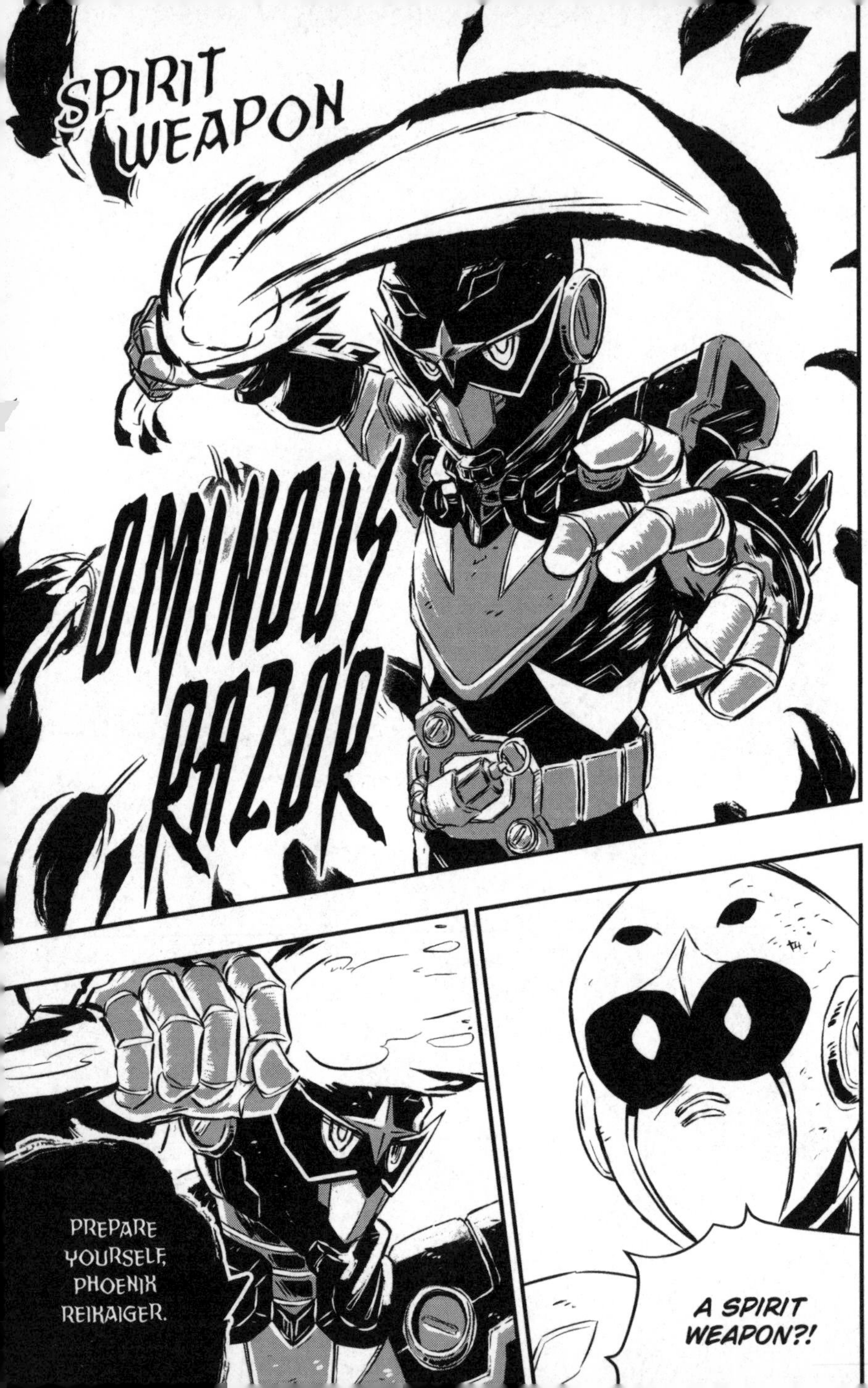
SPIRIT WEAPON
OMINOUS RAZOR
PREPARE YOURSELF, PHOENIX REIKAIGER.
A SPIRIT WEAPON?!

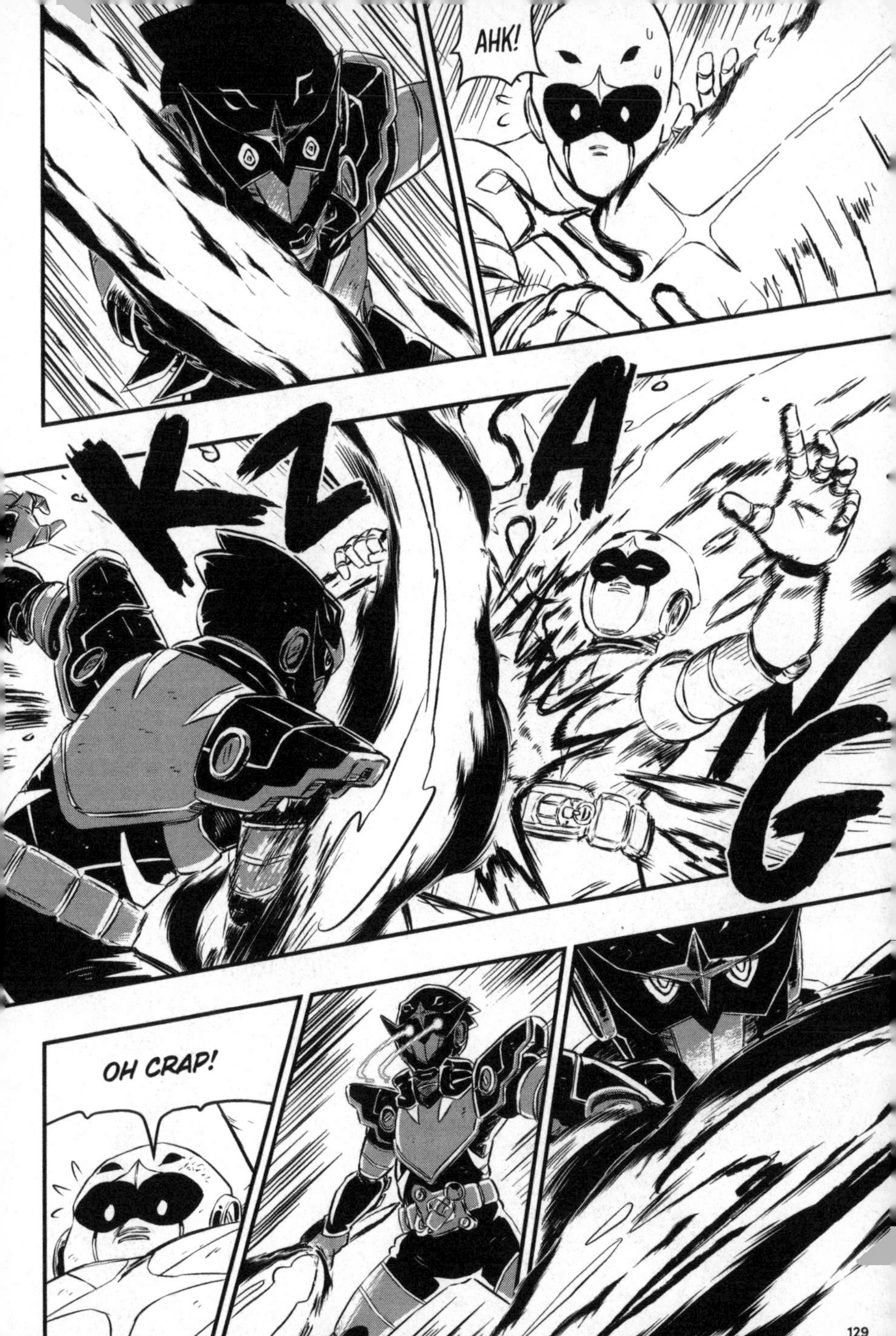
AHK!
KZANG
OH CRAP!

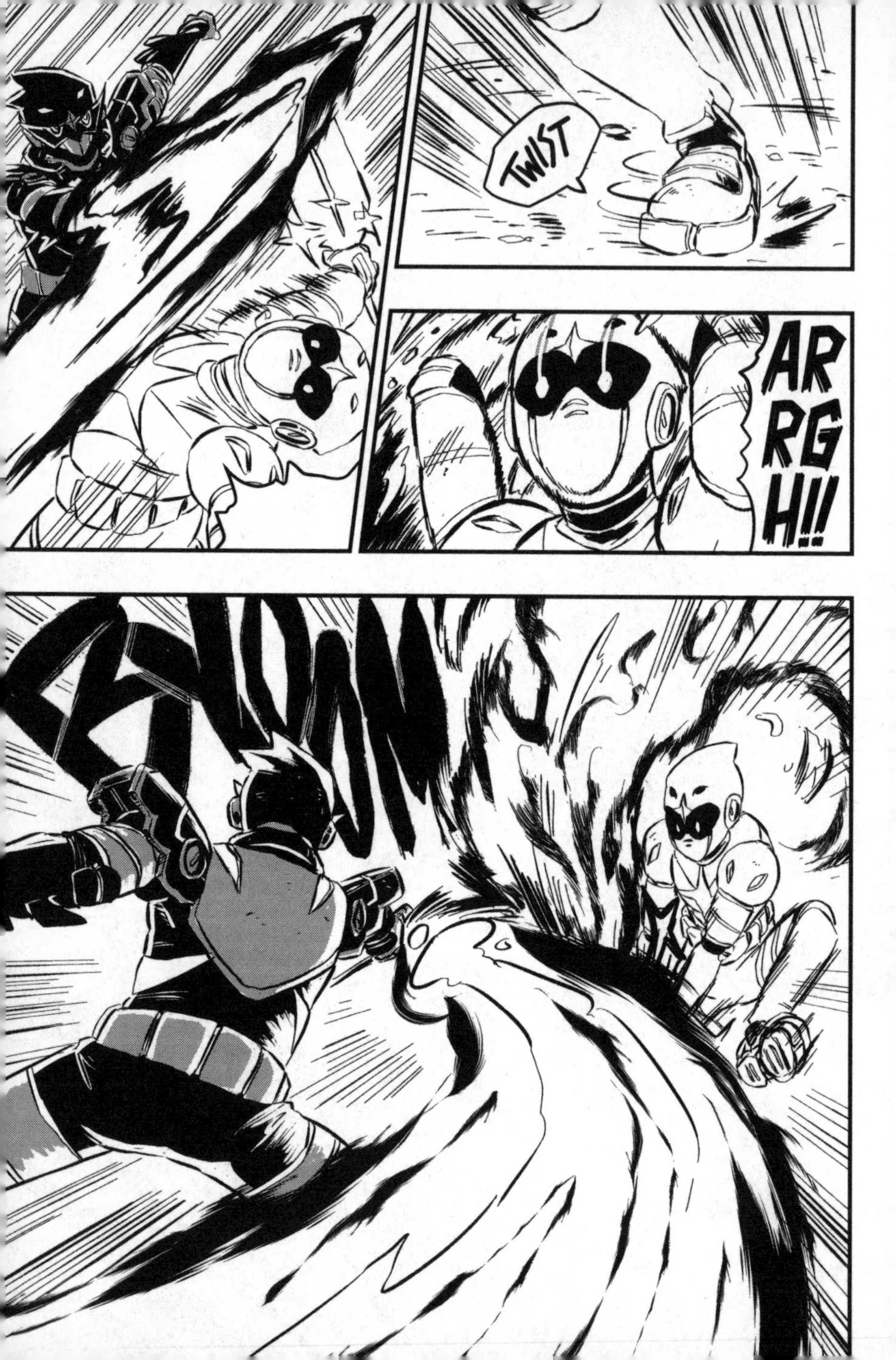
TWIST
ARRGH!!

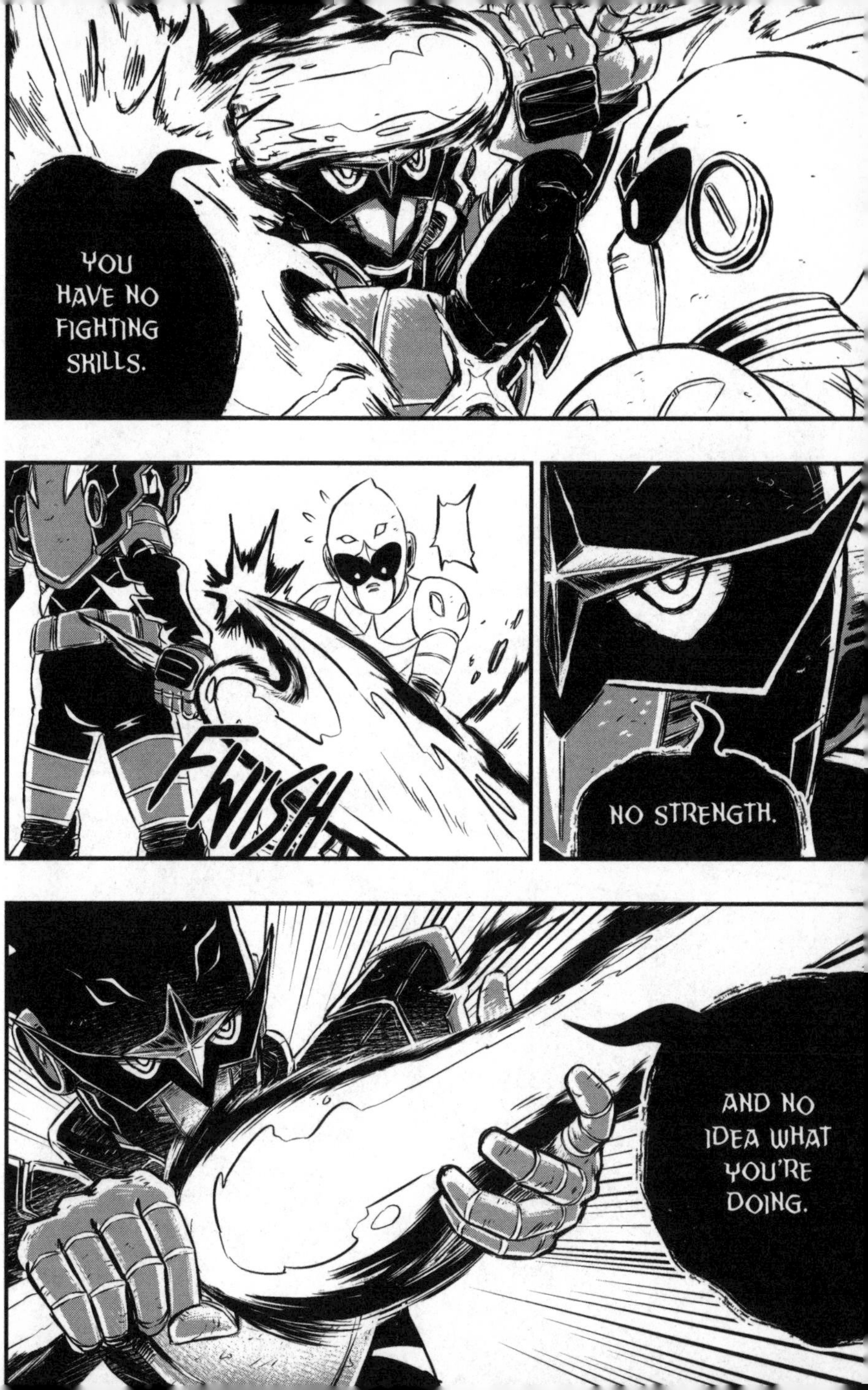
YOU HAVE NO FIGHTING SKILLS.
FWISH
NO STRENGTH.
AND NO IDEA WHAT YOU'RE DOING.

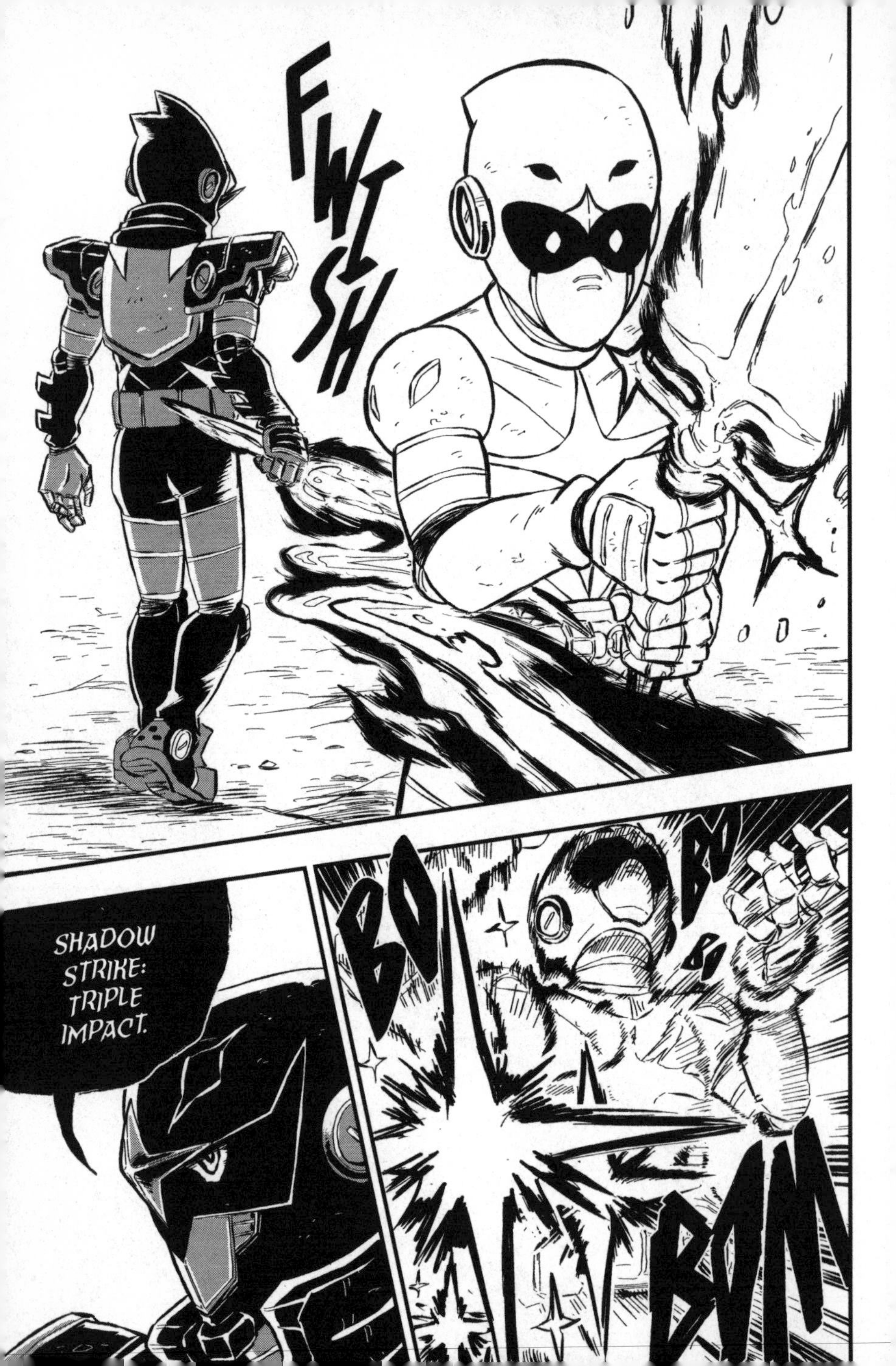
FWISH
SHADOW STRIKE: TRIPLE IMPACT.
BO
BO
BO
BOM

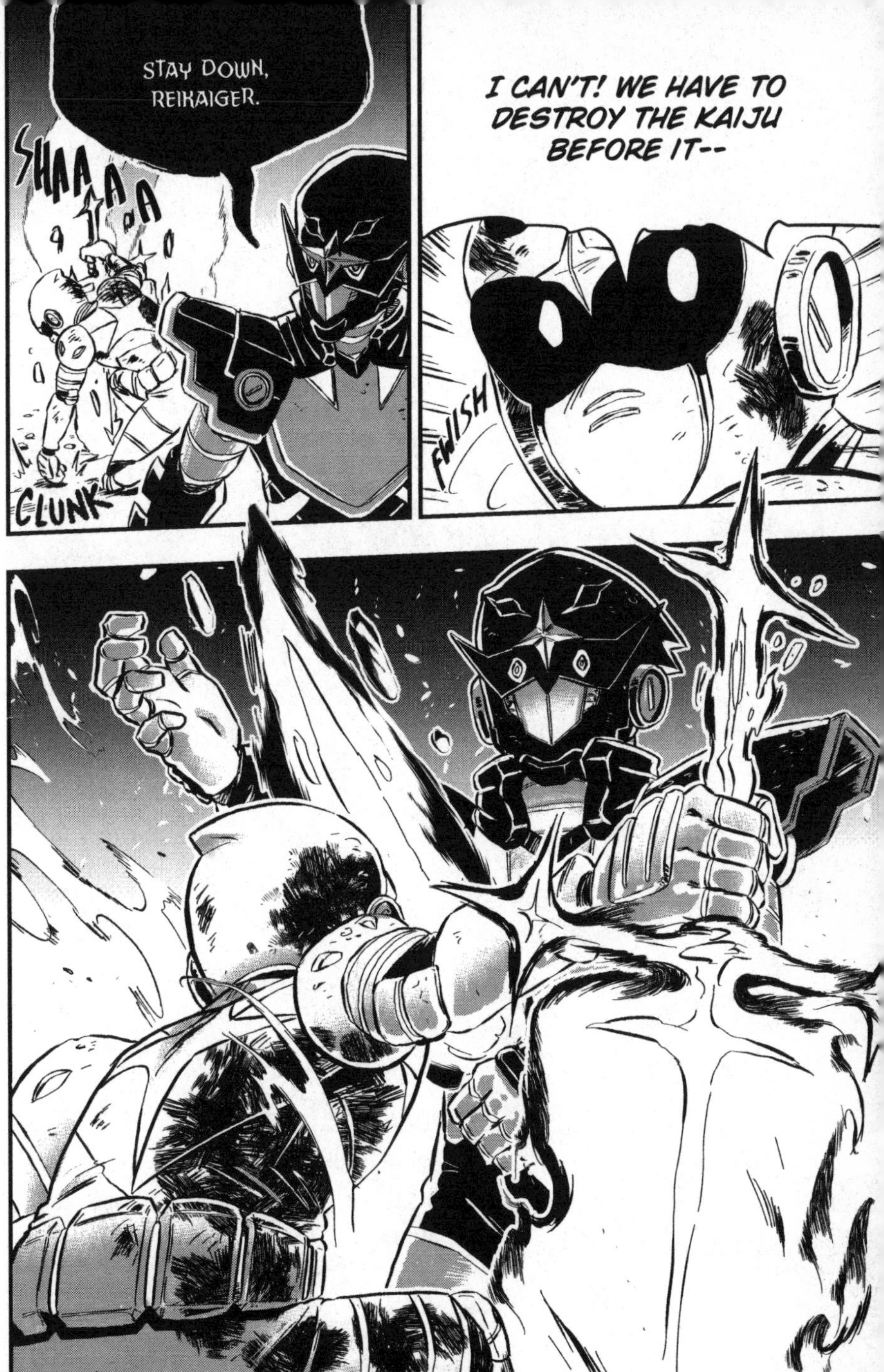
STAY DOWN, REIKAIGER.
SHAAAA
CLUNK
I CAN'T! WE HAVE TO DESTROY THE KAIJU BEFORE IT--
FWISH

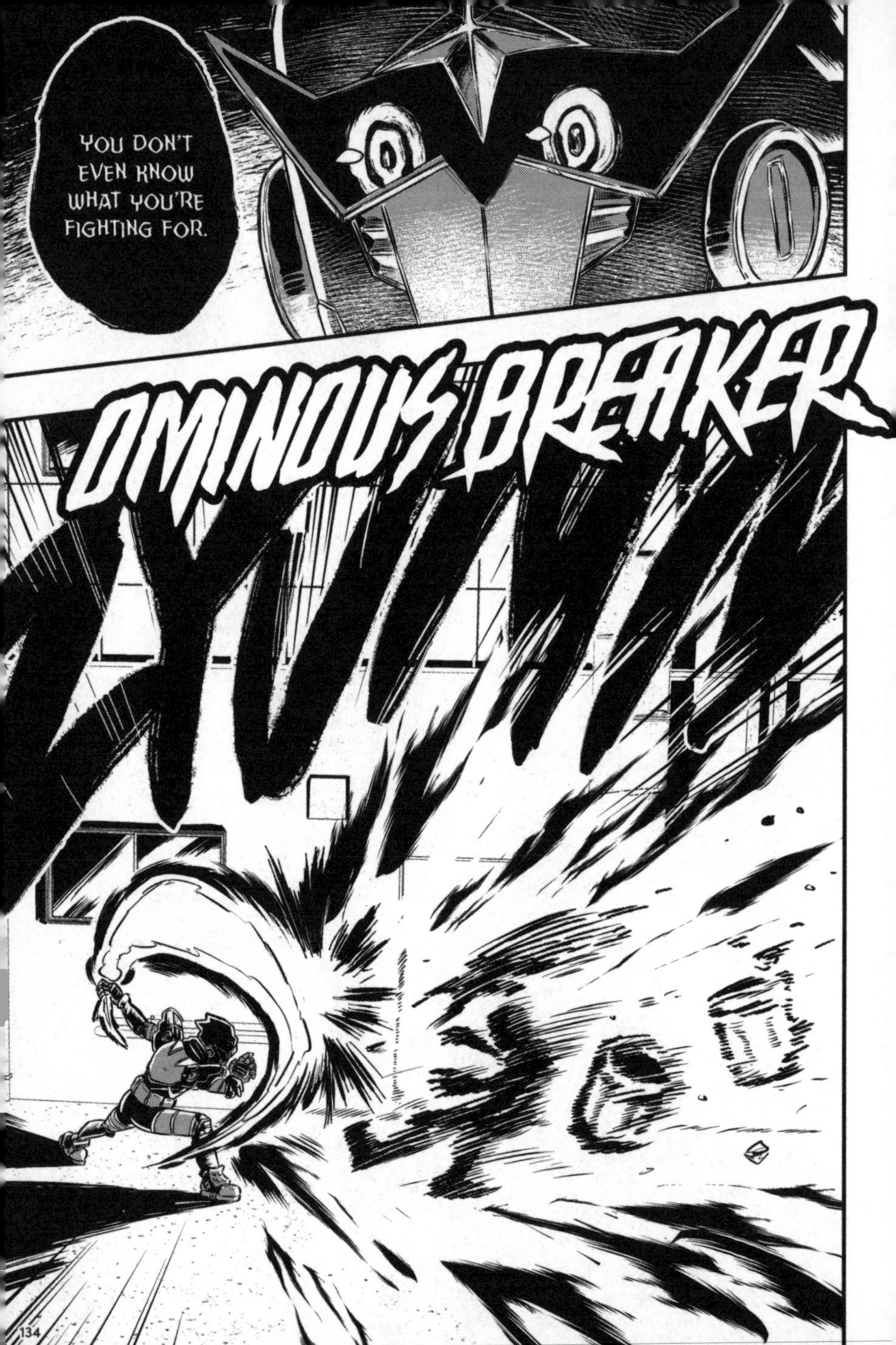
YOU DON'T EVEN KNOW WHAT YOU'RE FIGHTING FOR.
OMINOUS BREAKER

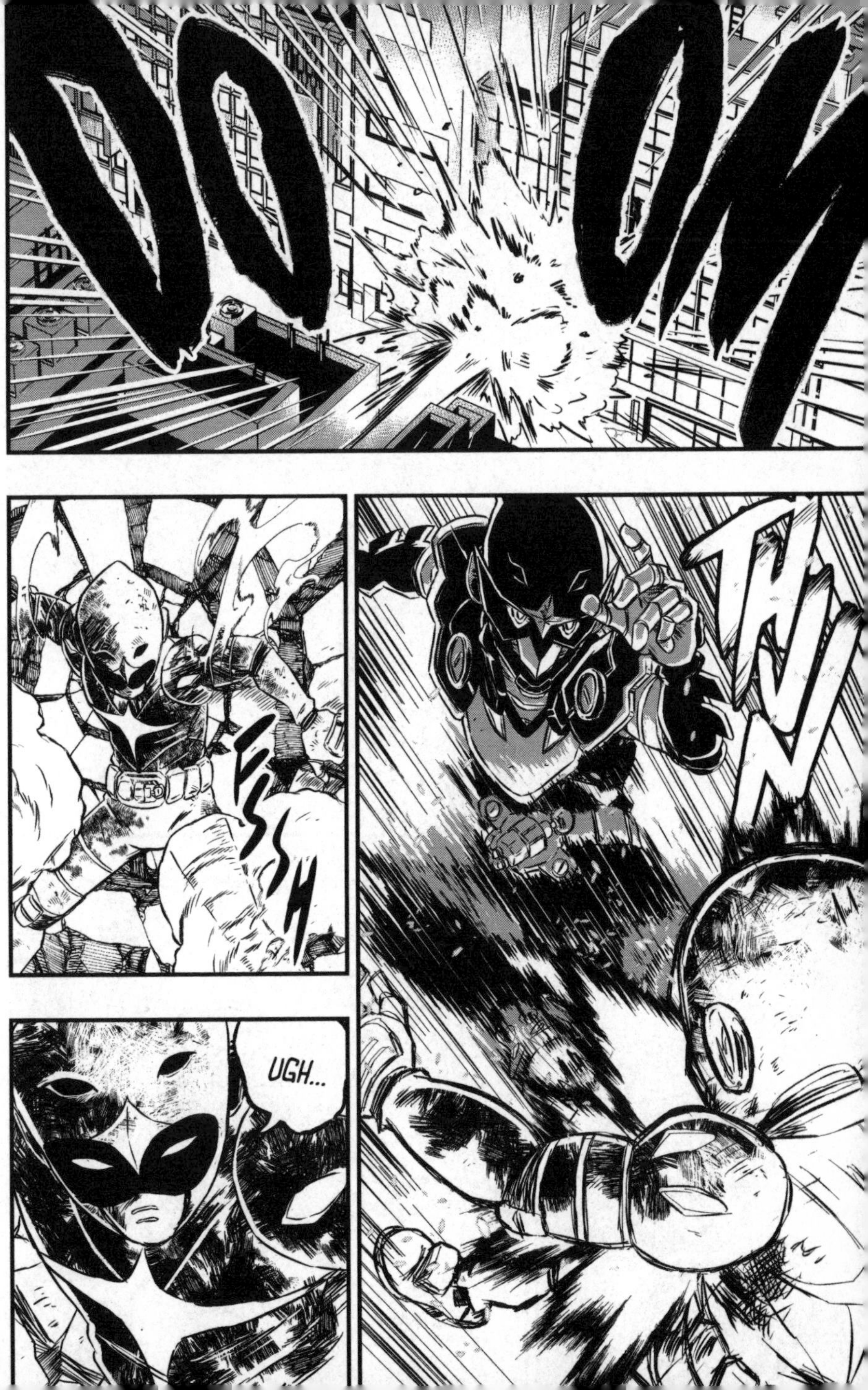
DOOM
FSSSH
THWN
UGH...

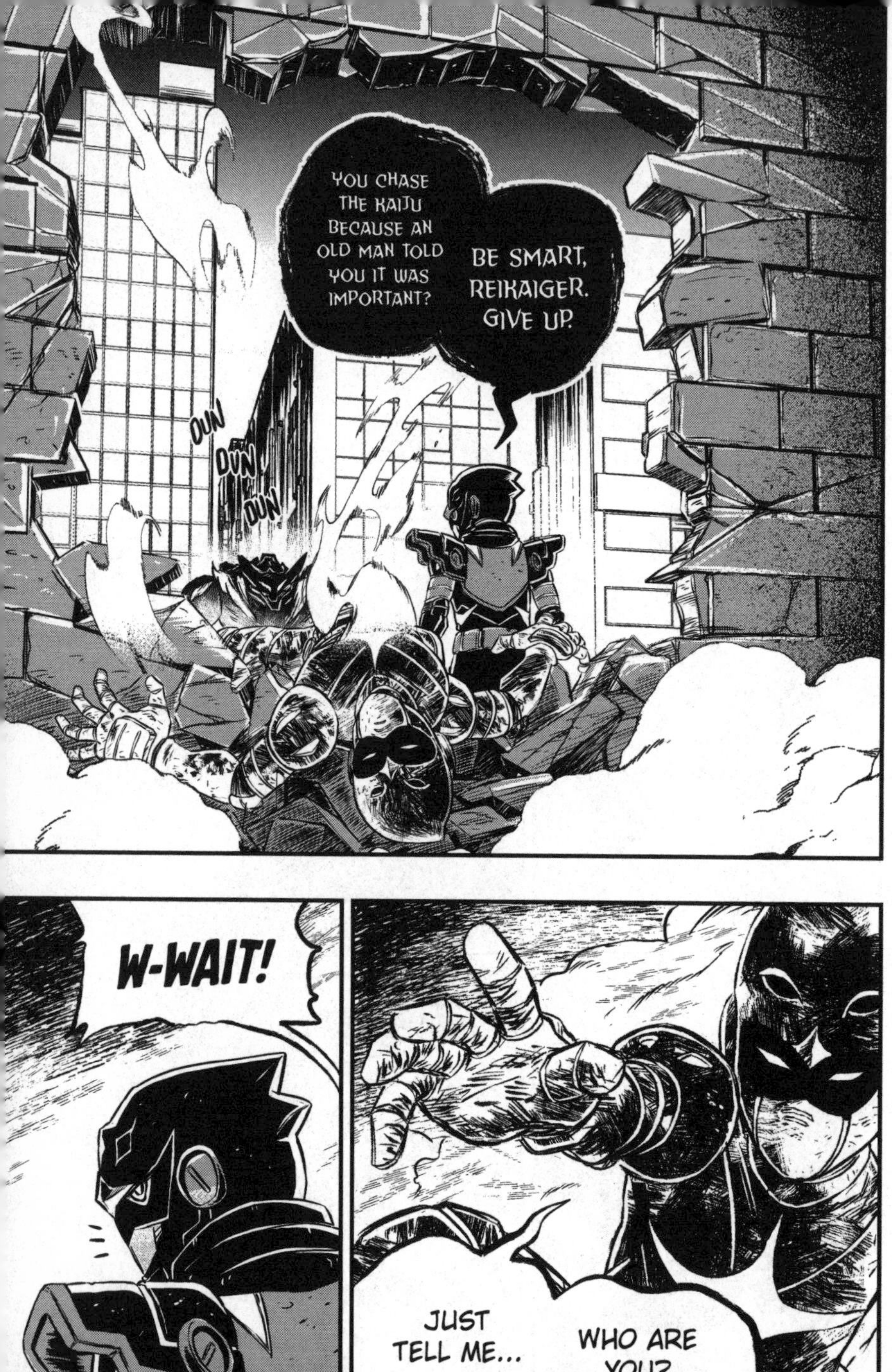
YOU CHASE THE KAIJU BECAUSE AN OLD MAN TOLD YOU IT WAS IMPORTANT?
BE SMART, REIKAIGER. GIVE UP.
DUN
DUN
DUN
W-WAIT!
JUST TELL ME...
WHO ARE YOU?

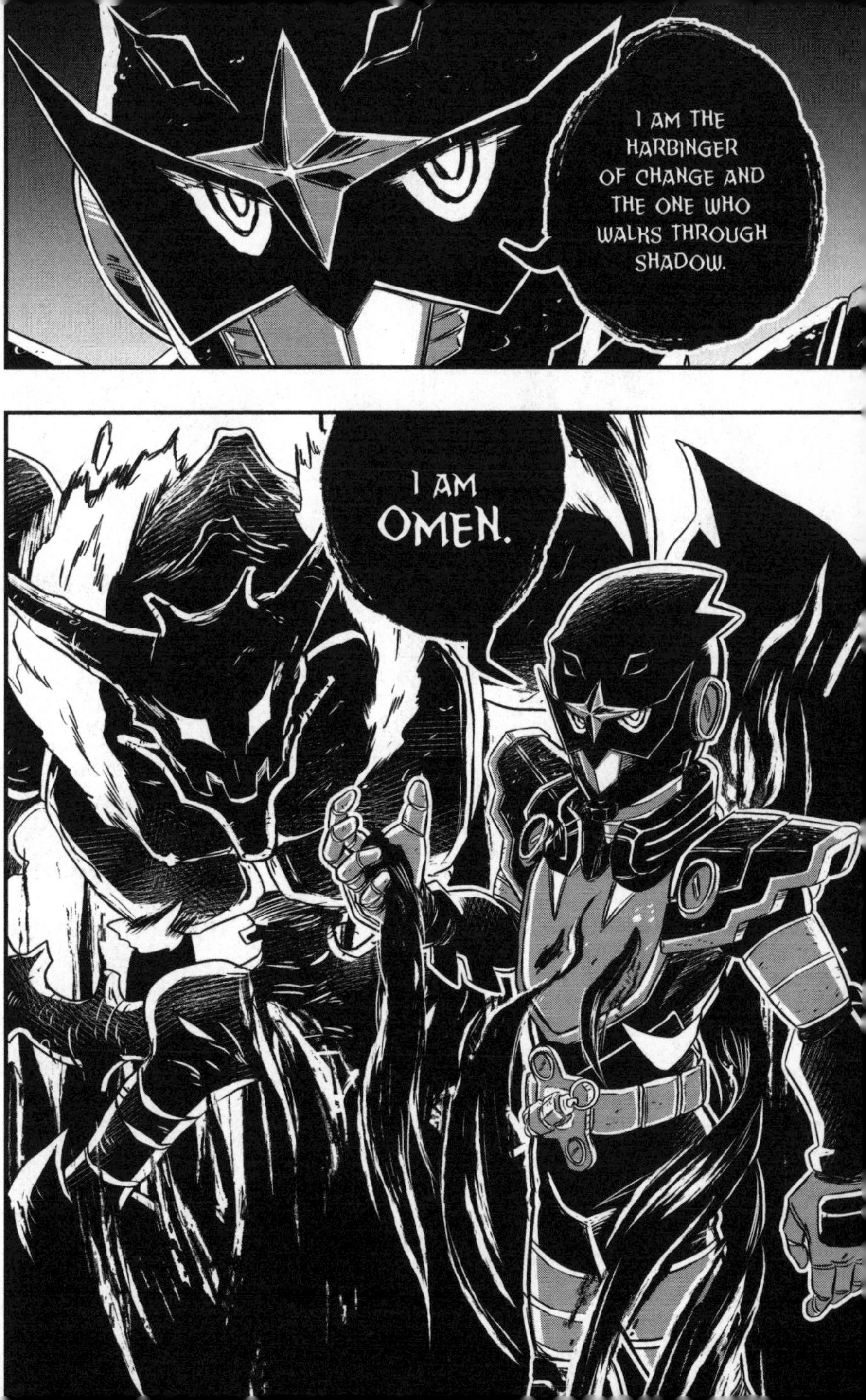
I AM THE HARBINGER OF CHANGE AND THE ONE WHO WALKS THROUGH SHADOW.
I AM OMEN.

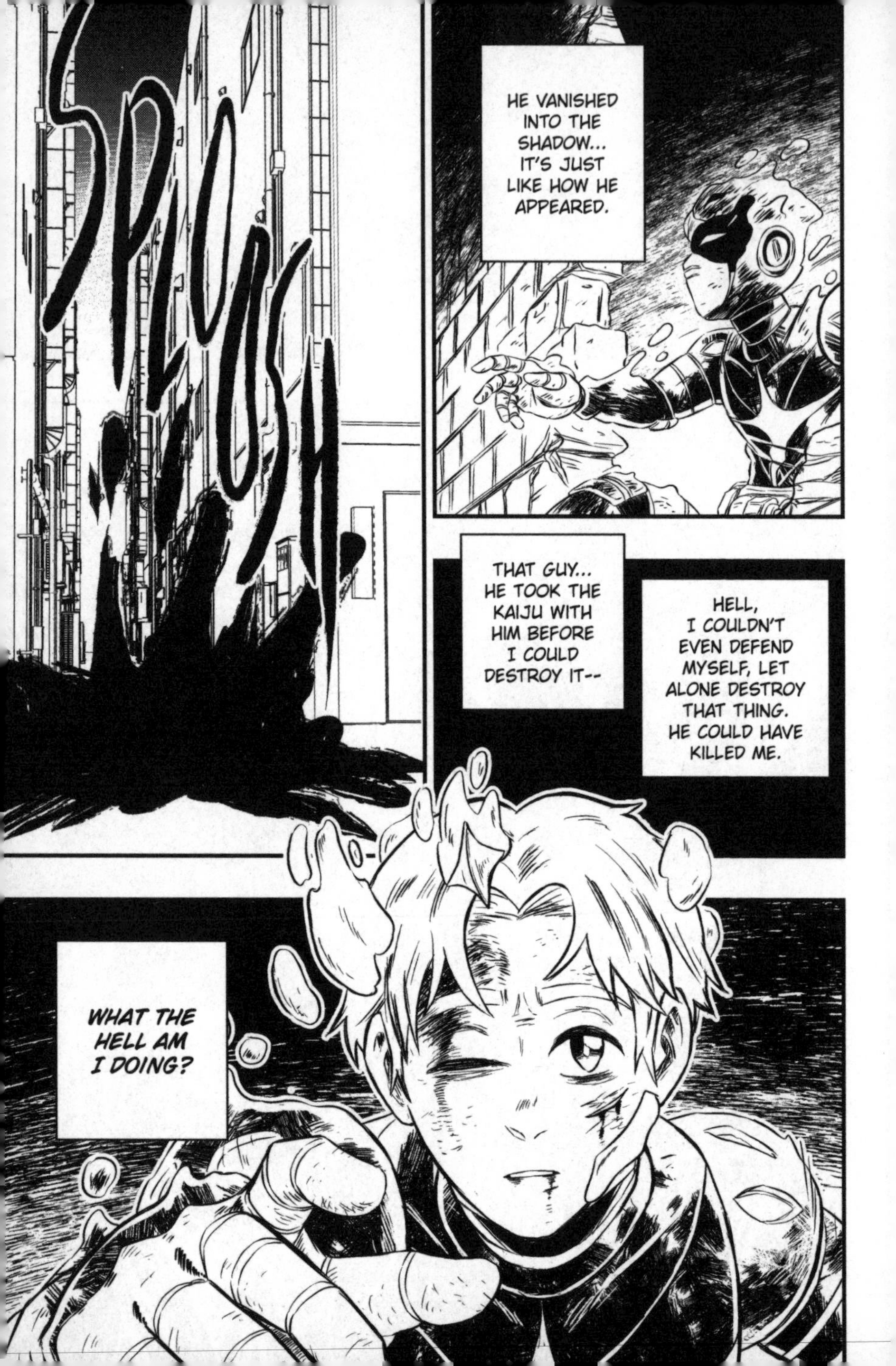
SPLOOSH
HE VANISHED INTO THE SHADOW... IT'S JUST LIKE HOW HE APPEARED.
THAT GUY... HE TOOK THE KAIJU WITH HIM BEFORE I COULD DESTROY IT--
HELL, I COULDN'T EVEN DEFEND MYSELF, LET ALONE DESTROY THAT THING. HE COULD HAVE KILLED ME.
WHAT THE HELL AM I DOING?

HENSHIN!

CHAPTER SEVEN

PRESSURE

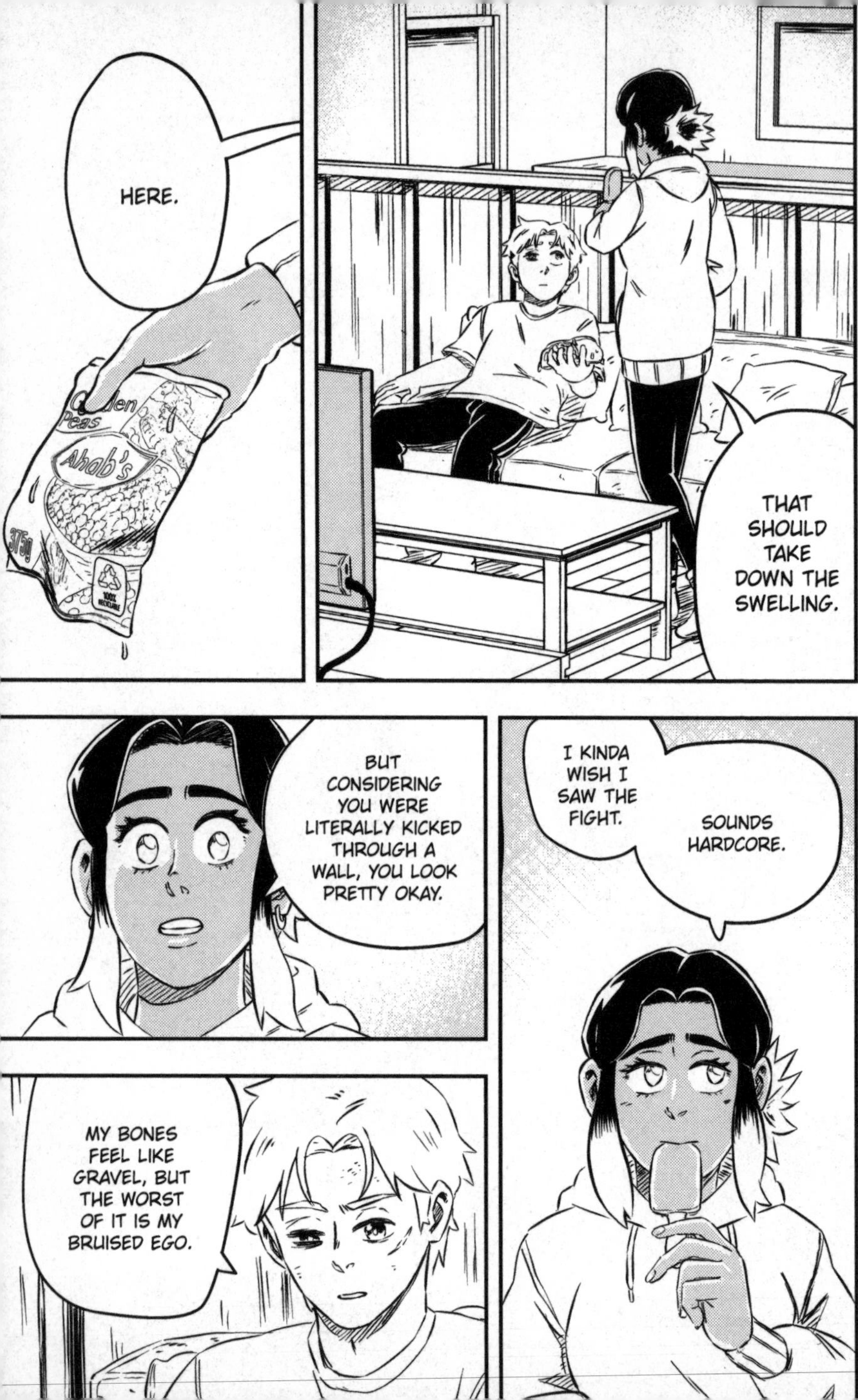
HERE.
Golden Peas
Ahab's
375g
100% RECYCLABLE
THAT SHOULD TAKE DOWN THE SWELLING.
BUT CONSIDERING YOU WERE LITERALLY KICKED THROUGH A WALL, YOU LOOK PRETTY OKAY.
I KINDA WISH I SAW THE FIGHT.
SOUNDS HARDCORE.
MY BONES FEEL LIKE GRAVEL, BUT THE WORST OF IT IS MY BRUISED EGO.

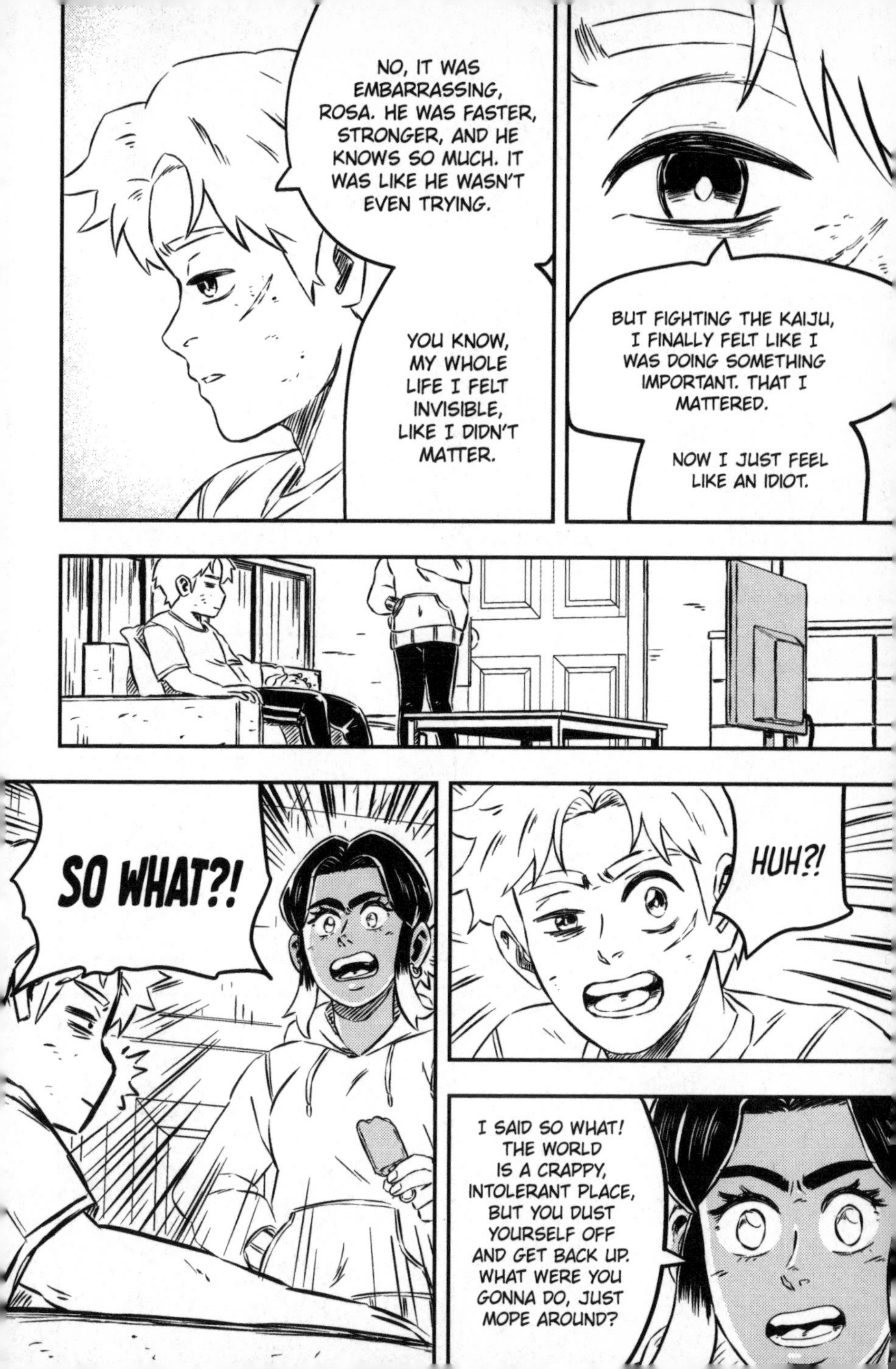
NO, IT WAS EMBARRASSING, ROSA. HE WAS FASTER, STRONGER, AND HE KNOWS SO MUCH. IT WAS LIKE HE WASN'T EVEN TRYING.
YOU KNOW, MY WHOLE LIFE I FELT INVISIBLE, LIKE I DIDN'T MATTER.
BUT FIGHTING THE KAIJU, I FINALLY FELT LIKE I WAS DOING SOMETHING IMPORTANT. THAT I MATTERED.
NOW I JUST FEEL LIKE AN IDIOT.
SO WHAT?!
HUH?!
I SAID SO WHAT! THE WORLD IS A CRAPPY, INTOLERANT PLACE, BUT YOU DUST YOURSELF OFF AND GET BACK UP. WHAT WERE YOU GONNA DO, JUST MOPE AROUND?

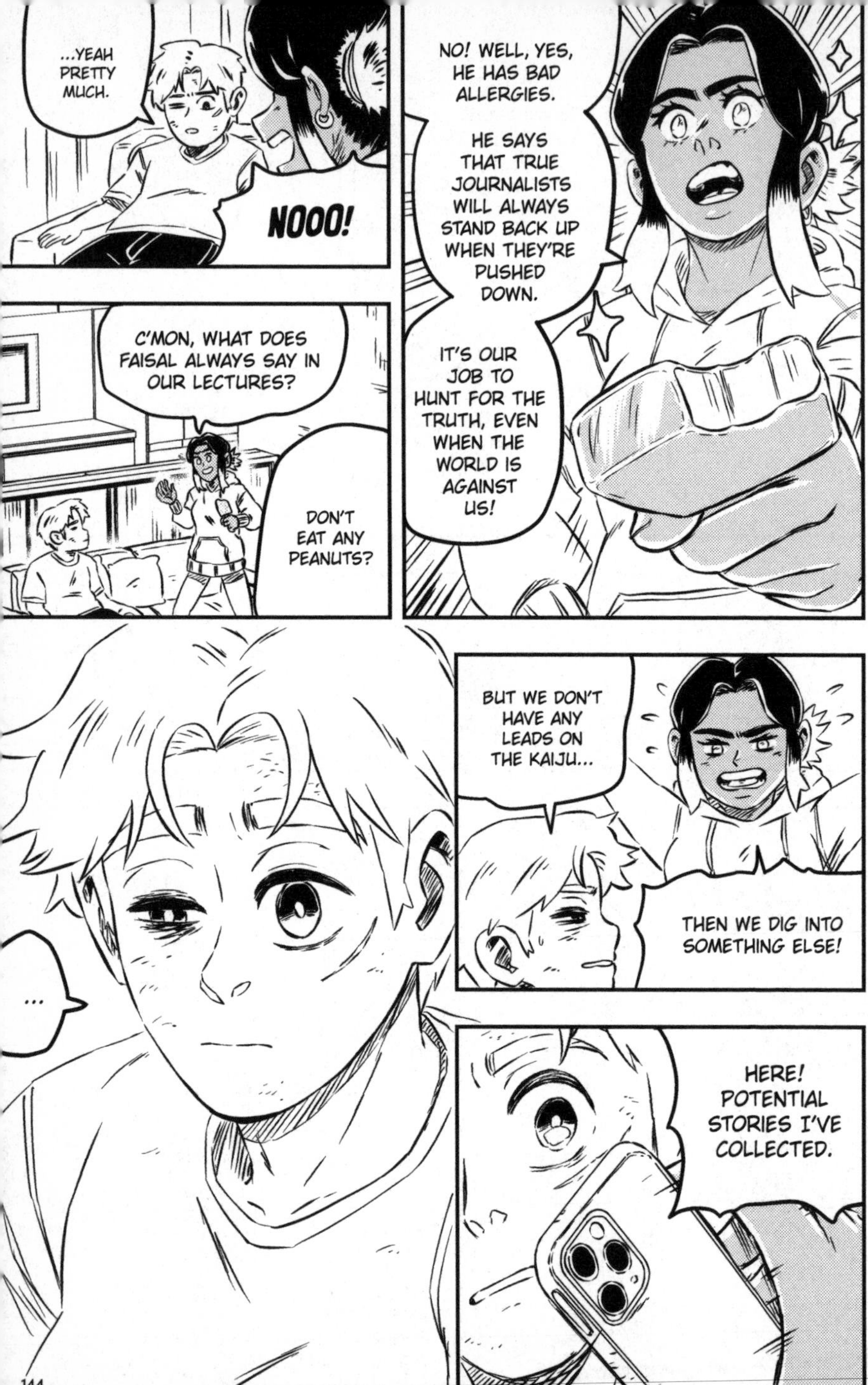
...YEAH PRETTY MUCH.
NOOO!
NO! WELL, YES, HE HAS BAD ALLERGIES.
C'MON, WHAT DOES FAISAL ALWAYS SAY IN OUR LECTURES?
DON'T EAT ANY PEANUTS?
HE SAYS THAT TRUE JOURNALISTS WILL ALWAYS STAND BACK UP WHEN THEY'RE PUSHED DOWN.
IT'S OUR JOB TO HUNT FOR THE TRUTH, EVEN WHEN THE WORLD IS AGAINST US!
BUT WE DON'T HAVE ANY LEADS ON THE KAIJU...
THEN WE DIG INTO SOMETHING ELSE!
...
HERE! POTENTIAL STORIES I'VE COLLECTED.

ARE POLITICIANS LIZARD PEOPLE... A DOG THAT CAN READ MINDS... KID WITH HAMMERS FOR HANDS?

YOU SAID THE SAME THING ABOUT THE MASKED HERO LAST WEEK.

I GUESS I DID, DIDN'T I?

OOH! WHAT ABOUT THIS ONE?

ROSA, THIS IS ALL *NONSENSE*.

PRIME MINISTER AND ALTON GRIEVES RUN SHADOW COUNCIL, PULLING ALL THE STRINGS IN SOCIETY?

I THOUGHT YOU SAID TO DROP GRIEVES?

HEHE, I GUESS I DID...

HE'S *REGGIE CANNON*. CEO OF THE *BOX GROUP*, THEY OWN LOADS OF CLUBS AND BARS IN THE CITY. I REMEMBER HIM FROM RESEARCHING GRIEVES.

HE WAS LET OFF THE HOOK FOR MILLIONS IN TAX FRAUD, EVEN THOUGH HE WAS BASICALLY CAUGHT RED-HANDED.

A SECRET CABAL SEEMS A BIT MUCH--

HEY, WAIT A SECOND...

BUT WHAT DOES THAT HAVE TO DO WITH GRIEVES?

9:23

HOLLOWSTONE POST

Support Us

News Opinion Sport Culture Lifestyle

...ie Cannon cleared of ...rges, set to return

...n not-guilty is

Anya Pretrov

...open and shut cause of tax
...against the entrepreneur
...d that has become an

WELL, HIS BROTHER IS A MINISTER, AND A GRIEVES SUBSIDIARY COMPANY IS ONE OF HIS CAMPAIGN DONORS.

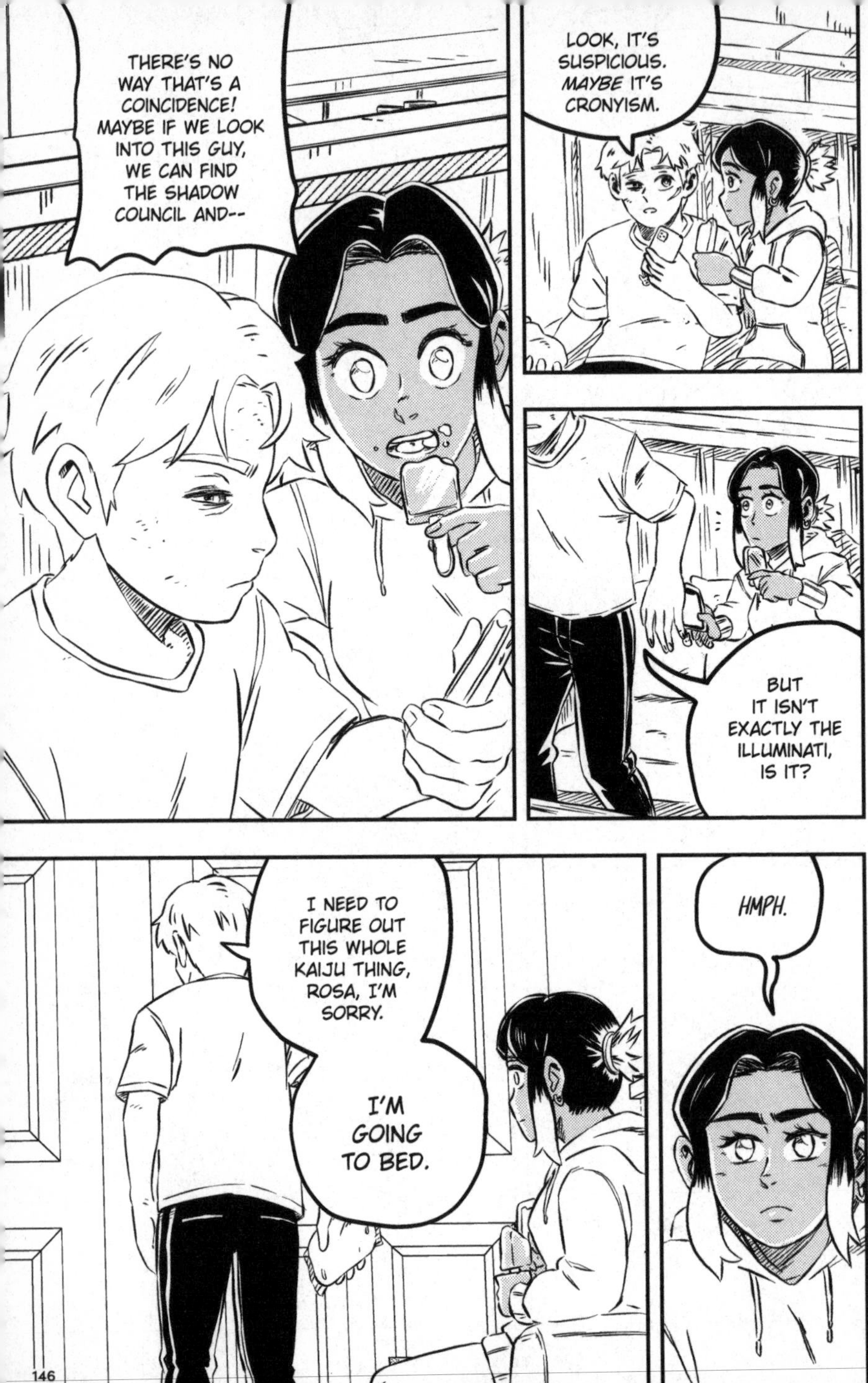
THERE'S NO WAY THAT'S A COINCIDENCE! MAYBE IF WE LOOK INTO THIS GUY, WE CAN FIND THE SHADOW COUNCIL AND--
LOOK, IT'S SUSPICIOUS. *MAYBE* IT'S CRONYISM.
BUT IT ISN'T EXACTLY THE ILLUMINATI, IS IT?
I NEED TO FIGURE OUT THIS WHOLE KAIJU THING, ROSA, I'M SORRY.
I'M GOING TO BED.
HMPH.

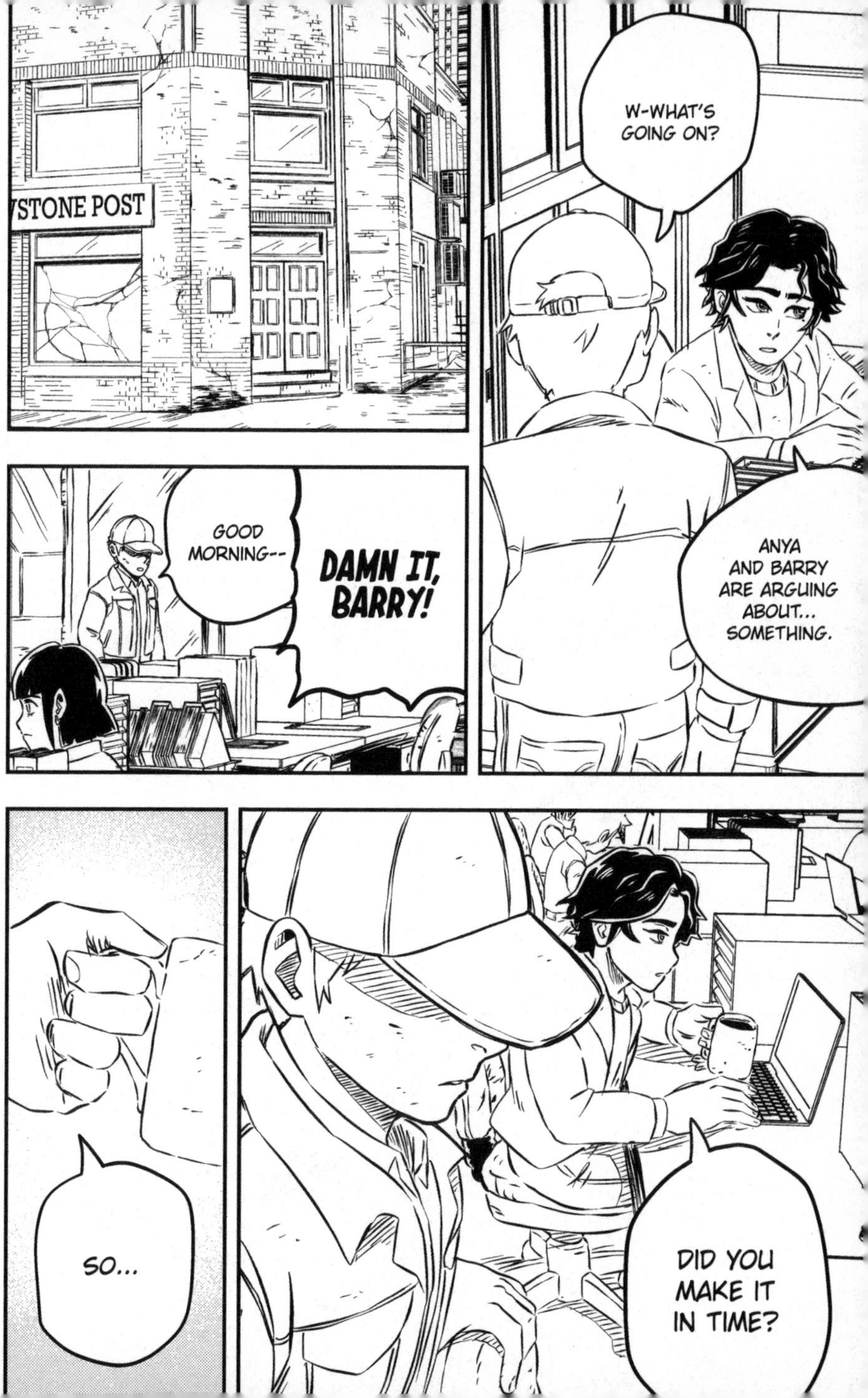
STONE POST
W-WHAT'S GOING ON?
GOOD MORNING--
DAMN IT, BARRY!
ANYA AND BARRY ARE ARGUING ABOUT... SOMETHING.
SO...
DID YOU MAKE IT IN TIME?

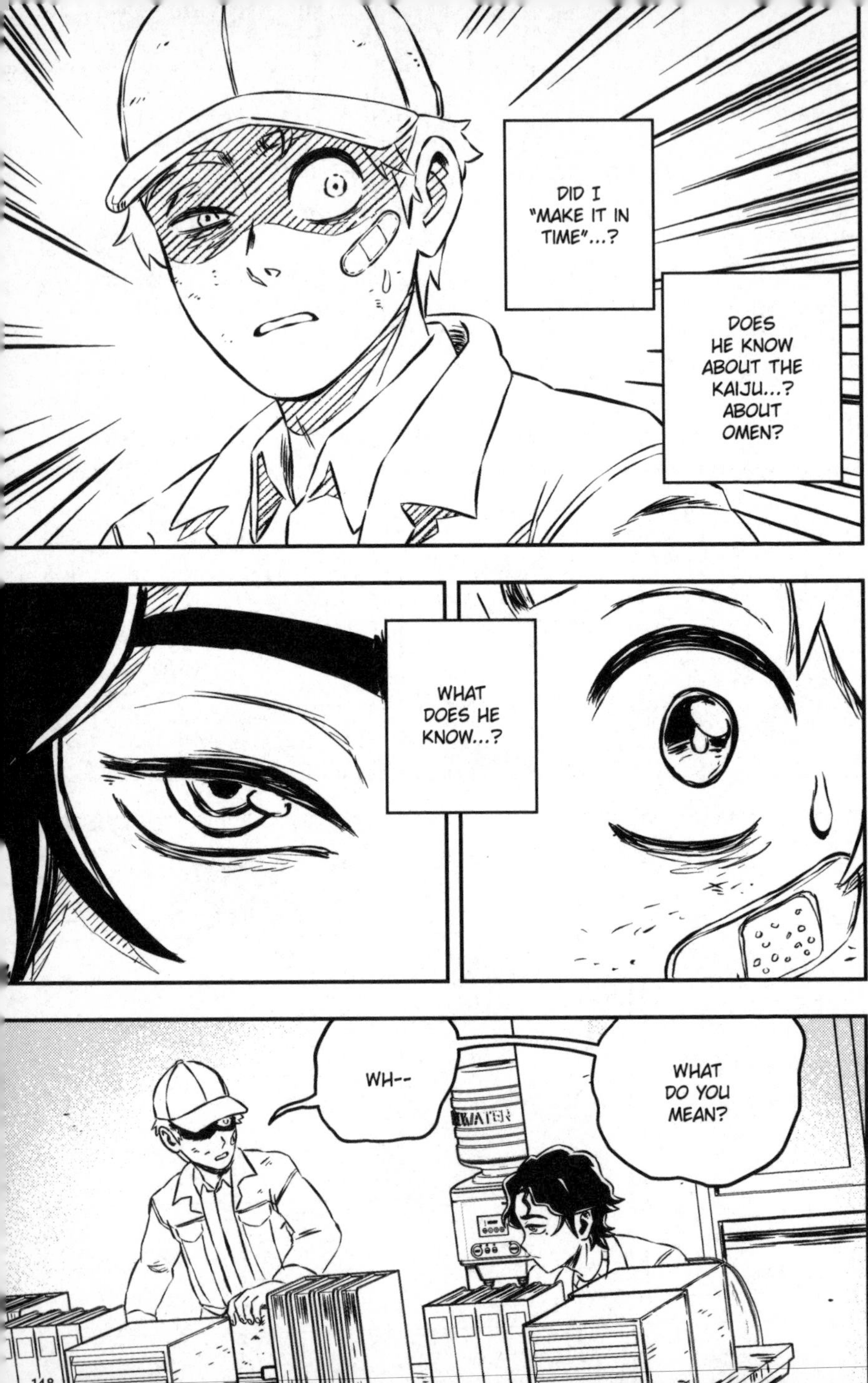
DID I "MAKE IT IN TIME"...?
DOES HE KNOW ABOUT THE KAIJU...? ABOUT OMEN?
WHAT DOES HE KNOW...?
WH--
WHAT DO YOU MEAN?
WATER

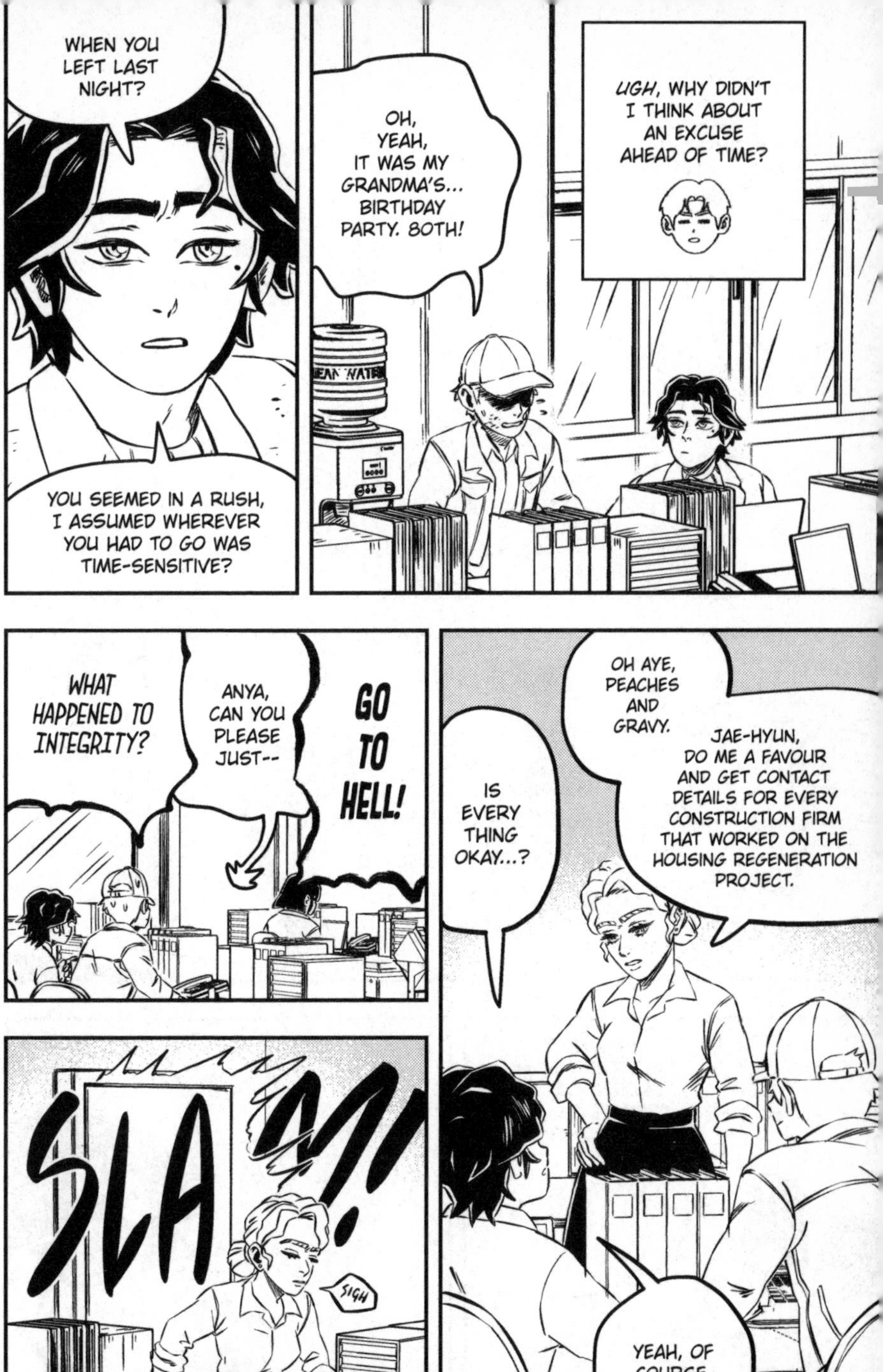
WHEN YOU LEFT LAST NIGHT?
YOU SEEMED IN A RUSH, I ASSUMED WHEREVER YOU HAD TO GO WAS TIME-SENSITIVE?
OH, YEAH, IT WAS MY GRANDMA'S... BIRTHDAY PARTY. 80TH!
UGH, WHY DIDN'T I THINK ABOUT AN EXCUSE AHEAD OF TIME?
WHAT HAPPENED TO INTEGRITY?
ANYA, CAN YOU PLEASE JUST--
GO TO HELL!
SLAM!
SIGH
IS EVERY THING OKAY...?
OH AYE, PEACHES AND GRAVY.
JAE-HYUN, DO ME A FAVOUR AND GET CONTACT DETAILS FOR EVERY CONSTRUCTION FIRM THAT WORKED ON THE HOUSING REGENERATION PROJECT.
YEAH, OF COURSE.

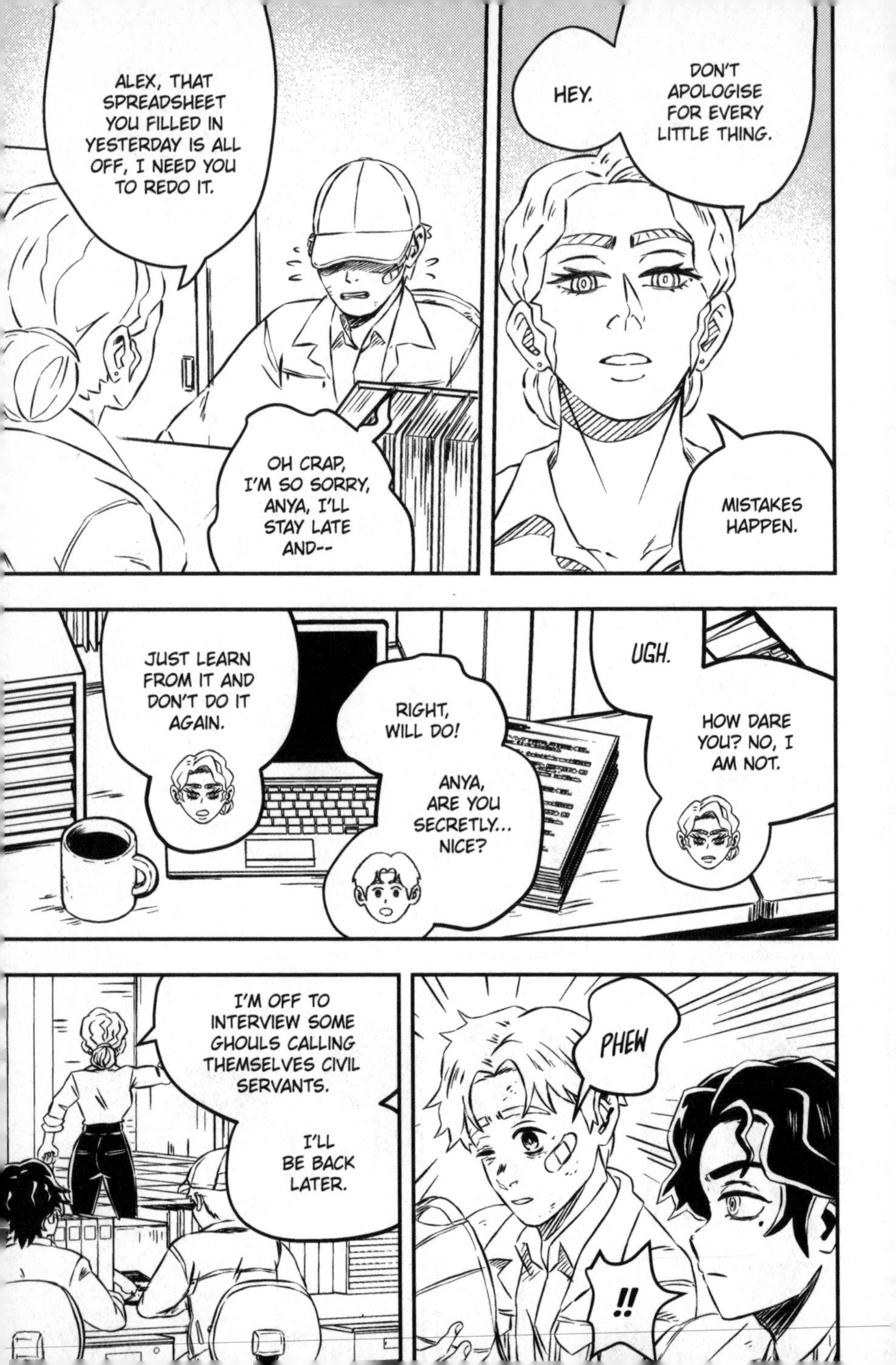
ALEX, THAT SPREADSHEET YOU FILLED IN YESTERDAY IS ALL OFF, I NEED YOU TO REDO IT.
OH CRAP, I'M SO SORRY, ANYA, I'LL STAY LATE AND--
HEY.
DON'T APOLOGISE FOR EVERY LITTLE THING.
MISTAKES HAPPEN.
JUST LEARN FROM IT AND DON'T DO IT AGAIN.
RIGHT, WILL DO!
ANYA, ARE YOU SECRETLY... NICE?
UGH.
HOW DARE YOU? NO, I AM NOT.
I'M OFF TO INTERVIEW SOME GHOULS CALLING THEMSELVES CIVIL SERVANTS.
I'LL BE BACK LATER.
PHEW
!!

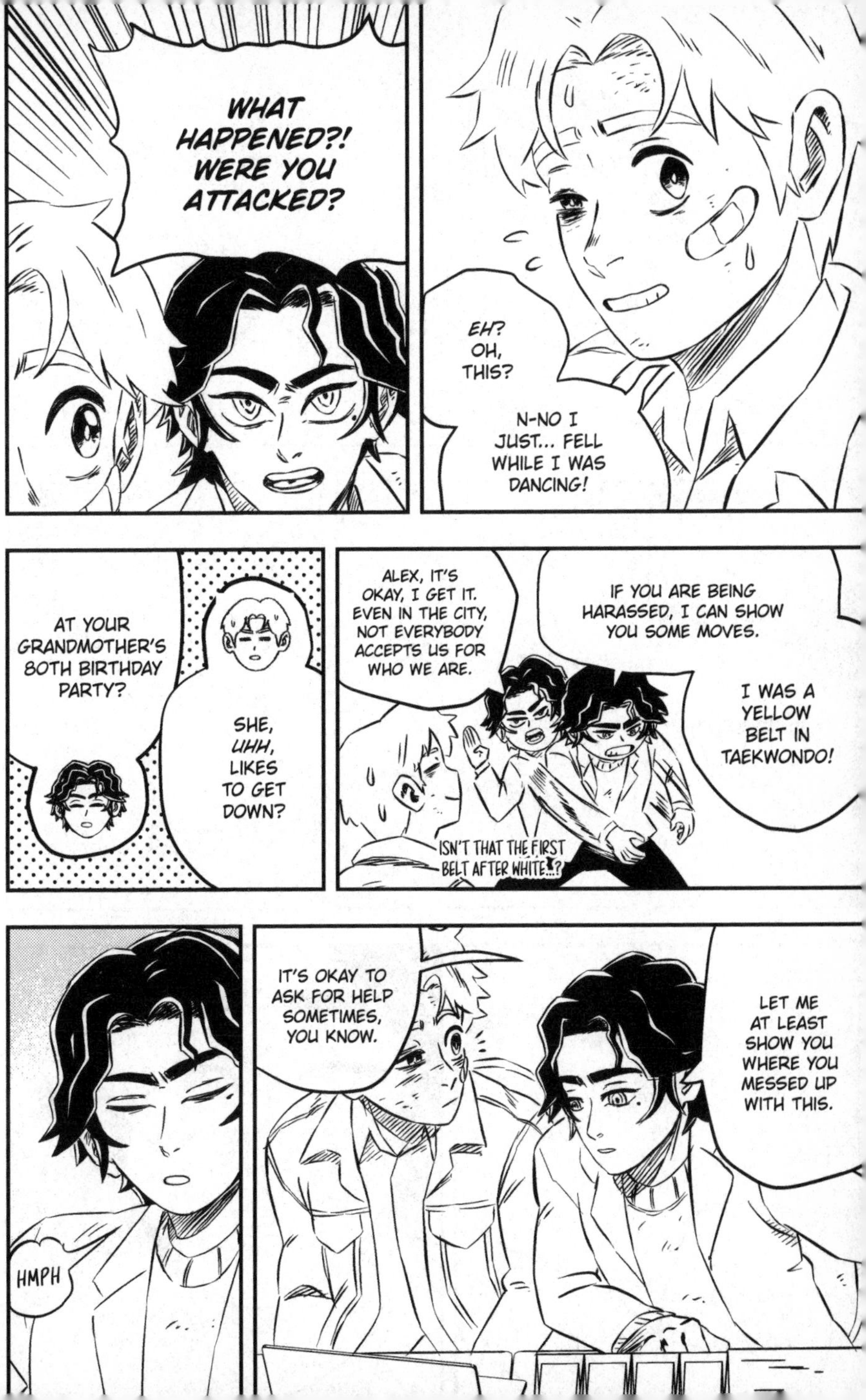
WHAT HAPPENED?! WERE YOU ATTACKED?
EH? OH, THIS?
N-NO I JUST... FELL WHILE I WAS DANCING!
AT YOUR GRANDMOTHER'S 80TH BIRTHDAY PARTY?
SHE, UHH, LIKES TO GET DOWN?
ALEX, IT'S OKAY, I GET IT. EVEN IN THE CITY, NOT EVERYBODY ACCEPTS US FOR WHO WE ARE.
IF YOU ARE BEING HARASSED, I CAN SHOW YOU SOME MOVES.
I WAS A YELLOW BELT IN TAEKWONDO!
ISN'T THAT THE FIRST BELT AFTER WHITE...?
HMPH
IT'S OKAY TO ASK FOR HELP SOMETIMES, YOU KNOW.
LET ME AT LEAST SHOW YOU WHERE YOU MESSED UP WITH THIS.

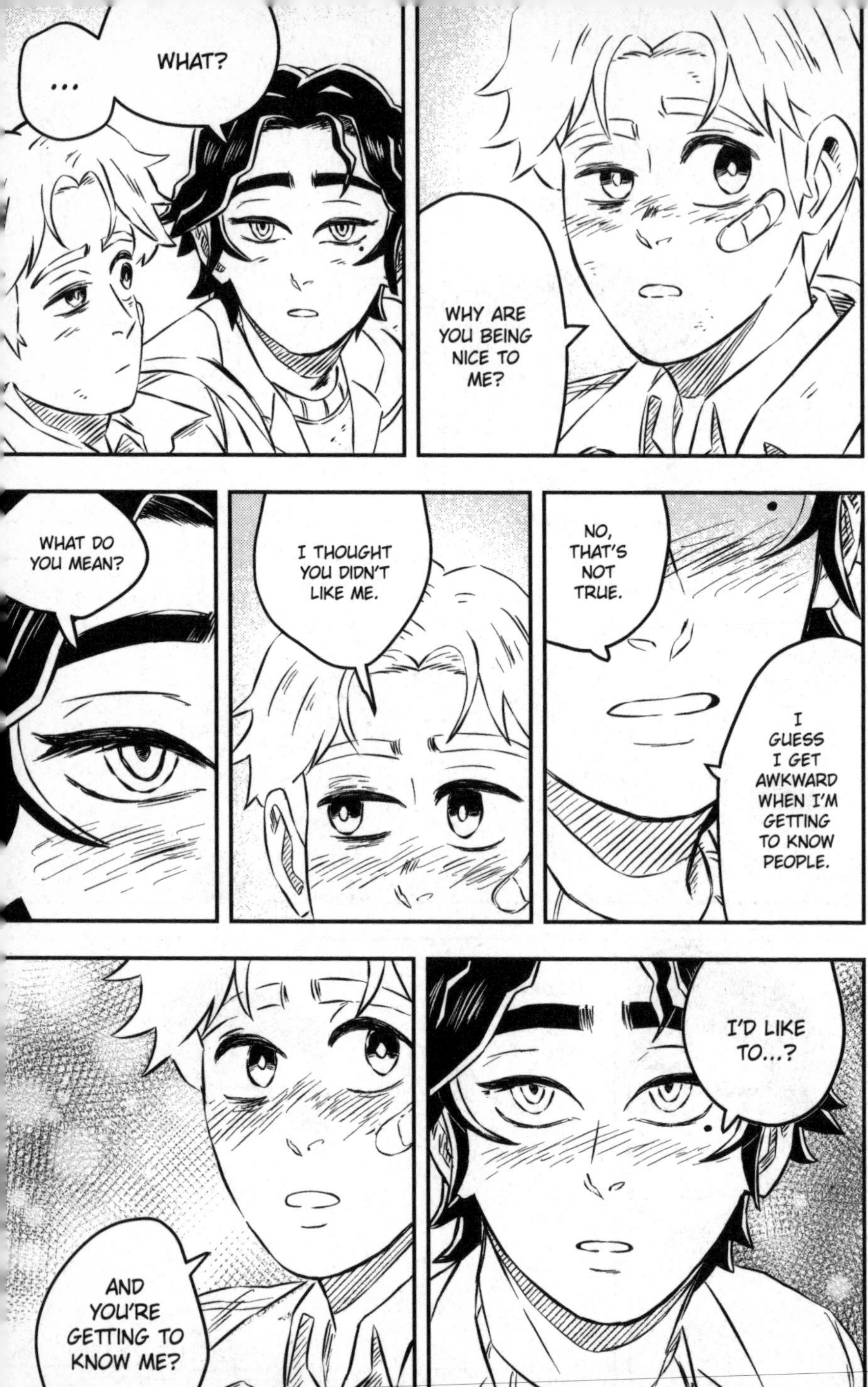
...
WHAT?
WHY ARE YOU BEING NICE TO ME?
WHAT DO YOU MEAN?
I THOUGHT YOU DIDN'T LIKE ME.
NO, THAT'S NOT TRUE.
I GUESS I GET AWKWARD WHEN I'M GETTING TO KNOW PEOPLE.
AND YOU'RE GETTING TO KNOW ME?
I'D LIKE TO...?

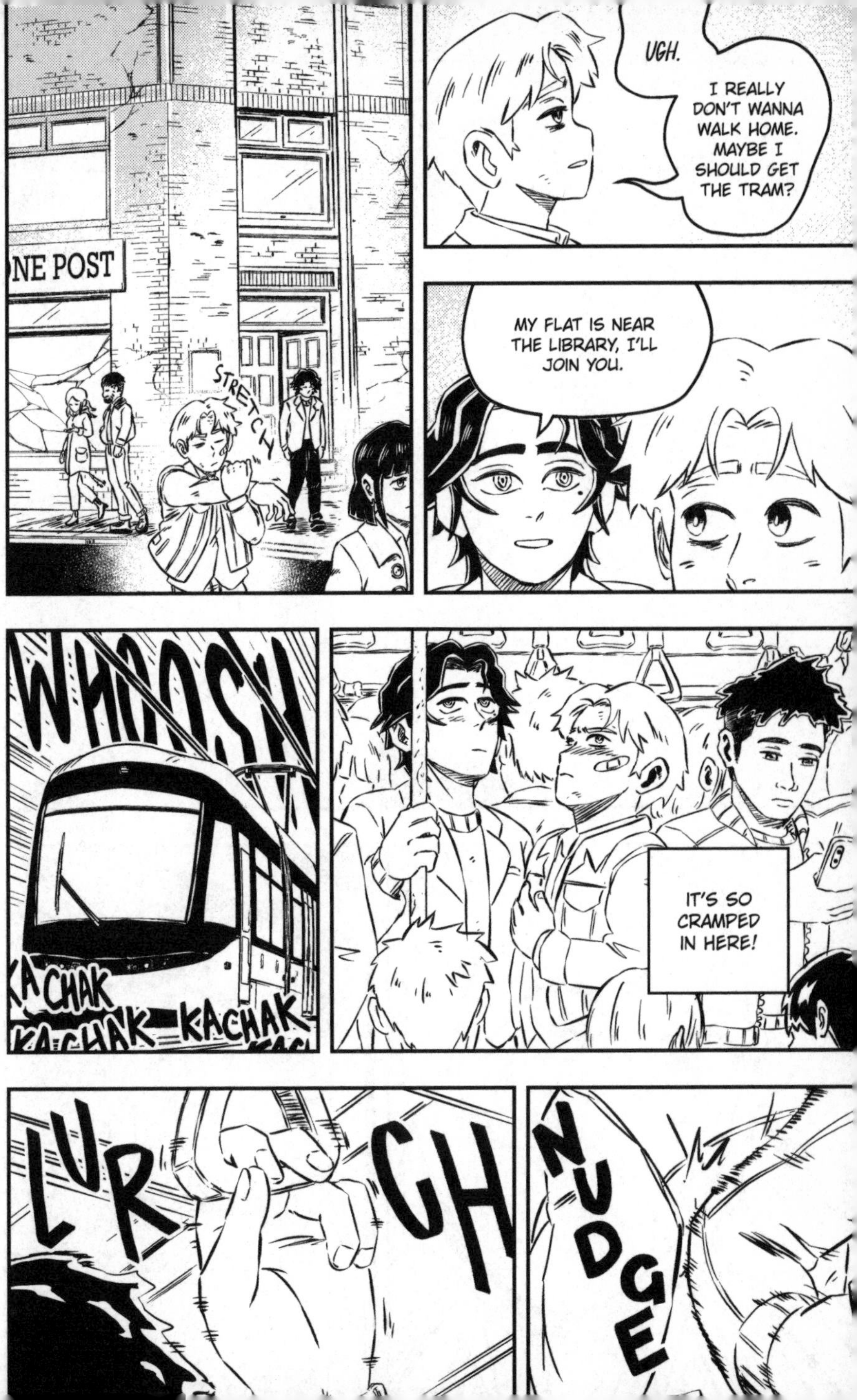
ONE POST
STRETCH
UGH.
I REALLY DON'T WANNA WALK HOME. MAYBE I SHOULD GET THE TRAM?
MY FLAT IS NEAR THE LIBRARY, I'LL JOIN YOU.
WHOOSH
KACHAK
KACHAK KACHAK
IT'S SO CRAMPED IN HERE!
LURCH
NUDGE

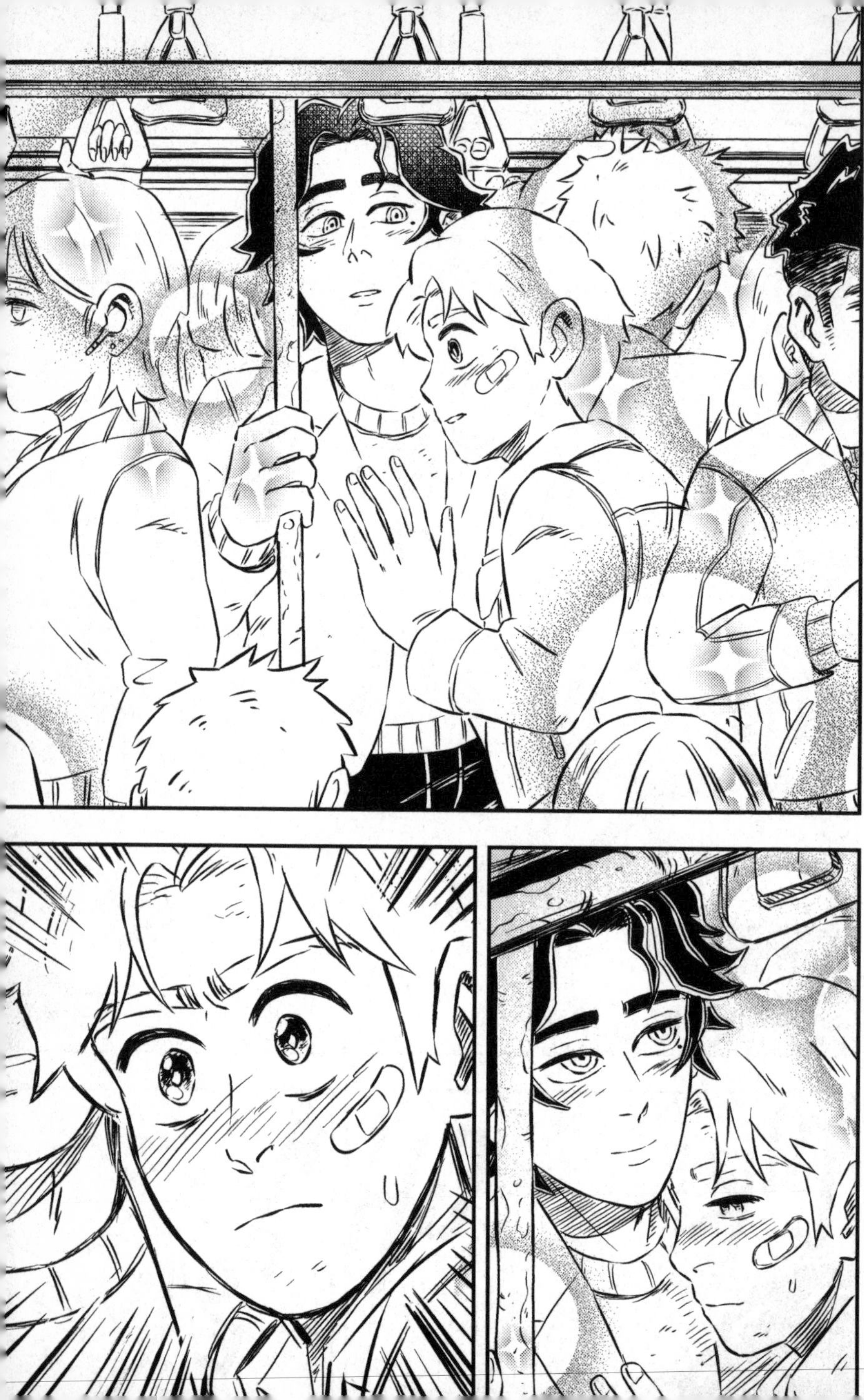

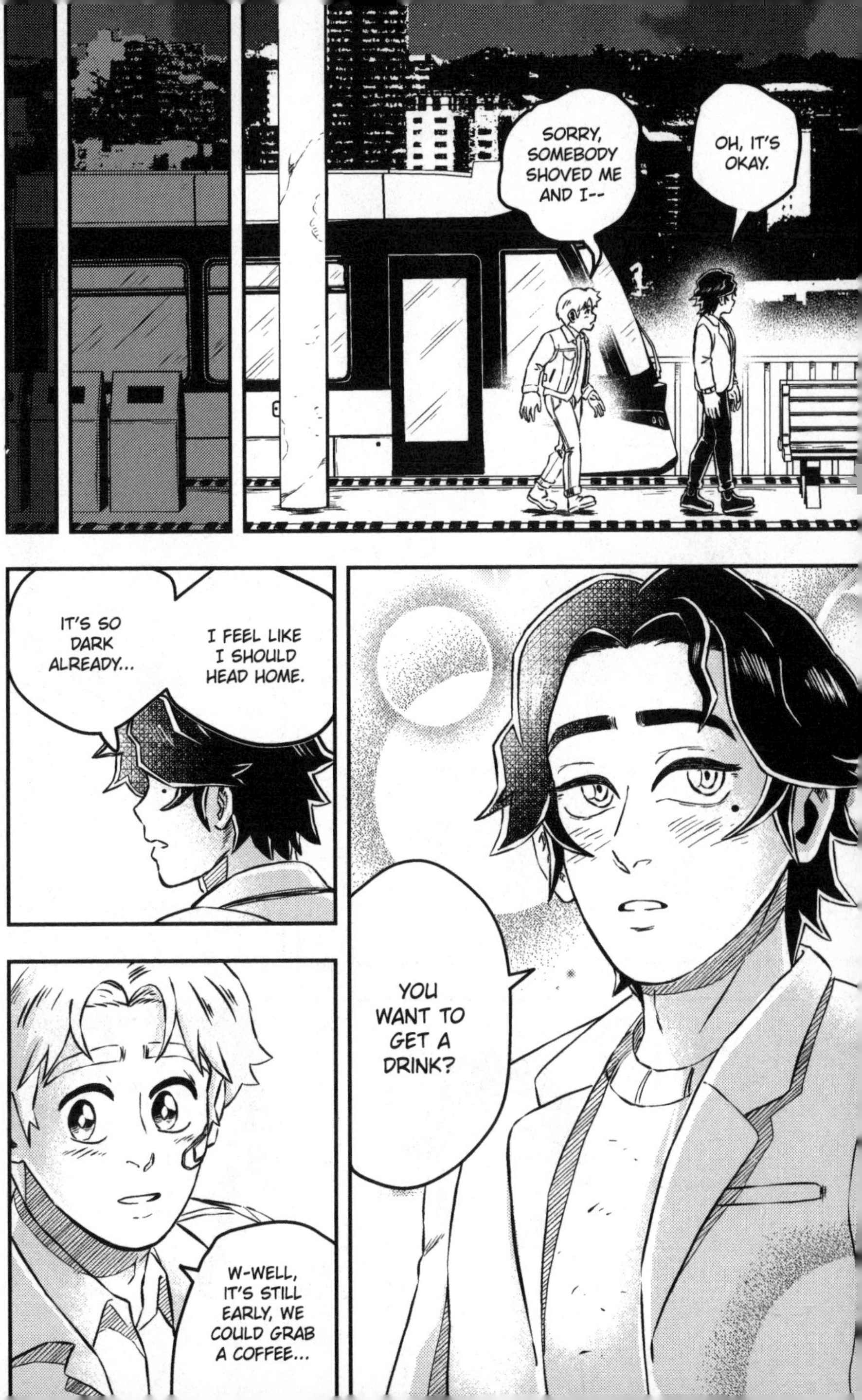
SORRY, SOMEBODY SHOVED ME AND I--
OH, IT'S OKAY.
IT'S SO DARK ALREADY...
I FEEL LIKE I SHOULD HEAD HOME.
YOU WANT TO GET A DRINK?
W-WELL, IT'S STILL EARLY, WE COULD GRAB A COFFEE...

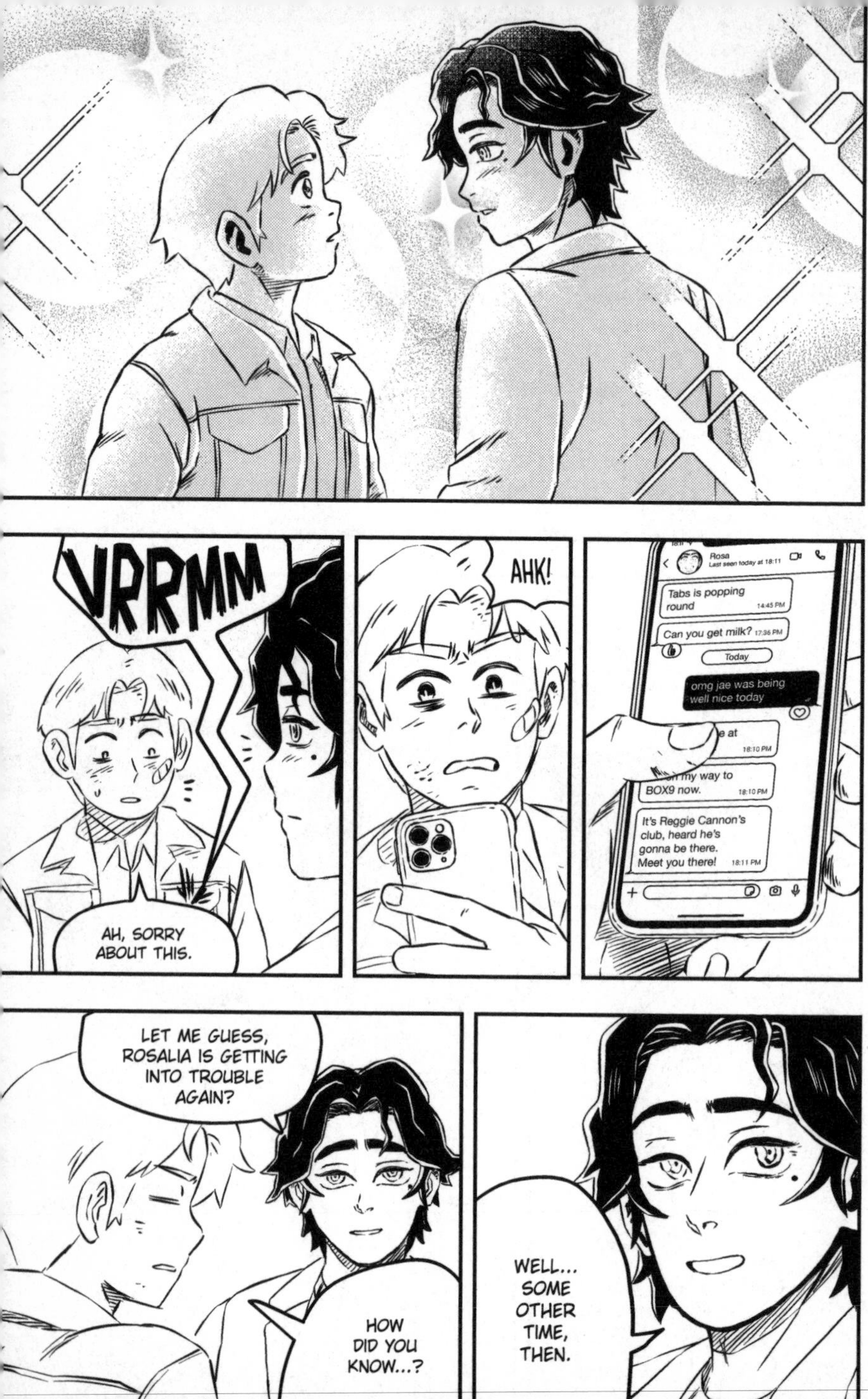
VRRMM
AH, SORRY ABOUT THIS.
AHK!
Rosa
Last seen today at 18:11
Tabs is popping round 14:45 PM
Can you get milk? 17:36 PM
Today
omg jae was being well nice today
18:10 PM
my way to BOX9 now. 18:10 PM
It's Reggie Cannon's club, heard he's gonna be there. Meet you there! 18:11 PM
LET ME GUESS, ROSALIA IS GETTING INTO TROUBLE AGAIN?
HOW DID YOU KNOW...?
WELL... SOME OTHER TIME, THEN.

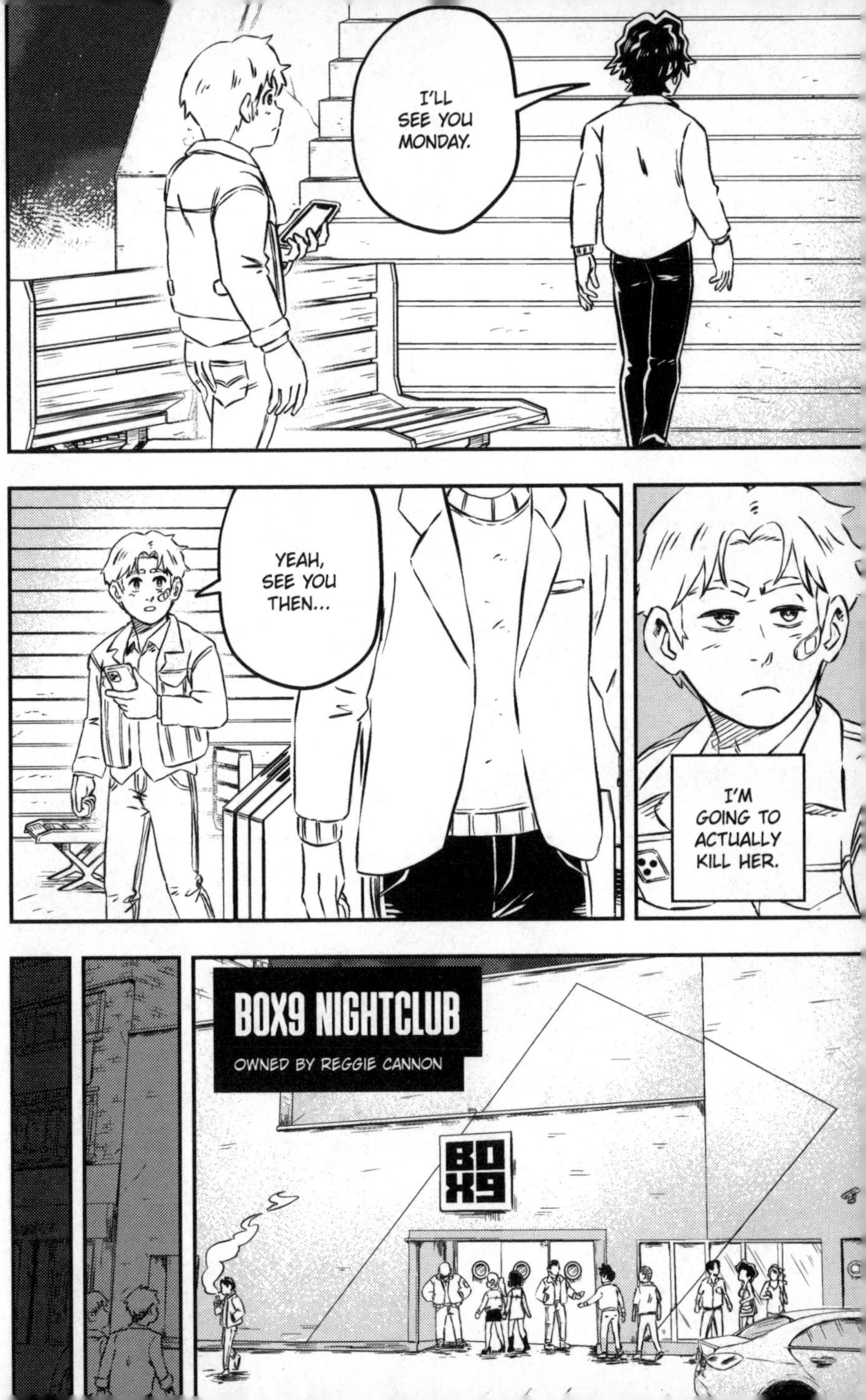
I'LL SEE YOU MONDAY.
YEAH, SEE YOU THEN...
I'M GOING TO ACTUALLY KILL HER.
BOX9 NIGHTCLUB
OWNED BY REGGIE CANNON
BOX9

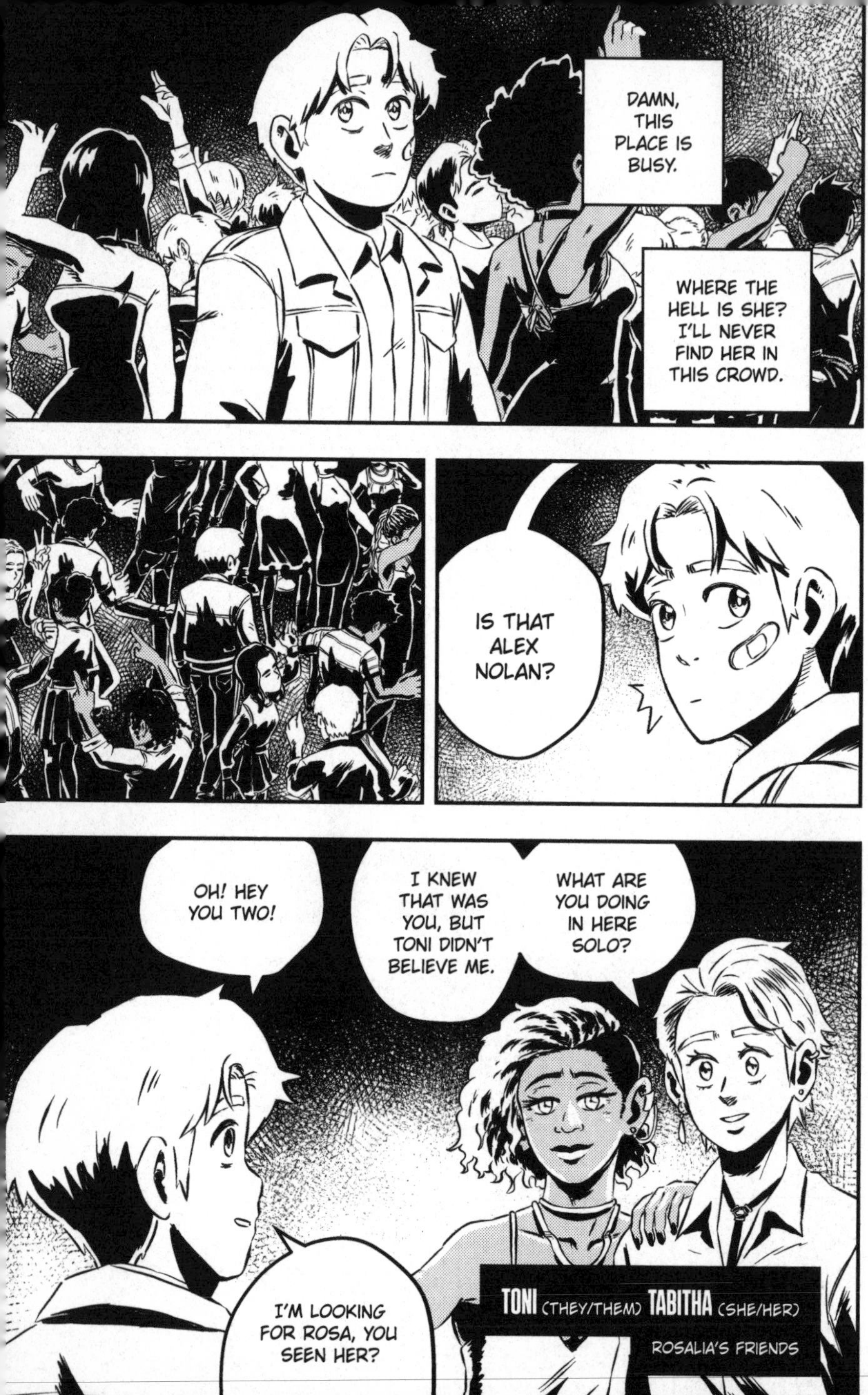
DAMN, THIS PLACE IS BUSY.
WHERE THE HELL IS SHE? I'LL NEVER FIND HER IN THIS CROWD.
IS THAT ALEX NOLAN?
OH! HEY YOU TWO!
I KNEW THAT WAS YOU, BUT TONI DIDN'T BELIEVE ME.
WHAT ARE YOU DOING IN HERE SOLO?
TONI (THEY/THEM) TABITHA (SHE/HER)
ROSALIA'S FRIENDS
I'M LOOKING FOR ROSA, YOU SEEN HER?

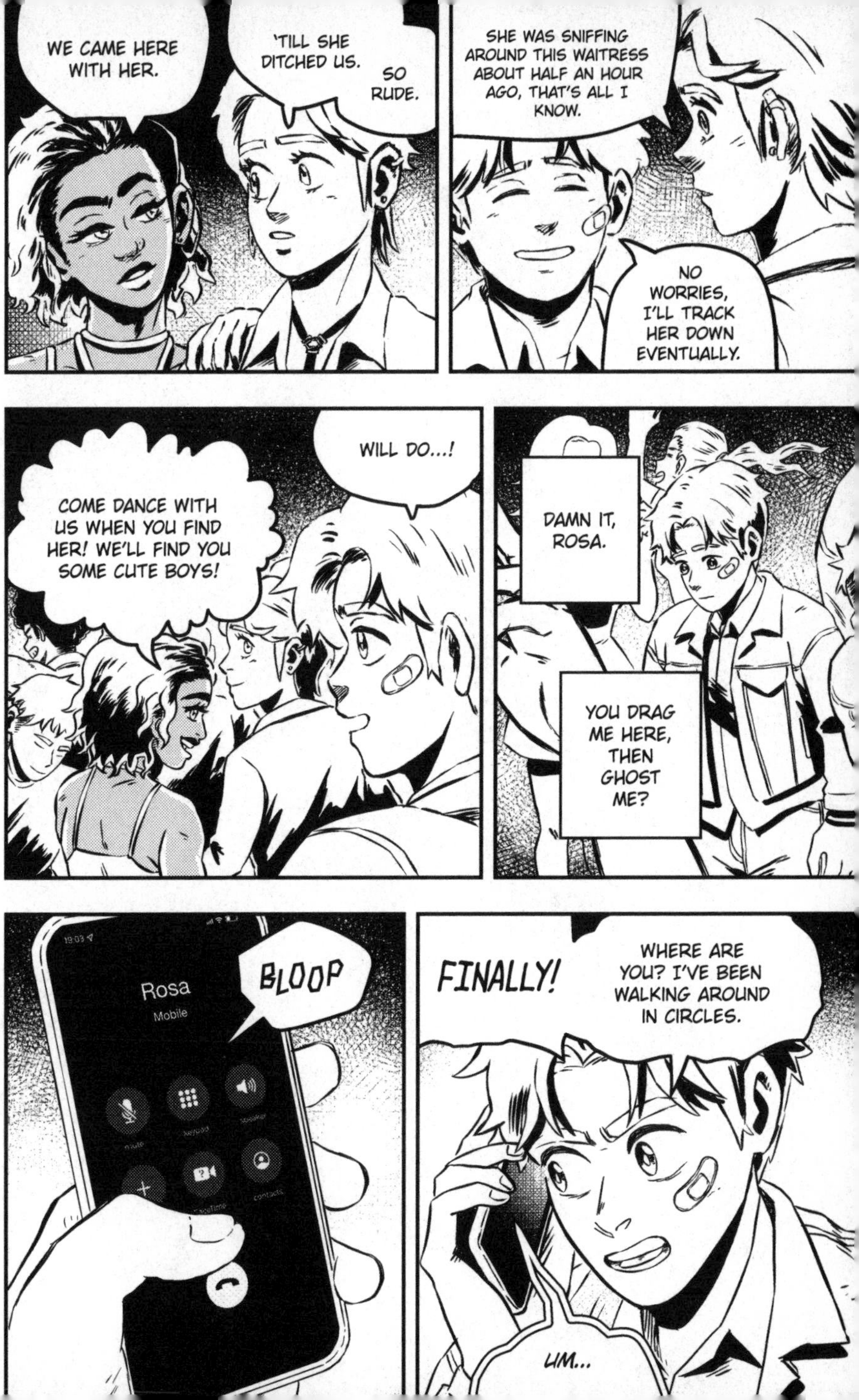
WE CAME HERE WITH HER.
'TILL SHE DITCHED US.
SO RUDE.
SHE WAS SNIFFING AROUND THIS WAITRESS ABOUT HALF AN HOUR AGO, THAT'S ALL I KNOW.
NO WORRIES, I'LL TRACK HER DOWN EVENTUALLY.
COME DANCE WITH US WHEN YOU FIND HER! WE'LL FIND YOU SOME CUTE BOYS!
WILL DO...!
DAMN IT, ROSA.
YOU DRAG ME HERE, THEN GHOST ME?
Rosa
Mobile
BLOOP
FINALLY!
WHERE ARE YOU? I'VE BEEN WALKING AROUND IN CIRCLES.
UM...

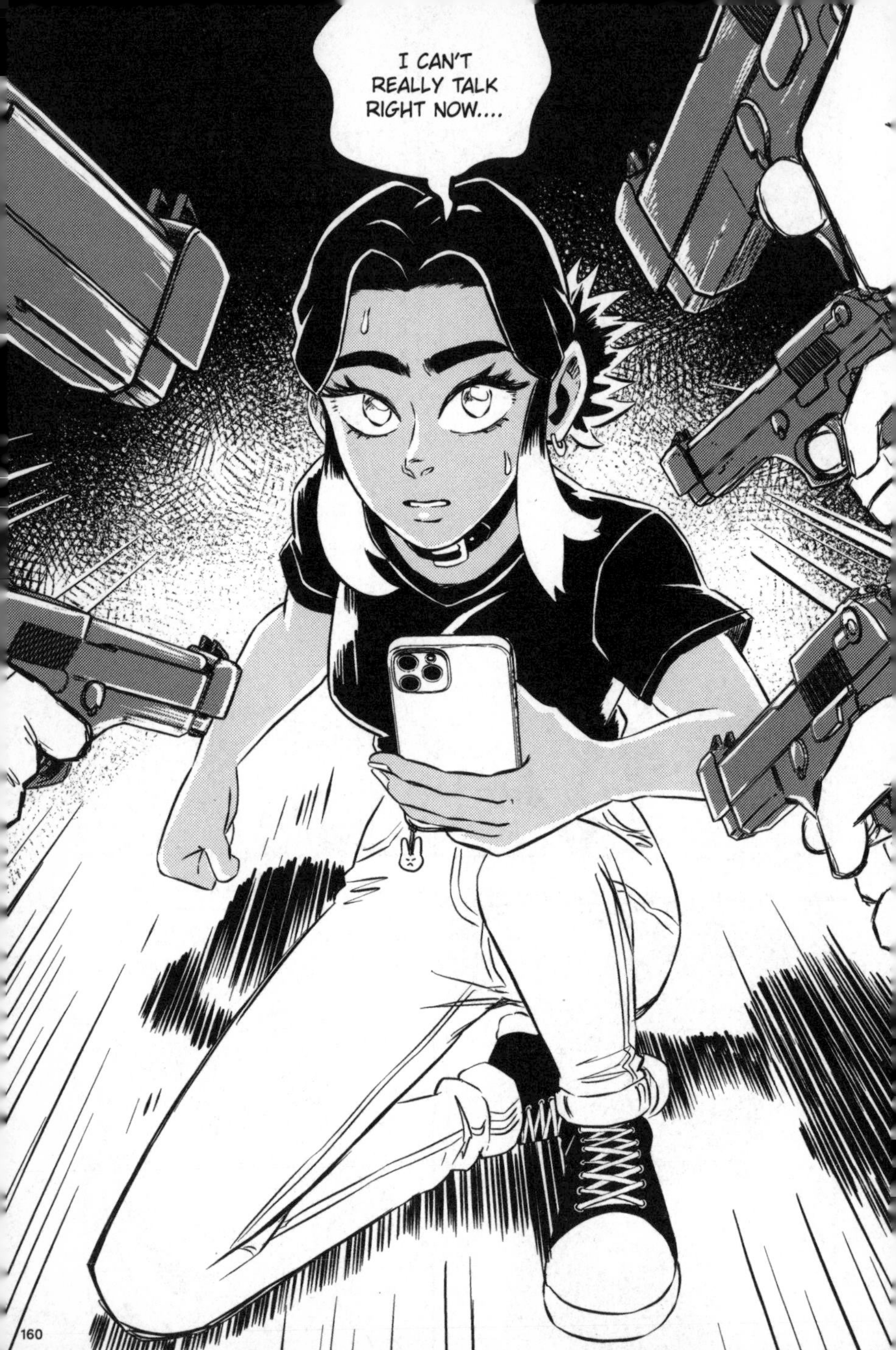
I CAN'T REALLY TALK RIGHT NOW....

CHAPTER EIGHT
DOWN THE RABBIT HOLE

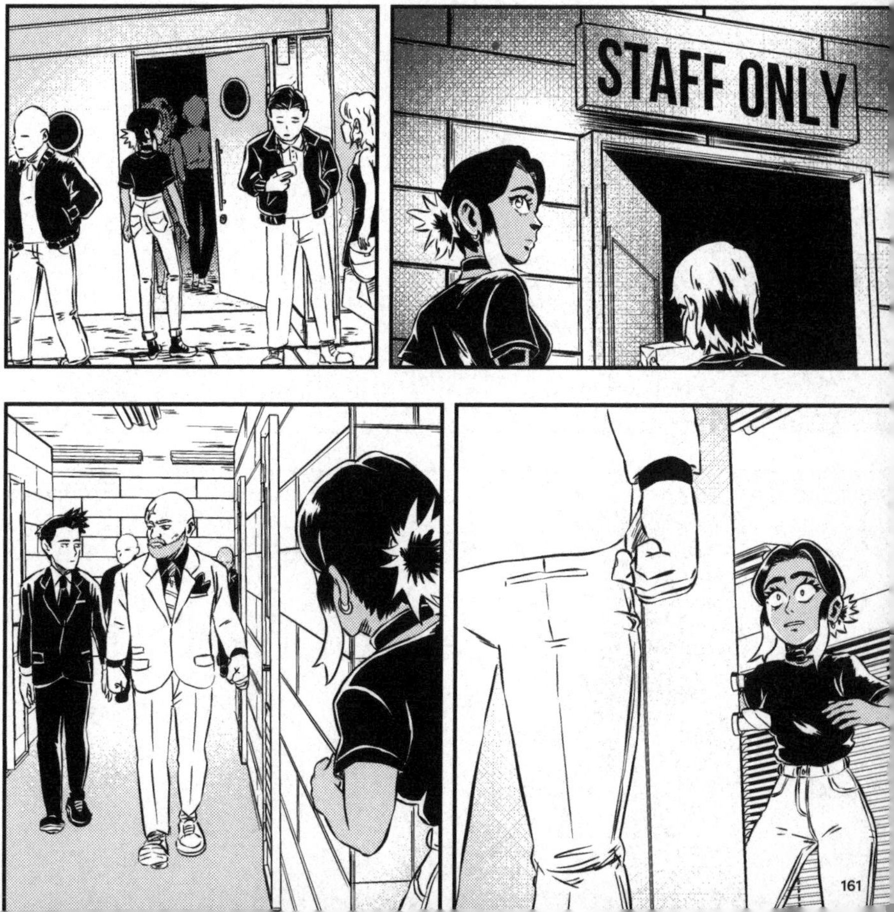
STAFF ONLY

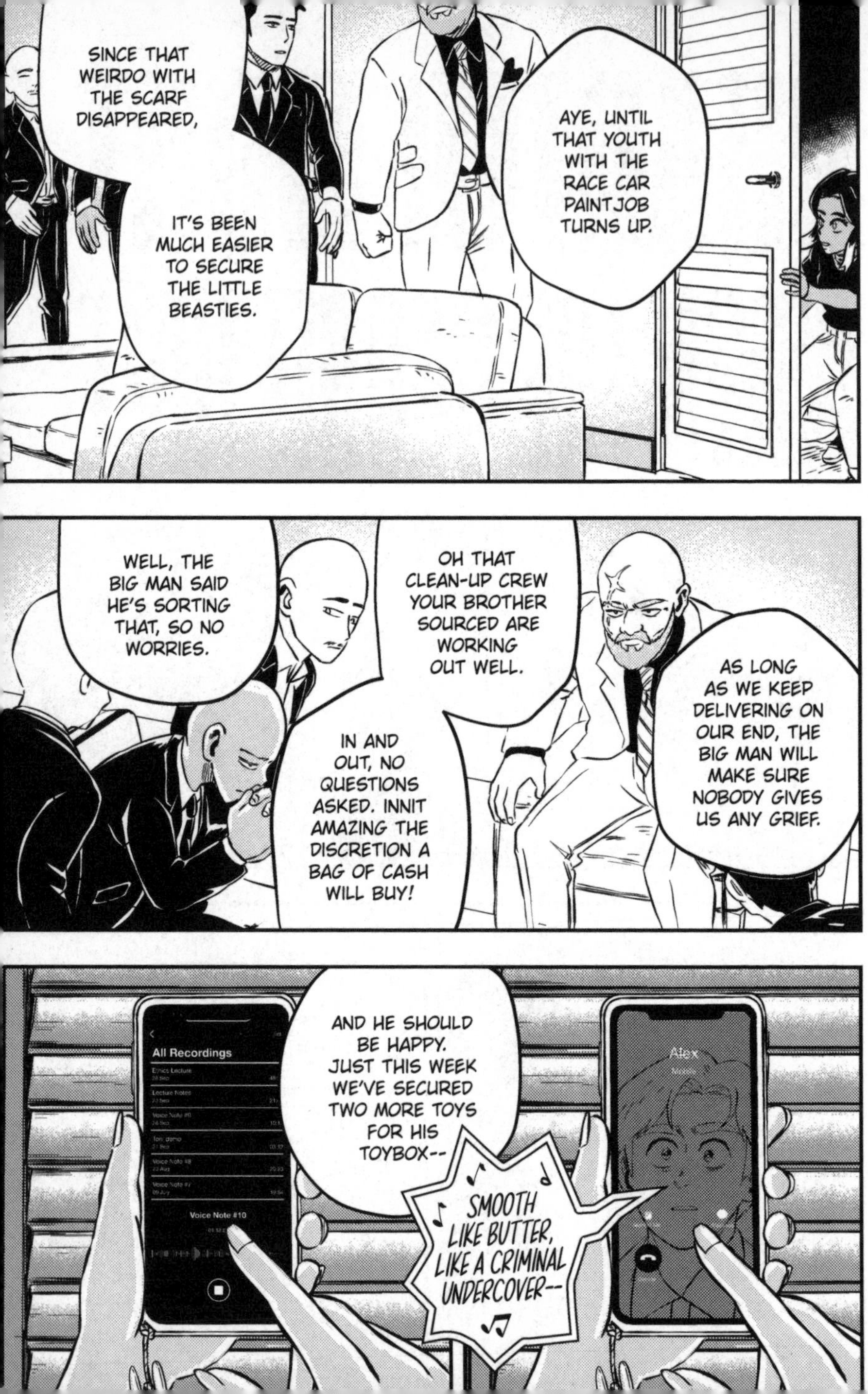
SINCE THAT WEIRDO WITH THE SCARF DISAPPEARED,
IT'S BEEN MUCH EASIER TO SECURE THE LITTLE BEASTIES.
AYE, UNTIL THAT YOUTH WITH THE RACE CAR PAINTJOB TURNS UP.
WELL, THE BIG MAN SAID HE'S SORTING THAT, SO NO WORRIES.
OH THAT CLEAN-UP CREW YOUR BROTHER SOURCED ARE WORKING OUT WELL.
IN AND OUT, NO QUESTIONS ASKED. INNIT AMAZING THE DISCRETION A BAG OF CASH WILL BUY!
AS LONG AS WE KEEP DELIVERING ON OUR END, THE BIG MAN WILL MAKE SURE NOBODY GIVES US ANY GRIEF.
All Recordings
Voice Note #10
AND HE SHOULD BE HAPPY. JUST THIS WEEK WE'VE SECURED TWO MORE TOYS FOR HIS TOYBOX--
Alex
SMOOTH LIKE BUTTER, LIKE A CRIMINAL UNDERCOVER--

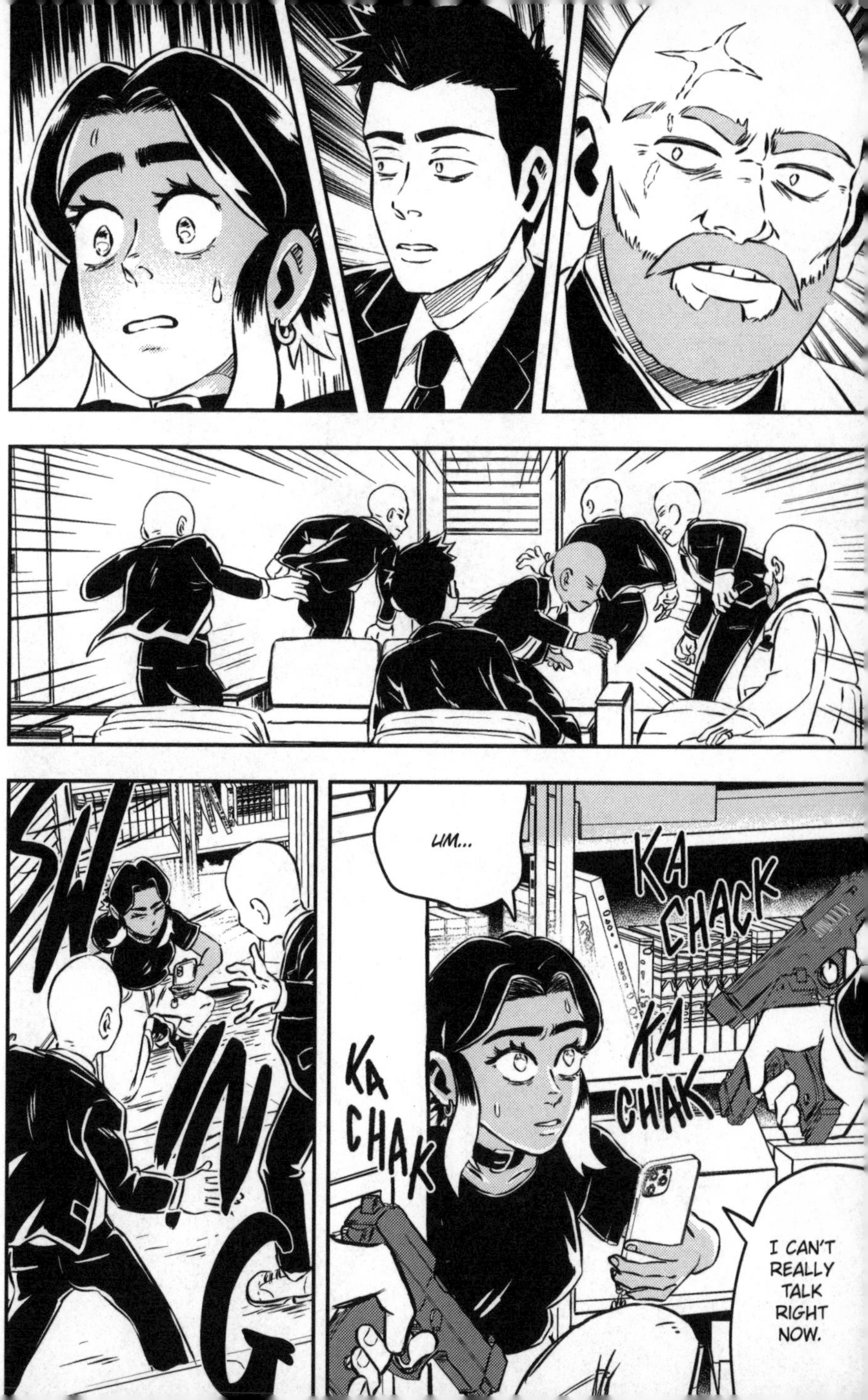
UM...
KA CHACK
KA CHAK
KA CHAK
I CAN'T REALLY TALK RIGHT NOW.

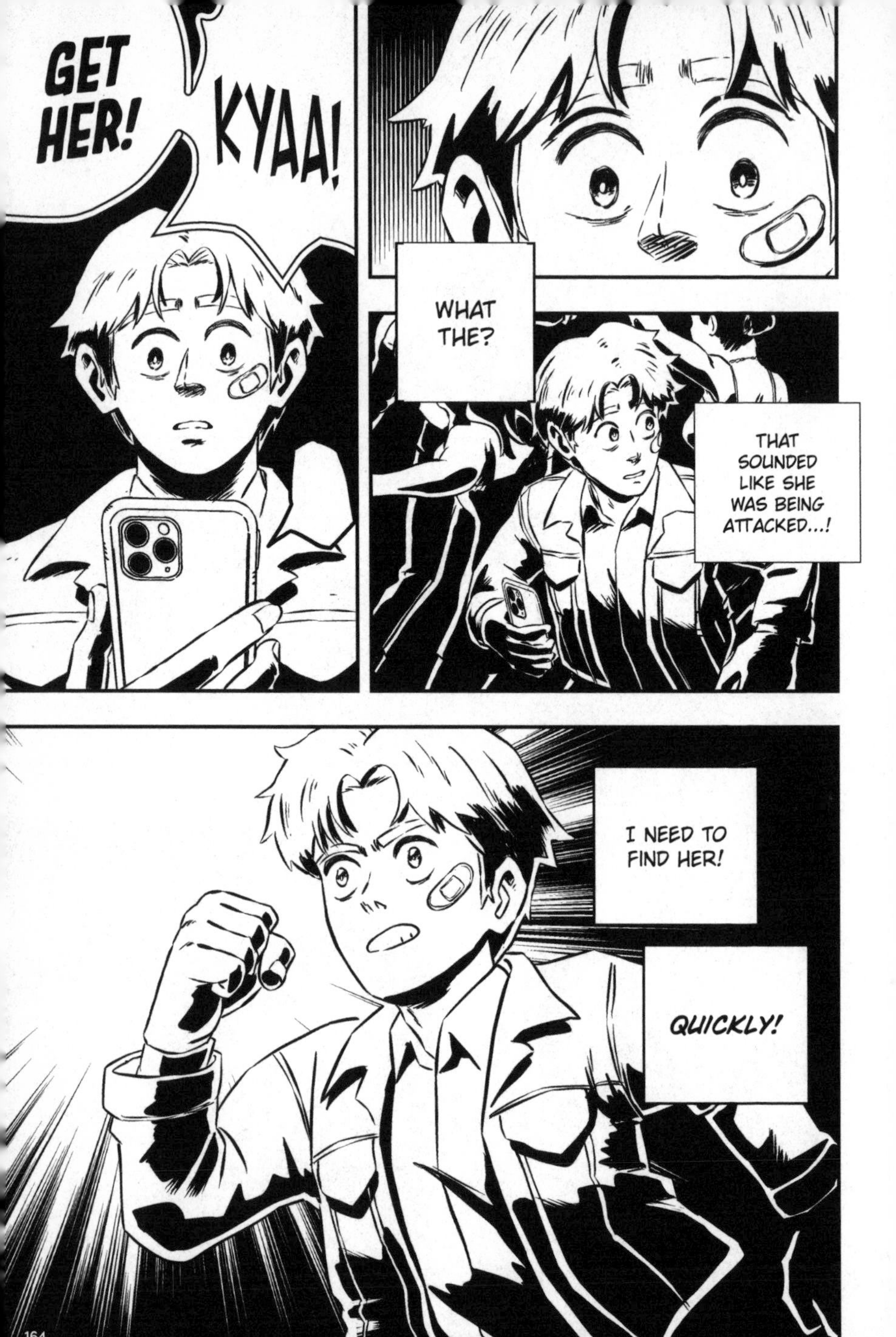
GET HER!
KYAA!
WHAT THE?
THAT SOUNDED LIKE SHE WAS BEING ATTACKED...!
I NEED TO FIND HER!
QUICKLY!

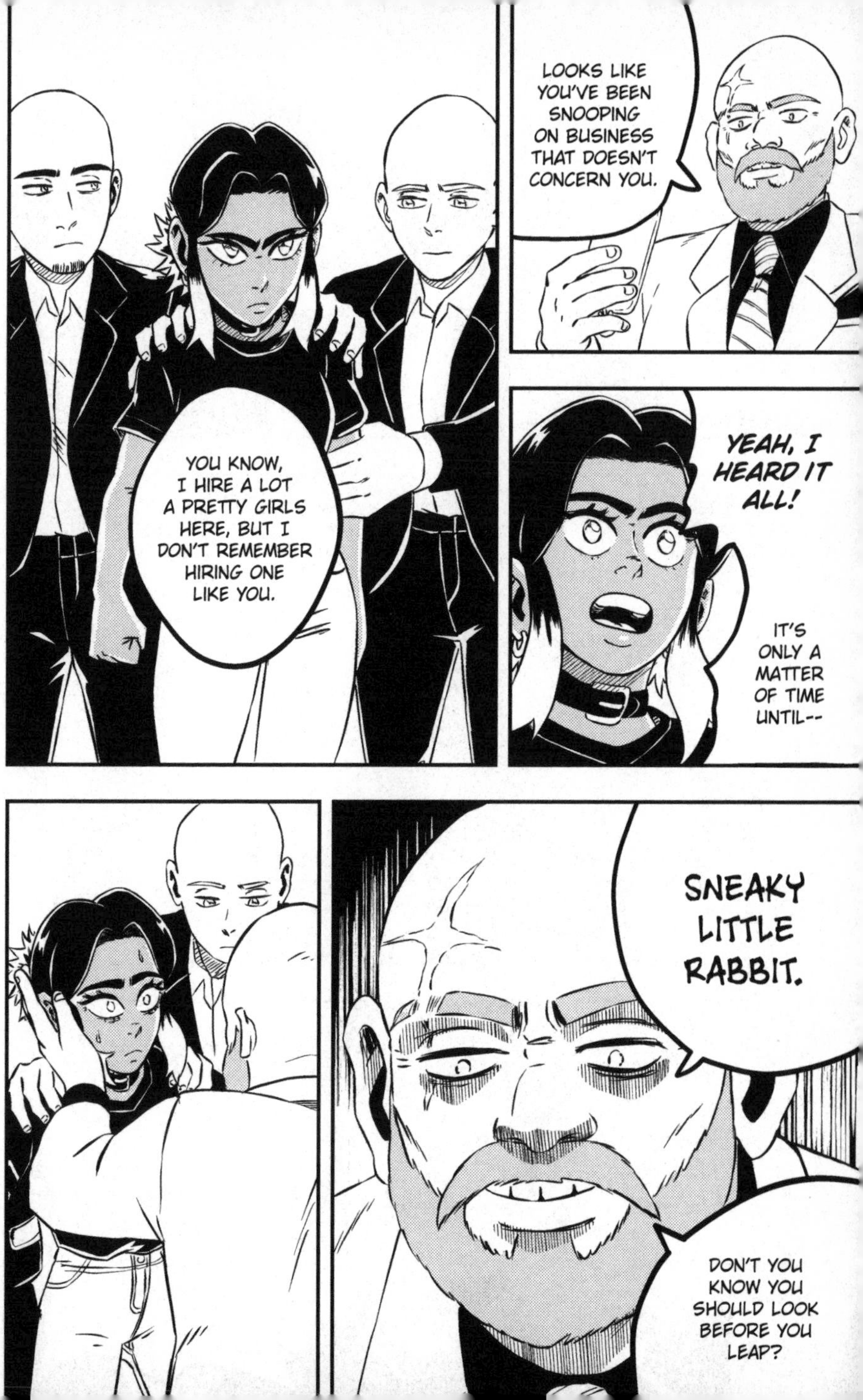
LOOKS LIKE YOU'VE BEEN SNOOPING ON BUSINESS THAT DOESN'T CONCERN YOU.
YOU KNOW, I HIRE A LOT A PRETTY GIRLS HERE, BUT I DON'T REMEMBER HIRING ONE LIKE YOU.
YEAH, I HEARD IT ALL!
IT'S ONLY A MATTER OF TIME UNTIL--
SNEAKY LITTLE RABBIT.
DON'T YOU KNOW YOU SHOULD LOOK BEFORE YOU LEAP?

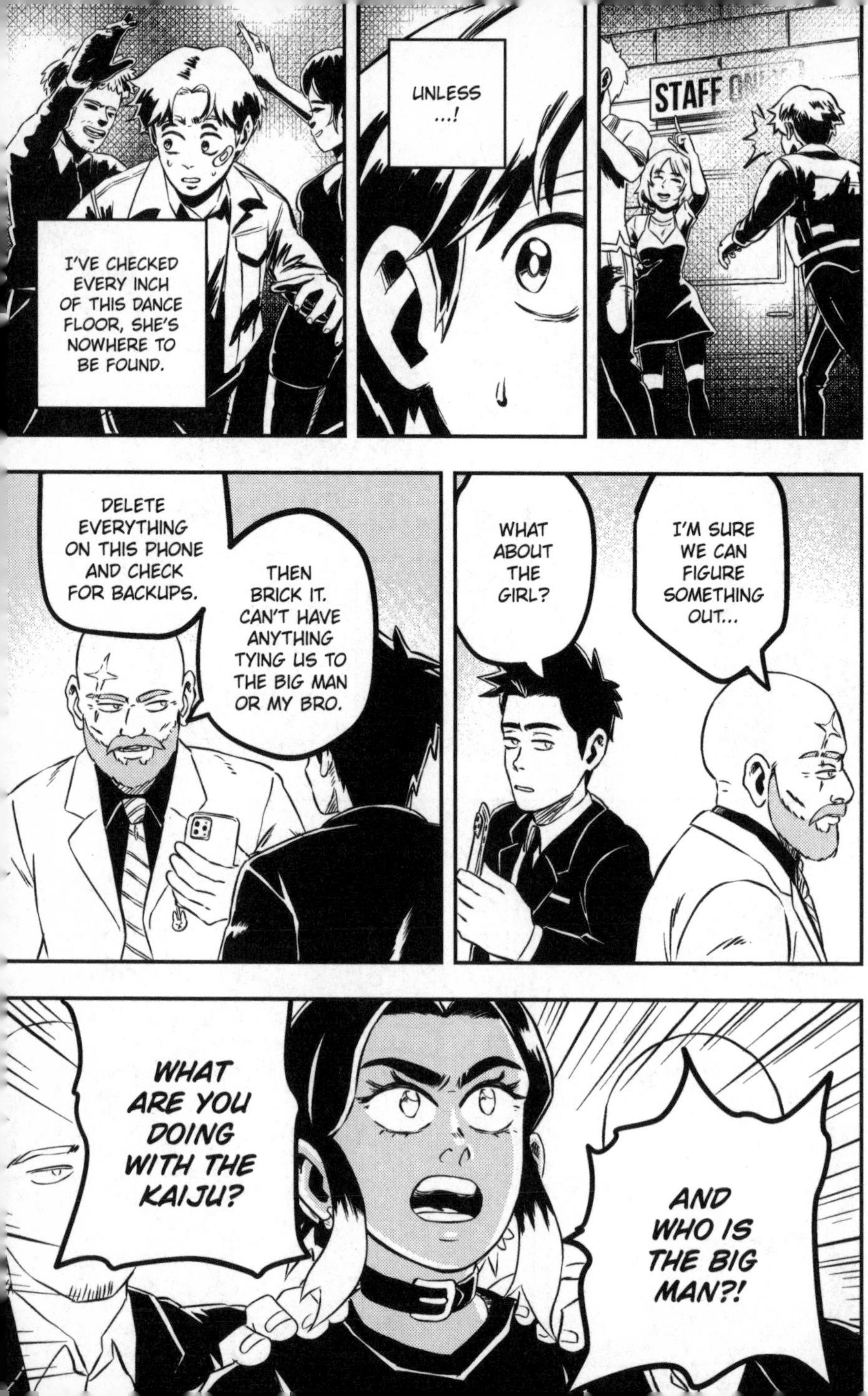
I'VE CHECKED EVERY INCH OF THIS DANCE FLOOR, SHE'S NOWHERE TO BE FOUND.
UNLESS ...!
STAFF
DELETE EVERYTHING ON THIS PHONE AND CHECK FOR BACKUPS.
THEN BRICK IT. CAN'T HAVE ANYTHING TYING US TO THE BIG MAN OR MY BRO.
WHAT ABOUT THE GIRL?
I'M SURE WE CAN FIGURE SOMETHING OUT...
WHAT ARE YOU DOING WITH THE KAIJU?
AND WHO IS THE BIG MAN?!

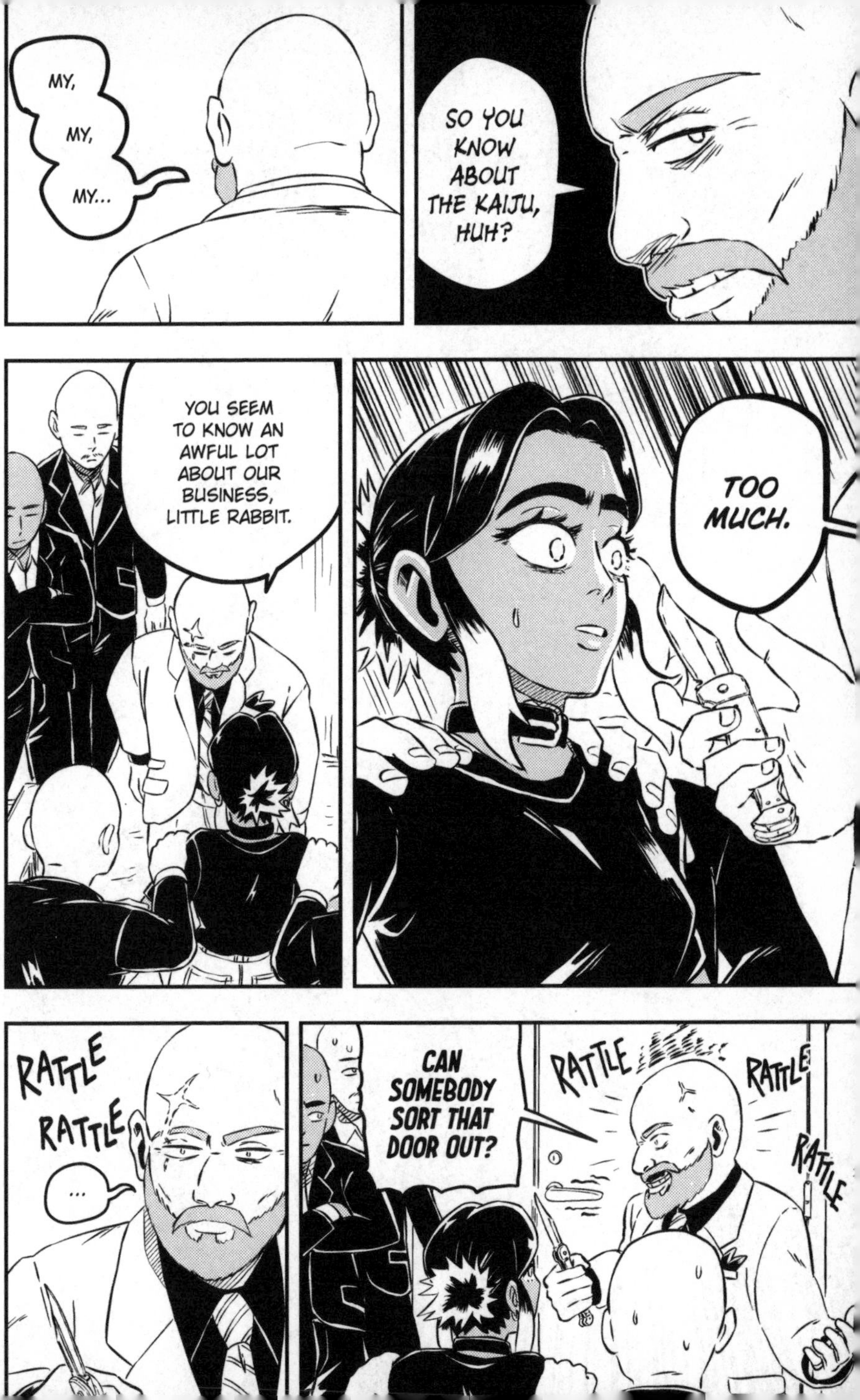
MY,
MY,
MY...
SO YOU KNOW ABOUT THE KAIJU, HUH?
YOU SEEM TO KNOW AN AWFUL LOT ABOUT OUR BUSINESS, LITTLE RABBIT.
TOO MUCH.
RATTLE
RATTLE
...
CAN SOMEBODY SORT THAT DOOR OUT?
RATTLE
RATTLE
RATTLE

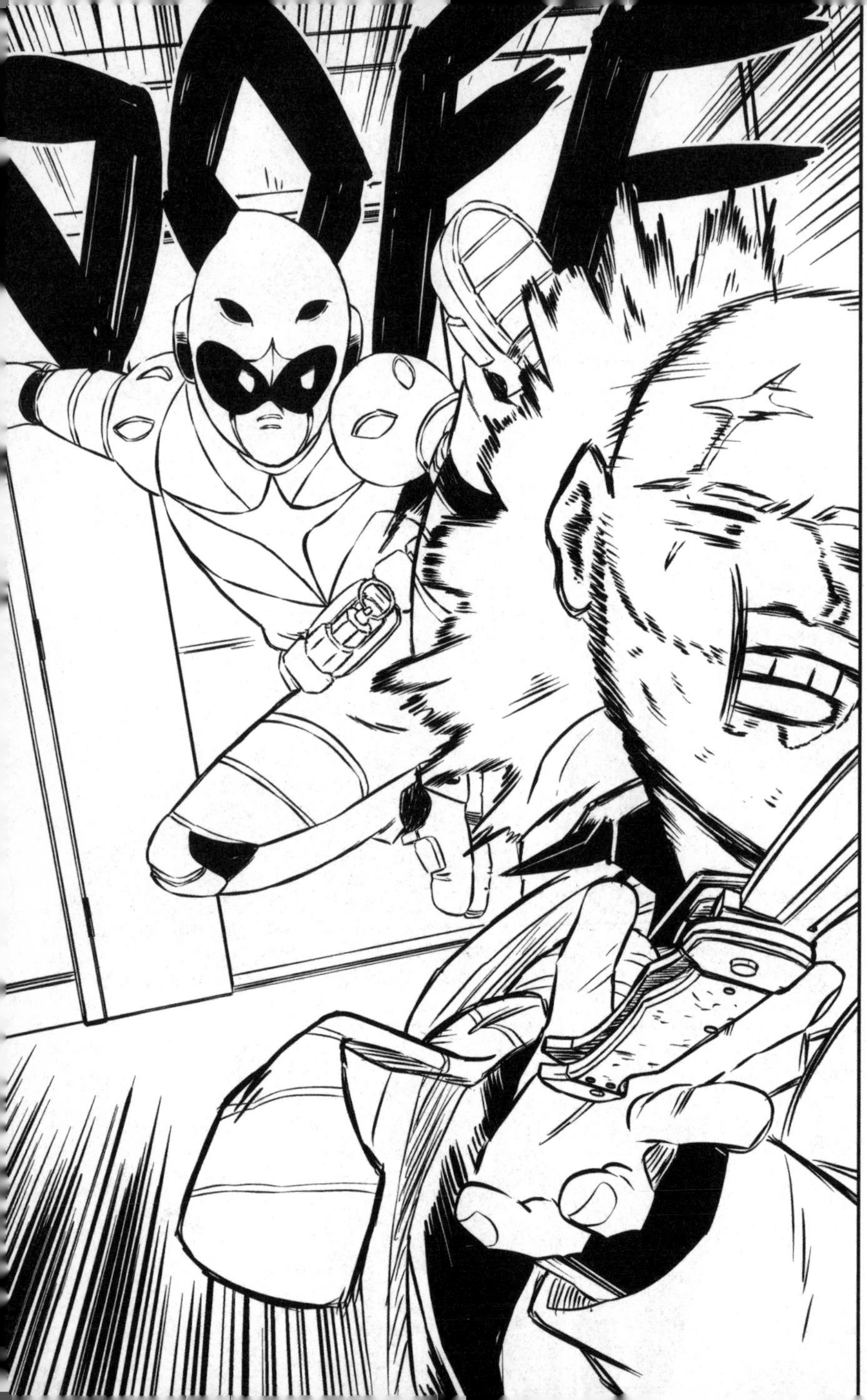
DOFF

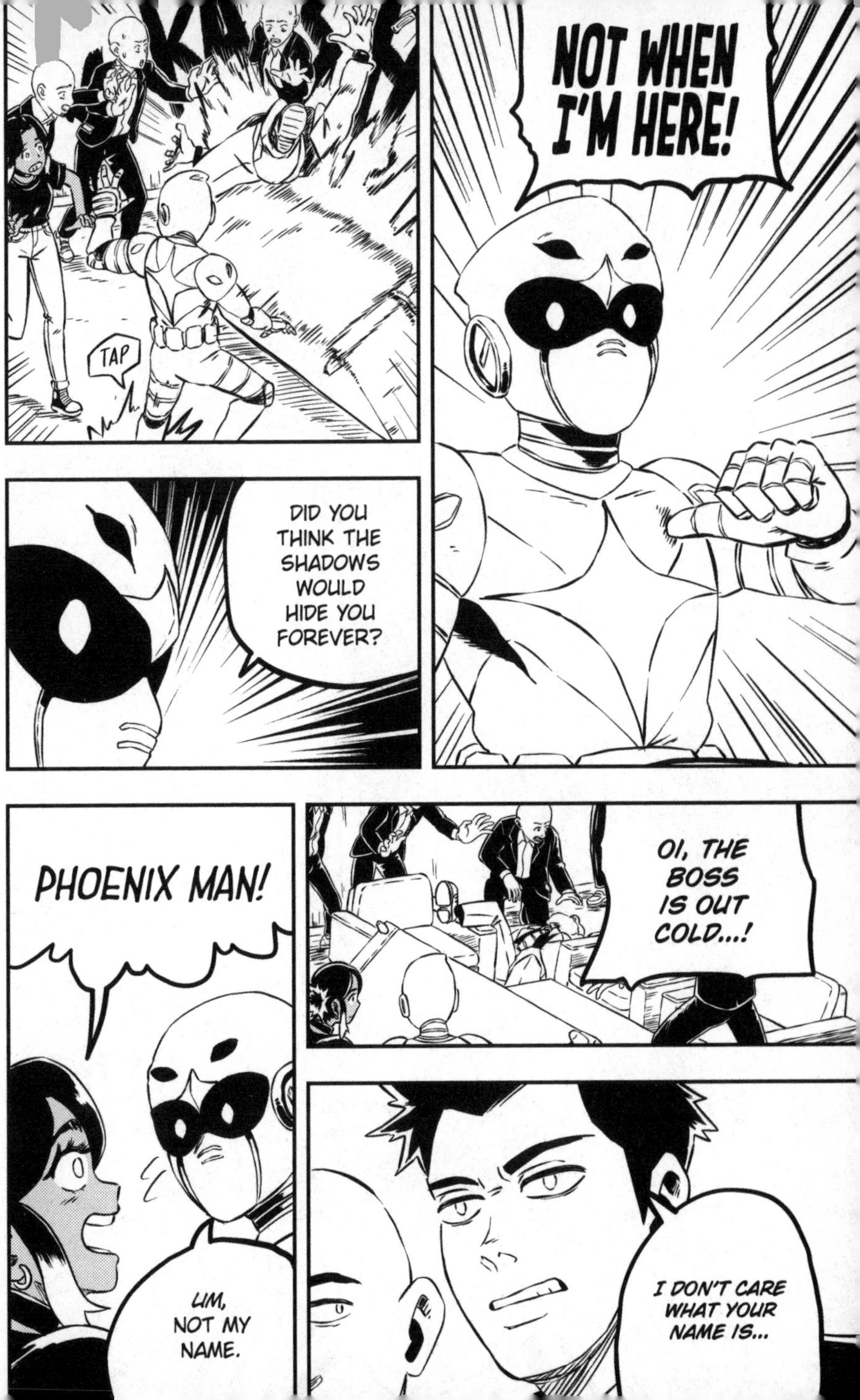
TAP
NOT WHEN I'M HERE!
DID YOU THINK THE SHADOWS WOULD HIDE YOU FOREVER?
PHOENIX MAN!
UM, NOT MY NAME.
OI, THE BOSS IS OUT COLD...!
I DON'T CARE WHAT YOUR NAME IS...

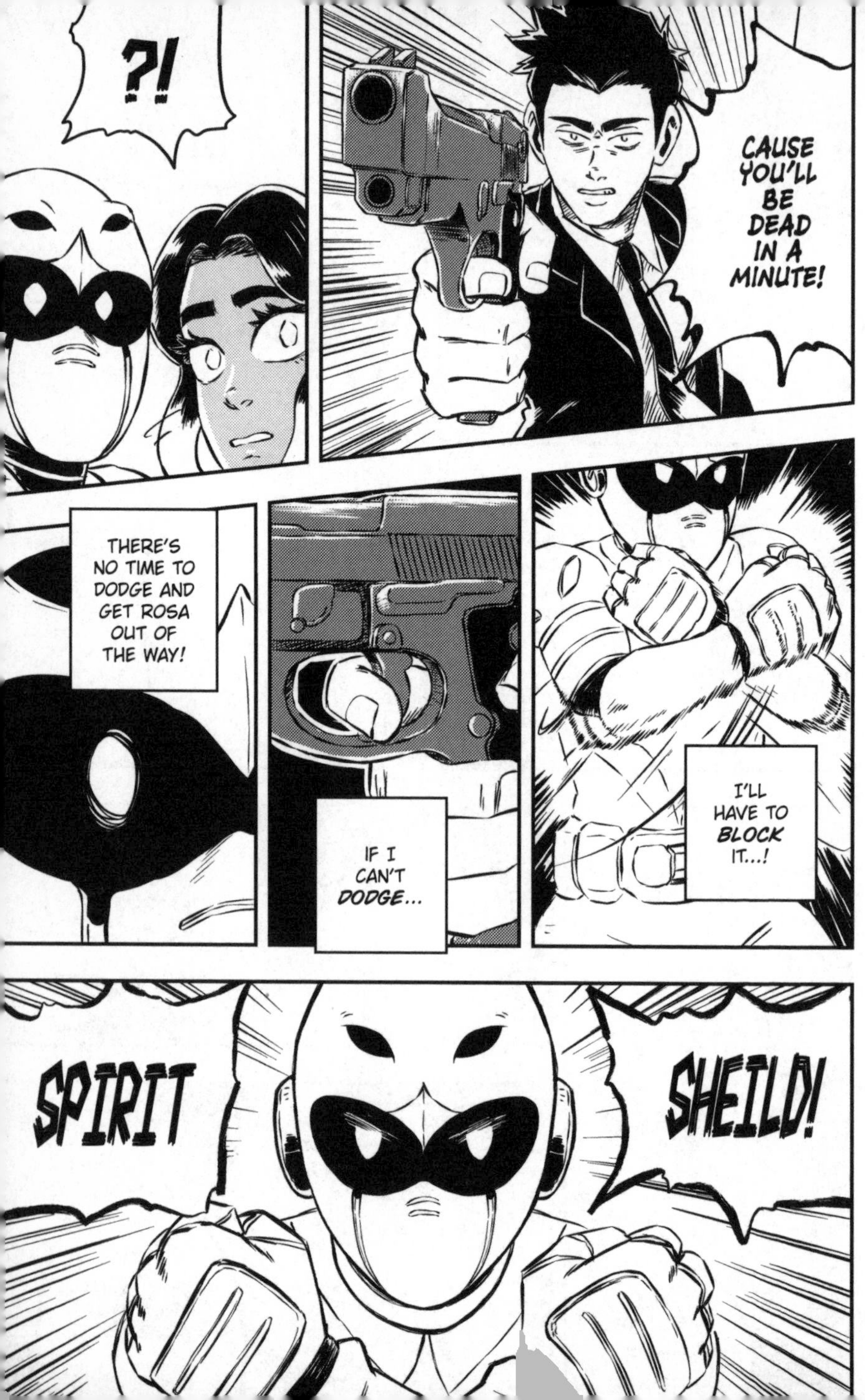
?!
CAUSE YOU'LL BE DEAD IN A MINUTE!
THERE'S NO TIME TO DODGE AND GET ROSA OUT OF THE WAY!
IF I CAN'T DODGE...
I'LL HAVE TO BLOCK IT...!
SPIRIT
SHEILD!

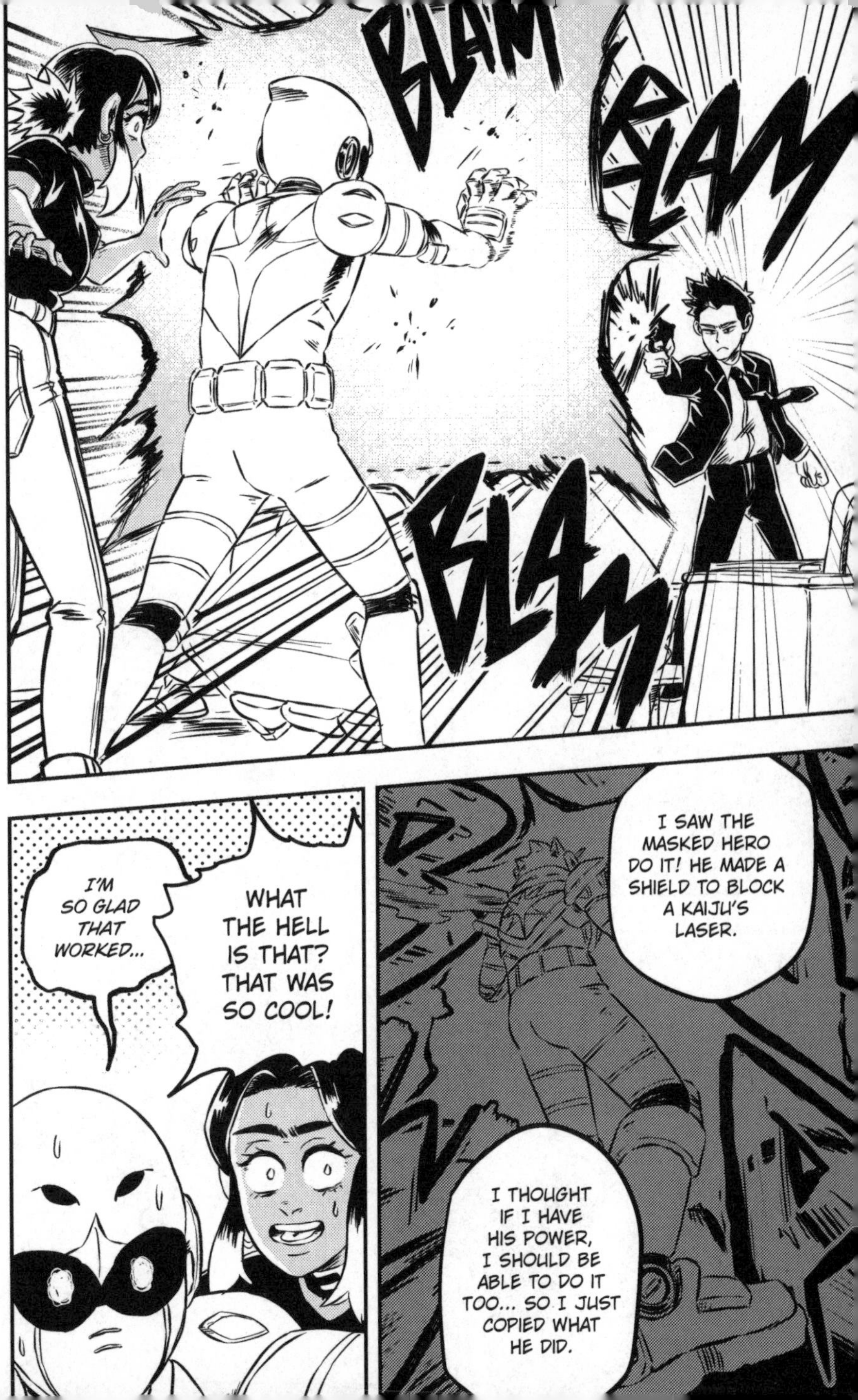
BLAM
BLAM
BLAM
I SAW THE MASKED HERO DO IT! HE MADE A SHIELD TO BLOCK A KAIJU'S LASER.
WHAT THE HELL IS THAT? THAT WAS SO COOL!
I'M SO GLAD THAT WORKED...
I THOUGHT IF I HAVE HIS POWER, I SHOULD BE ABLE TO DO IT TOO... SO I JUST COPIED WHAT HE DID.

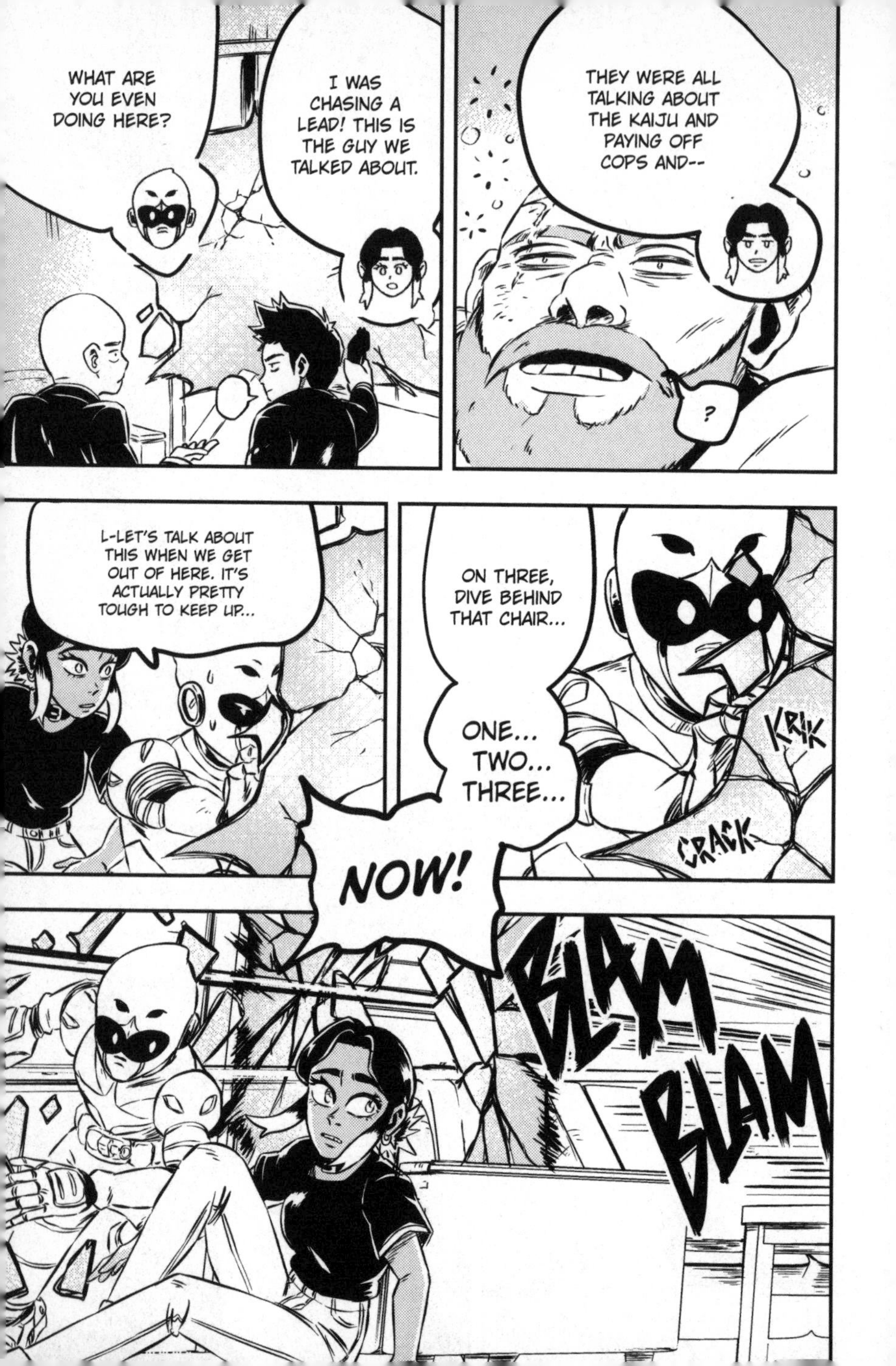
WHAT ARE YOU EVEN DOING HERE?
I WAS CHASING A LEAD! THIS IS THE GUY WE TALKED ABOUT.
THEY WERE ALL TALKING ABOUT THE KAIJU AND PAYING OFF COPS AND--
?
L-LET'S TALK ABOUT THIS WHEN WE GET OUT OF HERE. IT'S ACTUALLY PRETTY TOUGH TO KEEP UP...
ON THREE, DIVE BEHIND THAT CHAIR...
ONE... TWO... THREE...
KRIK
CRACK
NOW!
BLAM
BLAM

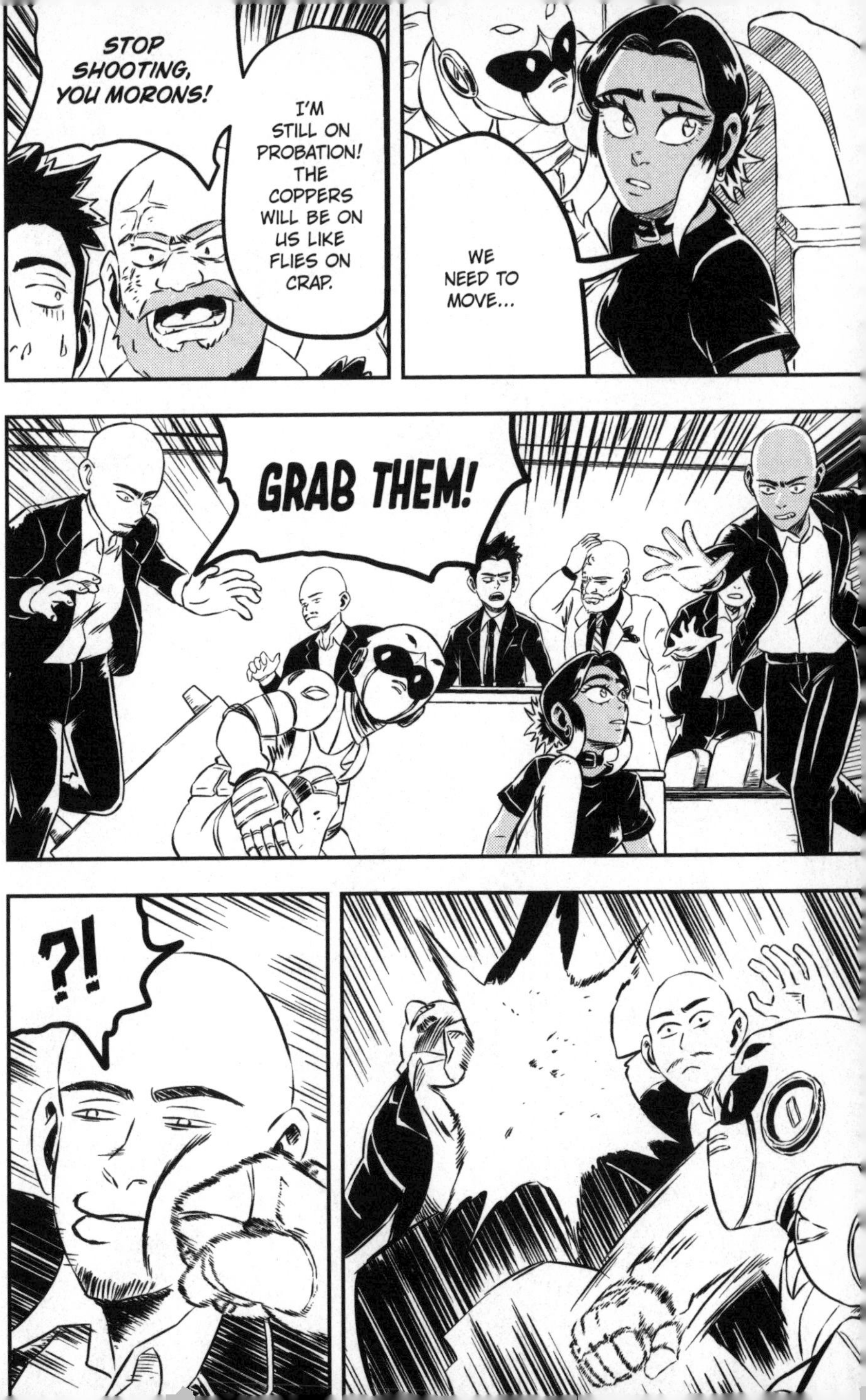
STOP SHOOTING, YOU MORONS!
I'M STILL ON PROBATION! THE COPPERS WILL BE ON US LIKE FLIES ON CRAP.
WE NEED TO MOVE...
GRAB THEM!
?!

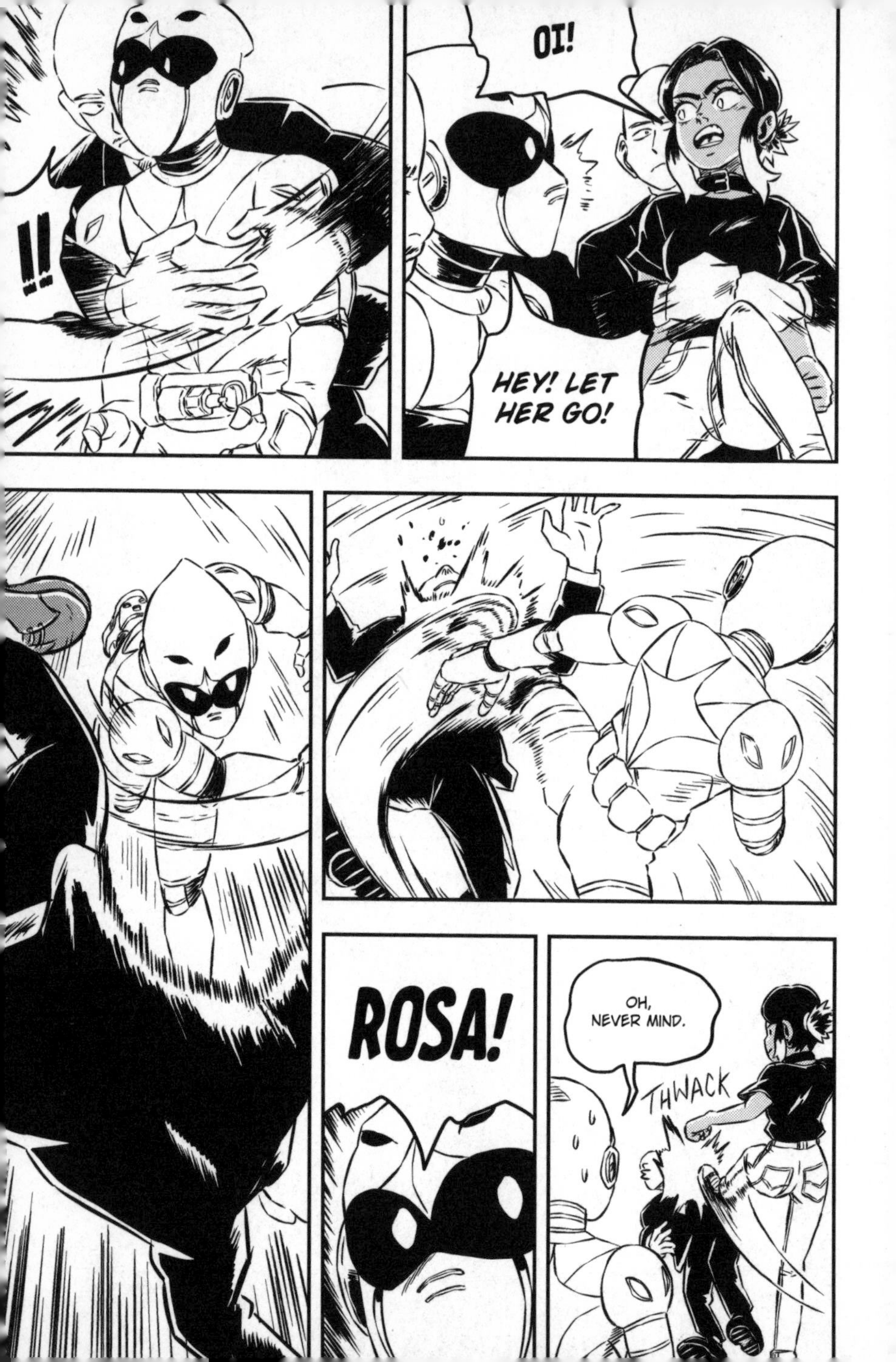
!!
OI!
HEY! LET HER GO!
ROSA!
OH, NEVER MIND.
THWACK

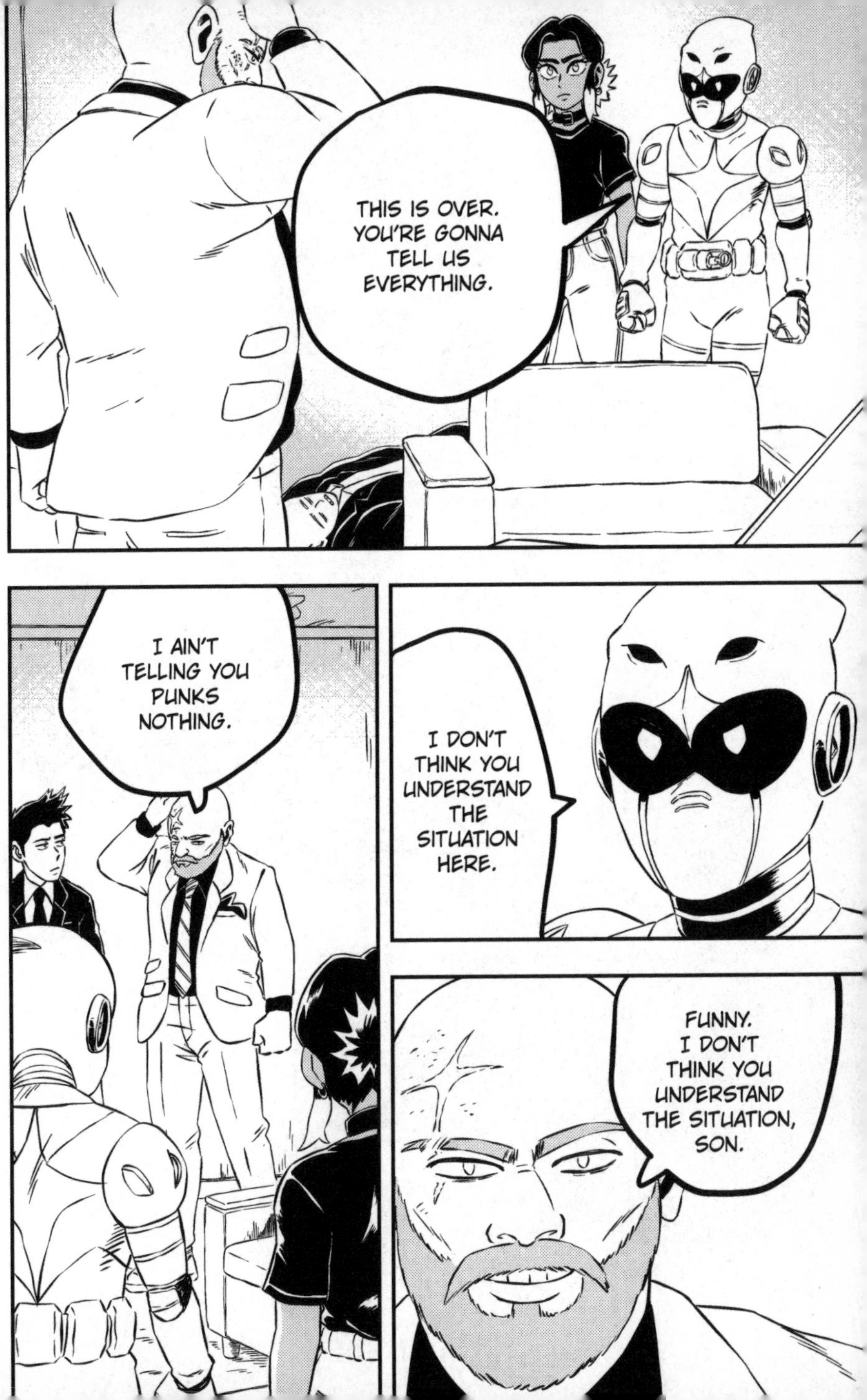
THIS IS OVER. YOU'RE GONNA TELL US EVERYTHING.
I AIN'T TELLING YOU PUNKS NOTHING.
I DON'T THINK YOU UNDERSTAND THE SITUATION HERE.
FUNNY. I DON'T THINK YOU UNDERSTAND THE SITUATION, SON.

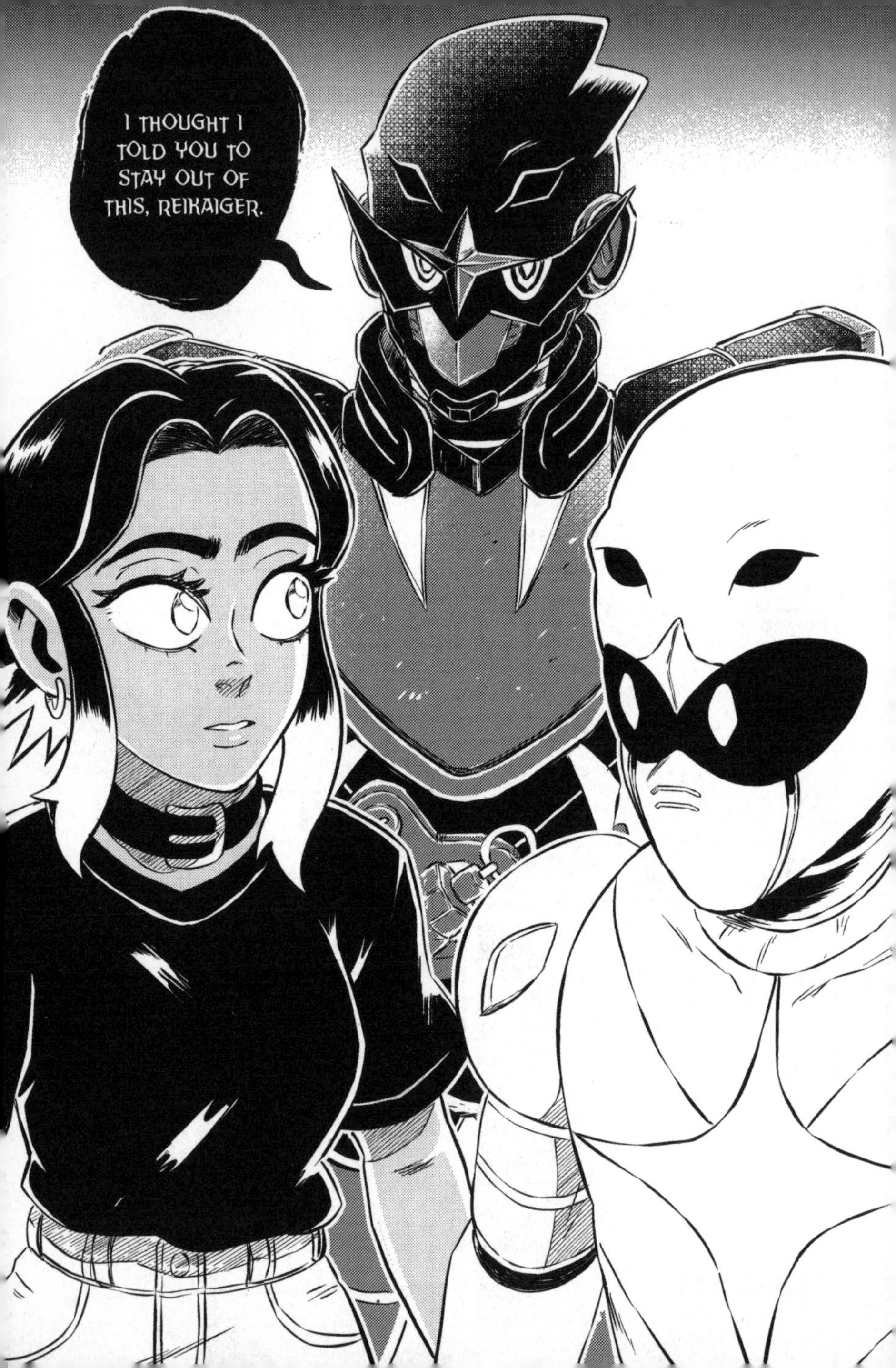
I THOUGHT I TOLD YOU TO STAY OUT OF THIS, REIKAIGER.

HENSHIN!

CHAPTER NINE

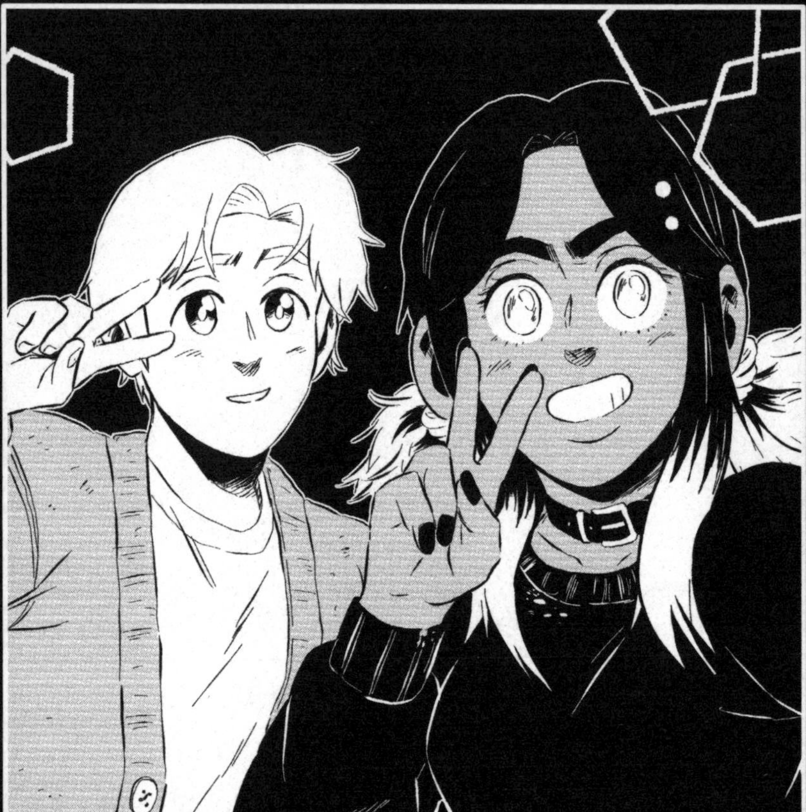

BRAWL

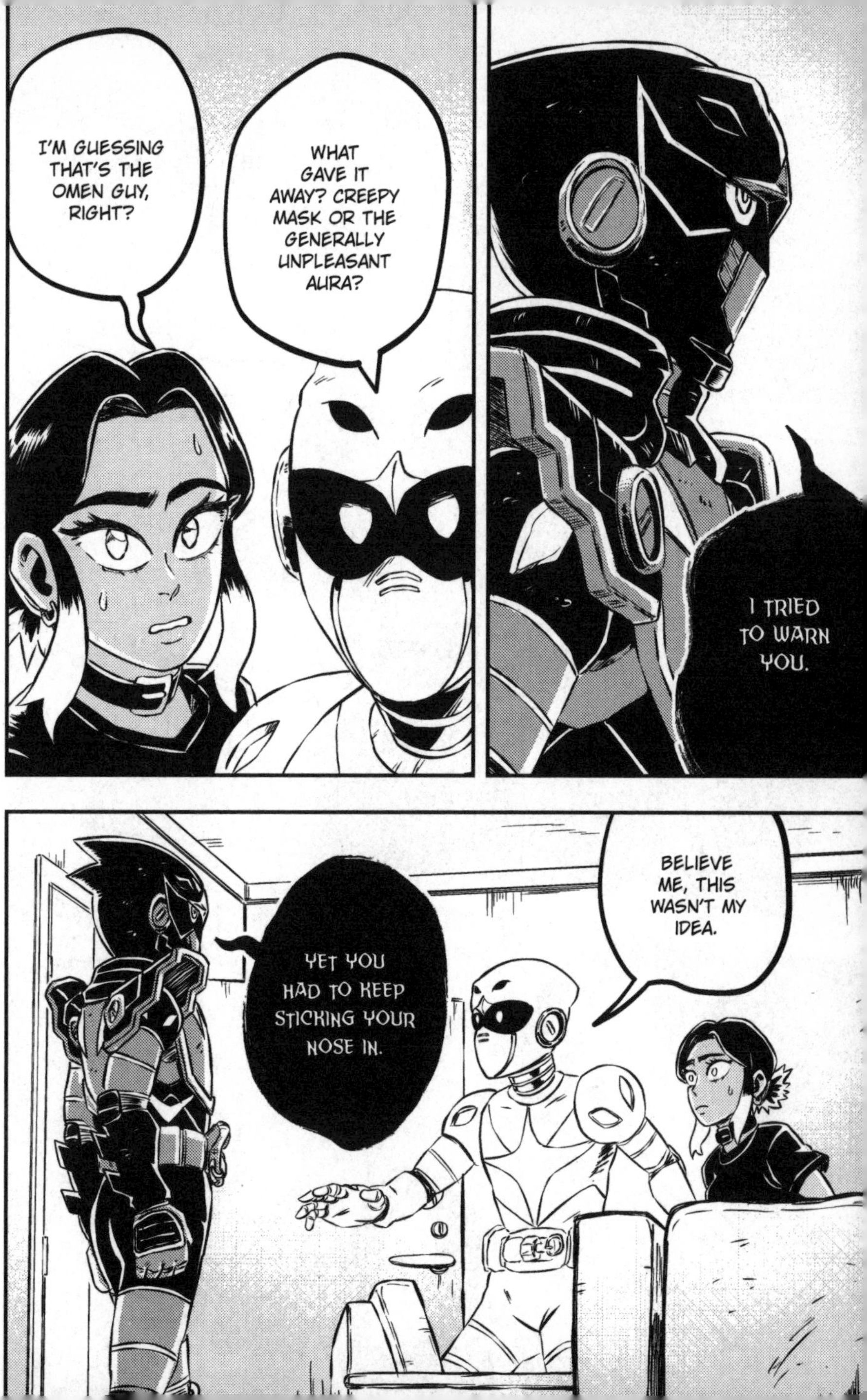
I'M GUESSING THAT'S THE OMEN GUY, RIGHT?
WHAT GAVE IT AWAY? CREEPY MASK OR THE GENERALLY UNPLEASANT AURA?
I TRIED TO WARN YOU.
BELIEVE ME, THIS WASN'T MY IDEA.
YET YOU HAD TO KEEP STICKING YOUR NOSE IN.

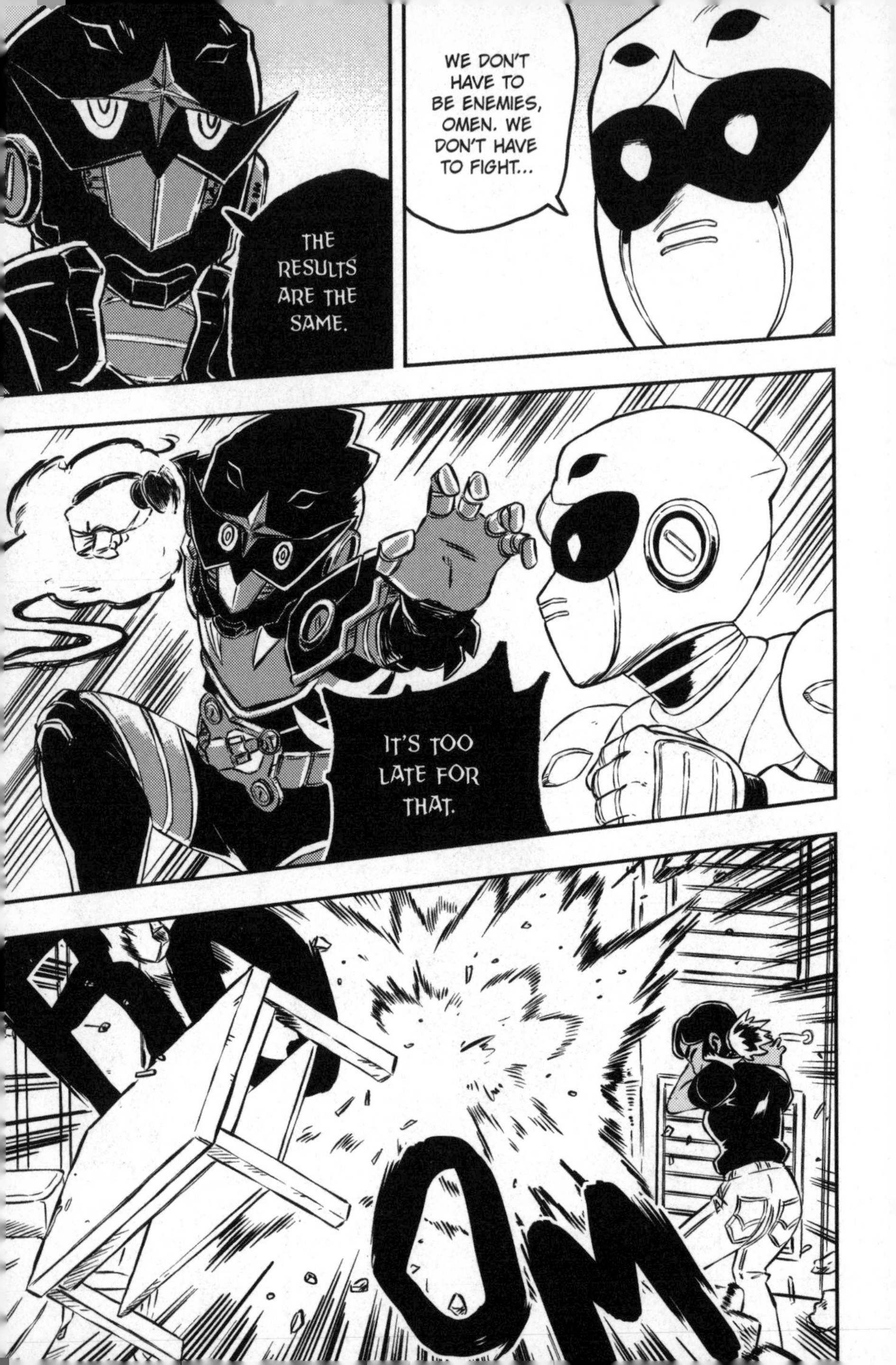
THE RESULTS ARE THE SAME.
WE DON'T HAVE TO BE ENEMIES, OMEN. WE DON'T HAVE TO FIGHT...
IT'S TOO LATE FOR THAT.

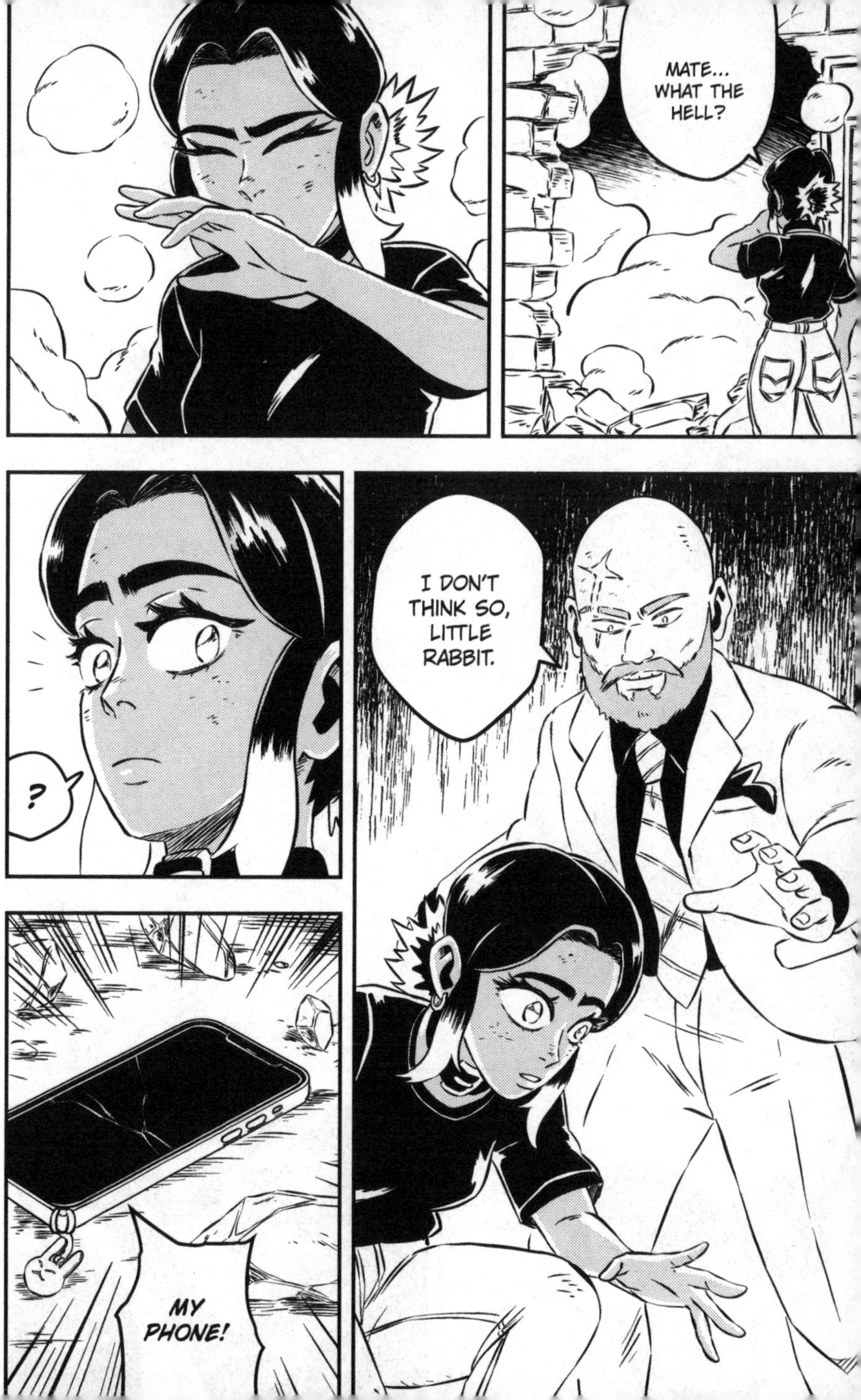
MATE... WHAT THE HELL?
?
I DON'T THINK SO, LITTLE RABBIT.
MY PHONE!

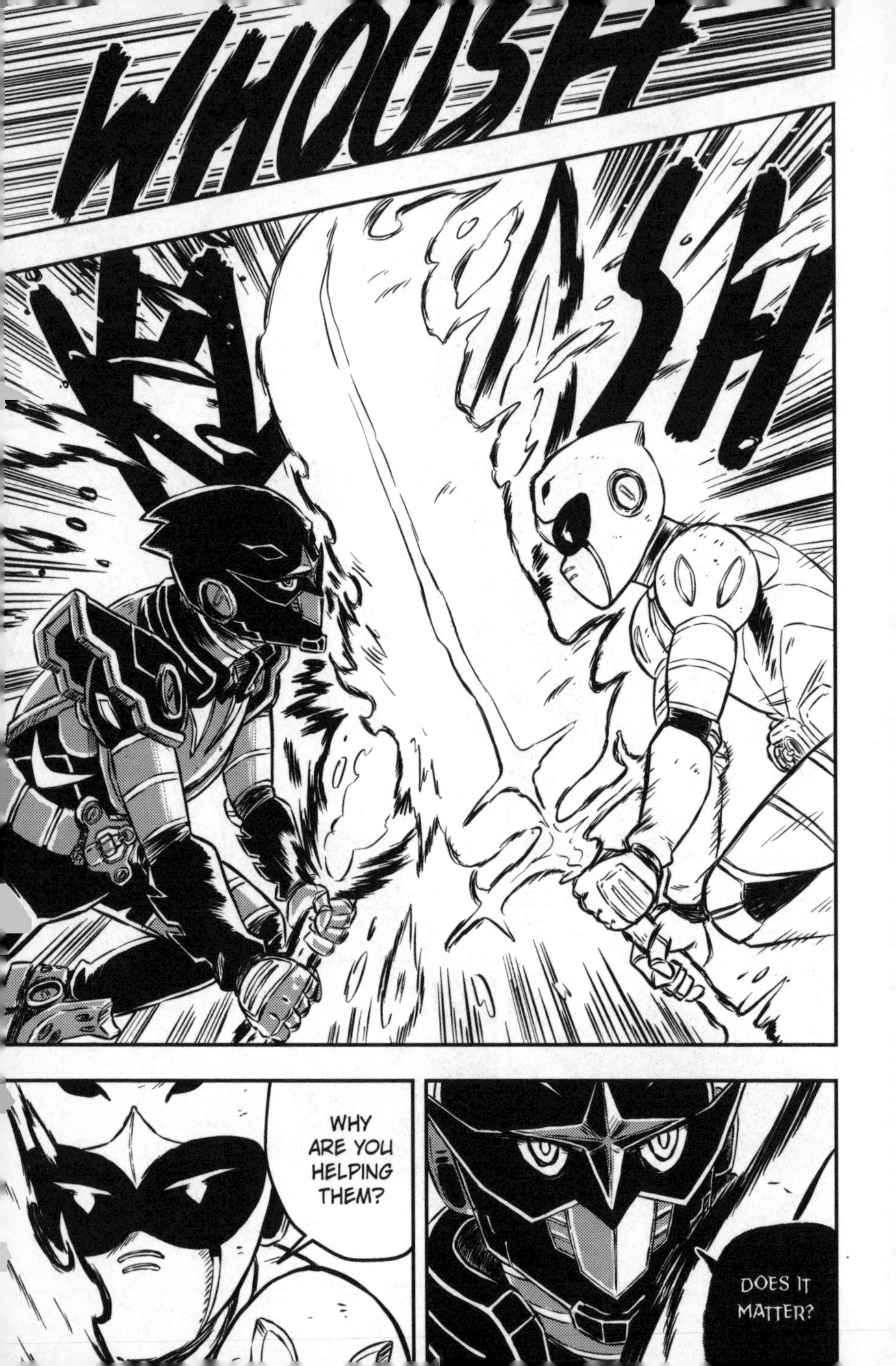
WHOOSH
KLASH
WHY ARE YOU HELPING THEM?
DOES IT MATTER?

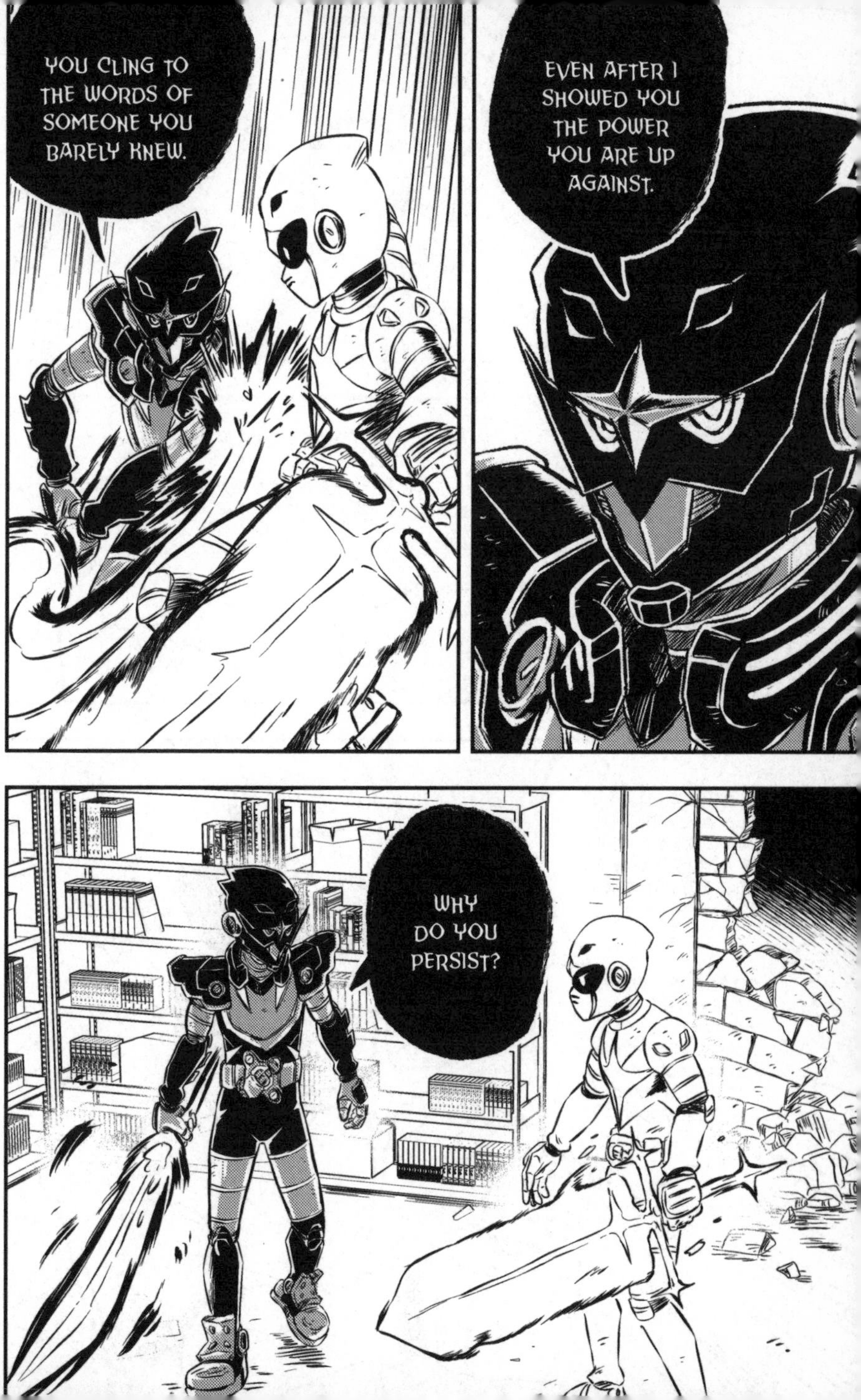
YOU CLING TO THE WORDS OF SOMEONE YOU BARELY KNEW.
EVEN AFTER I SHOWED YOU THE POWER YOU ARE UP AGAINST.
WHY DO YOU PERSIST?

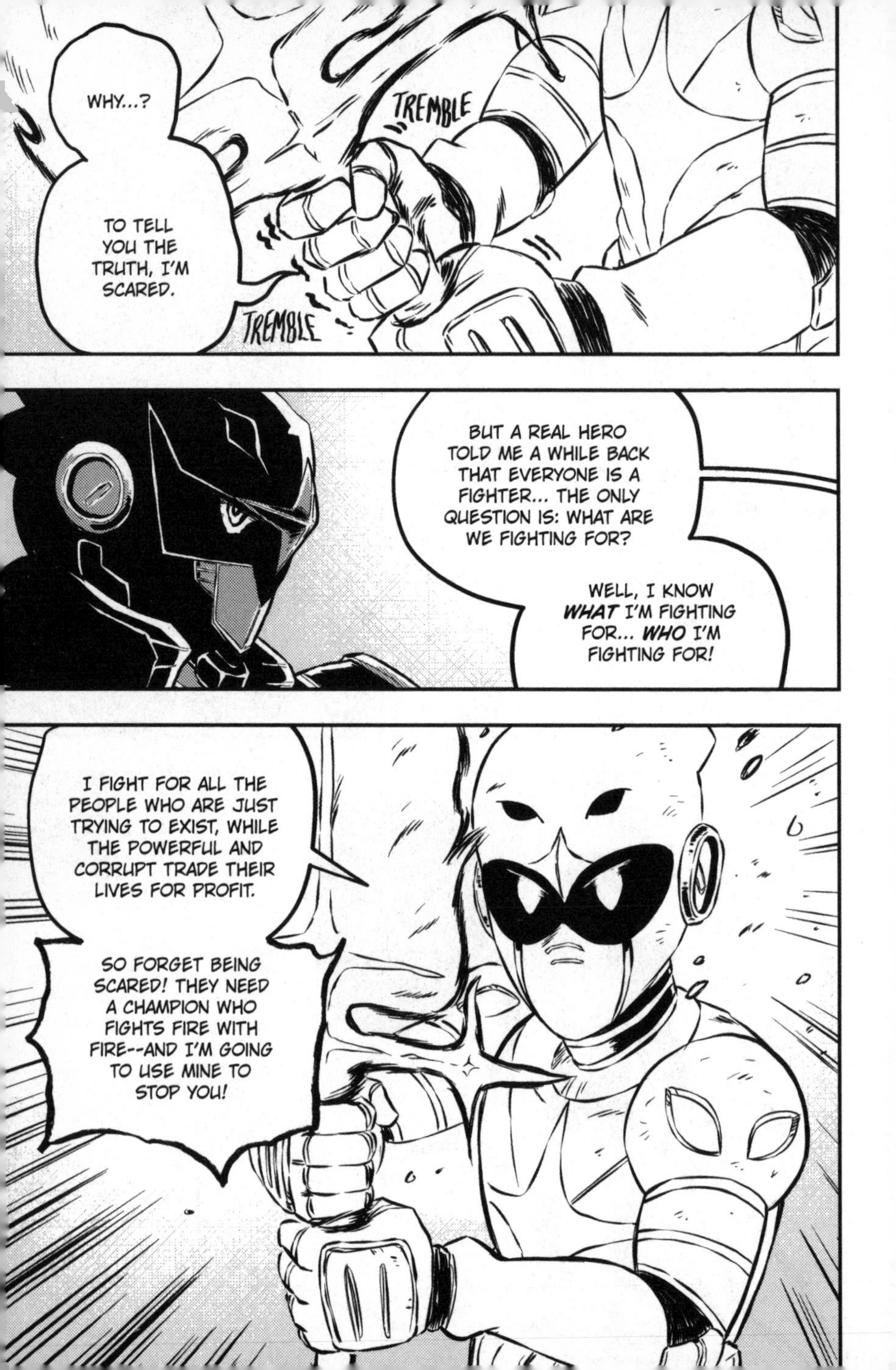
WHY...?
TREMBLE
TO TELL YOU THE TRUTH, I'M SCARED.
TREMBLE
BUT A REAL HERO TOLD ME A WHILE BACK THAT EVERYONE IS A FIGHTER... THE ONLY QUESTION IS: WHAT ARE WE FIGHTING FOR?
WELL, I KNOW *WHAT* I'M FIGHTING FOR... *WHO* I'M FIGHTING FOR!
I FIGHT FOR ALL THE PEOPLE WHO ARE JUST TRYING TO EXIST, WHILE THE POWERFUL AND CORRUPT TRADE THEIR LIVES FOR PROFIT.
SO FORGET BEING SCARED! THEY NEED A CHAMPION WHO FIGHTS FIRE WITH FIRE--AND I'M GOING TO USE MINE TO STOP YOU!

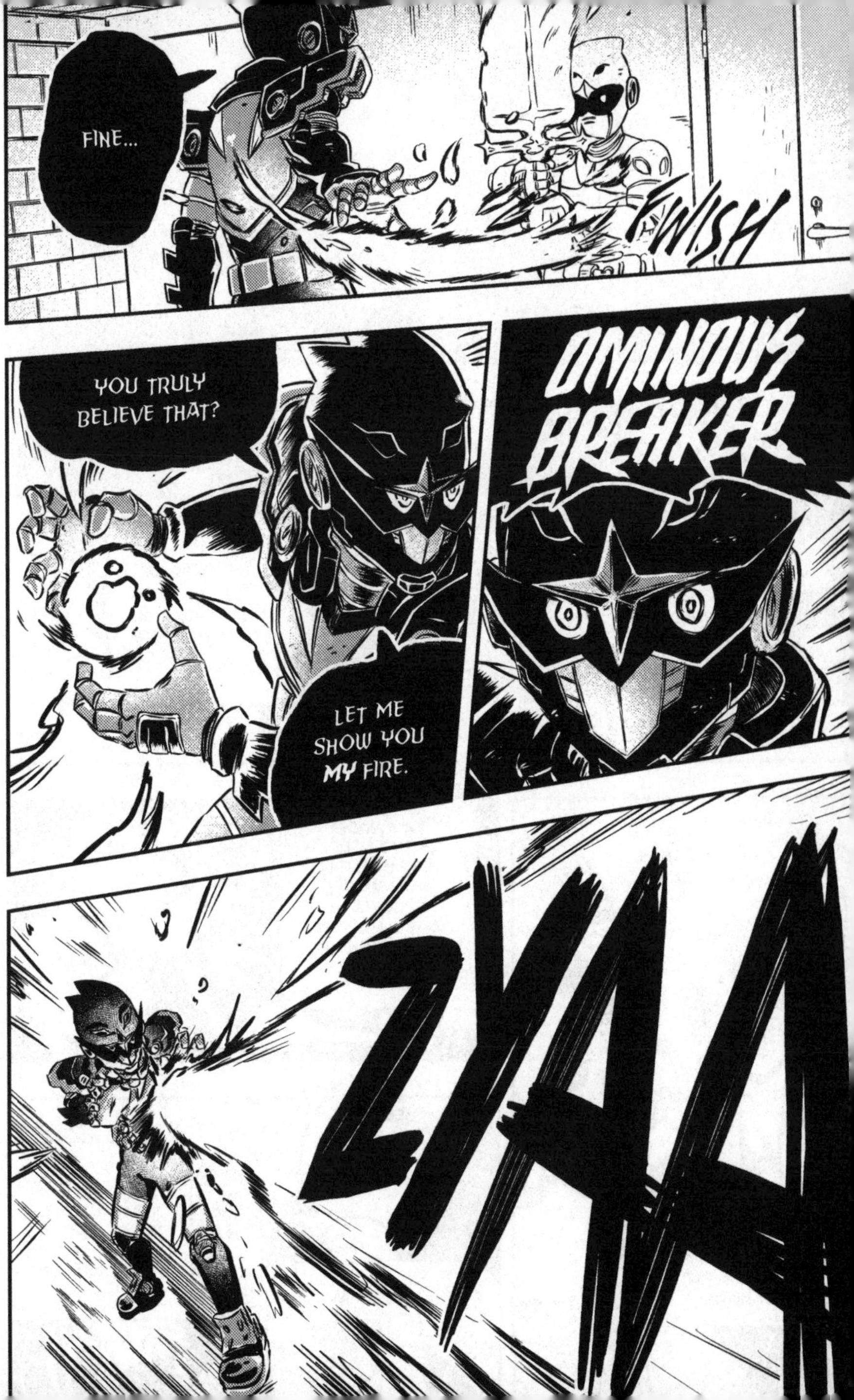
FINE...
FINISH
YOU TRULY BELIEVE THAT?
LET ME SHOW YOU MY FIRE.
OMINOUS BREAKER
ZYAA

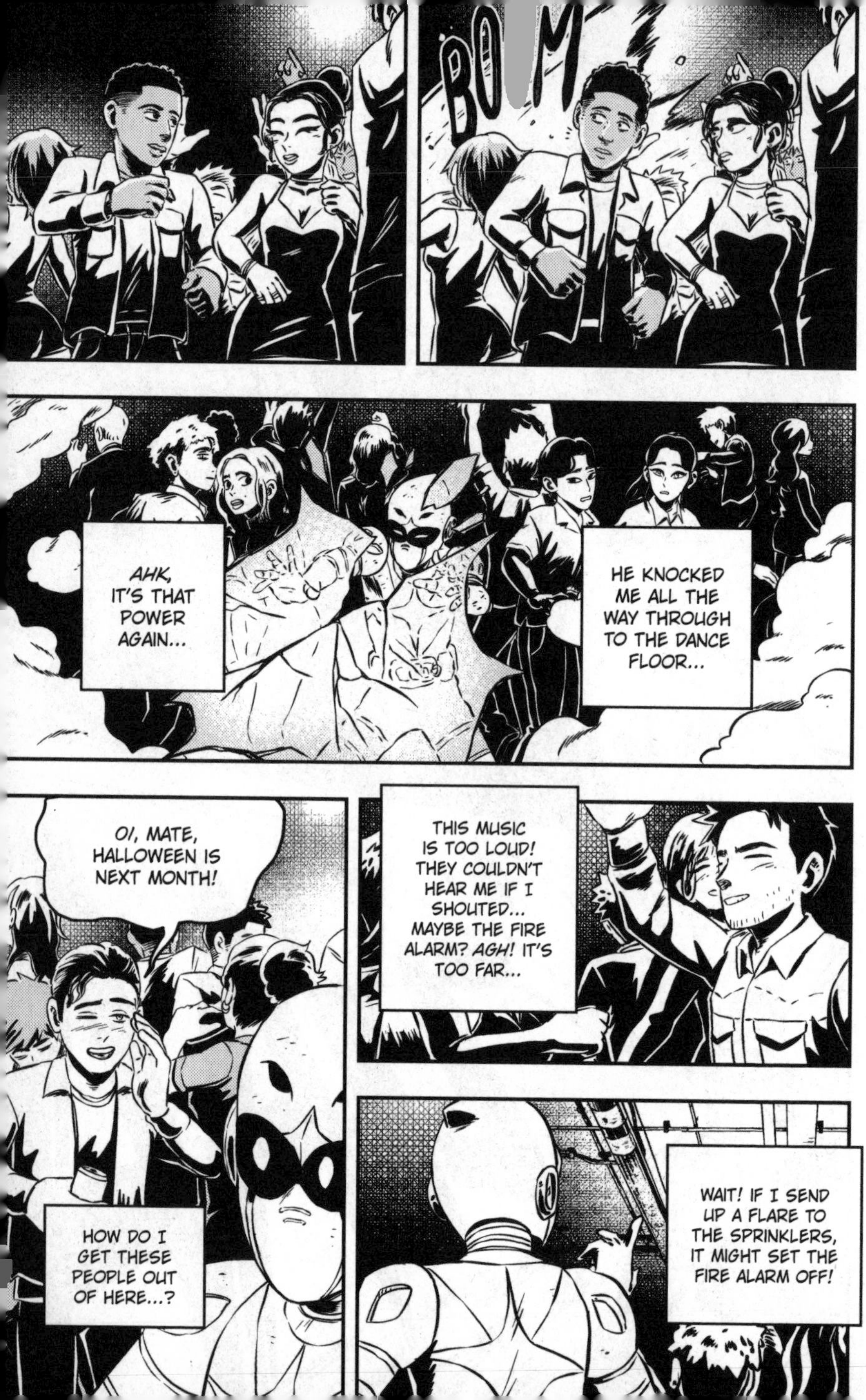
BOOM
AHK, IT'S THAT POWER AGAIN...
HE KNOCKED ME ALL THE WAY THROUGH TO THE DANCE FLOOR...
OI, MATE, HALLOWEEN IS NEXT MONTH!
THIS MUSIC IS TOO LOUD! THEY COULDN'T HEAR ME IF I SHOUTED... MAYBE THE FIRE ALARM? AGH! IT'S TOO FAR...
HOW DO I GET THESE PEOPLE OUT OF HERE...?
WAIT! IF I SEND UP A FLARE TO THE SPRINKLERS, IT MIGHT SET THE FIRE ALARM OFF!

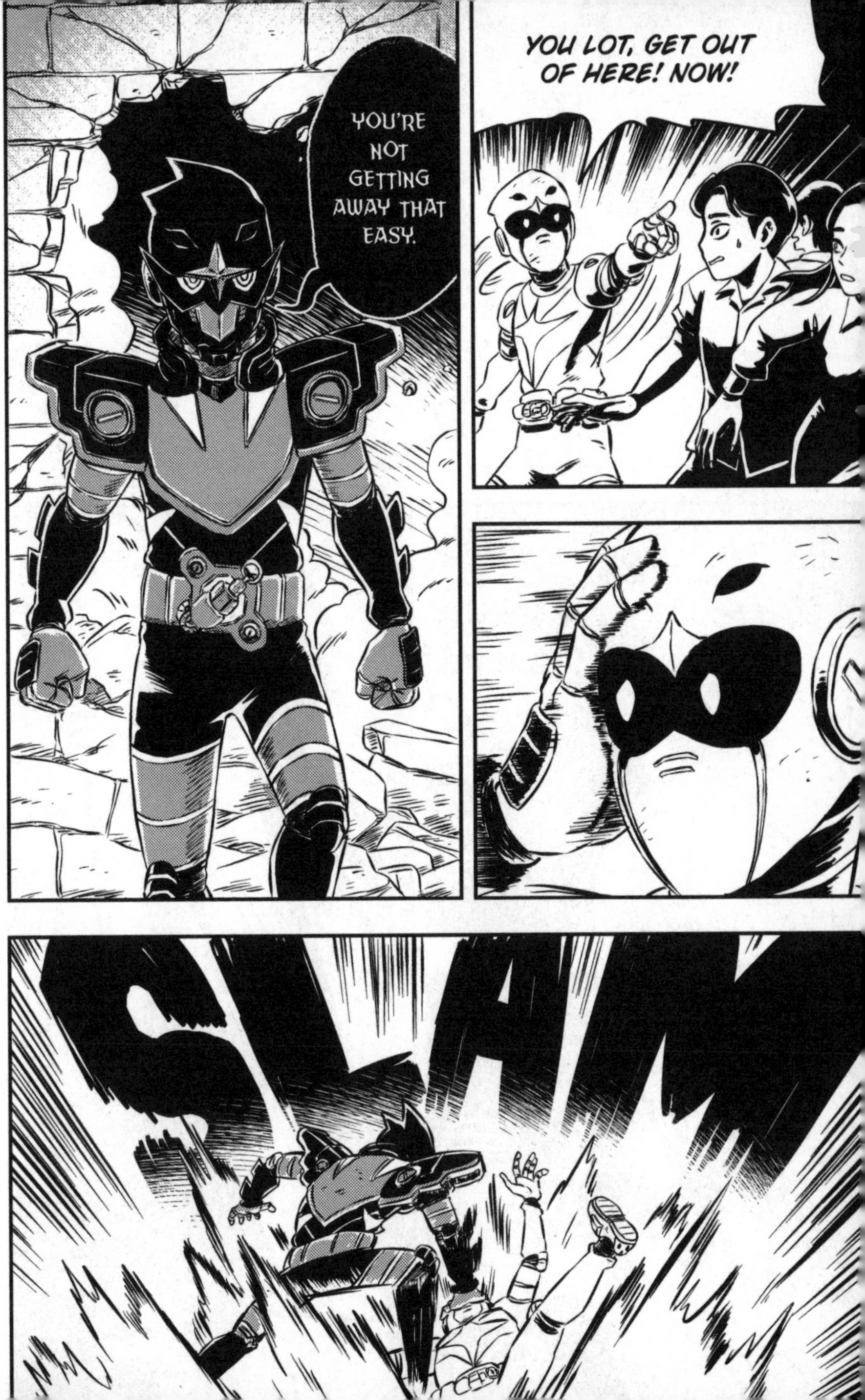
YOU'RE NOT GETTING AWAY THAT EASY.
YOU LOT, GET OUT OF HERE! NOW!
SLAM

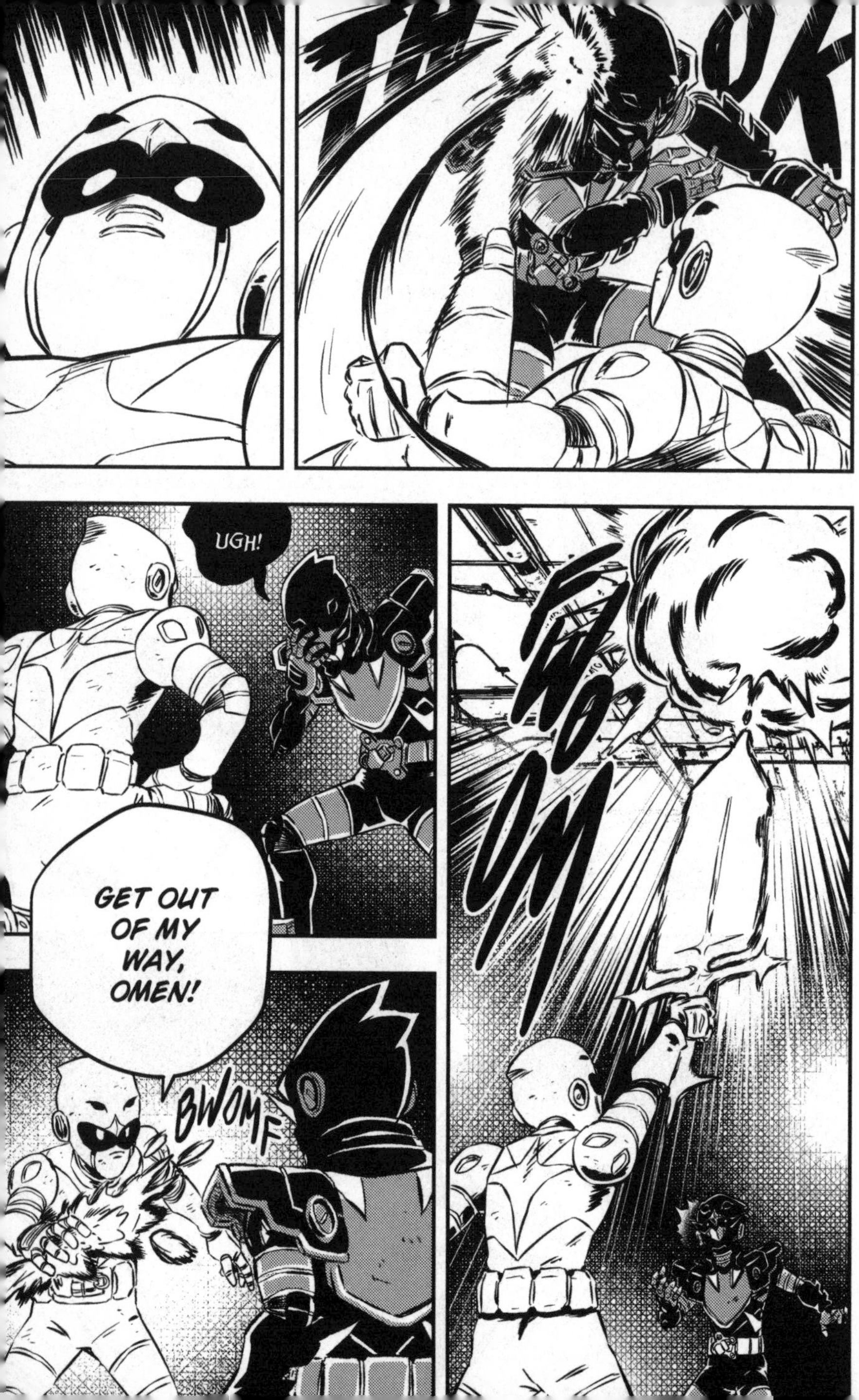
THOK
UGH!
FWOOOM
GET OUT OF MY WAY, OMEN!
BWOMF

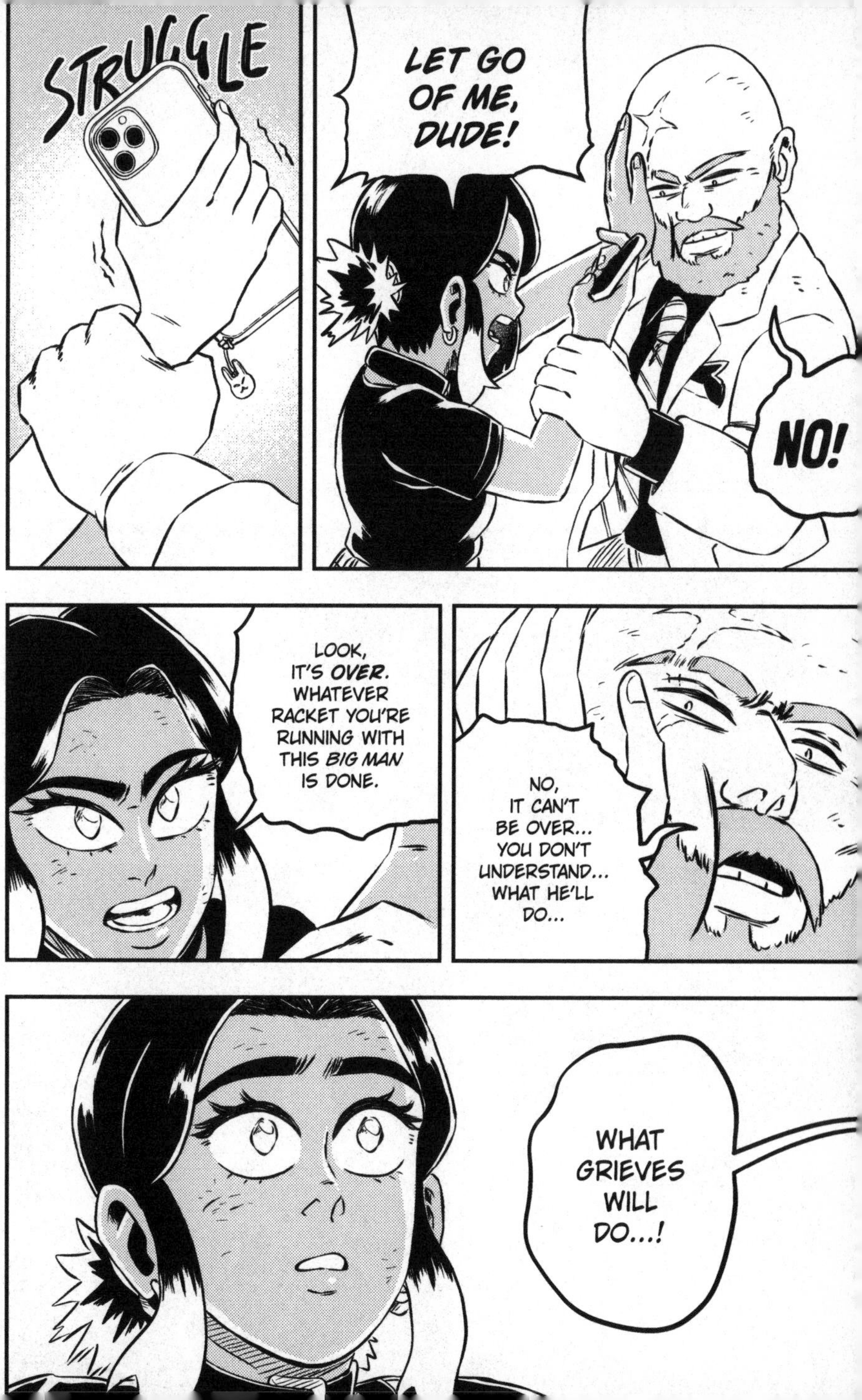
STRUGGLE
LET GO OF ME, DUDE!
NO!
LOOK, IT'S OVER. WHATEVER RACKET YOU'RE RUNNING WITH THIS BIG MAN IS DONE.
NO, IT CAN'T BE OVER... YOU DON'T UNDERSTAND... WHAT HE'LL DO...
WHAT GRIEVES WILL DO...!

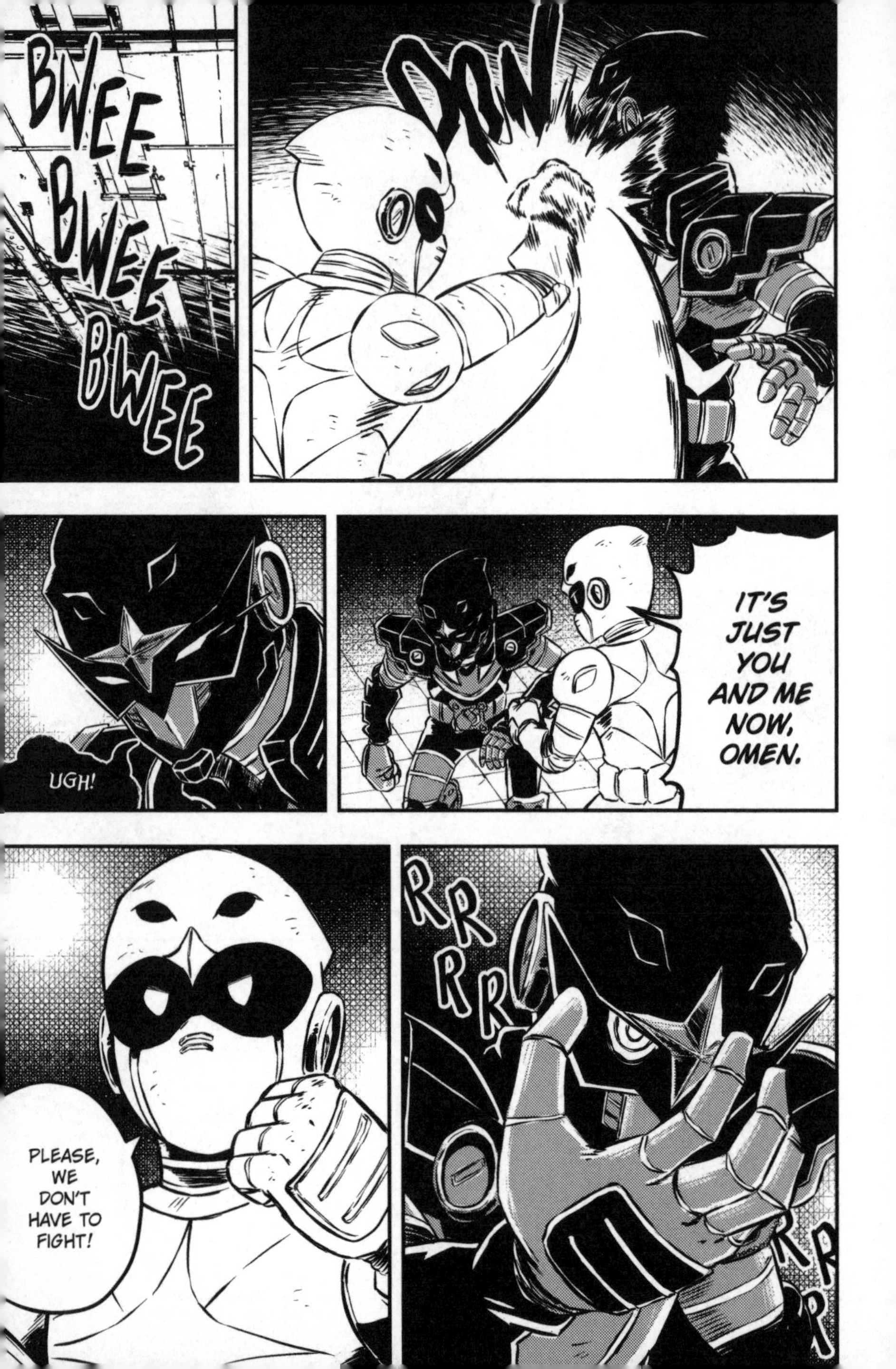
BWEE BWEE BWEE BWEE
DON
UGH!
IT'S JUST YOU AND ME NOW, OMEN.
PLEASE, WE DON'T HAVE TO FIGHT!
RRRRR
RRR

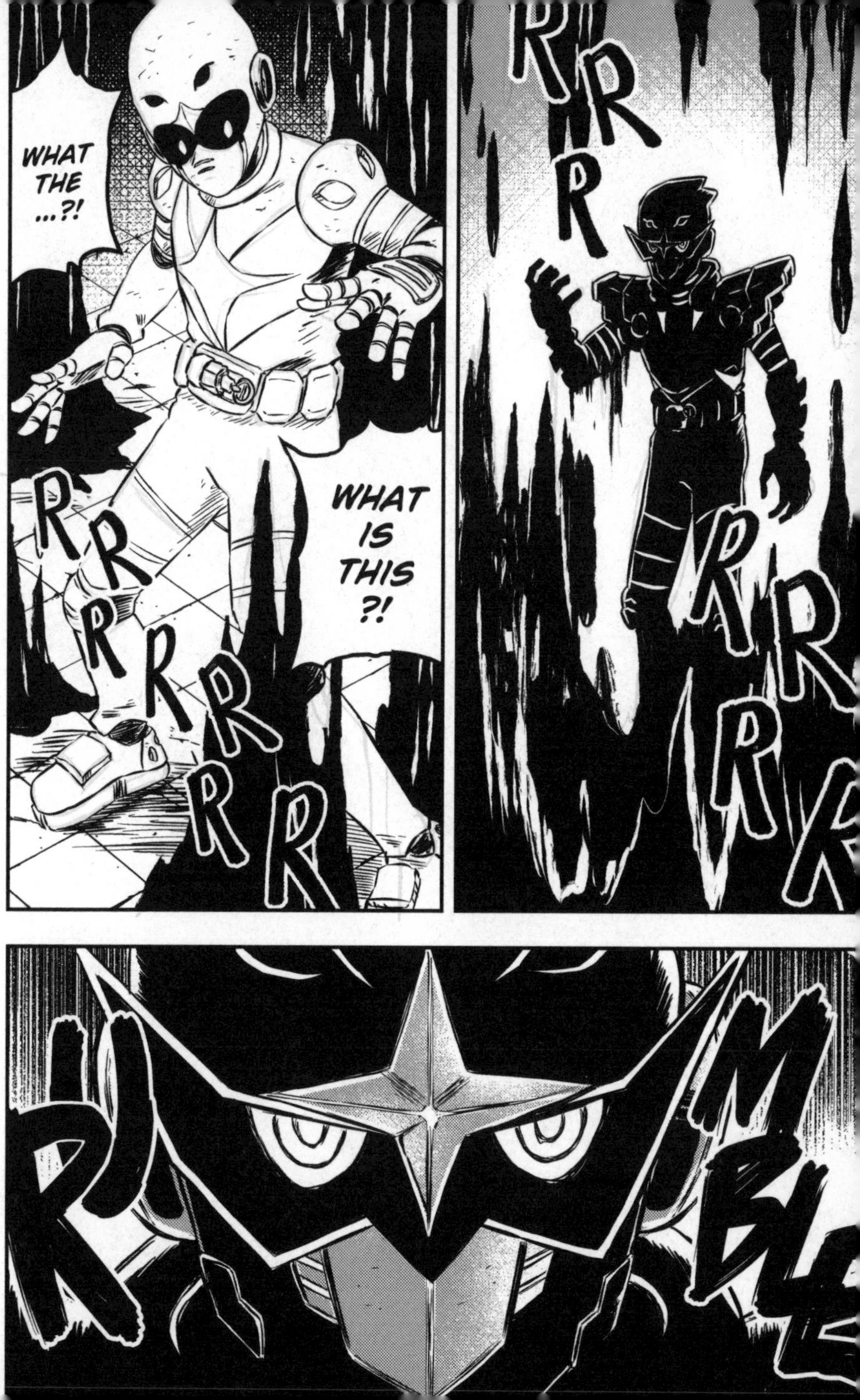
WHAT THE ...?!
WHAT IS THIS ?!

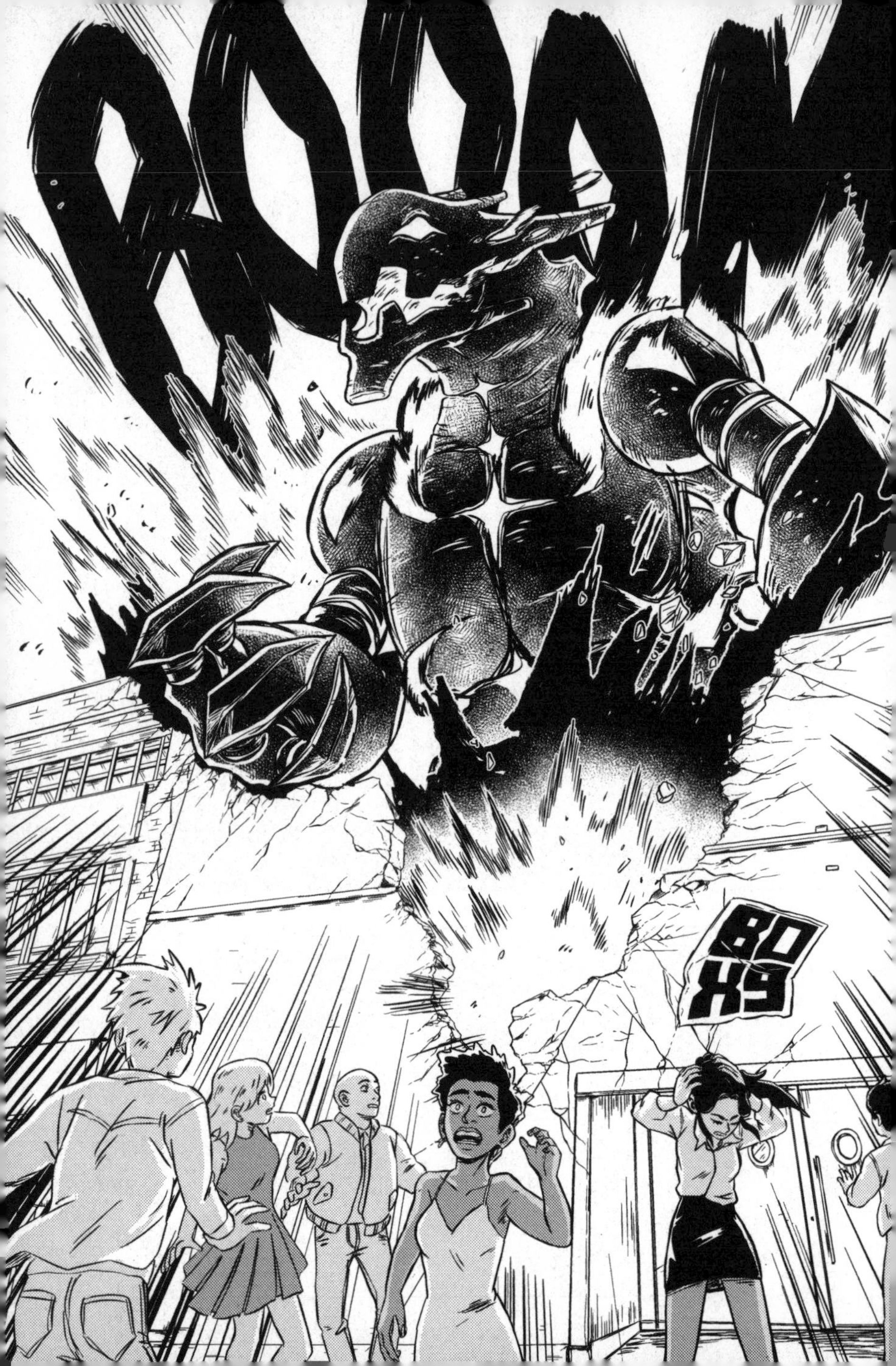
BOOM

HENSHIN!

CHAPTER TEN
BLAZE

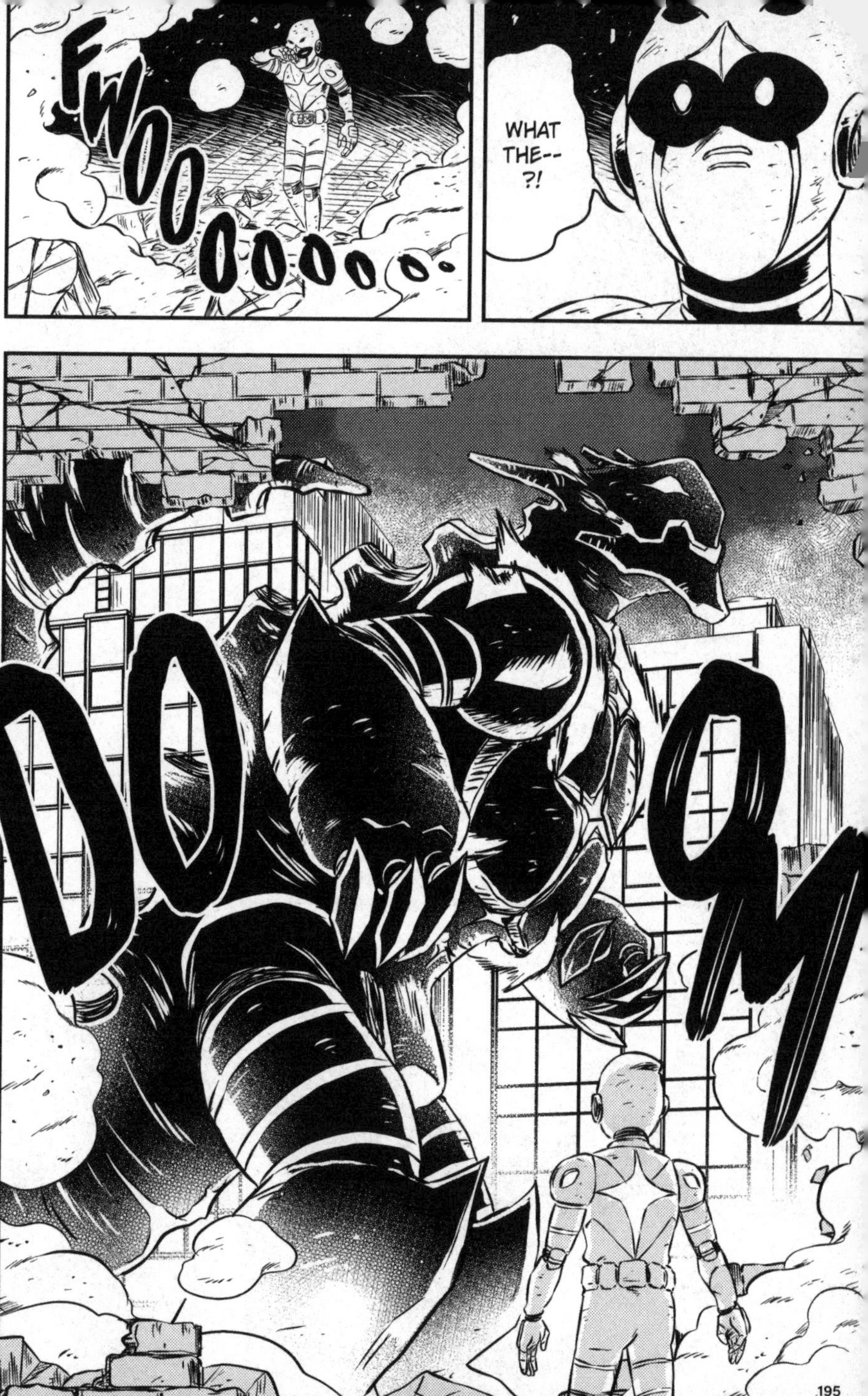
FWOOOOOOOOO
WHAT THE-- ?!
DOOOM

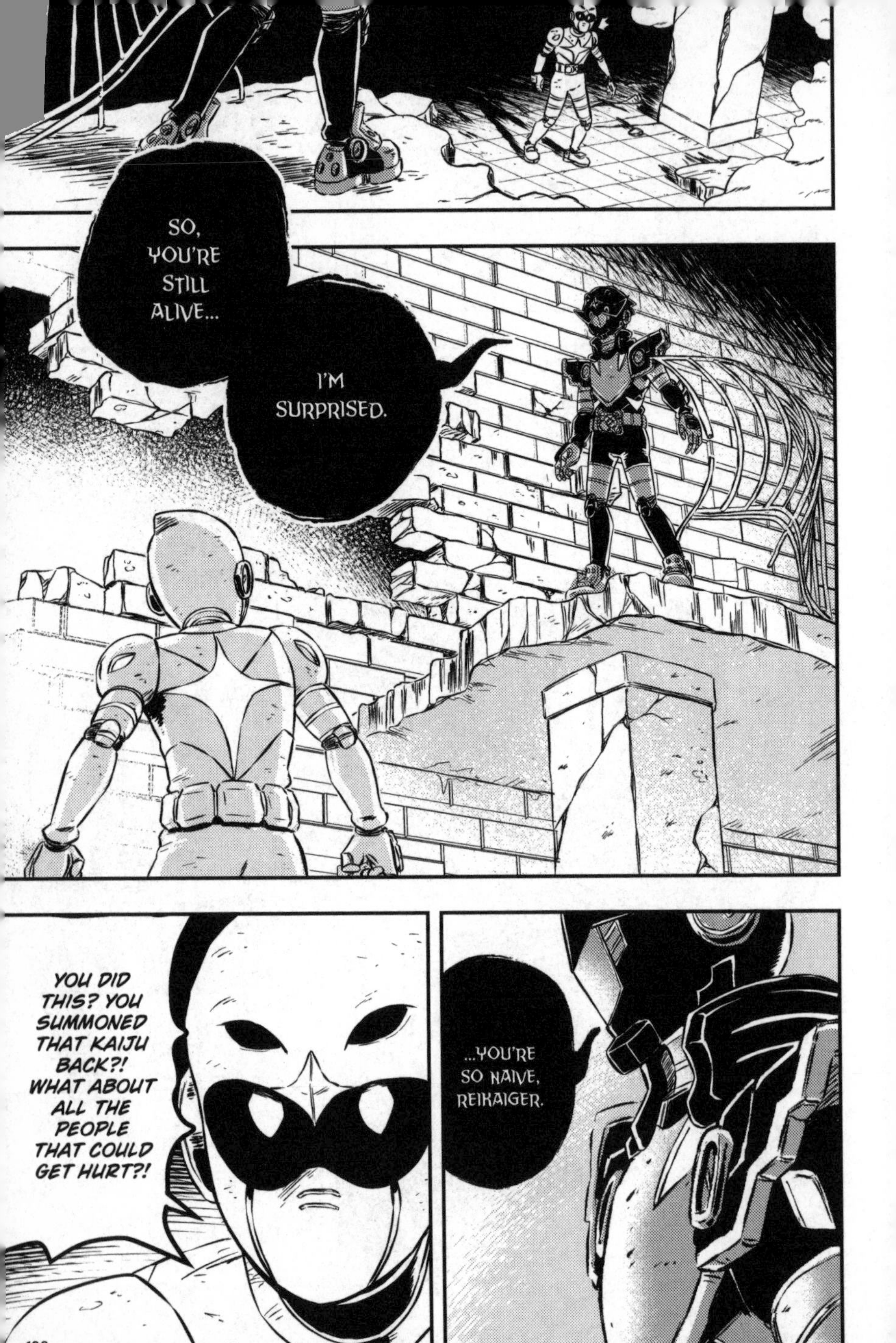
SO, YOU'RE STILL ALIVE...
I'M SURPRISED.
YOU DID THIS? YOU SUMMONED THAT KAIJU BACK?! WHAT ABOUT ALL THE PEOPLE THAT COULD GET HURT?!
...YOU'RE SO NAIVE, REIKAIGER.

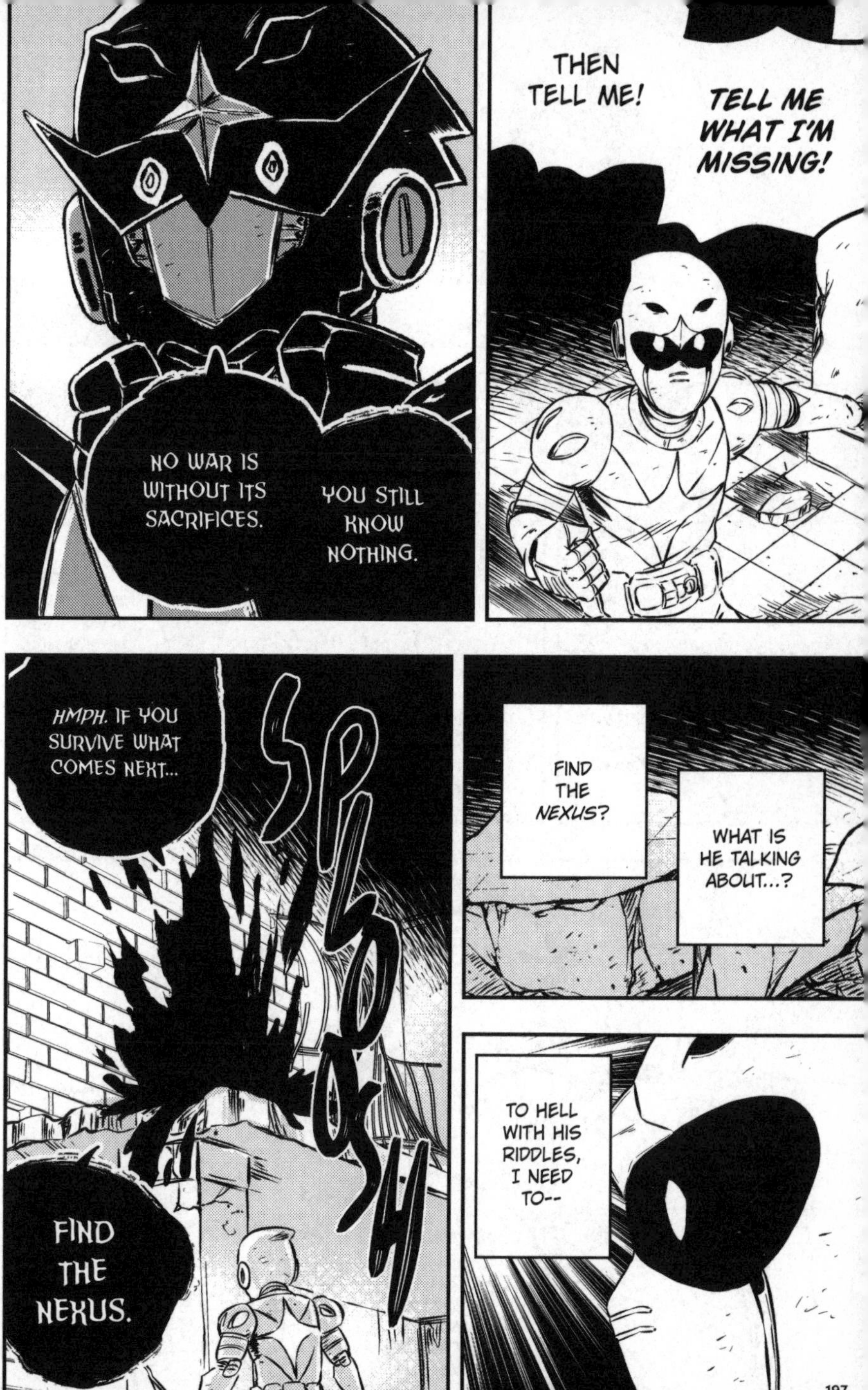
NO WAR IS WITHOUT ITS SACRIFICES.
YOU STILL KNOW NOTHING.
THEN TELL ME!
TELL ME WHAT I'M MISSING!
HMPH. IF YOU SURVIVE WHAT COMES NEXT...
FIND THE NEXUS.
SPLOOSH
FIND THE *NEXUS?*
WHAT IS HE TALKING ABOUT...?
TO HELL WITH HIS RIDDLES, I NEED TO--

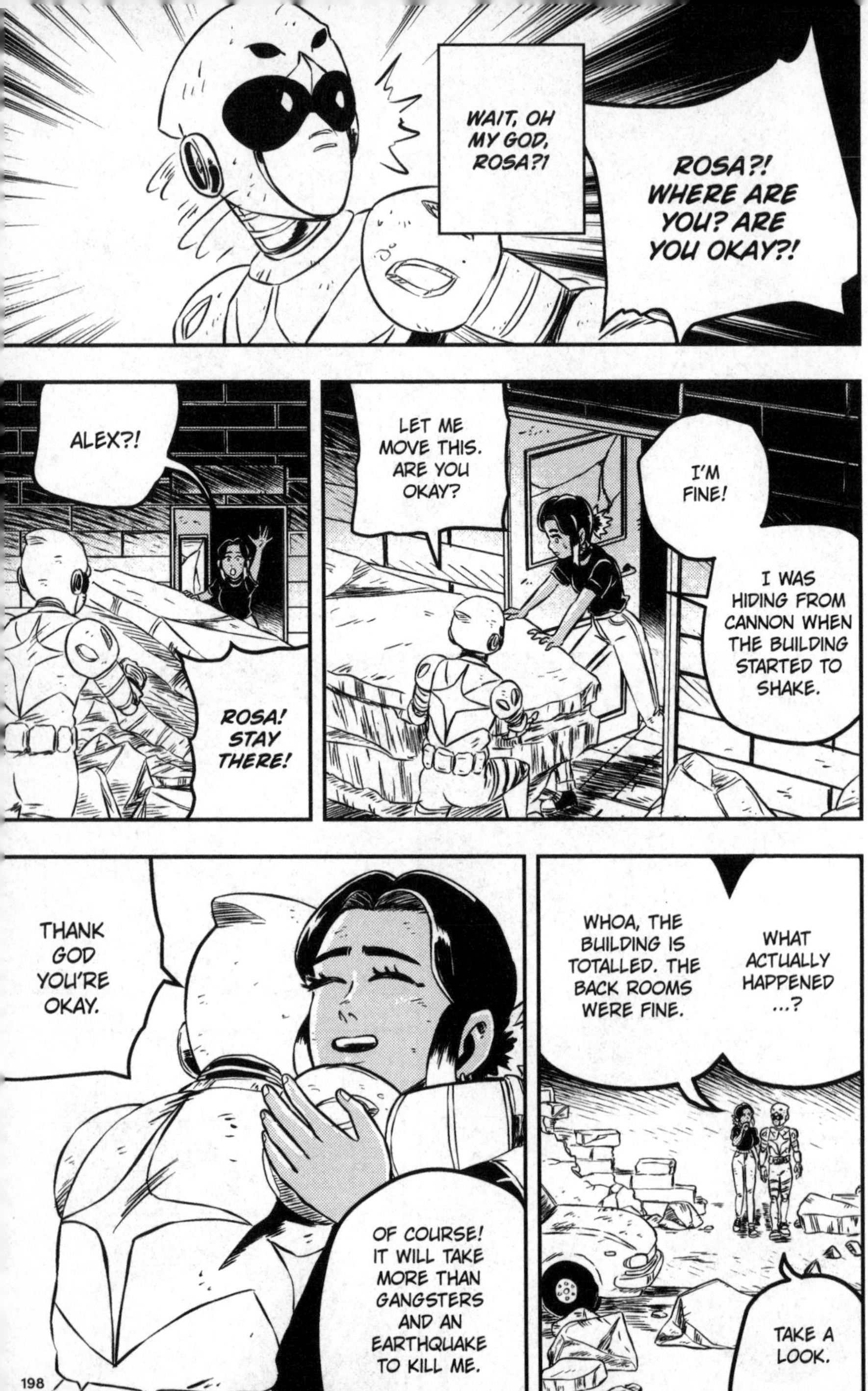
WAIT, OH MY GOD, ROSA?!
ROSA?! WHERE ARE YOU? ARE YOU OKAY?!
ALEX?!
ROSA! STAY THERE!
LET ME MOVE THIS. ARE YOU OKAY?
I'M FINE!
I WAS HIDING FROM CANNON WHEN THE BUILDING STARTED TO SHAKE.
THANK GOD YOU'RE OKAY.
OF COURSE! IT WILL TAKE MORE THAN GANGSTERS AND AN EARTHQUAKE TO KILL ME.
WHOA, THE BUILDING IS TOTALLED. THE BACK ROOMS WERE FINE.
WHAT ACTUALLY HAPPENED ...?
TAKE A LOOK.

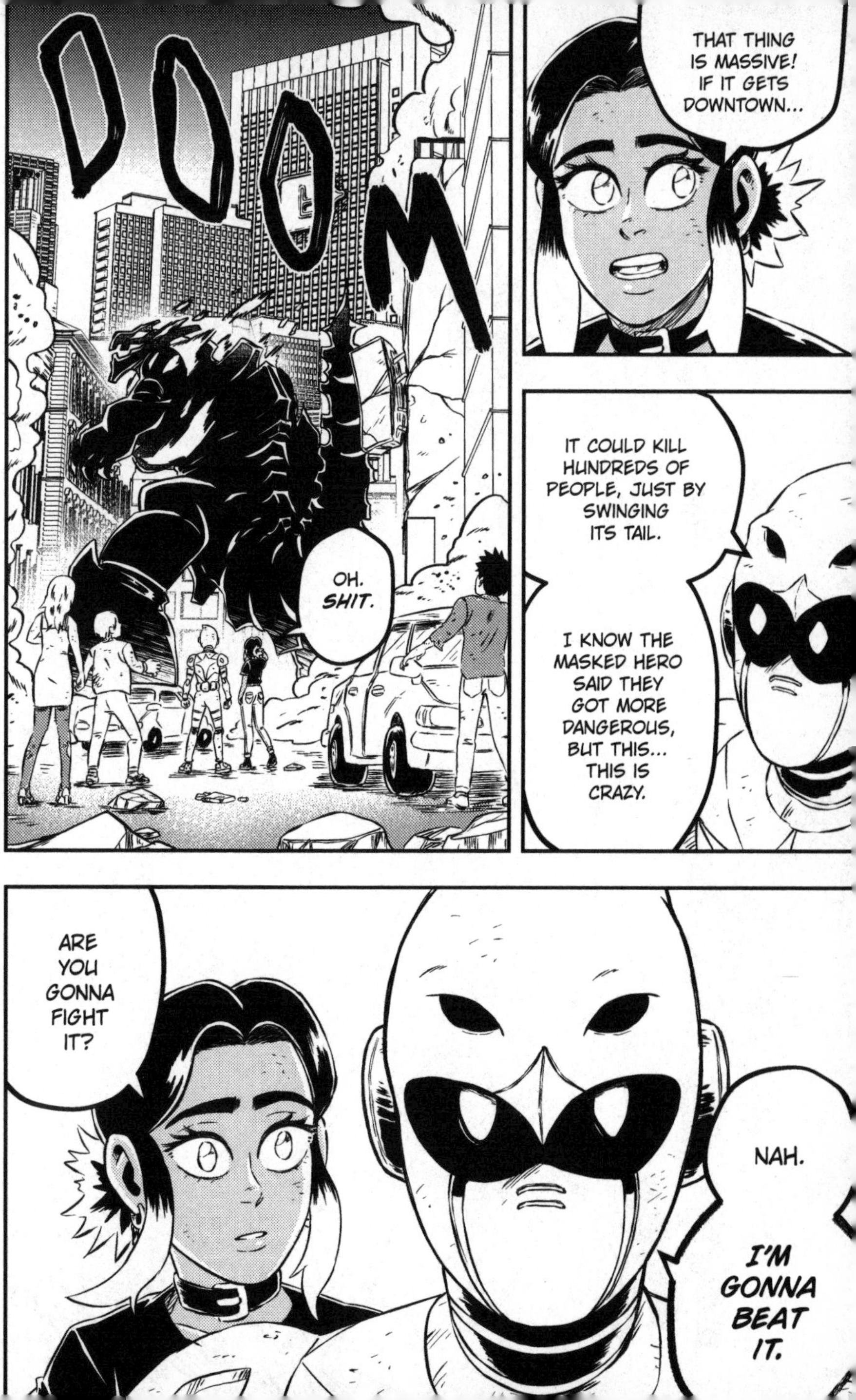
DOOOM
OH. SHIT.
THAT THING IS MASSIVE! IF IT GETS DOWNTOWN...
IT COULD KILL HUNDREDS OF PEOPLE, JUST BY SWINGING ITS TAIL.
I KNOW THE MASKED HERO SAID THEY GOT MORE DANGEROUS, BUT THIS... THIS IS CRAZY.
ARE YOU GONNA FIGHT IT?
NAH.
I'M GONNA BEAT IT.

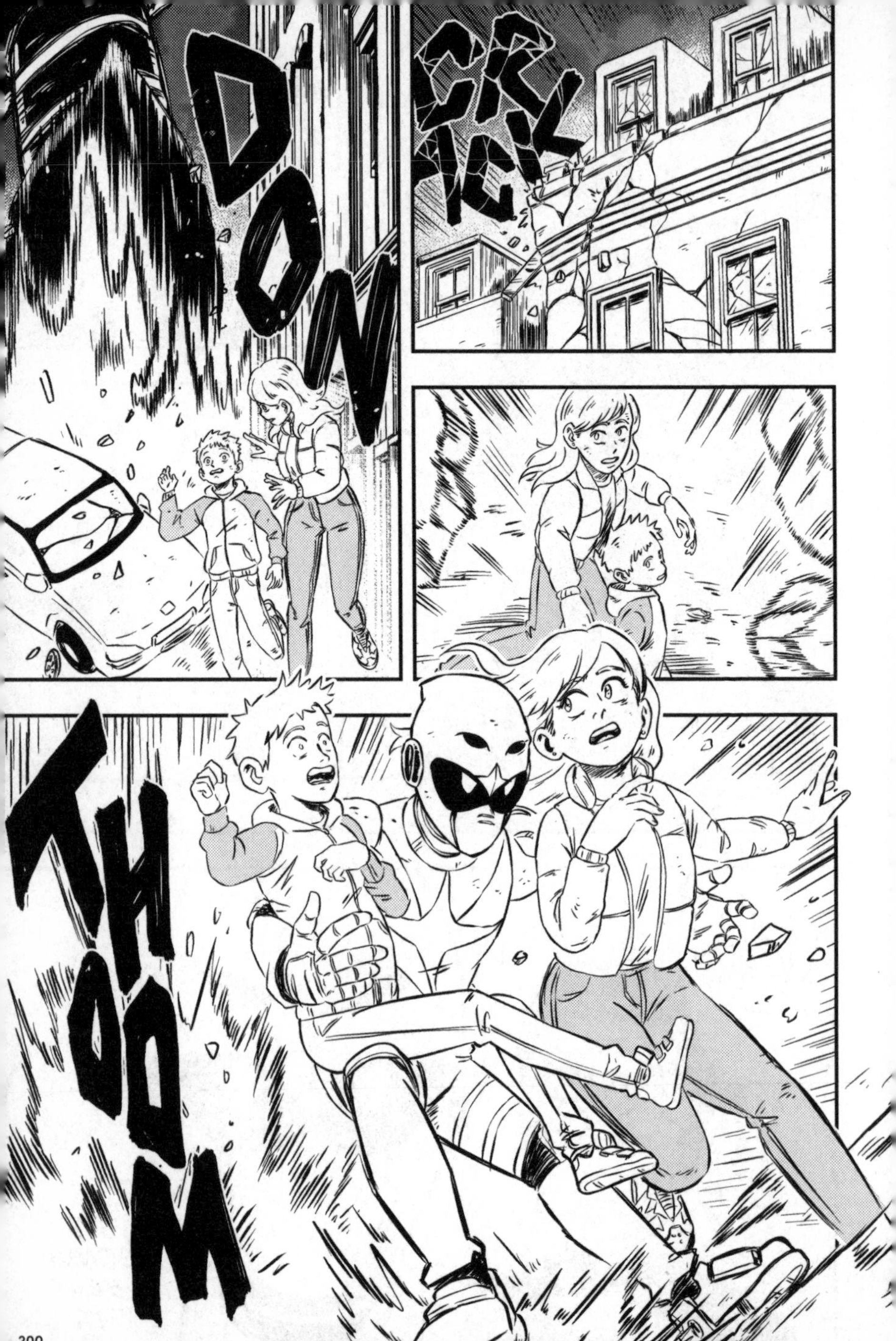
DON
CRACK
THOOM

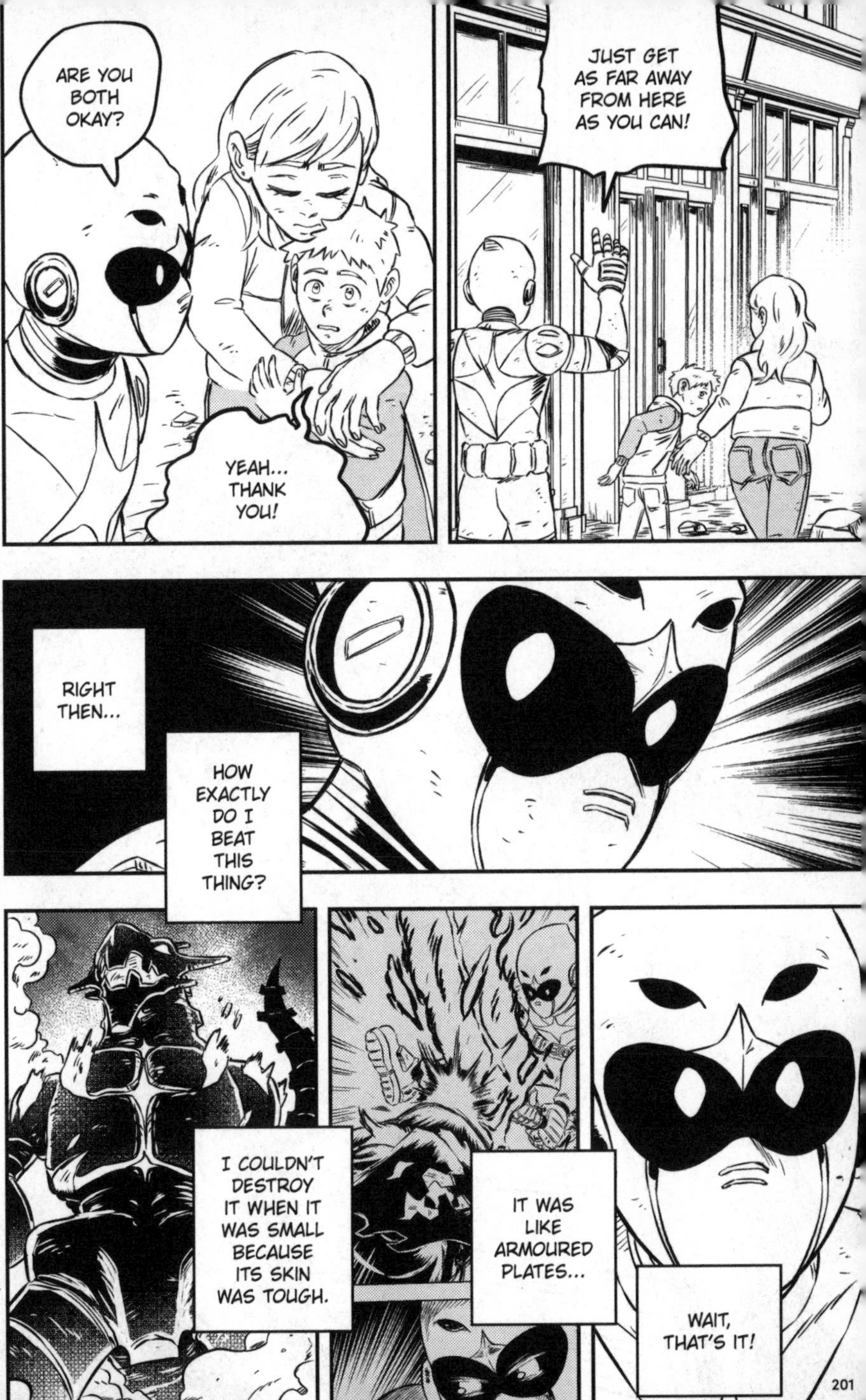

ARE YOU BOTH OKAY?
YEAH... THANK YOU!
JUST GET AS FAR AWAY FROM HERE AS YOU CAN!
RIGHT THEN...
HOW EXACTLY DO I BEAT THIS THING?
I COULDN'T DESTROY IT WHEN IT WAS SMALL BECAUSE ITS SKIN WAS TOUGH.
IT WAS LIKE ARMOURED PLATES...
WAIT, THAT'S IT!

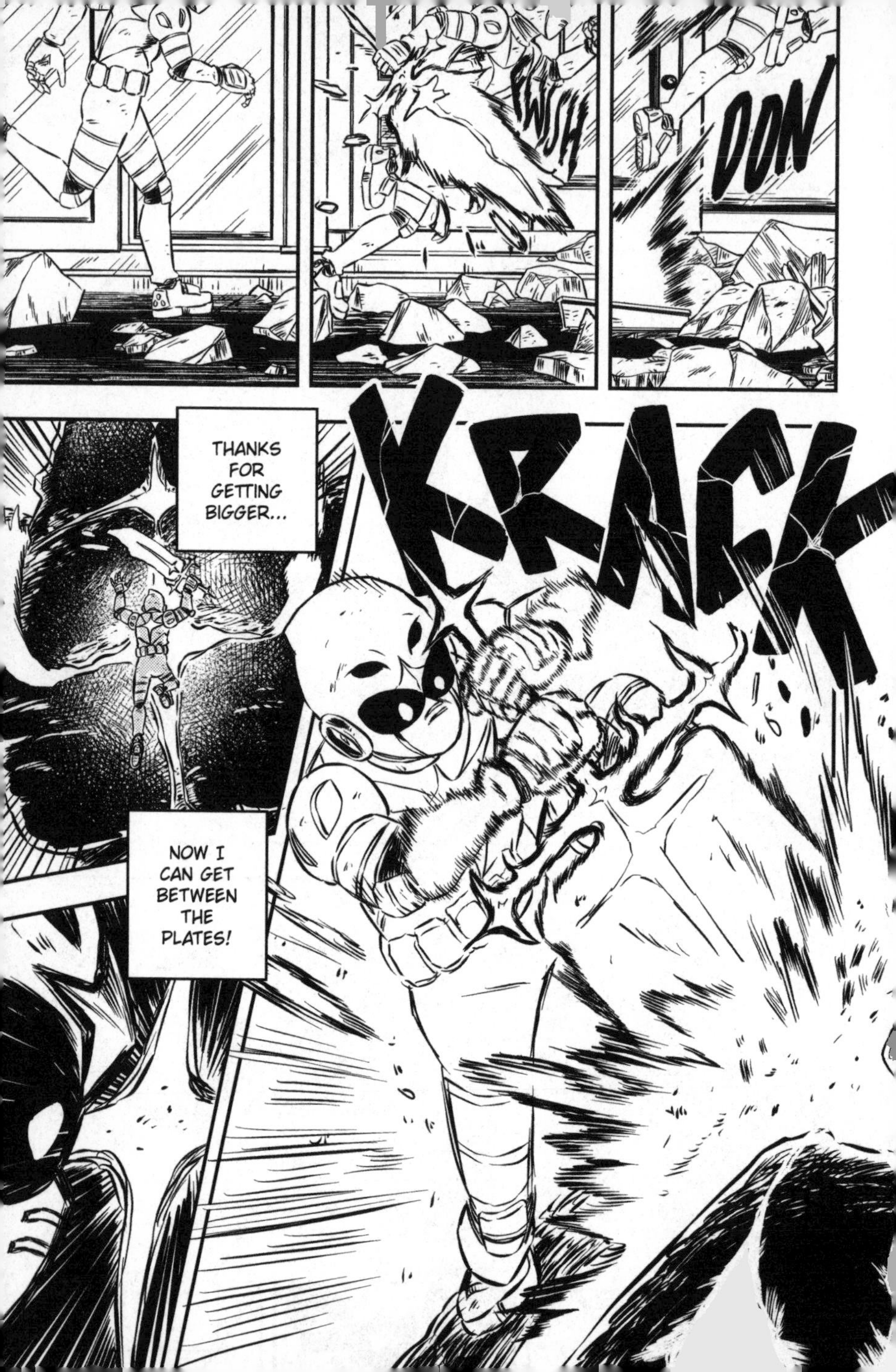
PWUSH
DON
THANKS FOR GETTING BIGGER...
KRACK
NOW I CAN GET BETWEEN THE PLATES!

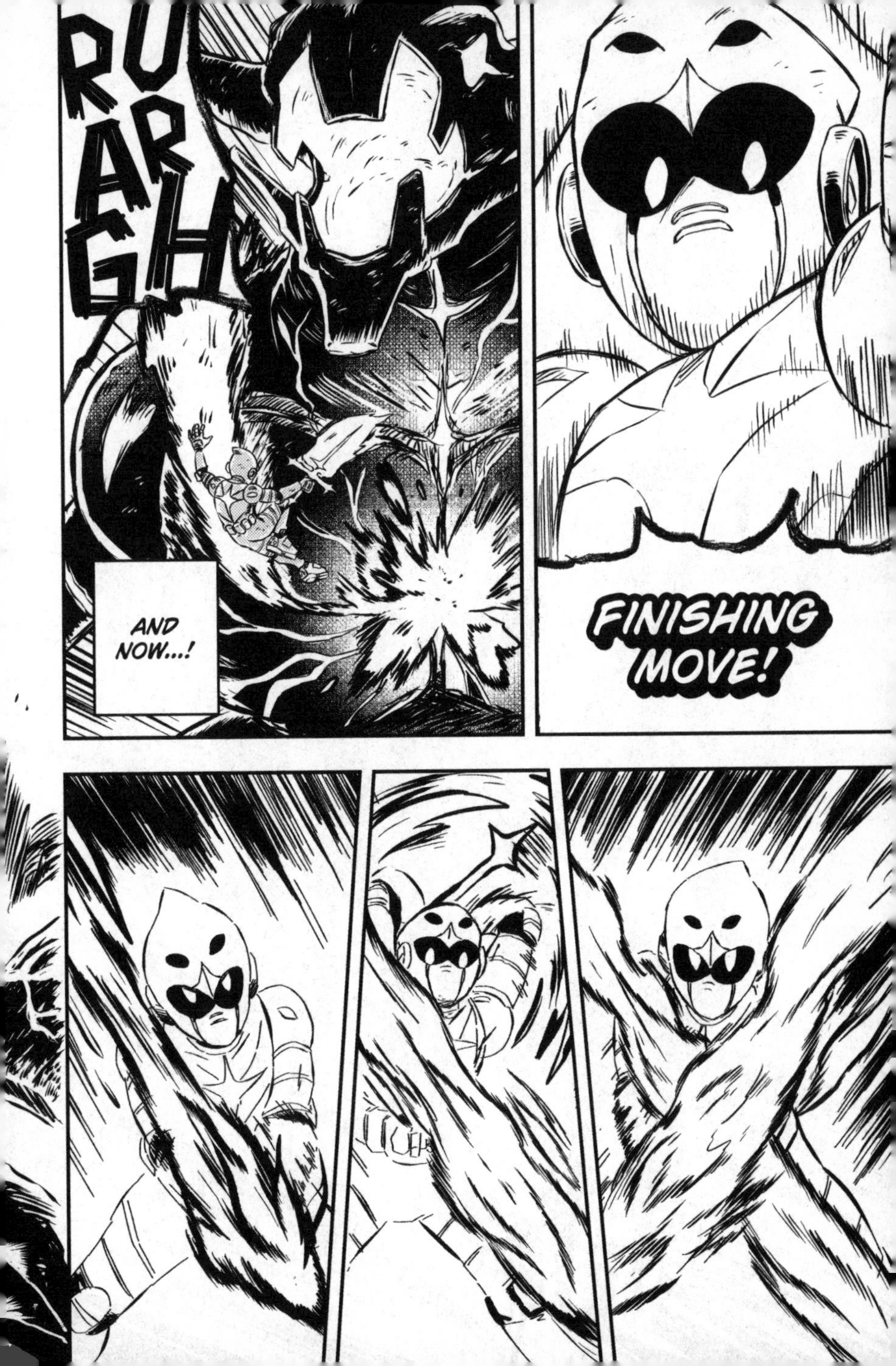
RUARGH
AND NOW...!
FINISHING MOVE!

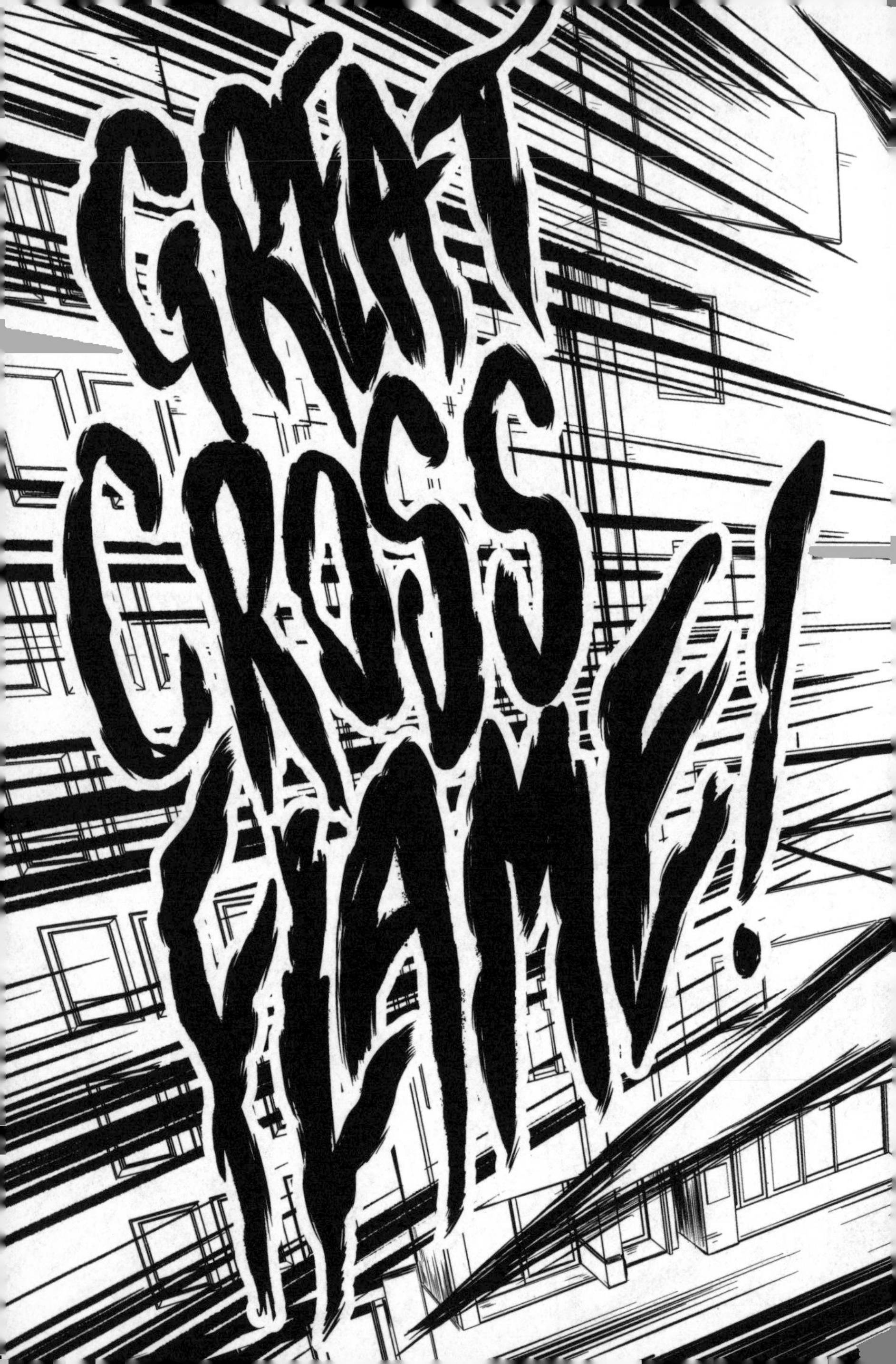
GREAT CROSS FLAME!

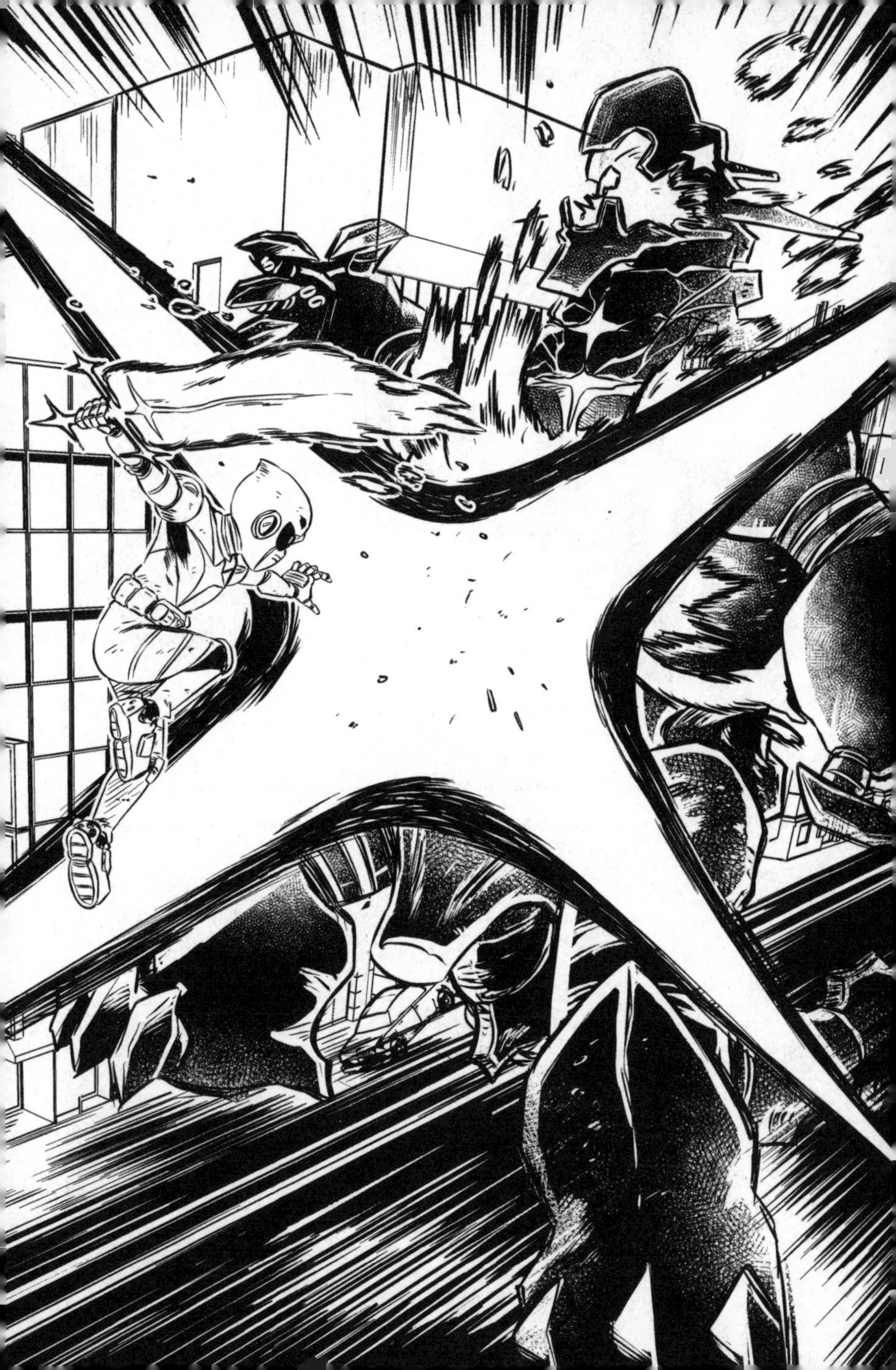

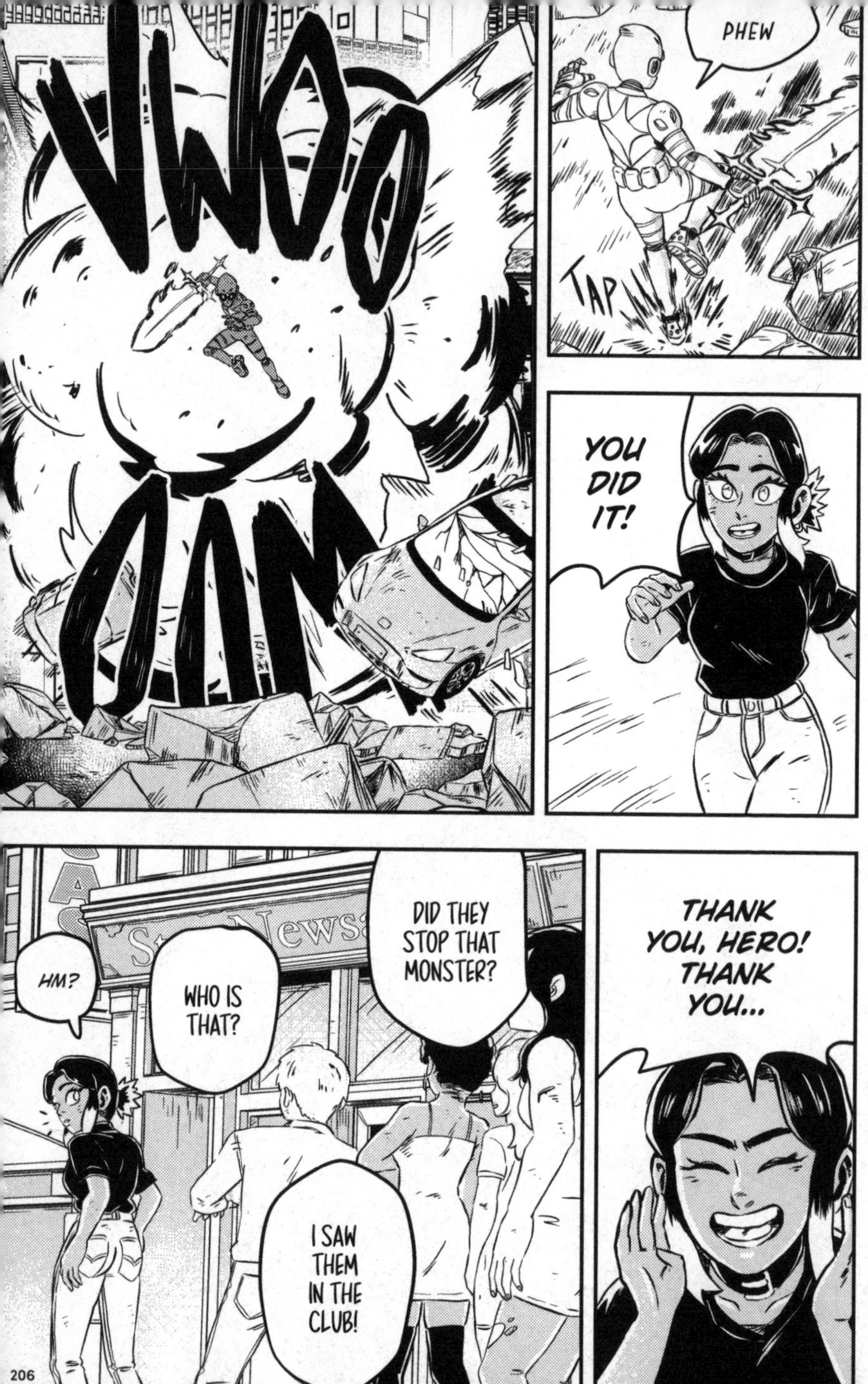

PHEW
TAP
YOU DID IT!
HM?
WHO IS THAT?
DID THEY STOP THAT MONSTER?
I SAW THEM IN THE CLUB!
THANK YOU, HERO! THANK YOU...

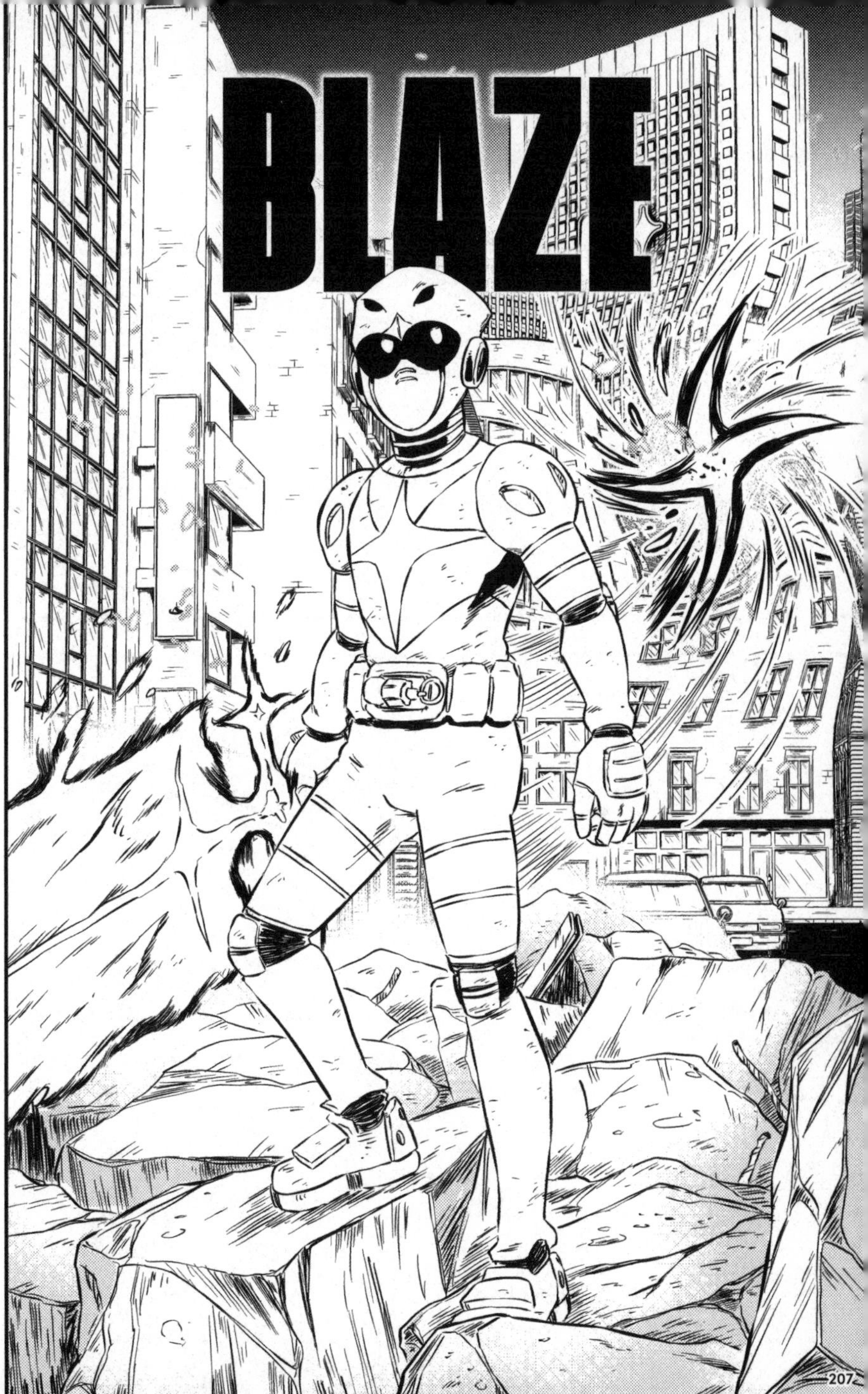
BLAZE

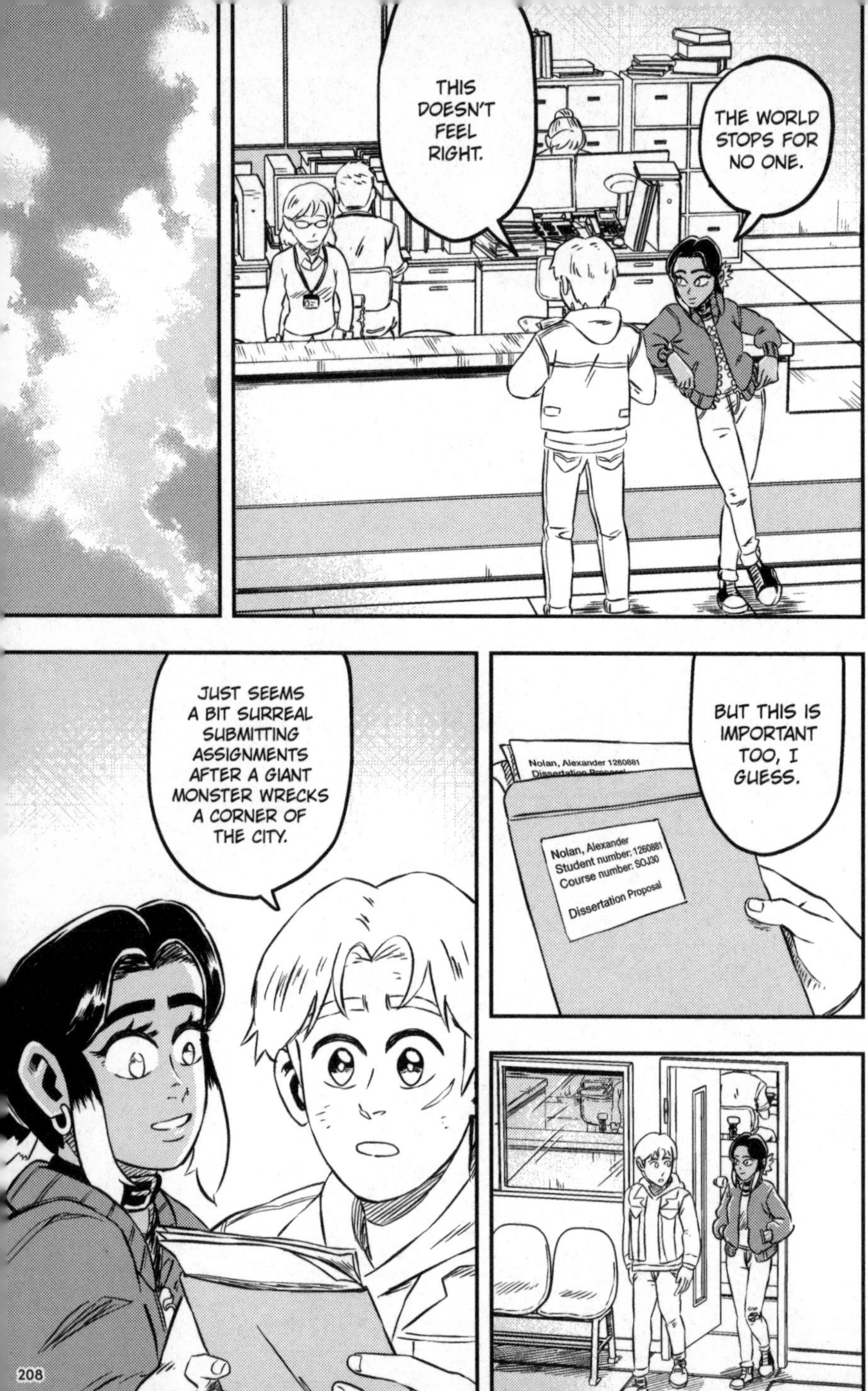
THIS DOESN'T FEEL RIGHT.
THE WORLD STOPS FOR NO ONE.
JUST SEEMS A BIT SURREAL SUBMITTING ASSIGNMENTS AFTER A GIANT MONSTER WRECKS A CORNER OF THE CITY.
BUT THIS IS IMPORTANT TOO, I GUESS.
Nolan, Alexander 1260881
Nolan, Alexander
Student number: 1260881
Course number: SOJ30
Dissertation Proposal

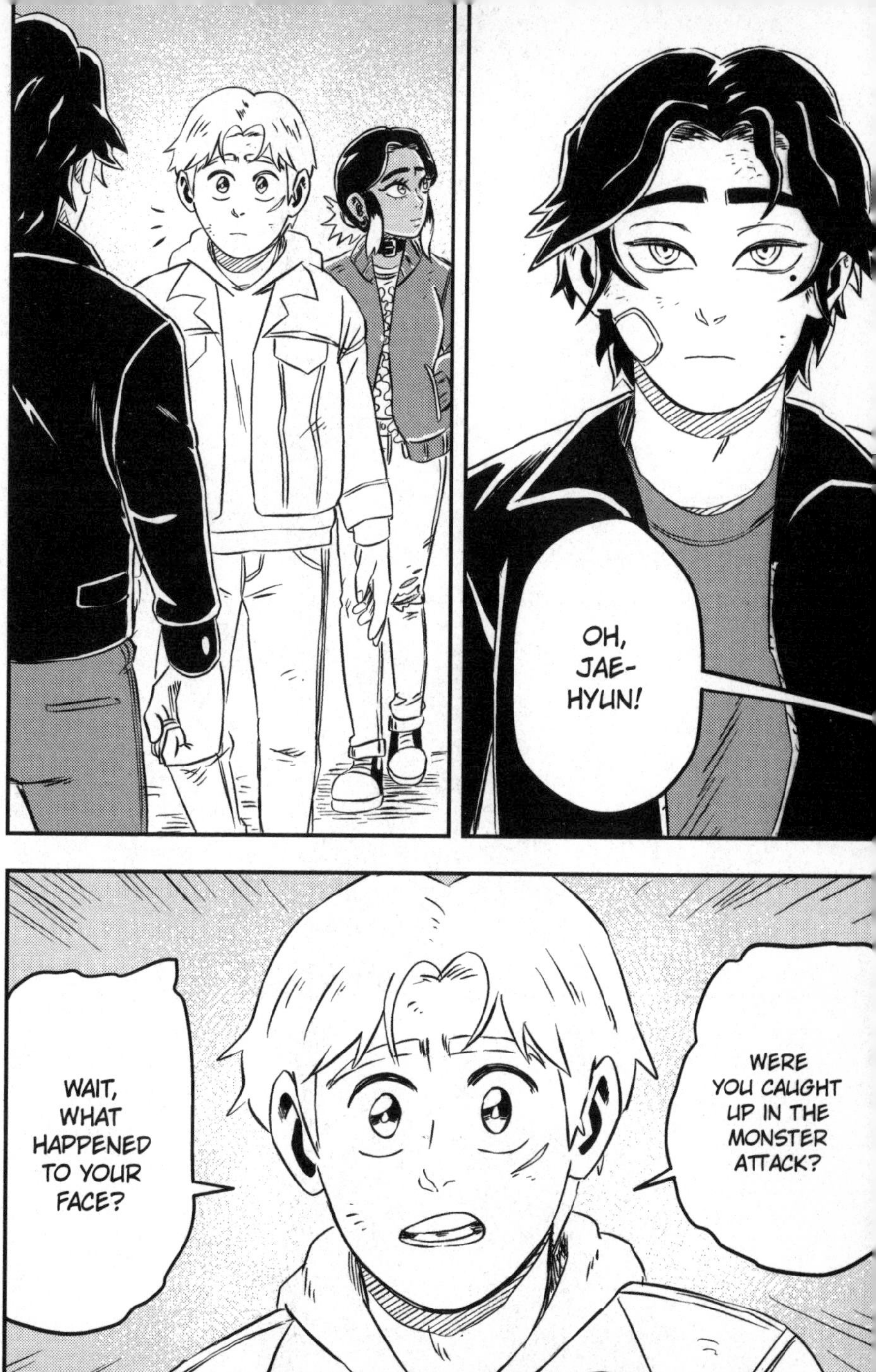
OH, JAE-HYUN!
WERE YOU CAUGHT UP IN THE MONSTER ATTACK?
WAIT, WHAT HAPPENED TO YOUR FACE?

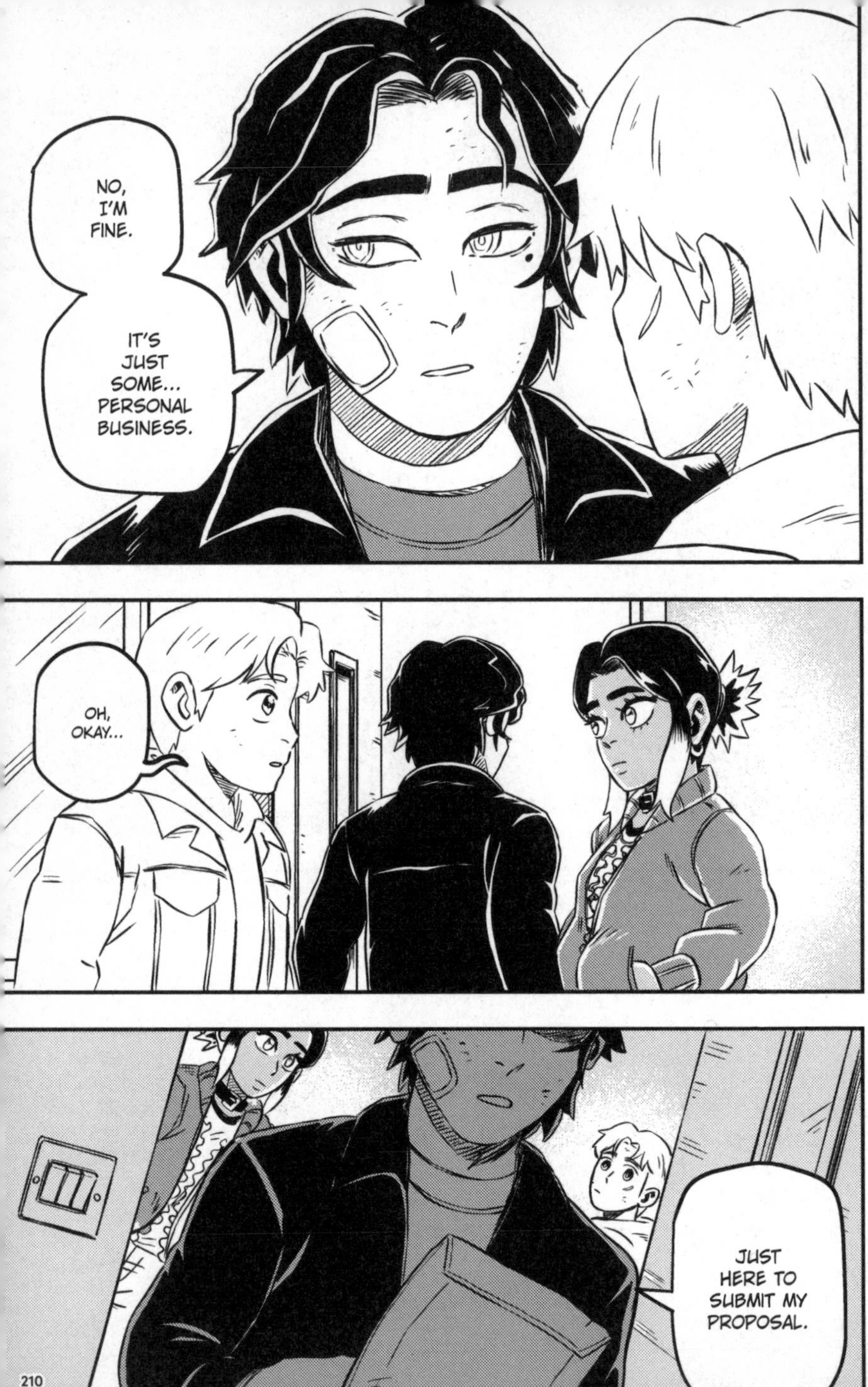
NO, I'M FINE.
IT'S JUST SOME... PERSONAL BUSINESS.
OH, OKAY...
JUST HERE TO SUBMIT MY PROPOSAL.

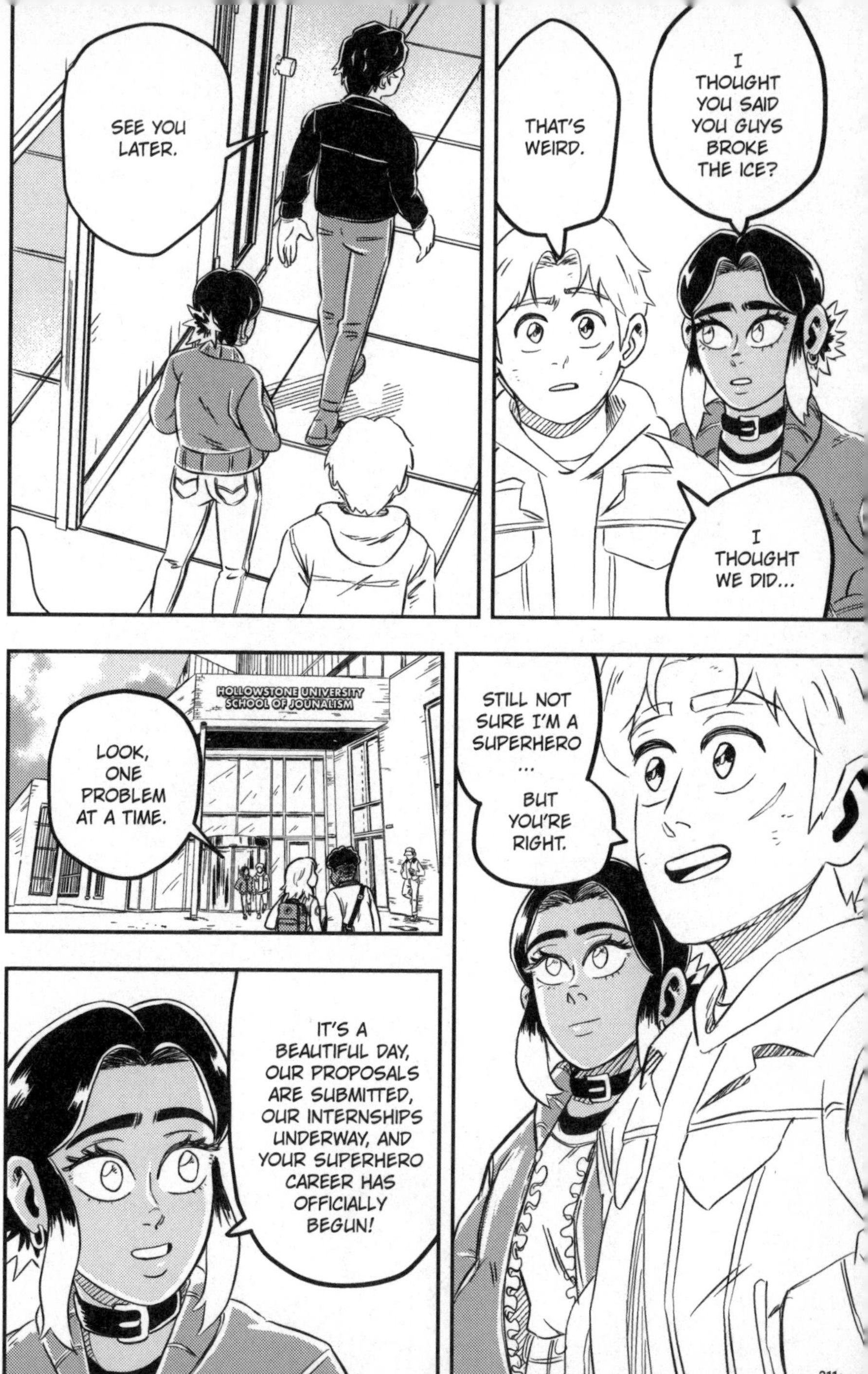
SEE YOU LATER.
THAT'S WEIRD.
I THOUGHT YOU SAID YOU GUYS BROKE THE ICE?
I THOUGHT WE DID...
HOLLOWSTONE UNIVERSITY SCHOOL OF JOUNALISM
LOOK, ONE PROBLEM AT A TIME.
IT'S A BEAUTIFUL DAY, OUR PROPOSALS ARE SUBMITTED, OUR INTERNSHIPS UNDERWAY, AND YOUR SUPERHERO CAREER HAS OFFICIALLY BEGUN!
STILL NOT SURE I'M A SUPERHERO ...
BUT YOU'RE RIGHT.

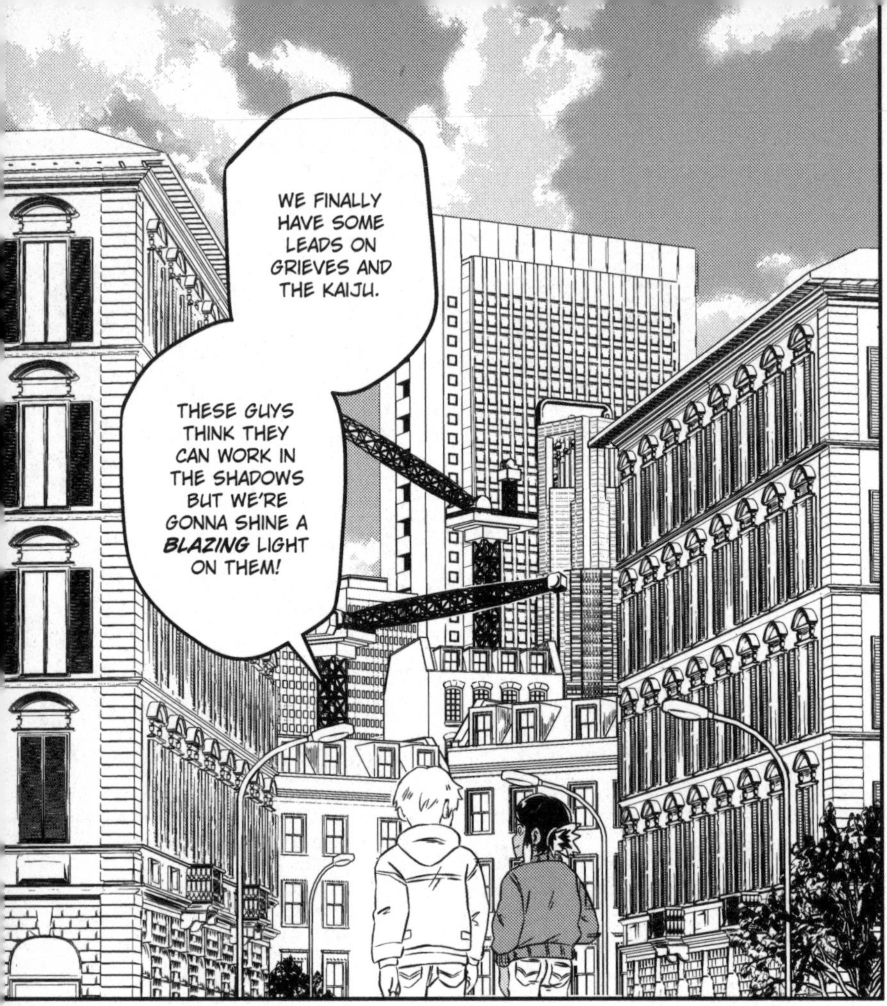
WE FINALLY HAVE SOME LEADS ON GRIEVES AND THE KAIJU.
THESE GUYS THINK THEY CAN WORK IN THE SHADOWS BUT WE'RE GONNA SHINE A *BLAZING* LIGHT ON THEM!

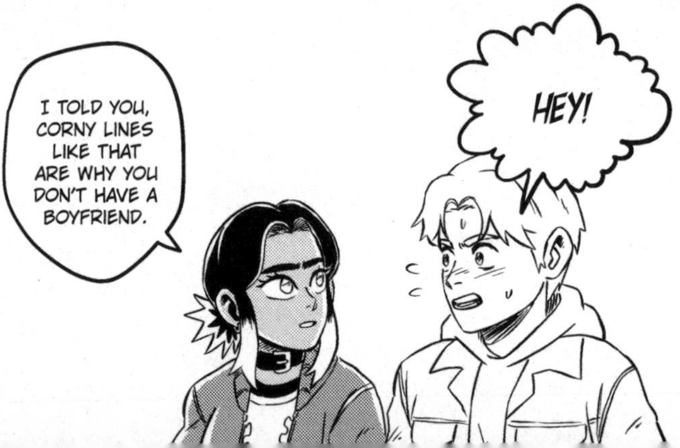
I TOLD YOU, CORNY LINES LIKE THAT ARE WHY YOU DON'T HAVE A BOYFRIEND.
HEY!

HENSHIN!

END OF VOLUME 1

ABOUT THE AUTHOR

BON IDLE

Bon Idle (Mitch Proctor) is the creator of
HENSHIN! and a graphic designer from
Nottingham, England, where he lives with
his cat, Ricky.

Graduate of the University of Lincoln, he has
worked in the marketing industry as a graphic
designer and published several small-press
titles before joining Saturday AM as a creator
and graphic designer.

ACKNOWLEDGMENTS

"IF THIS IS YOUR FIRST TIME READING THIS STORY, THANK YOU FOR PICKING UP THE BOOK. IF YOU'VE FOLLOWED THE STORY IN SATURDAY BRUNCH, THANK YOU FOR STICKING WITH ME AND READING IT AGAIN!

"I'VE REDRAWN AND REWORKED *A LOT* OF THIS BOOK FROM THE ORIGINAL SERIALISED VERSION. CHARACTERS HAVE BEEN INTRODUCED SOONER, DIALOGUE HAS BEEN REWORKED, PAGE LAYOUTS ADJUSTED AND WHOLE NEW PAGES HAVE BEEN ADDED. BEING ABLE TO REVISIT THIS FIRST ARC AND LOOK AT IT AS A WHOLE WAS A VERY TOUGH BUT FULFILLING EXPERIENCE.

"THIS STORY OBVIOUSLY OWES SO MUCH TO JAPANESE TOKUSATSU. IT'S A JOY TO BE ABLE TO CREATE MY OWN WORLD AND TRY AND TELL THE TYPE OF STORIES YOU DON'T TYPICALLY SEE IN THAT GENRE AND TRY TO REFLECT THE DIVERSE AND BEAUTIFUL WORLD I SEE AROUND ME.

"I'M ALREADY HARD AT WORK ON THE NEXT PART OF *HENSHIN!* AND I THINK IF YOU ENJOYED THIS BOOK, YOU'RE GONNA LOVE THE NEXT ONE. IT'S GOING TO BE BIGGER, BOLDER AND BLOODY BONKERS.

"THANKS FOR READING. I'LL SEE YOU NEXT TIME!"

—Bon Idle (Mitch Proctor)

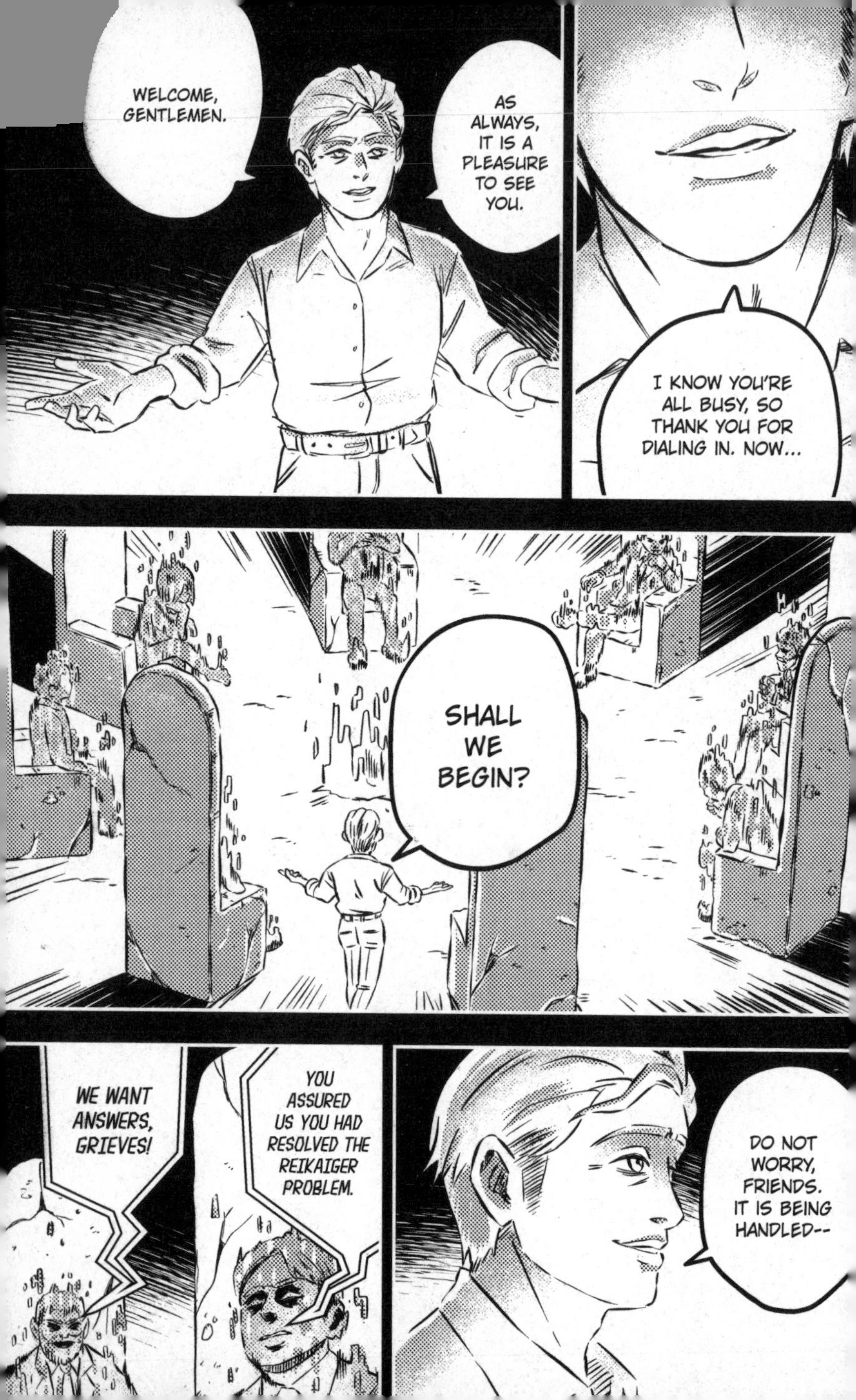

WELCOME, GENTLEMEN.
AS ALWAYS, IT IS A PLEASURE TO SEE YOU.
I KNOW YOU'RE ALL BUSY, SO THANK YOU FOR DIALING IN. NOW...
SHALL WE BEGIN?
WE WANT ANSWERS, GRIEVES!
YOU ASSURED US YOU HAD RESOLVED THE REIKAIGER PROBLEM.
DO NOT WORRY, FRIENDS. IT IS BEING HANDLED--

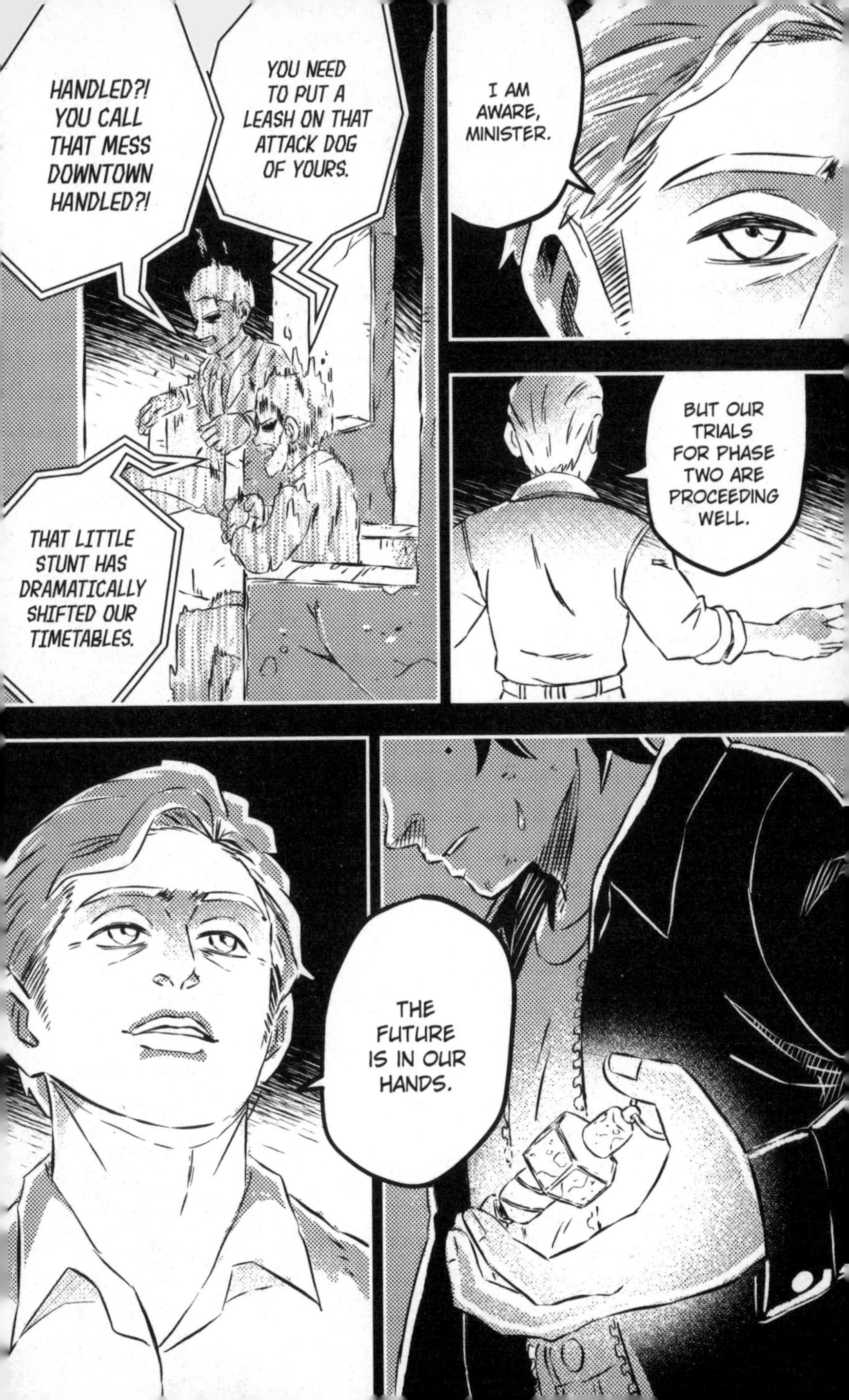
HANDLED?! YOU CALL THAT MESS DOWNTOWN HANDLED?!
YOU NEED TO PUT A LEASH ON THAT ATTACK DOG OF YOURS.
THAT LITTLE STUNT HAS DRAMATICALLY SHIFTED OUR TIMETABLES.
I AM AWARE, MINISTER.
BUT OUR TRIALS FOR PHASE TWO ARE PROCEEDING WELL.
THE FUTURE IS IN OUR HANDS.

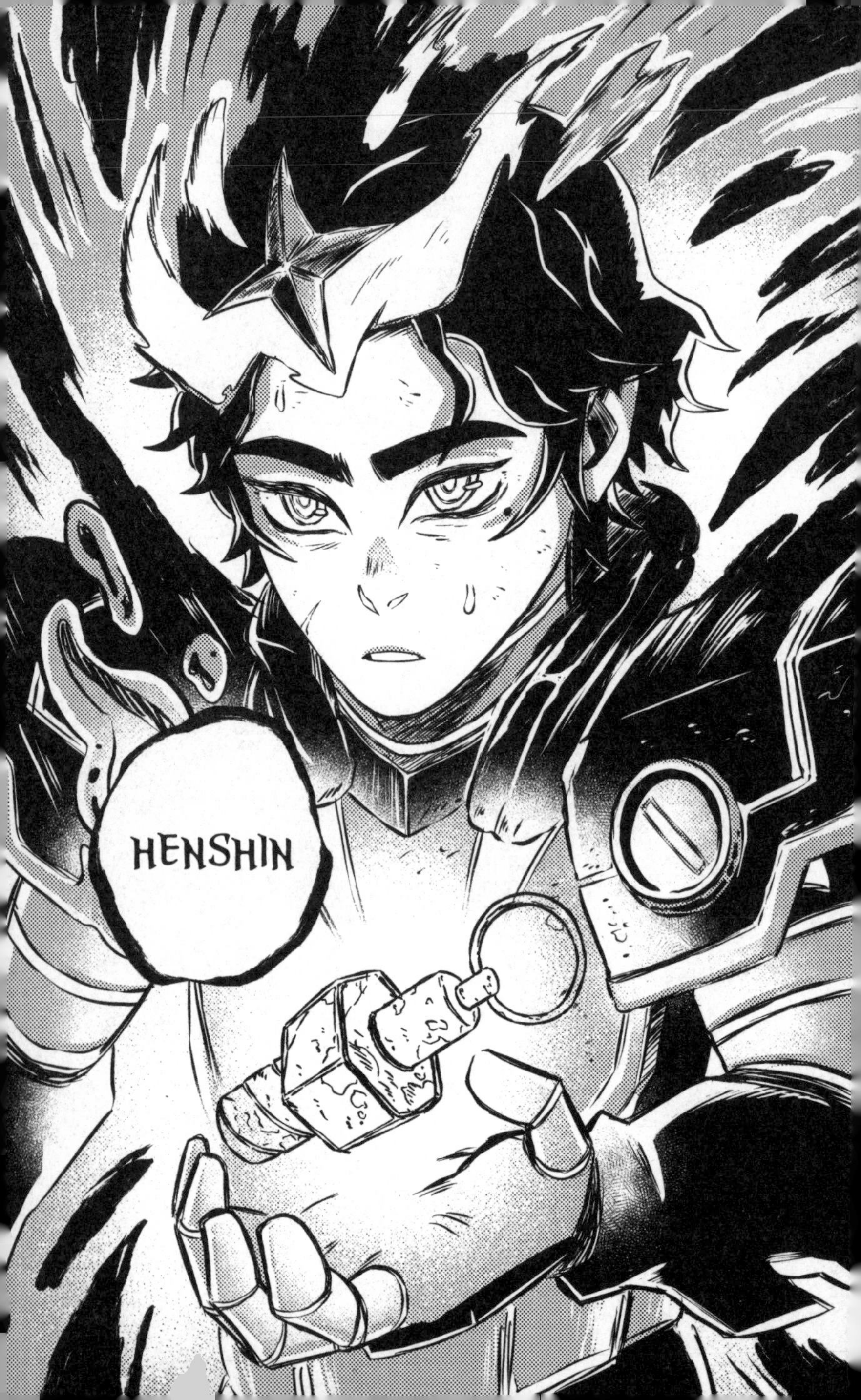
HENSHIN

HENSHIN!

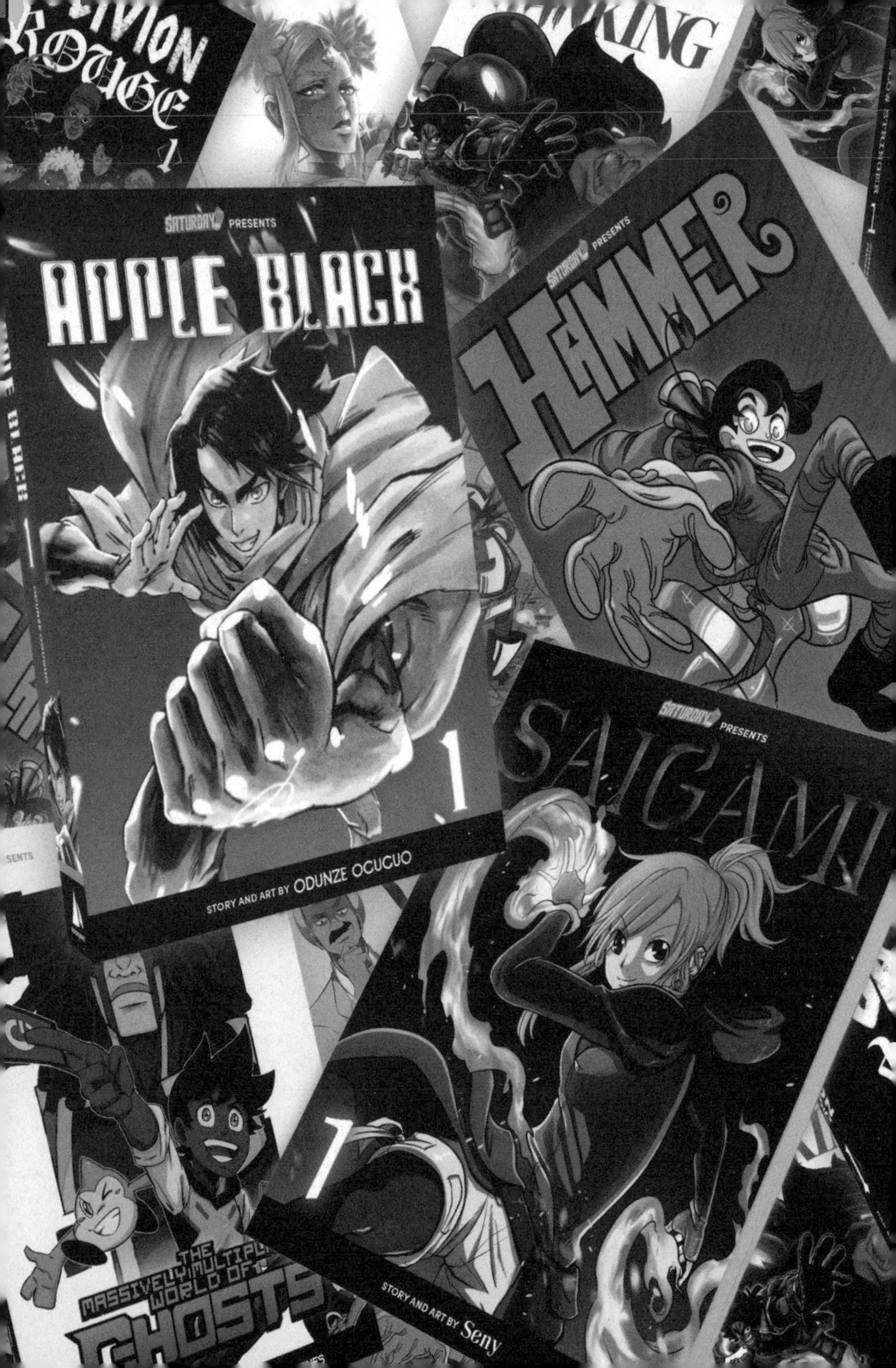

ROUGE
1
SATURDAY PRESENTS
APPLE BLACK
1
STORY AND ART BY ODUNZE OGUGUO
SATURDAY PRESENTS
HAMMER
SATURDAY PRESENTS
SAIGAMI
1
STORY AND ART BY Seny
THE
MASSIVELY MULTIPL
WORLD OF
GHOSTS

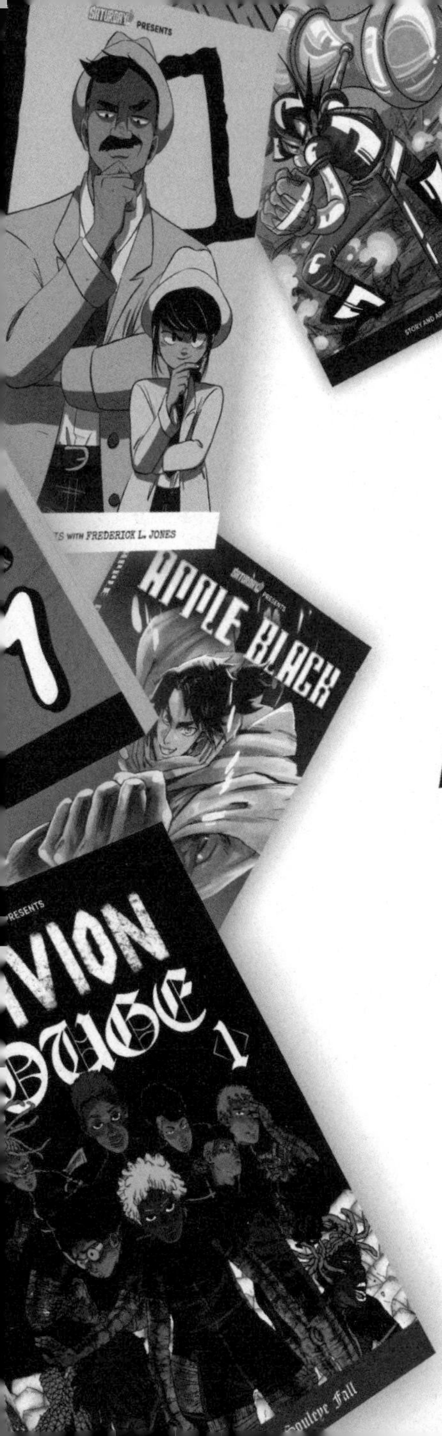
SATURDAY AM PRESENTS
STORY AND ART BY JEVODIN
WITH FREDERICK L. JONES
APPLE BLACK
Odunze Oguguo
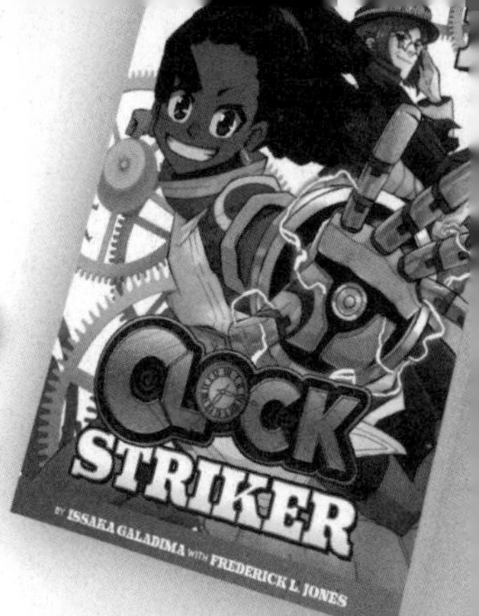
CLOCK STRIKER
BY ISSAKA GALADIMA WITH FREDERICK L. JONES
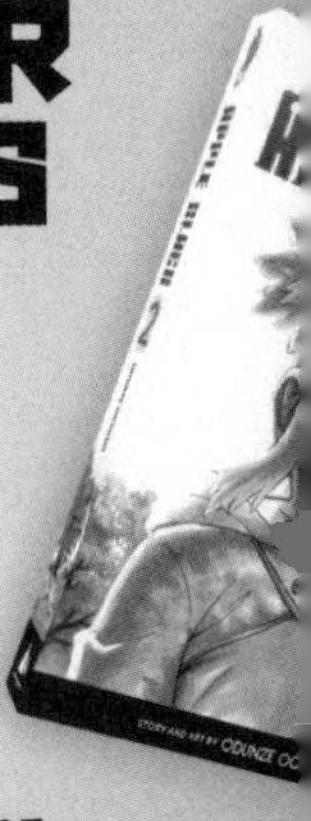